8.

THE MERMAID SERIES.

EDITED BY HAVELOCK ELLIS.

THE BEST PLAYS OF THE OLD DRAMATISTS.

THOMAS DEKKER.

" What things have we seen
Done at the Mermaid ! heard words that have been
So nimble, and so full of subtle flame,
As if that every one from whence they came
Had meant to put his whole wit in a jest,
And had resolved to live a fool the rest
Of his dull life."

Master Francis Beaumont to Ben Jonson.

—⚬⚬⚬⦚⚬⚬—

" Souls of Poets dead and gone,
    What Elysium have ye known,
    Happy field or mossy cavern,
    Choicer than the Mermaid Tavern ? "

Keats.

LONDON :
BRADBURY, AGNEW, & CO., PRINTERS, WHITEFRIARS.

CONTENTS.

		PAGE
THOMAS DEKKER	. . . . . .	vii
THE SHOEMAKER'S HOLIDAY	. . . . .	I
THE HONEST WHORE.—Part the First	. . .	89
THE HONEST WHORE.—Part the Second	. . .	191
OLD FORTUNATUS	. . . . . .	287
THE WITCH OF EDMONTON	. . . .	387

THOMAS DEKKER.

IN Henslowe's Diary, among the curious items which Alleyn's fellow manager in the Fortune and other theatres set down concerning his transactions in the plays of the time, the name of a certain " Mr. Dickers," will be found under date 8th of January, 1597. In this way, the adventure of Thomas Dekker into the precarious field of dramatic authorship is first recorded for us. The entry refers to some twenty shillings "lent unto Thomas Dowton" to buy a book of Dekker's, no doubt the MS. of some play written by him, the name of which, however, is not given. A week later, a second entry notes again a disbursement, this time of four pounds, also for a book of his "called Fayeton" (Phaeton), possibly a further part of the same work. The third entry referring to him is ominous : "Lent unto the companey, the 4 of febreary 1598, to disecharge Mr. Dicker owt of the

cownter in the powltrey, the some of fortie shillings.
I saye dd to Thomas Dowton. . . . . xxxx^{s}."
In the sorry indication of these three entries,
showing first the promising emergence of the young
playwright, and then immediately the coming of
disaster upon him, and his being lodged for debt
in "the Counter in the Poultry," we have at once
the key to Dekker's career. Dekker, perhaps the
most original and most striking figure among
the lesser known men of that brilliant array which
follows Marlowe, is at the same time one of the
most unfortunate in his life and its artistic outcome, judged by the standard of his own genius.
It was as if Fortune, to take a figure from his own
play, having first presented him with the gift
which, as a poet of the time, he most desired,—the
playwright's great opportunity, then turned upon
him, and said,—

" But now go dwell with cares, and quickly die."

If, however, he lived with cares, he laughed at
them, and he was too strong to let them kill him
outright.   But, nevertheless, there they were ;
they never perhaps quite upset that undaunted
good-humour of his, but they defeated him as an
artist, they allied themselves insidiously with his
own natural weaknesses to defeat the consumma-
tion of a really great poetic faculty.

Dekker, however, is one of those authors whose
personal effect tends to outgo the purely artistic
one. He has the rare gift of putting heart into

everything he says, and because of this abounding heartiness of his, it is hard to measure him by the absolute standards of criticism. Indeed, after the endless shortcomings and disappointments of his verse and prose have been estimated and written against him, he remains, after all has been set down, still the same lovable, elusive being, a man of genius, a child of nature. For this reason, it is disappointing that so little is to be actually known of his life. As one reads his plays, and marks the strong individuality shown in them, the desire to know how he adjusted himself to the everyday life, and took its little defeats and encouragements, springs very strongly. It is the natural interest that one takes in men of his cordial humanity, and it is disappointing to be balked of its satisfaction.

The outline of Dekker's life is indeed singularly blank. We do not know exactly when he was born, or where; there is scarcely any clue to the important period of his youth, and his early struggles as a poet and playwright; we do not even know when he died. A few further entries in Henslowe's Diary, whose value an uneasy sense of J. Payne Collier's editorial methods tends to depreciate, and a few incidental references in Dekker's own works, chiefly in the dedications and introductions to his plays, form the whole of the exact record which we have to rely upon.

In the dedication to *Match Me in London,* perhaps the most interesting of all the plays by him

not included in this volume, which was published
in 1631, he says, sadly enough, "I have been a
Priest in Apollo's Temple many years, my voice is
decaying with my Age, yet yours being clear and
above mine shall much honour me, if you but listen
to my old tunes." Again in 1637, in the dedicatory
epistle of his prose tract, *English Villainies Seven
Several Times Pressed to Death*, he refers more
definitely to his "three-score years." Sixty years
back from 1637 gives us 1577, but as Collier [1] tells us
that he was married before 1594, and as we know
that he had already won recognition as a young
playwright in 1597, it will be well to read the
term "three-score years" pretty freely, as meaning
generally the term between sixty and seventy, and
to put down the date of his birth at about the year
1569—70, or even a little earlier.

There is less uncertainty about his birthplace :
various references in his prose tracts prove pretty
certainly that he was born in London, as seems so
fit in one of the most devoted of those poets who
have celebrated the English capital. "O thou
beautifullest daughter of two united Monarchies !"
he cries, in his *Seven Deadly Sins of London ;*
"from thy womb received I my being, from thy
breasts my nourishment." This is confirmed by
similar passages in the *Dead Term, The Rod for
Runaways*, and other of the prose pamphlets. The
particular spot in London where he was born
is not however to be learnt, although Collier sur-

---

[1] "Memoirs of Actors," xvi., xvii,

mises that he was born in Southwark. The name itself,—whether Dekker or Decker, suggests a Dutch origin, which is further corroborated by the curious knowledge shown in the plays and prose tracts of Dutch people and Dutch books, to say nothing of the frequent Dutch realism of Dekker's dramatic method. Dr. Grosart, whose indefatigable energy of research was probably never exercised to so little purpose in the case of any author, discovered on the title-page of one copy of the civic " Entertainment " by Dekker, *Troia-Nova-Triumphans, or London Triumphing*, the words " Merchant-Tailor " written opposite his name, as if by one who had known him. From this we may again conjecture that his father was a tailor, and that possibly the boy went to Merchant Tailor's School, and was intended for that trade. The intimate knowledge of the daily routine of tailors' and shoemakers' shops displayed in *The Shoemaker's Holiday*, and other of the plays, bear every evidence of being drawn from actual experience. It is not a very wild imagination, therefore, to imagine that the boy Dekker may have been apprenticed in the ordinary way as a shoemaker or tailor, making escape from the craftsman's life as his poetic ambition grew hot, and at last inevitable, in its hazardous issue upon the path of a playwright and man of letters.

It is only by free inference from his works that we can possibly fill up the early part of his life, until, in 1597, as already noted, we find him com-

mitted to the life of an author and playwright, and
tasting, no doubt, of its sweets, as in the early part
of 1598 he had a sharp foretaste of its bitterness.
Much of the description in his plays casts a vivid
light upon this wild life of the playhouse and
tavern which he, with other young poets of the extraordinary decade terminating the sixteenth century must have lived. Some of the scenes in *The
Honest Whore*, and again in *Satiromastix* and
other of the lesser known comedies, are full of
this interest; and luminous passages also occur
in the plays of his various collaborators. In
some of his own prose works, especially in his
singular guide to the gallant's life in Elizabethan
London, *The Gull's Horn Book*, Dekker has indirectly supplied a still more realistic account of
the life lived by the young bloods who frequented
the playhouses and taverns. From this inimitable
book one gathers much curious detail for the picture
of Dekker's daily surroundings. In Chapter V.,
which is headed, " How a Gallant should behave
himself in an Ordinary," the young hero of the
period is advised to repair to the "ordinary," or
eating-house, so early as "some half-hour after
eleven ; for then you shall find most of your
fashion-mongers planted in the room waiting for
meat." Amongst the types of gallant to whom
Dekker gives special advice as to behaviour at the
ordinary, is the poet :—

"If you be a Poet," he says, "and come into the Ordinary ;
though it can be no great glory to be an ordinary Poet ; order yourself

thus. Observe no man ; doff not cap to that gentleman to-day at dinner, to whom, not two nights since, you were beholden for a supper ; but, after a turn or two in the room, take occasion, pulling out your gloves, to have some *Epigram*, or *Satire*, or *Sonnet* fastened in one of them . . . Marry, if you chance to get into your hands any witty thing of another man's, that is some-what better ; I would counsel you then, if demand be made who composed it, you may say : 'Faith, a learned Gentleman, a very worthy friend.' And this seeming to lay it on another man will be counted either modesty in you, or a sign that you are not ambitious of praise, or else that you dare not take it upon you for fear of the sharpness it carries with it."

At dinner, directions are given in the same vein of irony, as to the manner of eating and so forth ; and after dinner, among other occupations and diversions proposed for the afternoon figures the play. The next chapter is devoted accordingly to expounding "How a Gallant should behave himself in a Playhouse." From the point of view of Dekker's dramatic work, this is naturally the most interesting part of the book. It gives us a vivid idea of the associations which would colour his thoughts as, the dinner hour over, the stream of gallants, 'prentices and so forth, issued from the ordinaries, the fashionable promenade in the Middle Aisle of St. Paul's, and elsewhere, and wended their way at afternoon to the play. Dekker, it is quite evident, speaks feelingly, remembering his own troubles, in these ironical counsellings to the "Gull," who in his seat on the stage seems to have acted as a sort of irresponsible *chorus*, hinder-ing rather than aiding the understanding of the play, however, and resented equally by the playwright and the playgoers in pit or gallery. " Whither," proceeds the Horn Book,—

" Whither therefore the gatherers of the public, or private Play-house stand to receive the afternoon's rent ; let our Gallant having paid it, presently advance himself up to the Throne of the stage ; I mean not into the lord's room, which is now but the stage's suburbs ; no, ... but on the very rushes where the comedy is to dance, yea, and under the state of Cambyses himself, must our feathered ostrich, like a piece of ordnance, be planted valiantly, because im-pudently, beating down the mews and hisses of the opposed rascality." Here it continues—" By sitting on the stage, you may, without travelling for it, at the very next door ask whose play it is ; and, by that *Quest* of *Inquiry*, the law warrants you to avoid much mistaking ; if you know not the author, you may rail against him, and peradventure so behave yourself, that you may enforce the author to know you."

The refinements of torture to which the Eliza-bethan playwright was subject under this arrange-ment, must indeed have been infinite. Dekker further enlarges with the piteous irony of a long-suffering experience :—

" It shall crown you with rich commendation, to laugh aloud in the middest of the most serious and saddest scene of the terriblest tragedy ; and to let that clapper, your tongue, be tossed so high, that all the house may ring of it."

Again, even more suggestively—

" Now, sir ; if the writer be a fellow that hath either epigrammed you, or hath had a flirt at your mistress, or hath brought either your feather, or your red beard, or your little legs, etc., on the stage ; you shall disgrace him worse than by tossing him in a blanket, or giving him the bastinado in a tavern, if, in the middle of his play, be it Pastoral or Comedy, Moral or Tragedy, you rise with a screwed and discontented face from your stool to be gone."

From another passage, it is clear that the first arrival of the gallant upon the stage, as seen from the front of the house, must have been almost as striking as this precipitate exit.

> "Present not yourself on the stage," it advises "especially at a new play, until the quaking Prologue hath, by rubbing, got colour into his cheeks, and is ready to give the trumpets their cue that he is upon point to enter; for then it is time, as though you were one of the properties, or that you dropt out of the hangings, to creep from behind the arras, with your tripos or three-footed stool, in one hand, and a teston (tester,—sixpence) mounted between a forefinger and a thumb in the other."

From the ordinary to the playhouse, from the playhouse to the tavern, the satirist follows still as good-humouredly:—"the next places that are filled, after the playhouses be emptied are, or ought to be, taverns; into a tavern then let us next march, where the brains of one hogshead must be beaten out to make up another."

The ordinary, the playhouse, the tavern:—Dekker no doubt knew them only too well, but it is not to be inferred because of this that his life was an idle one. His extraordinary energy, at the beginning of his career at any rate, becomes clear when we turn to the record of his plays. We have already referred to those which he had been engaged to write for Henslowe, and which no doubt were written and duly performed before the appearance of *The Shoemaker's Holiday*, the first of those actually remaining to us. The year 1599 especially, towards the middle of which *The Shoemaker's Holiday* was published, must have been a year of immense activity. On the 9th and 16th April, Henslowe records a play by Dekker

Lacy in his disguise as Hans, the Dutchman. Of the female characters, Eyre's wife is a good sample of foolish, conventional femininity, well realised in the little she has to say and do. The most taking of the female parts, however, is Jane: the whole episode of Ralph's going to the wars, his delayed return to her, her wooing by Hammon, and her final rescue at the last moment by the band of shoemakers, is worked out with singular sweetness, and with great feeling for simple dramatic effect. One of the prettiest scenes in the whole of Dekker, is that where Jane is shown sitting alone in the shop sewing when Hammon approaches, and tries by fair means and foul to win her love. Compared with her, Rose, the heroine in chief, is indistinct. Sybil, the maid, however, is an excellent counterpart to Firk, the feminine to his masculine, —as unabashed in her innuendo as he in his blunt animalism.

Taken all through, this "Pleasant Comedy of the Gentle Craft" is one to be remembered with the score or so of the best comedies of pure joy of life which were produced by the Elizabethans; and remembered it probably will be even when Dekker's stronger and maturer work is overlooked. The abounding happiness that fills it is contagious; only here and there the note of trouble for Ralph and Jane occurs to set off the unadulterated comedy of the rest. The whole spirit of the play is expressed in the words of Simon Eyre when he sums up his philosophy for the edification of the Lord Mayor,

who says to him, laughing—" Ha, ha, ha ! I had
rather than a thousand pound, I had an heart but
half so light as yours ; " and Eyre replies, " Why,
what should I do, my Lord ? A pound of care
pays not a dram of debt. Hum, let's be merry
whiles we are young ; old age, sack and sugar, will
steal upon us, ere we be aware." As pointed out
in the notes to the play, it is worth remembering
that Robert Herrick, who was a goldsmith's apprentice in London when the play was first performed
there, seems to have in part appropriated these
words of Eyre's, and paraphrased them in one of
his inimitable verses. Dekker has himself twice
overflowed into song in the play, and the shoemaker's drinking-song shows at once the exquisite
lyric faculty which he possessed. Its chorus lingers
long in the memory as an echo of the happy, bois-
terous life, well nourished with cakes and ale, of the
Elizabethan craftsman :—

> " Trowl the bowl, the jolly nut-brown bowl,
> And here, kind mate, to thee :
> Let's sing a dirge for Saint Hugh's soul,
> And down it merrily."

The Shoemaker's Holiday serves well as an instance of Dekker's realistic method. One sees in it
a natural outcome of his prentice life in London,
as a shoemaker, a "seamster," or what not. In
coming to *Old Fortunatus* on the other hand, we
have Dekker as pure poet and idealist. Instead of
the lusty zest of comedy, we have the romantic
spirit in its perfection ; the glamour of romance is

cast over everything.   Founded upon one of those
fabulous histories in which the sixteenth century
so loved to indulge its imagination, the play appeals
directly to the sense of wonder and adventure
which the poets, playwrights and story-tellers of
the day, could always count upon in their audience.
As pointed out in the preliminary note to the play,
Dekker's version is founded upon an earlier one
which was performed some three years before he
began his.   It would be interesting to discover what
the character of the original version was, both in its
general lines and in its details.   In his admirable
book, " Studies in the Literary Relations of England
and Germany in the sixteenth century," Mr. C. H.
Herford has pointed out the resemblance in certain
parts of the original legend and of the play to the
story of Faustus.   This indirectly leads us to the
consideration of how far the writer of the earlier
play may have been influenced, if at all, by the
dramatic method of Marlowe.   For in some
parts of Dekker's version, the resemblance in
the structure of the blank verse on occasion,
and in the scenic and other detail, to Marlowe
is striking.   Only, in the verse, it is *Tamburlaine*
rather than *Dr. Faustus* that is suggested, as for
instance in Fortune's address to Fortunatus, when
she appears to him with her array of discrowned
kings and kings new-created.

> " These have I ruined, and exalted those :
> These hands have conquered Spain : these brows fill up
> The golden circle of rich Portugal,

Viriat a monarch now, but born a shepherd :
This Primislaus, a Bohemian King,
Last day a carter ; this monk Gregory,
Now lifted to the Papal dignity."

The preceding passage, beginning " Thou shalt be one of Fortune's minions," which contains too a direct reference to—

" that great Scythian swain,
Fortune's best minion, warlike Tamburlaine,"

is still more like Marlowe. Dekker's verse, it is true, does not march mail-clad like Marlowe's : it has a plasticity and a suppleness which the other's " mighty line " lacked, while it fails to achieve the same state and sustained dignity. But after all differences are allowed for, there is much in the blank verse in some parts of *Old Fortunatus*, which only Marlowe could have inspired.

This is not said with any thought of depreciating Dekker, who has so often been depreciated in order to add to the lustre of others, but because it marks an interesting point in his development as a poet and dramatist. Two things were enough in themselves to prevent his carrying on the tradition of Marlowe : one, and an insuperable one, his faculty of humour ; the second, springing from the first, his lack of that sense of his own artistic dignity, failing which his genius never rose to its potential height. Signs of the power to achieve the very highest in poetry are scattered extravagantly all through *Old Fortunatus*, so that one does not wonder at Charles Lamb's tremendous compliment. There are lines in it which have rarely been surpassed, and there are fewer lapses in the play than is usual with Dekker, in the inspired recklessness of his method. Dekker's theory of blank verse, in especial, was not a severe one. It admitted of a free interspersion of rhymed lines, and of other dubious modifications of the strict measure. But it is remarkable how successful many of the passages are in spite of these irregularities. Dekker had the privilege of genius, and the faculty of putting into words that rhythmical unction and natural charm which defy the exacter laws of prosody.

Part of the structural defects of the play are due to one of those exigencies to which the Elizabethan playwrights were peculiarly liable. Mr. C. H. Herford, in the book before alluded to, has shewn that Dekker had practically finished the play on the lines of the original fable of Fortunatus, when it was ordered for performance at Court, whereupon further special additions were made with a view to this. Thus, it will be perceived that there are two prologues ; while a serious interference with the original lines of the play is shown in the intrusion of Virtue and Vice, in the fashion of a " Masque " or " Triumph," so as to upset the simple dramatic motive of the supremacy of Fortune. In this way, as Mr. Herford says, the right moral tension of the tragedy gives way to the decorous conventionalities of the

Masque. For, the apparent moral effect gained by the triumph of Virtue over Vice and over Fortune is only one of appearance. Dekker had already, according to his wont, moralised the original story, which is innocent of moral intention. For instance, Andelocia, who like Fortunatus is in Dekker's hands a prodigal upon whom Fortune wreaks a tragic retribution, is in the original romance a hero to the last, using the immoral supremacy afforded by the Purse and Wishing Cap without either moral recoil or material injury to himself.

There are other parts, fine in themselves, but insufficiently related to the main line of the plot, whose inconsequence can not be excused because of any exterior later addition, as for instance, the Orleans episode. It is hard, at the same time, to have to find fault with an intrusion which has resulted so delightfully in itself; and we may best take leave of the play in the tempered eulogy of Mr. J. Addington Symonds, who, after speaking of certain of these defects, goes on to say, " Among the poet's most perfect achievements, however, are the scenes in which Orleans indulges a lover's lunacy in a passion of wild fancies. To quote passages would be to murder the effect. Nothing can be imagined finer than the paradoxes of this witty fanatic, in whose opinion the whole world is mad and he the only wise man left ; who scorns the scorn of sober folk, extols deformity, and adores the very horns that sprout upon his lady's brow.

The mastery of Dekker is shown throughout this comedy in the flesh and blood reality which he has given to abstractions ; even the subordinate characters define each a clearly defined quality. Fortunatus and his sons have a higher degree of reality ; while Virtue, Vice, and Fortune, withdrawn from human action and anxiety, survey the world from thrones and feel such passions only as befits immortals. They enter and depart in pomps and pageants to solemn strains of music. . . . . To have conceived the comedy of *Old Fortunatus* proves Dekker a poet of no common order. A little more firmness in its ground-plan would have made it a masterpiece."[1]

It may seem that undue attention has been given to these two plays, but in them will be found so characteristic an embodiment of Dekker's qualities as a playwright,—as a realistic writer of comedy and as a romantic poet, that they serve as an admirable illustration of the whole of his dramatic works. The next play of which we have any record is the famous burlesque upon Ben Jonson, *Satiromastix*, which was published in 1602. As an artistic whole, this deserves, no doubt, all that has been said against it ; Dekker's awkward fashion of interweaving two more or less inconsequent dramatic motives was never displayed more unfortunately. But as a young poet's retort upon an unsparing antagonist of Ben Jonson's autocratic position, the thing is surely not contemptible.

[1] "The Academy," vol. v., 1874, pp. 136-7.

The exaggerated reproduction of Jonson's Captain Tucca, in especial, which has been pointed to as proving a lack of invention on Dekker's part, was no doubt one of the favourite hits of the piece, an out-Heroding of Herod which could not fail to immensely tickle the playgoers of the day. And the appearance of Horace cleverly got up in imitation of the author of *The Poetaster*, labouring over an ode by candlelight, must have brought down the house.

" O me thy priest inspire,
   For I to thee and thine immortal name,
   In—sacred raptures flowing, flowing—swimming, swimming :
   In sacred raptures swimming,
   Immortal name, game, dame, tame, lame, lame, lame,
   —— —— hath,—shame, proclaim, oh ?—
   In sacred raptures flowing, will proclaim, not—
   O me thy priest inspire !
   For I to thee and thine immortal name,
   In flowing numbers filled with sprite and flame,
   (Good, Good !) In flowing numbers filled with sprite and flame."

What is remarkable about Dekker's retort is its perfect good-humour ; there is not a trace of vindictiveness in all its satire. Dekker probably took up the cudgels, as beforetime he first entered upon the literary career, more " for the fun of it," than with any very deliberate or serious intention. Though the episode of Cœlestine has no conceivable reference to the " Untrussing of the Humourous Poet," it is worth turning to for its own sake. Mr. Swinburne's conjecture that this part of the play was originally designed for another purpose, and was only used here for want of material to fill out

the Jonson burlesque to the required length, is
probably the correct one.

The reputation which Dekker won by *Satiromastix*
seems to have been the cause of something of a
new departure in the year following its publication;
we find him then appearing for the first time as a
prose-writer.   He had already been engaged in
writing *Canaan's Calamity; the Destruction of
Jerusalem,* in sensational doggrel,—the wretched
hack-work of a few hasty hours, no doubt, written
for some urgent bookseller, which I am afraid there
is no sufficient reason to think with Mr. Swinburne
that he did not compose.   And now he may be said
to have seriously begun his career as a man of
letters, as distinct from a playwright, by the publication of an interesting work whose title-page
well suggests its contents.   The title runs:—*The
Wonderful Year:* " Wherein is shewed the picture
of London lying sick of the Plague.   At the end
of all (like a merry Epilogue to a dull Play) certain
tales are cut out in sundry fashions of purpose to
shorten the lives of long winter's nights, that lie
watching in the dark for us."   Passages in this work
show clearly enough that Dekker had the making
in him too of a prose writer, if he could only learn
to master and rightly direct his faculty of words,
but there is no pervading sense of the art of prose
in it.   Immediately following *The Wonderful
Year,* however, came another prose-work which
in its way is perfect.   *The Bachelor's Banquet* is
a delightful satire on the life matrimonial, " plea-

santly discoursing the variable humours of women, their quickness of wits and unsearchable deceits." Here we have Dekker at his best. His facile humour for once served him capably from beginning to end, and the result is a satire of inimitable pleasantry, full of his hearty spontaneity of fun, and all the more effective because, like *Satiromastix*, it is so devoid of any real offence. As if to offer atonement for having satirised woman-kind at all, it must have been about this time that he collaborated with Haughton and Chettle, in *The Pleasant Comedy of Patient Grissill*, with its charming picture of a woman's ideal patience. As this play is to be given in a later volume, it need not be examined at length here.

And now, in 1604, we come to the work, of all Dekker's, which most fully and characteristically represents his genius, with its fund of great qualities and great defects — *The Honest Whore*. The second part of the play, it is true, was not published until many years later, but it will be convenient to take both parts together in considering it here, noting only significant changes in style and so forth. With the play as a whole, Hazlitt's well-known criticism has become so inseparably identified and forms so incomparable an exposition, that I prefer to give it here instead of commentary of my own, completing it by what further notes seem to be required.

" Old honest Dekker's Signior Orlando Friscobaldo I shall never forget ! I became only of late acquainted with this last-mentioned

worthy character ! but the bargain between us is, I trust, for life.
We sometimes regret that we had not sooner met with characters
like this, that seem to raise, revive, and give a new zest to our
being. . . . . The execution is, throughout, as exact as the
conception is new and masterly. There is the least colour possible
used ; the pencil drags ; the canvas is almost seen through : but
then, what precision of outline, what truth and purity of tone, what
firmness of hand, what marking of character ! The words and
answers all along are so true and pertinent, that we seem to see the
gestures, and to hear the tone with which they are accompanied. So
when Orlando, disguised, says to his daughter, 'You'll forgive me,'
and she replies, 'I am not marble, I forgive you ;' or again, when
she introduces him to her husband, saying simply, 'It is my father,'
there needs no stage-direction to supply the relenting tones of voice
or cordial frankness of manner with which these words are spoken.
It is as if there were some fine art to chisel thought, and to embody
the inmost movements of the mind in every-day actions and familiar
speech.

" Simplicity and extravagance of style, homeliness and quaintness,
tragedy and comedy, interchangeably set their hands and seals to
this admirable production. We find the simplicity of prose with the
graces of poetry. The stalk grows out of the ground ; but the
flowers spread their flaunting leaves in the air. The mixture of
levity in the chief character bespeaks the bitterness from which it
seeks relief ; it is the idle echo of fixed despair, jealous of observation
or pity. The sarcasm quivers on the lip, while the tear stands con-
gealed on the eyelid. This 'tough senior,' this impracticable old
gentleman, softens into a little child ; this choke-pear melts in the
mouth like marmalade. In spite of his resolute professions of mis-
anthropy, he watches over his daughter with kindly solicitude ; plays
the careful housewife ; broods over her lifeless hopes ; nurses the
decay of her husband's fortune, as he had supported her tottering
infancy ; saves the high-flying Matheo from the gallows more than
once, and is twice a father to them. The story has all the romance
of private life, all the pathos of bearing up against silent grief, all the
tenderness of concealed affection : there is much sorrow patiently
borne, and then comes peace. . . . . . The manner too in
which Infelice, the wife of Hippolito, is made acquainted with her
husband's infidelity, is finely dramatic ; and in the scene where she
convicts him of his injustice, by taxing herself with incontinence
first, and then turning his most galling reproaches to her into up-
braidings against his own conduct, she acquits herself with infinite
spirit and address. The contrivance by which, in the first part, after
being supposed dead, she is restored to life, and married to Hippolito,
though perhaps a little far-fetched, is affecting and romantic."

It must be constantly borne in mind, when reading the two parts of the play, that an interval of twenty-five years separates them, and that Orlando Friscobaldo is the creation of an obviously more matured imagination than are the characters of the earlier part. Indeed, the way in which Bellafront's casual mention of her father's name in the earlier part is developed into so masterly a characterisation is very significant. In the period between, Dekker had gone through strange and bitter experience. According to Collier, he married early, and a daughter was baptised in his name as early as 1594, and we can only wonder what dark sorrow he had known, that he came to shape out of himself the inexpressible tragi-comedy of Bellafront's shame and her father's love. There is all the difference between youth and age, indeed, in the two parts ; and it is impressive to note how a conception, prompted mainly by the humourist's artistic interest in the first instance, came to be wrought out and carried to the end with such a bitter freight of actuality. In this grim masterpiece, Dekker has used his realistic method with terrible sincerity, and yet, with so cunning a grasp of the nettle of shame that with its sting it yields a fragrance as of the perfect flower of love. The weakest parts of the play are those where Dekker conforms most to conventional dramatic methods, as in the forensic contest between Bellafront and Hippolito, which is dramatically weak, though in passages not ineffective. In

Henslowe's Diary, Middleton is mentioned as a collaborator in the play with Dekker, and there are parts of it which might very well be from his hand. Mr. A. H. Bullen conjectures that the scenes where Bellafront is first discovered in her chamber and again the shop scenes where the gallants try to irritate Candido, are chiefly Middleton's. Mr. J. Addington Symonds considers also that the play as a whole has "the movement of one of Middleton's acknowledged plays." Making due allowance for every assistance of the kind, the essential merit of the whole work is so unmistakeably Dekker's, however, that the reader may safely leave Middleton out of court in considering the play as a whole, and put it down as Dekker's to all intents and purposes.

Before the publication of the first part, Dekker had, in 1603, in his *Magnificent Entertainment given to King James,* inserted some lines of Middleton's, which proves that they were in contact about the time when the play was being written. After its publication Dekker apparently gave himself up for a while to prose-writing. In 1606, one of his best known pamphlets, *The Seven Deadly Sins of London,* appeared, which he himself affirmed on the title-page was only a week's work, "Opus Septem Dierum." The satire, though here and there forced, and roughly written, is not unimpressive, and contains many passages of vivid imaginative power. The Seven Deadly Sins, or as Dekker has it, "The Names

of the Actors in this Old Interlude of Iniquity,"
are not at all what one would be likely to expect.
The terms by which they are designated are
extravagantly metaphorical, and including " Politic
Bankruptism," " Candlelight," and " Shaving," and
there is a special addendum to say that " Seven
may easily play this, but not without a Devil."
Published in the same year, *News from Hell,
brought by the Devil's Carrier,* which resolves
itself into " The Devil's Answer to Pierce Penny-
lesse," is a confused, gruesomely humoresque description of the nether regions, and of a Mephis-
tophelian journey thence to London and other
places in the upper world. *The Double PP,* a
rather ungainly satire on the Papists, partly in
prose, partly in verse, inspired by the Gunpowder
Plot of 1605, also appeared in 1606.

The year 1607 shows Dekker at his worst as a
playwright. The production of *The Whore of
Babylon* marks the low-water mark of his unfortunate career. It is a sort of allegory, presenting
Elizabeth as Titania, and other national and inter-
national topics in a hopelessly cumbrous disguise.
As a rule Dekker illuminates even his hastiest
productions with some gleam of true humour or
imagination, but here there is hardly a redeeming
touch of either, or, if one does exist, the dull
atmosphere of the whole keeps it hidden from
sight. Dekker atoned a little for his sins as a
playwright in this year, however, by the issue of an
interesting miscellany of prose writings, whose

comprehensive title may be quoted in full :—*Jests to make you Merry*: "With the Conjuring up of Cock Watt (the Walking Spirit of Newgate) to tell tales. Unto which is added the Misery of a Prison, and a Prisoner. And a Paradox in Praise of Serjeants. Written by T. D. and George Wilkins." George Wilkins, says Dr. Grosart, "was in a small way a contemporary playwright ;" and it is impossible to say exactly what share he may have had in this strange composition. But some of the little stories among the "Jests" bear very clearly Dekker's touch, and "The Misery of a Prison and a Prisoner" is unmistakeably the pitiful and bitter expression of his own sorry experiences. In this year was also re-issued under the new title of *A Knight's Conjuring done in Earnest, discovered in Jest*, the before-mentioned *News from Hell*, without anything to show that the book was chiefly a republication. There are some few additions to it, however, including an interesting vision of Chaucer, Spenser, Marlowe, Greene, Peele, and Nash in the haunts of Apollo.

Now, too, we find Dekker in collaboration with Webster, in the plays *Westward Ho, Northward Ho*, and *Sir Thomas Wyatt*. Of these, the first two are lively comedies of intrigue, affording many striking pictures of contemporary life, grossly realistic often, but not more so than is usual in comedies of the time. In *Northward Ho* the social diversions of the Greenshields and the Mayberrys are amusingly contrived, and there are passages

in *Westward Ho* of a higher and poetic kind, as
in the passage (Act iv., Sc. ii.) quoted by Mr. J.
A. Symonds in his essay on Dekker :—

> " Go let Music
> Charm with her excellent voice an awful silence
> Through all this building, that her sphery soul
> May, on the wings of air, in thousand forms,
> Invisibly fly, yet be enjoyed."

The speeches of the earl in this play contain other
rare imaginative touches, in strange contrast with
the reckless farcical tenour of the piece generally.
Sir Thomas Wyatt is less satisfactory, a medley of
absurd printer's errors adding to the confusion of
what was probably a confused work at best.
Marston's protest, as to the unfairness of taking
seriously and critically plays which were hastily
and carelessly written to meet the demand of the
hour, must be remembered in judging plays like
this. In addition to the plays which their authors
revised and set forth with their deliberate *impri-
matur*, many were written without any idea of
publication ; the playwrights looked upon them
merely as a sort of journalism, which they did
not wish to have judged by permanent artistic
standards. It would be waste of time to deliberate
over the exact share to be alloted to Dekker and
Webster in these three plays. It will be noted,
however, in the two comedies, that certain of the
characters, as the Welsh captain and Hans in
Northward Ho, speak in a dialect suspiciously like
that of the dialect parts in Dekker's other plays.

For the next two or three years Dekker appears to have occupied himself again chiefly with prose. In 1608 appeared *The Bellman of London*, which is a sort of unconventional cyclopedia of thieving and vagabondage, containing much curious information about the shady side of Elizabethan life. Its importance in relation to Dekker's fondness for the same subject-maker in his plays, however, is somewhat lessened when we discover that the work is partly appropriated from a book first published about forty years before, in 1567, entitled *A Caveat or Warning for Common Cursitors, vulgarly called Vagabonds;* by Thomas Harman. *The Bellman of London* seems to have been successful; for it was followed the next year by a second book of the same kind, *Lanthorn and Candle-light; or, The Bellman's Second Night Walk:* also in part taken from Harman. In 1609 *The Gull's Horn-book*, which has already been referred to, was published,—by far the most important and interesting of all Dekker's prose works. Its value will be apparent from the passages already quoted, but to anyone who wishes to realise intimately the every-day life of the time, and its relation to Dekker's own environment, the book is simply indispensable. The initial conception, like most of Dekker's conceptions, was not original. The idea of it is taken from a Dutch book which Dekker had thought of translating into English verse, but, finding difficulties in the way, he decided instead to write a new prose work on the same lines. The earlier parts of the book are the least reliable, as here Dekker made free use of the Dutch original ; but from Chap. iv., "How a Gallant should behave Himself in Paul's Walk," onwards, the book is probably as true as it is humorously realistic in its descriptions, forming a delightful prose complement to the plays. The rest of Dekker's prose works, interesting as they are in themselves, have not enough bearing upon the plays to warrant me in any lengthy examination of them. Between the two "Bellman" books appeared *The Dead Term ; or, Westminster's Complaint for Long Vacations and Short Terms,* which, amid some extravagance, contains a great deal in the way of description of London life, which is picturesque and historically valuable. In 1609 two other works followed or preceded *The Gull's Horn-book.* The most valuable of the two is entitled, *Work for Armourers ; or, the Peace is Broken,* which contains some suggestive autobiographical references to Dekker's delight in history, to the hard lot of poetry and the drama, and to many other matters, interesting, personally, in approaching its main fancifully treated thesis of the struggle between *Poverty and Money. The Raven's Almanack,* the second of the two, is chiefly a budget of stories, with "A Song sung by an Old Woman in a Meadow," which has something of Dekker's rougher lyrical quality in it.

In 1611 Dekker and Middleton came together again, and wrote conjointly *The Roaring Girl,* a vigorous comedy, whose heroine, Moll Cutpurse, goes about in the guise of a gallant, and wreaks summary vengeance upon offenders. In spite of her aggressive masculinity, she is somehow made in her way really attractive. Some of the scenes, as those in the "Sempster's" shop, and those in which the Gallipots and Tiltyards go duck-hunting, are full of contemporary colour. The Mayoralty Pageant of 1612 has already been mentioned. In that year also appeared an absurd semi-allegorical dramatic fantasy by Dekker, founded upon Machiavelli's "Belphegor,"—*If this be not a Good Play the Devil is in it,* in which Devils, Zanies, Friars, Dancing Girls, and other human and superhuman elements are wrought into a curious medley of utter nonsense with real humour and fancy. From 1613 to 1616, Oldys informs us that Dekker was in prison again. An interesting and pathetic letter exists from him to Alleyne, who must have acted generously towards him throughout; the letter is dated " King's Bench, Sept. 12, 1616." It is significant that in the first year of his re-imprisonment, he issued a very remarkable book of prayers, entitled *The Four Birds of Noah's Ark,* to the profound eloquence and power of devotional expression in which, as in "A Prayer for a Soldier," Mr. Swinburne has paid a well-deserved tribute. With *A Strange Horse-Race,* published also in 1613, were included the singular piece of humour,—"The Devil's last Will and Testament," and another prose fantasy, "The Bankrupt's Banquet." A much more

notable work is *Dekker his Dream*, which is mainly
in verse. It is a rough and unpolished piece of
work, most interesting autobiographically, but full
of vigorous and sometimes very imaginative
descriptions, and with occasional fine passages, as
two lines, taken almost at random, will testify :—

> " Each man was both the lion and the prey,
>   And every corn-field an Aceldema."

Dekker did not emerge again as a playwright
until 1622, when he appears with still another
collaborator, the last man whom one would have
expected him to work with,—Massinger. They
wrote together *The Virgin Martyr*, which is, as
might be expected, a patchwork of incongruous
qualities. Dekker probably supplied both the
weakest and the strongest parts of the play, the
atrocious humorous passages, equally with the ex-
quisitely tender scene, for instance, between
Dorothea, the Virgin Martyr, and Angelo, "a good
spirit, serving Dorothea in the habit of a Page."
This is the scene which won from Charles Lamb in
his " Specimens of the Elizabethan Dramatists,"
his unbounded tribute to Dekker's genius ; and
as the scene can be turned to there, I need not
repeat it here, as I should otherwise be inclined
to do.

There is no record of the next five years of
Dekker's life. In 1628 and 1629 he again wrote
the Mayoralty pageants under title *Britannia's
Honour*, and *London's Tempe*, which at best con-

tain glimpses of his true quality. In 1631, *Match Me in London*, a comedy of court intrigue in civic life, has something of his real genius again. It was in the dedicatory note of this play, to "The Noble Lover, and deservedly beloved, of the Muses, Ludovick Carlisle, Esquire, Gentleman of the Bows, and Groom of the King and Queen's Privy-Chamber," that Dekker so pathetically referred to his voice, "Decaying with my Age." But comparatively with some of the second-rate pieces of ten, and even twenty years before, there is little sign of decay. *Match Me in London* shows, it is true, the prose side of Dekker's dramatic faculty, rather than its side of poetic exuberance; but the piece is as full of Dekker's old picturesque realism and genial humanity, as ever. The street and shop scenes, supposed to be placed chiefly in Seville, might just as well be in London : Dekker transfers the 'Counter' there without hesitation, and except for occasional doubtful attempts at Spanish local colour, the whole play is as native as anything Dekker has done. The plot turns chiefly upon the attempt of the King to corrupt Tormiella, one of the brightest and most taking of all Dekker's heroines, whose guileless fidelity to her husband is delicately portrayed. The usual sub-plot in which Don John, the King's brother, conspires for the throne, is less inconsequent than most of Dekker's supplementary plots, and the whole comedy is managed with a higher sense of dramatic form than Dekker often showed. *Match Me in*

London, as being entirely Dekker's own composition, certainly deserves to rank with his half-dozen best plays, and I am sorry that it was not possible to find room for it in this edition, although the same ground has already been partly covered in his other comedies.

I confess I find it hard to understand how anyone can seriously prefer *The Wonder of a Kingdom*, which appeared some few years later, to *Match Me in London*, as Mr. J. A. Symonds has done. In the former we find Dekker for once working without any real pervading humanity ; there are touches of his usual heartiness in it, but as a whole it is a heartless production—more a cold study of motives and passions than a sympathetic re-creation of them in forms of art. It was highly appropriate, indeed, that Dekker long before had been chosen as a champion to meet Ben Jonson, for the two men mark very clearly two types of poet and artist. Jonson in his plays worked largely from the mere curiosity about men's passions and motives, he wrought conceptions which sprang too often from an analytical interest, rather than the emotional human impulse which drives the poet to reflect men's strifes and destinies for simple love's sake. With Dekker it was different. Without perhaps consciously realising it, he worked mainly from this impulse of the heart, putting himself passionately into all that he characterised, in his exuberant, careless way. For once, however, in *The Wonder of a Kingdom*, he

seems to have laid aside something of his natural
kindliness. The episode of old Lord Vanni's intrigue
with Alphonsina is repulsive, unvisited as it is by
even ordinary comedy retribution. It is only
fair to allow, however, that Dekker's kindlier
quality crops up in some scenes of the play,
and Hazlitt's testimony to Gentili, "that truly ideal
character of a magnificent patron," may be set
against the comment of the German critic, Dr.
Schmidt, who has said very truly,—"That the
youthful fire which fills *Fortunatus* is in this drama
extinguished."

Although the two remaining plays which
Dekker wrote with Ford, *The Sun's Darling* and
The Witch of Edmonton, were not published till
1656 and 1658 respectively, they were certainly
written and performed long before *Match Me in
London*, probably helping to fill up the five blank
years following that in which *The Virgin Martyr*
appeared. *The Sun's Darling* is a charming conception, inadequately wrought out, but nevertheless full of facile and exuberant poetic quality.
The lyrics, especially, the best of which are undoubtedly Dekker's, are so fresh and full of impulse that one inclines to think that they date
back to the first half of his life. Some of these
have found their way, infrequently, into the anth-
ologies, as that beginning, "What bird so sings,
yet so does wail," and again the delightful country
song, in which one can forgive the mixture of musk-
roses and daffodils, haymaking and hunting, lambs

and partridges, in defiance of all rustic tradition, for the sake of its catching tune :—

> " Hay-makers, rakers, reapers and mowers,
>   Wait on your Summer Queen.
> Dress up with musk-rose her eglantine bowers,
>   Daffadils strew the green. . . ."

The hero of this Moral Masque, as the authors term it,—Raybright, "The Sun's Darling," is shown in progression through the seasons under the Sun's guidance, which he perverts in his restless pursuit of sensuous pleasure. All these scenes are full of suggestions of beauty, but they are imperfectly realised. Exquisite passages occur, however, as in the scene where Spring, Health, Youth, and Delight appear to Raybright, and Spring, wooing him in vain, proffers him the bay-tree :—

> " That tree shall now be thine, about it sit
> All the old poets, with fresh laurel crowned,
> Singing in verse the praise of chastity."

When it is too late, Raybright, filled with love for the Spring, is seized with remorse : so in turn all the seasons pass by, while Humour and Folly lead him always astray. The Sun's peroration in addressing Raybright at the end of his foiled career is a solemn and profound, if rather fanciful, summing-up of life. Altogether *The Sun's Darling* forms a valuable later complement to *Old Fortunatus,* and it is only to be regretted that its authors did not bestow upon it the longer, patient labour which would have made it worthy of its conception.

The Witch of Edmonton, the second play in

which Ford and Dekker worked conjointly, is so utterly different to *The Sun's Darling* that one finds it difficult to believe that the same hands can have been concerned in its production. Possibly the initial conception was Rowley's, and though it would not be easy to differentiate his exact share in any special scene or passage, there is a considerable residuum which marks itself off as unlike the work of Dekker or Ford. Dekker's share is more apparent. The scenes where Cuddy Banks and his fellow villagers disport themselves, some of those where the Witch herself appears, and again those of Susan's love and sorrow, have by general critical consent been awarded to him. Part of the severer tragedy in the terrible hallucination of Mother Sawyer, however, which has generally been considered Dekker's, I fancy bears the stamp of Ford. In his essay on Ford, Mr. Swinburne has essayed a comparison of the parts due severally to Dekker and to Ford, which is too important to be overlooked. He would assign the part of Mother Sawyer chiefly to Dekker. " In all this part of the play I trace the hand of Dekker; his intimate and familiar sense of wretchedness, his great and gentle spirit of compassion for the poor and suffering with whom his own lot in life was so often cast, in prison and out." The part of Susan also, he allots to Dekker; and of the scene where Frank Thorney's guilt is discovered, he remarks suggestively : " The interview of Frank with the disguised Winifred in this scene may be compared by the student of dramatic style with the parting of the same characters at the close; the one has all the poignant simplicity of Dekker, the other all the majestic energy of Ford."

The dates of publication of the two last plays bring us far beyond the time of Dekker's death, of which, however, we have no record at all. None of his prose works reach so late a period; the last is *A Rod for Runaways*, published in 1625. Collier, who always made his evidence go as far as possible, himself admits that there is no further trace of him after 1638, the year when Milton wrote *Lycidas*, the year when Scotland was ominously signing the Covenant. In the further oncoming of the Civil War, Dekker disappears altogether, as uncertainly as he first entered the scene.

In summing up this strange life and its dramatic outcome, it is easily seen what is to be said on the adverse side. Dekker had, let us admit, great defects. He was the type of the prodigal in literature,—the kindhearted, irresponsible poet whom we all know, and love, and pardon seventy times seven. But it is sad to think that with a little of the common talent which every successful man of affairs counts as part of his daily equipment, he might have left a different record. He never attained the serious conception of himself and his dignity as a worker which every poet, every artist must have, who would take effect proportionate to his genius. He never seemed to become conscious in any enduring way of his artistic function, and he constantly threw aside, under pressure of the moment, those standards of excellence which none knew better than he how to estimate. But after all has been said, he remains, by his faults as well as by his faculties, one of the most individual, one of the most suggestive, figures of the whole Elizabethan circle. Because of the breath of simple humanity in them, his works leave a sense of brightness and human encouragement whose charm lingers when many more careful monuments of literary effort are forgotten. His artistic sincerity has resulted in a picture of life as he saw it, unequalled for its sentiment, for its living spirit of tears and laughter, as well as for its outspoken truth. His homely realism brings before us all the pleasant everyday bustle of the Elizabethan streets—the craftsmen and prentices, the citizens at their shop doors, the gallants in the Middle Aisle of St. Paul's. The general feeling is that of a summer's morning in the pleasant Cheapside of those days—more like the street of a little market-town than the Cheapside of to-day—where in the clear sunny air the alert cry of the prentices, "What do you lack?" rings out cheerily, and each small incident of the common life is touched with vivid colour. And if the night follows, dark and haunted by grim passions and sorrows, and the King's Bench waits for poor poets not far away, this poet who had known the night and the prison only too well! sang so undauntedly, that the terrors of them fell away at the sound.

As he had this faith in the happy issue out of his own troubles, so Dekker looked unflinchingly as a poet upon the grim and dark side of human life, seeing it to emerge presently, bright in the higher vision of earth and Heaven. Much that at first seems gratuitously obscene and terrible in his dramatic presentation may in this way be accepted with the same vigorous apprehension of the comedy and tragedy of life, which he himself showed. The whole justification of his lifework, indeed, is to be found in these words of his, from the dedicatory epistle to *His Dream*, which we may well take as his parting behest :—" So in these of mine, though the Devil be in the one, God is in the other : nay in both. What I send you, may perhaps seem bitter, yet it is wholesome ; your best physic is not a julep ; sweet sauces leave rotten bodies. There is a Hell named in our Creed, and a Heaven, and the Hell comes before ; if we look not into the first, we shall never live in the last."

ERNEST RHYS.

NOTE : Students of Dekker will find Pearson's Edition of his Plays in 4 Vols., published in 1873, and Dr. Grosart's edition of his Non-Dramatic Works, in 5 Vols., published in the Huth Library, 1885-6, sufficient for all ordinary purposes. There are no notes, however, in Dr. Grosart's reprint, and the notes to the plays in Pearson's edition are few and far between. Mr. Swinburne's article on Dekker (*Nineteenth Century*, January, 1887), will be found valuable also.

THE OLD FORTUNE THEATRE.

(*See Frontispiece.*)

THE original Fortune Theatre was built on the site of an old tim-
ber house standing in a large garden near Golden Lane, Cripplegate,
and said to have been formerly a nursery for Henry the Eighth's
children, who were sent to this then suburban spot for the benefit of
the air. Edward Alleyn the actor acquired the lease of the house
and grounds on December 22, 1599, and, early the following year,
supported by the Lord Admiral (the Earl of Nottingham), to whose
company of players he belonged, he, in conjunction with Henslowe,
his father-in-law, employed Peter Streete to build there "a newe
house and stadge for a Plaiehowse" for the sum of £440.

Alleyn notes his acquisition of the lease and his expenditure upon
the new theatre in the following terms :—

"What the Fortune cost me Novemb., 1599 [1600].
First for the leas to Brew, £240.
Then for the building the playhouse, £520.
For other privat buildings of myn owne, £120.
So in all it has cost me for the leasse, £880.
Bought the inheritance of the land of the Gills of the Ile of Man,
which is the Fortune, and all the howses in Whight crosstrett and
Gowlding lane, in June, 1610, for the some of £340.
Bought in John Garretts lease in revertion from the Gills for
21 years, for £100.
So in all itt cost me £1320.
Blessed be the Lord God everlasting."

It was at the Fortune that Alleyn's fame as an actor reached its
height. He was especially popular in the character of Barabas in
Marlowe's *Jew of Malta*, which he revived at the new theatre.
Here also many of the plays written in the whole or part by Dekker
were originally performed, as Dekker generally wrote for the Lord
Admiral's company, who played regularly at the Fortune under
Alleyn and Henslowe's management, while the Lord Chamberlain's
company, with whom Shakespeare and Burbadge were associated,
played at the Globe.

Some twenty years after the erection of the theatre Alleyn
records in his diary under date December 9, 1621, "This night, att
12 of ye clock, ye Fortune was burnt." The year following the
theatre was rebuilt, and leased by Alleyn to various persons, he
having then decided to retire from the stage. On the suppression
of the theatres by the Puritans the inside of the Fortune was
destroyed by a company of soldiers, and the lessees failed to pay
their rent, whereby a considerable loss was sustained by the
authorities of Dulwich College, in whom the property of the
Fortune was vested. This eventually led to the Court of Assistants
ordering the more dilapidated portions of the theatre to be pulled
down, and to their leasing the ground belonging to it for building
purposes. So recently, however, as the year 1819, the front of the
old theatre was still standing, as represented in the frontispiece to
the present volume—a reduced copy of an engraving in Wilkinson's
"Londina."

THE SHOEMAKER'S HOLIDAY;

OR A PLEASANT COMEDY OF

THE GENTLE CRAFT.

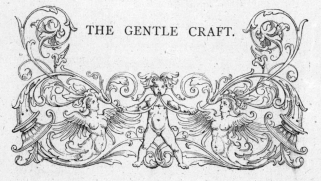

Dekker.

B

HE SHOEMAKER'S HOLIDAY, or a Pleasant Comedy of the Gentle Craft, was first published in 1599, as we learn from a passage in Henslowe's Diary; but the earliest known edition is the quarto of 1600, which describes the play as "acted before the Queen's most excellent Maiestie New-years day at night last, by the right honourable the Earle of Nottingham, Lord High Admirall of England, his seruants." Other editions followed in 1610, 1618, and 1657. Of modern editions, Germany has produced the only one which is at all reliable, and upon this edition, admirably collated and edited by Drs. Karl Warnke and Ludwig Proescholdt, and published at Halle in 1886, the present reprint is based, the excellence of text, notes and introduction, leaving little beyond the modernising and some elucidation here and there to be done.

Dekker appears to have had a collaborator in the play in Robert Wilson, the actor, who is said to have created the part of Firk on its performance, but although Wilson may have provided some of the situations and dialogue, the credit of the play as a whole is undoubtedly Dekker's. *The Shoemaker's Holiday* is the first of Dekker's plays, in order of publication, which has survived, although according to Henslowe he began to write for the stage in 1596.

The conception of Simon Eyre, the Shoemaker, is taken from a real person of that name, who, according to Stow, was an upholsterer, and afterwards a draper. He built Leadenhall in 1419, as referred to by Dekker in Act V.,

Sc. 5, became Sheriff of London in 1434, was elected Lord Mayor in 1445, and died in 1459. About his character nothing certain is known. "It may well be," say the editors of the Halle edition, "that long after Eyre's death the builder of Leadenhall was supposed to have been a shoemaker himself, merely because Leadenhall was used as a leather-market. This tradition was probably taken up by the poet, who formed out of it one of the most popular comedies of the age."

TO ALL GOOD FELLOWS, PROFESSORS OF THE GENTLE CRAFT,[1] OF WHAT DEGREE SOEVER.

Kind gentlemen and honest boon companions, I present you here with a merry-conceited Comedy, called *The Shoemaker's Holiday*, acted by my Lord Admiral's Players this present Christmas before the Queen's most excellent Majesty, for the mirth and pleasant matter by her Highness graciously accepted, being indeed no way offensive. The argument of the play I will set down in this Epistle: Sir Hugh Lacy, Earl of Lincoln, had a young gentleman of his own name, his near kinsman, that loved the Lord Mayor's daughter of London; to prevent and cross which love, the Earl caused his kinsman to be sent Colonel of a company into France: who resigned his place to another gentleman his friend, and came disguised like a Dutch shoemaker to the house of Simon Eyre in Tower Street, who served the Mayor and his household with shoes: the merriments that passed in Eyre's house, his coming to be Mayor of London, Lacy's getting his love, and other accidents, with two merry Three-men's-songs. Take all in good worth that is well intended, for nothing is purposed but mirth; mirth lengtheneth long life, which, with all other blessings, I heartily wish you. Farewell!

[1] Shoemaking was called "the Gentle Craft," possibly in part because the patron saints of shoemakers, St. Crispin and St. Hugh, were said to be of noble, and even royal, blood; possibly because of the sedentary nature of the occupation.

PROLOGUE

As it was pronounced before the Queen's Majesty.

As wretches in a storm (expecting day),
With trembling hands and eyes cast up to heaven,
Make prayers the anchor of their conquered hopes,
So we, dear goddess, wonder of all eyes,
Your meanest vassals, through mistrust and fear
To sink into the bottom of disgrace
By our imperfect pastimes, prostrate thus
On bended knees, our sails of hope do strike,
Dreading the bitter storms of your dislike.
Since then, unhappy men, our hap is such,
That to ourselves ourselves no help can bring,
But needs must perish, if your saint-like ears
(Locking the temple where all mercy sits)
Refuse the tribute of our begging tongues :
Oh grant, bright mirror of true chastity,
From those life-breathing stars, your sun-like eyes,
One gracious smile : for your celestial breath
Must send us life, or sentence us to death.

DRAMATIS PERSONÆ.

THE KING.
THE EARL OF CORNWALL.
SIR HUGH LACY, Earl of Lincoln.
ROWLAND LACY, otherwise HANS, ⎫
ASKEW   ⎬ His Nephews.
SIR ROGER OATELEY, Lord Mayor of London.
Master HAMMON ⎫
Master WARNER ⎬ Citizens of London.
Master SCOTT ⎭
SIMON EYRE, the Shoemaker.
ROGER, commonly called ⎫
    HODGE [1]   ⎪
                          ⎬ EYRE'S Journeymen.
FIRK   ⎪
RALPH   ⎭
LOVELL, a Courtier.
DODGER, Servant to the EARL OF LINCOLN.
A DUTCH SKIPPER.
A BOY.
 Courtiers, Attendants, Officers, Soldiers, Hunters,
    Shoemakers, Apprentices, Servants.

ROSE, Daughter of SIR ROGER.
SYBIL, her Maid.
MARGERY, Wife of SIMON EYRE.
JANE, Wife of RALPH.

SCENE—LONDON and OLD FORD.

[1] A diminutive of Roger.

THE SHOEMAKER'S HOLIDAY.

ACT THE FIRST.

SCENE I.—*A Street in London.*

Enter the LORD MAYOR *and the* EARL OF LINCOLN.

INCOLN. My lord mayor, you have
   sundry times
   Feasted myself and many courtiers
    more :
   Seldom or never can we be so kind
   To make requital of your courtesy.
But leaving this, I hear my cousin Lacy
Is much affected to your daughter Rose.

 L. Mayor. True, my good lord, and she loves him so
  well
That I mislike her boldness in the chase.

 Lincoln. Why, my lord mayor, think you it then a
  shame,
To join a Lacy with an Oateley's name ?

 L. Mayor. Too mean is my poor girl for his high birth ;
Poor citizens must not with courtiers wed,
Who will in silks and gay apparel spend
More in one year than I am worth, by far :
Therefore your honour need not doubt my girl.

 Lincoln. Take heed, my lord, advise you what you do !

A verier unthrift lives not in the world,
Than is my cousin; for I'll tell you what :
'Tis now almost a year since he requested
To travel countries for experience ;
I furnished him with coin, bills of exchange,
Letters of credit, men to wait on him,
Solicited my friends in Italy
Well to respect him.   But to see the end :
Scant had he journeyed through half Germany,
But all his coin was spent, his men cast off,
His bills embezzled,[1] and my jolly coz,
Ashamed to show his bankrupt presence here,
Became a shoemaker in Wittenberg,
A goodly science for a gentleman
Of such descent !   Now judge the rest by this :
Suppose your daughter have a thousand pound,
He did consume me more in one half year ;
And make him heir to all the wealth you have,
One twelvemonth's rioting will waste it all.
Then seek, my lord, some honest citizen
To wed your daughter to.

 L. Mayor.   I thank your lordship.
(Aside) Well, fox, I understand your subtilty.
As for your nephew, let your lordship's eye
But watch his actions, and you need not fear,
For I have sent my daughter far enough.
And yet your cousin Rowland might do well,
Now he hath learned an occupation ;
And yet I scorn to call him son-in-law.

 Lincoln. Ay, but I have a better trade for him :
I thank his grace, he hath appointed him
Chief colonel of all those companies
Mustered in London and the shires about,
To serve his highness in those wars of France.
See where he comes !—

---

[1] Wasted, squandered.

Enter LOVELL, LACY, *and* ASKEW.

Lovell, what news with you?

Lovell. My Lord of Lincoln, 'tis his highness' will,
That presently your cousin ship for France
With all his powers ; he would not for a million,
But they should land at Dieppe within four days.

Lincoln. Go certify his grace, it shall be done.

[*Exit* LOVELL.

Now, cousin Lacy, in what forwardness
Are all your companies ?

Lacy.   All well prepared.
The men of Hertfordshire lie at Mile-end,
Suffolk and Essex train in Tothill-fields,
The Londoners and those of Middlesex,
All gallantly prepared in Finsbury,
With frolic spirits long for their parting hour.

L. Mayor. They have their imprest,[1] coats, and
    furniture ;[2]
And, if it please your cousin Lacy come
To the Guildhall, he shall receive his pay ;
And twenty pounds besides my brethren
Will freely give him, to approve our loves
We bear unto my lord, your uncle here.

Lacy. I thank your honour.

Lincoln.   Thanks, my good lord mayor.

L. Mayor. At the Guildhall we will expect your
    coming.   [*Exit.*

Lincoln. To approve your loves to me?   No subtilty !
Nephew, that twenty pound he doth bestow
For joy to rid you from his daughter Rose.
But, cousins both, now here are none but friends,
I would not have you cast an amorous eye
Upon so mean a project as the love
Of a gay, wanton, painted citizen.

---

[1] Regimental badge or device.
[2] Weapons and martial equipment.

I know, this churl even in the height of scorn
Doth hate the mixture of his blood with thine.
I pray thee, do thou so !   Remember, coz,
What honourable fortunes wait on thee :
Increase the king's love, which so brightly shines,
And gilds thy hopes.   I have no heir but thee,—
And yet not thee, if with a wayward spirit
Thou start from the true bias of my love.

   Lacy. My lord, I will for honour, not desire
Of land or livings, or to be your heir,
So guide my actions in pursuit of France,
As shall add glory to the Lacys' name.

   Lincoln. Coz, for those words here's thirty Portuguese [1]
And, nephew Askew, there's a few for you.
Fair Honour, in her loftiest eminence,
Stays in France for you, till you fetch her thence.
Then, nephews, clap swift wings on your designs :
Begone, begone, make haste to the Guildhall ;
There presently I'll meet you.   Do not stay :
Where honour beckons, shame attends delay.   [*Exit.*

   Askew. How gladly would your uncle have you gone !
   Lacy. True, coz, but I'll o'erreach his policies.
I have some serious business for three days,
Which nothing but my presence can dispatch.
You, therefore, cousin, with the companies,
Shall haste to Dover ; there I'll meet with you :
Or, if I stay past my prefixèd time,
Away for France ; we'll meet in Normandy.
The twenty pounds my lord mayor gives to me
You shall receive, and these ten Portuguese,
Part of mine uncle's thirty.   Gentle coz,
Have care to our great charge ; I know, your wisdom
Hath tried itself in higher consequence.

   Askew. Coz, all myself am yours : yet have this care,
To lodge in London with all secrecy ;

---

[1] A gold coin, worth about three pounds twelve shillings.

Our uncle Lincoln hath, besides his own,
Many a jealous eye, that in your face
Stares only to watch means for your disgrace.

Lacy. Stay, cousin, who be these?

Enter SIMON EYRE, MARGERY *his wife*, HODGE, FIRK,
JANE, *and* RALPH *with a pair of shoes.*[1]

Eyre. Leave whining, leave whining! Away with this whimpering, this puling, these blubbering tears, and these wet eyes! I'll get thy husband discharged, I warrant thee, sweet Jane; go to!

Hodge. Master, here be the captains.

Eyre. Peace, Hodge; hush, ye knave, hush!

Firk. Here be the cavaliers and the colonels, master.

Eyre. Peace, Firk; peace, my fine Firk! Stand by with your pishery-pashery,[2] away! I am a man of the best presence; I'll speak to them, an they were Popes. —Gentlemen, captains, colonels, commanders! Brave men, brave leaders, may it please you to give me audience. I am Simon Eyre, the mad shoemaker of Tower Street; this wench with the mealy mouth that will never tire, is my wife, I can tell you; here's Hodge, my man and my foreman; here's Firk, my fine firking journeyman, and this is blubbered Jane. All we come to be suitors for this honest Ralph. Keep him at home, and as I am a true shoemaker and a gentleman of the gentle craft, buy spurs yourselves, and I'll find ye boots these seven years.

Marg. Seven years, husband?

Eyre. Peace, midriff, peace! I know what I do. Peace!

Firk. Truly, master cormorant, you shall do God good service to let Ralph and his wife stay together. She's a young new-married woman; if you take her husband away

---

[1] The quarto has " with a piece." Piece (old Fr. *bobelin*) was sometimes loosely used for the shoe itself, as well as for the piece of leather used in repairs. See *Cotgrave*.

[2] Twiddle-twaddle.

from her a night, you undo her ; she may beg in the day-time ; for he's as good a workman at a prick and an awl, as any is in our trade.

Jane. O let him stay, else I shall be undone.

Firk. Ay, truly, she shall be laid at one side like a pair of old shoes else, and be occupied for no use.

Lacy. Truly, my friends, it lies not in my power :
The Londoners are pressed, paid, and set forth
By the lord mayor ; I cannot change a man.

Hodge. Why, then you were as good be a corporal as a colonel, if you cannot discharge one good fellow ; and I tell you true, I think you do more than you can answer, to press a man within a year and a day of his marriage.

Eyre. Well said, melancholy Hodge ; gramercy, my fine foreman.

Marg. Truly, gentlemen, it were ill done for such as you, to stand so stiffly against a poor young wife, con-sidering her case, she is new-married, but let that pass : I pray, deal not roughly with her ; her husband is a young man, and but newly entered, but let that pass.

Eyre. Away with your pishery-pashery, your pols and your edipols ! [1] Peace, midriff ; silence, Cicely Bum-trinket ! Let your head speak.

Firk. Yea, and the horns too, master.

Eyre. Too soon, my fine Firk, too soon ! Peace, scoun-drels ! See you this man ? Captains, you will not release him ? Well, let him go ; he's a proper shot ; let him vanish ! Peace, Jane, dry up thy tears, they'll make his powder dankish. Take him, brave men ; Hector of Troy was an hackney to him, Hercules and Termagant [2] scoundrels, Prince Arthur's Round-table—by the Lord of Ludgate [3]—ne'er fed such a tall, such a dapper swords-

---

[1] Apparently one of Eyre's frequent improvised phrases, referring here to his wife's trick of repeating herself, as in her previous speech.

[2] An imaginary Saracen god, represented in the old moralities and plays as of a quite ungodly tendency to violence.

[3] A nick-name, possibly, for some character of the day, used with a vague reference to King Lud.

man ; by the life of Pharaoh, a brave, resolute swordsman !
Peace, Jane ! I say no more, mad knaves.

Firk. See, see, Hodge, how my master raves in commendation of Ralph !

Hodge. Ralph, th'art a gull, by this hand, an thou
goest not.

Askew. I am glad, good Master Eyre, it is my hap
To meet so resolute a soldier.
Trust me, for your report and love to him,
A common slight regard shall not respect him.

Lacy. Is thy name Ralph ?

Ralph.   Yes, sir.

Lacy.   Give me thy hand ;
Thou shalt not want, as I am a gentleman.
Woman, be patient ; God, no doubt, will send
Thy husband safe again ; but he must go,
His country's quarrel says it shall be so.

Hodge. Th'art a gull, by my stirrup, if thou dost not go.
I will not have thee strike thy gimlet into these weak
vessels ; prick thine enemies, Ralph.

Enter DODGER.

Dodger. My lord, your uncle on the Tower-hill
Stays with the lord mayor and the aldermen,
And doth request you with all speed you may,
To hasten thither.

Askew.   Cousin, let's go.

Lacy. Dodger, run you before, tell them we come.—
This Dodger is mine uncle's parasite,   [*Exit* DODGER.
The arrant'st varlet that e'er breathed on earth ;
He sets more discord in a noble house
By one day's broaching of his pickthank tales,[1]
Than can be salved again in twenty years,
And he, I fear, shall go with us to France,
To pry into our actions.

---

[1] Tales told to curry favour.

Askew.   Therefore, coz,
It shall behove you to be circumspect.

Lacy. Fear not, good cousin.—Ralph, hie to your colours.

Ralph. I must, because there's no remedy;
But, gentle master and my loving dame,
As you have always been a friend to me,
So in mine absence think upon my wife.

Jane. Alas, my Ralph.

Marg. She cannot speak for weeping.

Eyre. Peace, you cracked groats,[1] you mustard tokens,[2] disquiet not the brave soldier.   Go thy ways, Ralph!

Jane. Ay, ay, you bid him go; what shall I do
When he is gone?

Firk. Why, be doing with me or my fellow Hodge; be not idle.

Eyre. Let me see thy hand, Jane.   This fine hand, this white hand, these pretty fingers must spin, must card, must work; work, you bombast-cotton-candle-quean;[3] work for your living, with a pox to you.—Hold thee, Ralph, here's five sixpences for thee; fight for the honour of the gentle craft, for the gentlemen shoemakers, the courageous cordwainers, the flower of St. Martin's, the mad knaves of Bedlam, Fleet Street, Tower Street and Whitechapel; crack me the crowns of the French knaves; a pox on them, crack them; fight, by the Lord of Ludgate; fight, my fine boy!

Firk. Here, Ralph, here's three twopences: two carry into France, the third shall wash our souls at part-ing, for sorrow is dry.   For my sake, firk the *Basa mon cues.*

Hodge. Ralph, I am heavy at parting; but here's a

---

[1] The groat was the silver fourpenny-piece.   The simile of a cracked coin is an obvious expression of worthlessness.

[2] Little yellow spots on the body which denoted the infection of the plague.

[3] Another of Eyre's improvised phrases, whose component parts sufficiently explain its meaning.

shilling for thee. God send thee to cram thy slops with
French crowns, and thy enemies' bellies with bullets.

Ralph. I thank you, master, and I thank you all.
Now, gentle wife, my loving lovely Jane,
Rich men, at parting, give their wives rich gifts,
Jewels and rings, to grace their lily hands.
Thou know'st our trade makes rings for women's heels:
Here take this pair of shoes, cut out by Hodge,
Stitched by my fellow Firk, seamed by myself,
Made up and pinked with letters for thy name.
Wear them, my dear Jane, for thy husband's sake;
And every morning, when thou pull'st them on,
Remember me, and pray for my return.
Make much of them; for I have made them so,
That I can know them from a thousand mo.

Drum sounds. Enter the LORD MAYOR, *the* Earl *of*
LINCOLN, LACY, ASKEW, DODGER, *and* Soldiers.
They pass over the stage; RALPH *falls in amongst
them;* FIRK *and the rest cry* "Farewell," *etc., and
so exeunt.*

ACT THE SECOND.

SCENE I.—*A Garden at Old Ford.*

Enter ROSE, *alone, making a garland.*

OSE. Here sit thou down upon this
flow'ry bank,
And make a garland for thy Lacy's
head.
These pinks, these roses, and these
violets,
These blushing gilliflowers, these marigolds,
The fair embroidery of his coronet,
Carry not half such beauty in their cheeks,
As the sweet countenance of my Lacy doth.
O my most unkind father! O my stars,
Why lowered you so at my nativity,
To make me love, yet live robbed of my love?
Here as a thief am I imprisonëd
For my dear Lacy's sake within those walls,
Which by my father's cost were builded up
For better purposes; here must I languish
For him that doth as much lament, I know,
Mine absence, as for him I pine in woe.

Enter SYBIL.

Sybil. Good morrow, young mistress. I am sure you
make that garland for me; against I shall be Lady of the
Harvest.

Rose. Sybil, what news at London?

Sybil. None but good; my lord mayor, your father, and master Philpot, your uncle, and Master Scot, your cousin, and Mistress Frigbottom by Doctors' Commons, do all, by my troth, send you most hearty commendations.

Rose. Did Lacy send kind greetings to his love?

Sybil. O yes, out of cry, by my troth. I scant knew him; here 'a wore a scarf; and here a scarf, here a bunch of feathers, and here precious stones and jewels, and a pair of garters,—O, monstrous! like one of our yellow silk curtains at home here in Old Ford house, here in Master Belly-mount's chamber. I stood at our door in Cornhill, looked at him, he at me indeed, spake to him, but he not to me, not a word; marry go-up, thought I, with a wanion![1] He passed by me as proud— Marry foh! are you grown humorous, thought I; and so shut the door, and in I came.

Rose. O Sybil, how dost thou my Lacy wrong!
My Rowland is as gentle as a lamb,
No dove was ever half so mild as he.

Sybil. Mild? yea, as a bushel of stamped crabs.[2] He looked upon me as sour as verjuice. Go thy ways, thought I; thou may'st be much in my gaskins,[3] but nothing in my nether-stocks. This is your fault, mistress, to love him that loves not you; he thinks scorn to do as he's done to; but if I were as you, I'd cry: Go by, Jeronimo, go by![4]

I'd set mine old debts against my new driblets,
And the hare's foot against the goose giblets,
For if ever I sigh, when sleep I should take,
Pray God I may lose my maidenhead when I wake.

Rose. Will my love leave me then, and go to France?
Sybil. I know not that, but I am sure I see him stalk before the soldiers. By my troth, he is a proper man;

---

[1] With a vengeance.   [2] Crushed crab apples.
[3] A kind of trousers, first worn by the Gascons.
[4] A phrase from Kyd's *Spanish Tragedy*.

Dekker.   C

but he is proper that proper doth. Let him go snick-
up,[1] young mistress.

Rose. Get thee to London, and learn perfectly,
Whether my Lacy go to France, or no.
Do this, and I will give thee for thy pains
My cambric apron and my Romish gloves,
My purple stockings and a stomacher.
Say, wilt thou do this, Sybil, for my sake?

Sybil. Will I, quoth a? At whose suit? By my troth,
yes I'll go. A cambric apron, gloves, a pair of purple
stockings, and a stomacher! I'll sweat in purple, mistress, for you; I'll take anything that comes a God's
name. O rich! a cambric apron! Faith, then have at
' up tails all.' I'll go jiggy-joggy to London, and be here
in a trice, young mistress.   [*Exit.*

Rose. Do so, good Sybil.   Meantime wretched I
Will sit and sigh for his lost company.   [*Exit.*

SCENE II.—*A Street in London.*

Enter LACY, *disguised as a Dutch Shoemaker.*

Lacy. How many shapes have gods and kings devised,
Thereby to compass their desired loves!
It is no shame for Rowland Lacy, then,
To clothe his cunning with the gentle craft,
That, thus disguised, I may unknown possess
The only happy presence of my Rose.
For her have I forsook my charge in France,
Incurred the king's displeasure, and stirred up
Rough hatred in mine uncle Lincoln's breast.
O love, how powerful art thou, that canst change
High birth to baseness, and a noble mind

---

[1] *i.e.* Go and be hanged!

To the mean semblance of a shoemaker !
But thus it must be.   For her cruel father,
Hating the single union of our souls,
Has secretly conveyed my Rose from London,
To bar me of her presence ; but I trust,
Fortune and this disguise will further me
Once more to view her beauty, gain her sight.
Here in Tower Street with Eyre the shoemaker
Mean I a while to work ; I know the trade,
I learnt it when I was in Wittenberg.
Then cheer thy hoping spirits, be not dismayed,
Thou canst not want : do Fortune what she can,
The gentle craft is living for a man.   [*Exit.*

SCENE III.--*An open Yard before* EYRE'S *House.*

Enter EYRE, *making himself ready.*[1]

Eyre. Where be these boys, these girls, these drabs,
these scoundrels ? They wallow in the fat brewiss [2] of my
bounty, and lick up the crumbs of my table, yet will not
rise to see my walks cleansed.   Come out, you powder-
beef [3] queans ! What, Nan ! what, Madge Mumble-crust.
Come out, you fat midriff-swag-belly-whores, and sweep
me these kennels that the noisome stench offend not
the noses of my neighbours.   What, Firk, I say ; what,
Hodge ! Open my shop-windows ! What, Firk, I say !

Enter FIRK.

Firk. O master, is't you that speak bandog[4] and Bed-

---

[1] *i.e.* Dressing himself.
[2] Bread soaked in pot liquor, and prepared *secundum artem.*—
Nares.   [3] Salted beef.
[4] A dog kept fastened up as a watch-dog, and therefore given to
loud barking.

lam this morning? I was in a dream, and mused what madman was got into the street so early; have you drunk this morning that your throat is so clear?

Eyre. Ah, well said, Firk; well said, Firk. To work, my fine knave, to work! Wash thy face, and thou'lt be more blest.

Firk. Let them wash my face that will eat it. Good master, send for a souse-wife,[1] if you'll have my face cleaner.

Enter HODGE.

Eyre. Away, sloven! avaunt, scoundrel! — Good-morrow, Hodge; good-morrow, my fine foreman.

Hodge. O, master, good-morrow; y'are an early stirrer. Here's a fair morning.—Good-morrow, Firk, I could have slept this hour. Here's a brave day towards.

Eyre. Oh, haste to work, my fine foreman, haste to work.

Firk. Master, I am dry as dust to hear my fellow Roger talk of fair weather; let us pray for good leather, and let clowns and ploughboys and those that work in the fields pray for brave days. We work in a dry shop; what care I if it rain?

Enter MARGERY.

Eyre. How now, Dame Margery, can you see to rise? Trip and go, call up the drabs, your maids.

Marg. See to rise? I hope 'tis time enough, 'tis early enough for any woman to be seen abroad. I marvel how many wives in Tower Street are up so soon. Gods me, 'tis not noon,—here's a yawling![2]

Eyre. Peace, Margery, peace! Where's Cicely Bum-trinket, your maid? She has a privy fault, she farts in her sleep. Call the quean up; if my men want shoe-thread, I'll swinge her in a stirrup.

---

[1] A woman who washed and pickled pigs' faces.
[2] Bawling.

Firk. Yet, that's but a dry beating ; here's still a sign of drought.

Enter LACY *disguised, singing.*

Lacy.   *Der was een bore van Gelderland*
       Frolick sie byen ;
      He was als dronck he cold nyet stand,
      Upsolce sie byen.
      Tap eens de canneken,
      Drincke, schone mannekin.[1]

Firk. Master, for my life, yonder's a brother of the gentle craft ; if he bear not Saint Hugh's bones,[2] I'll forfeit my bones ; he's some uplandish workman : hire him, good master, that I may learn some gibble-gabble ; 'twill make us work the faster.

Eyre. Peace, Firk ! A hard world ! Let him pass, let him vanish ; we have journeymen enow. Peace, my fine Firk !

Marg. Nay, nay, y'are best follow your man's counsel ; you shall see what will come on't : we have not men enow, but we must entertain every butter-box ; but let that pass.

Hodge. Dame, 'fore God, if my master follow your counsel, he'll consume little beef. He shall be glad of men, and he can catch them.

Firk. Ay, that he shall.

Hodge. 'Fore God, a proper man, and I warrant, a fine workman. Master, farewell ; dame, adieu ; if such a man as he cannot find work, Hodge is not for you.

                                [*Offers to go.*

Eyre. Stay, my fine Hodge.

[1] There was a boor from Gelderland,
      Jolly they be ;
He was so drunk he could not stand,
      Drunken they be :
Clink then the cannikin,
      Drink, pretty mannikin !
[2] St. Hugh was the patron saint of shoemakers, and his bones were supposed to have been made into shoemaker's tools, for which this came to be a common term.

Firk. Faith, an your foreman go, dame, you must take a journey to seek a new journeyman; if Roger remove, Firk follows. If Saint Hugh's bones shall not be set a-work, I may prick mine awl in the walls, and go play. Fare ye well, master; good-bye, dame.

Eyre. Tarry, my fine Hodge, my brisk foreman! Stay, Firk! Peace, pudding-broth! By the Lord of Ludgate, I love my men as my life. Peace, you galli-mafry![1] Hodge, if he want work, I'll hire him. One of you to him; stay,—he comes to us.

Lacy. Goeden dach, meester, ende u vro oak.[2]

Firk. Nails, if I should speak after him without drinking, I should choke. And you, friend Oake, are you of the gentle craft?

Lacy. Yaw, yaw, ik bin den skomawker.[3]

Firk. Den skomaker, quoth a! And hark you, *sko-maker*, have you all your tools, a good rubbing-pin, a good stopper, a good dresser, your four sorts of awls, and your two balls of wax, your paring knife, your hand- and thumb-leathers, and good St. Hugh's bones to smooth up your work?

Lacy. Yaw, yaw; be niet vorveard. Ik hab all de din-gen voour mack skooes groot and cleane.[4]

Firk. Ha, ha! Good master, hire him; he'll make me laugh so that I shall work more in mirth than I can in earnest.

Eyre. Hear ye, friend, have ye any skill in the mystery of cordwainers?

Lacy. Ik weet niet wat yow seg; ich verstaw you niet.[5]

Firk. Why, thus, man: *(Imitating by gesture a shoe-maker at work)* Ich verste u niet, quoth a.

Lacy. Yaw, yaw, yaw; ick can dat wel doen.[6]

[1] A dish of different hashed meats.
[2] Good day, master, and your wife too.
[3] Yes, yes, I am a shoemaker.
[4] Yes, yes; be not afraid. I have everything, to make boots big and little.
[5] I don't know what you say; I don't understand you.
[6] Yes, yes, yes; I can do that very well.

Firk. *Yaw, yaw!* He speaks yawing like a jackdaw that gapes to be fed with cheese-curds. Oh, he'll give a villanous pull at a can of double-beer; but Hodge and I have the vantage, we must drink first, because we are the eldest journeymen.

Eyre. What is thy name?

Lacy. Hans—Hans Meulter.

Eyre. Give me thy hand; th'art welcome.—Hodge, entertain him; Firk, bid him welcome; come, Hans. Run, wife, bid your maids, your trullibubs,[1] make ready my fine men's breakfasts. To him, Hodge!

Hodge. Hans, th'art welcome; use thyself friendly, for we are good fellows; if not, thou shalt be fought with, wert thou bigger than a giant.

Firk. Yea, and drunk with, wert thou Gargantua. My master keeps no cowards, I tell thee.—Ho, boy, bring him an heel-block, here's a new journeyman.

Enter Boy.

Lacy. *O, ich wersto you; ich moet een halve dossen cans betaelen; here, boy, nempt dis skilling, tap eens freelicke.*[2]

[*Exit* Boy.

Eyre. Quick, snipper-snapper, away! Firk, scour thy throat, thou shalt wash it with Castilian liquor.

Enter Boy.

Come, my last of the fives, give me a can. Have to thee, Hans; here, Hodge; here, Firk; drink, you mad Greeks, and work like true Trojans, and pray for Simon Eyre, the shoemaker.—Here, Hans, and th'art welcome.

Firk. Lo, dame, you would have lost a good fellow that will teach us to laugh. This beer came hopping in well.

---

[1] Slatterns, sluts.

[2] O, I understand you; I must pay for half-a-dozen cans; here, boy, take this shilling, tap this once freely.

Marg. Simon, it is almost seven.

Eyre. Is't so, Dame Clapper-dudgeon?[1] Is't seven a
clock, and my men's breakfast not ready? Trip and go,
you soused conger,[2] away! Come, you mad hyper-
boreans; follow me, Hodge; follow me, Hans; come
after, my fine Firk; to work, to work a while, and then
to breakfast! 　　　　　　　　　　　　　[*Exit.*

Firk. Soft! *Yaw, yaw,* good Hans, though my
master have no more wit but to call you afore me, I am
not so foolish to go behind you, I being the elder journeyman. 　　　　　　　　　　　　　　　[*Exeunt.*

SCENE IV.—*A Field near Old Ford.*

Holloaing within.   Enter Master WARNER *and*
Master HAMMON, *attired as* Hunters.

Ham. Cousin, beat every brake, the game's not far,
This way with wingèd feet he fled from death,
Whilst the pursuing hounds, scenting his steps,
Find out his highway to destruction.
Besides, the miller's boy told me even now,
He saw him take soil,[3] and he holloaed him,
Affirming him to have been so embost[4]
That long he could not hold.

Warn. 　　　　　　　　If it be so,
'Tis best we trace these meadows by Old Ford.

A noise of Hunters *within.   Enter a* Boy.

Ham. How now, boy? Where's the deer? speak,
saw'st thou him?

Boy. O yea; I saw him leap through a hedge, and

---

[1] Cant term for a beggar. 　　　　[2] Conger-eel.
[3] Take cover. 　　　　[4] Spent; panting with exhaustion.

then over a ditch, then at my lord mayor's pale, over he skipped me, and in he went me, and "holla" the hunters cried, and "there, boy; there, boy!" But there he is, 'a mine honesty.

Ham. Boy, God amercy. Cousin, let's away; I hope we shall find better sport to-day.   [*Exeunt.*

SCENE V.—*Another part of the Field.*

Hunting within.   Enter ROSE *and* SYBIL.

Rose. Why, Sybil, wilt thou prove a forester?

Sybil. Upon some, no; forester, go by; no, faith, mistress. The deer came running into the barn through the orchard and over the pale; I wot well, I looked as pale as a new cheese to see him. But whip, says Goodman Pin-close, up with his flail, and our Nick with a prong, and down he fell, and they upon him, and I upon them. By my troth, we had such sport; and in the end we ended him; his throat we cut, flayed him, unhorned him, and my lord mayor shall eat of him anon, when he comes.   [*Horns sound within.*

Rose. Hark, hark, the hunters come; y'are best take heed,
    They'll have a saying to you for this deed.

Enter Master HAMMON, Master WARNER, Huntsmen, *and* Boy.

Ham. God save you, fair ladies.

Sybil.   Ladies! O gross![1]

Warn. Came not a buck this way?

Rose.   No, but two does.

Ham. And which way went they?   Faith, we'll hunt at those.

[1] Stupid.

Sybil. At those? upon some, no : when, can you tell?

Warn. Upon some, ay?

Sybil.   Good Lord!

Warn.   Wounds! Then farewell!

Ham. Boy, which way went he?

Boy.   This way, sir, he ran.

Ham. This way he ran indeed, fair Mistress Rose;
Our game was lately in your orchard seen.

Warn. Can you advise, which way he took his flight?

Sybil. Follow your nose; his horns will guide you right.

Warn. Th'art a mad wench.

Sybil.   O, rich!

Rose.   Trust me, not I.
It is not like that the wild forest-deer
Would come so near to places of resort;
You are deceived, he fled some other way.

Warn. Which way, my sugar-candy, can you shew?

Sybil. Come up, good honeysops, upon some, no.

Rose. Why do you stay, and not pursue your game?

Sybil. I'll hold my life, their hunting-nags be lame.

Ham. A deer more dear is found within this place.

Rose. But not the deer, sir, which you had in chase.

Ham. I chased the deer, but this dear chaseth me.

Rose. The strangest hunting that ever I see.
But where's your park?   [*She offers to go away.*

Ham.   'Tis here :   O stay!

Rose. Impale me, and then I will not stray.

Warn. They wrangle, wench; we are more kind than
     they.

Sybil. What kind of hart is that dear heart, you seek?

Warn. A hart, dear heart.

Sybil.   Who ever saw the like?

Rose. To lose your heart, is't possible you can?

Ham. My heart is lost.

Rose.   Alack, good gentleman!

Ham. This poor lost hart would I wish you might find.

Rose. You, by such luck, might prove your hart a hind.

Ham. Why, Luck had horns, so have I heard some say.

Rose. Now, God, an't be his will, send Luck into your
  way.

Enter the LORD MAYOR *and* Servants.

L. Mayor. What, Master Hammon? Welcome to
  Old Ford !

Sybil. Gods pittikins, hands off, sir !   Here's my lord.

L. Mayor. I hear you had ill luck, and lost your game.

Ham. Tis true, my lord.

L. Mayor.   I am sorry for the same.
What gentleman is this?

Ham.   My brother-in-law.

L. Mayor. Y'are welcome both ; sith Fortune offers
  you
Into my hands, you shall not part from hence,
Until you have refreshed your wearied limbs.
Go, Sybil, cover the board !   You shall be guest
To no good cheer, but even a hunter's feast.

Ham. I thank your lordship.—Cousin, on my life,
For our lost venison I shall find a wife.   [*Exeunt.*

L. Mayor. In, gentlemen ; I'll not be absent long.—
This Hammon is a proper gentleman,
A citizen by birth, fairly allied ;
How fit an husband were he for my girl !
Well, I will in, and do the best I can,
To match my daughter to this gentleman.   [*Exit.*

ACT THE THIRD.

SCENE I.—*A Room in* Eyre's *House.*

Enter Lacy *otherwise* Hans, Skipper, Hodge, *and* Firk.

KIP. *Ick sal yow wat seggen, Hans ; dis skip, dat comen from Candy, is al vol, by Got's sacrament, van sugar, civet, almonds, cambrick, end alle dingen, towsand towsand ding. Nempt it, Hans, nempt it vor v meester. Daer be de bils van laden. Your meester Simon Eyre sal hae good copen. Wat seggen yow, Hans ?*[1]

Firk. Wat seggen de reggen de copen, slopen—laugh, Hodge, laugh !

Hans. Mine liever broder Firk, bringt Meester Eyre tot det signe vn Swannekin ; daer sal yow finde dis skipper end me. Wat seggen yow, broder Firk ? Doot it, Hodge.[2] Come, skipper. [*Exeunt.*

Firk. Bring him, quoth you ? Here's no knavery, to bring my master to buy a ship worth the lading of two or

[1] I'll tell you what, Hans ; this ship that is come from Candia, is quite full, by God's sacrament, of sugar, civet, almonds, cambric, and all things ; a thousand, thousand things. Take it, Hans, take it for your master. There are the bills of lading. Your master, Simon Eyre, shall have a good bargain. What say you, Hans ?

[2] My dear brother Firk, bring Master Eyre to the sign of the Swan ; there shall you find this skipper and me. What say you, brother Firk ? Do it, Hodge.—[There were at this time two inns with the sign of the Swan in London, one at Dowgate, the other in Old Fish Street.]

three hundred thousand pounds.   Alas, that's nothing ; a trifle, a bauble, Hodge.

Hodge. The truth is, Firk, that the merchant owner of the ship dares not shew his head, and therefore this skipper that deals for him, for the love he bears to Hans, offers my master Eyre a bargain in the commodities. He shall have a reasonable day of payment ; he may sell the wares by that time, and be an huge gainer himself.

Firk. Yea, but can my fellow Hans lend my master twenty porpentines as an earnest penny ?

Hodge. Portuguese,[1] thou wouldst say ; here they be, Firk ; hark, they jingle in my pocket like St. Mary Overy's bells.[2]

Enter EYRE *and* MARGERY.

Firk. Mum, here comes my dame and my master. She'll scold, on my life, for loitering this Monday ; but all's one, let them all say what they can, Monday's our holiday.

Marg. You sing, Sir Sauce, but I beshrew your heart,
      I fear, for this your singing we shall smart.

Firk. Smart for me, dame ; why, dame, why ?

Hodge. Master, I hope you'll not suffer my dame to take down your journeymen.

Firk. If she take me down, I'll take her up ; yea, and take her down too, a button-hole lower.

Eyre. Peace, Firk ; not I, Hodge ; by the life of Pharaoh, by the Lord of Ludgate, by this beard, every hair whereof I value at a king's ransom, she shall not meddle with you.—Peace, you bombast-cotton-candle-quean ; away, queen of clubs ; quarrel not with me and my men, with me and my fine Firk ; I'll firk you, if you do.

---

[1] A coin worth about three pounds twelve shillings.

[2] "East from the Bishop of Winchester's house, directly over against it, stands a fair church, called St. Mary over the Rie, or Overie, that is, over the water."—*Stow's Survey of London.*

Marg. Yea, yea, man, you may use me as you please ; but let that pass.

Eyre. Let it pass, let it vanish away; peace ! Am I not Simon Eyre ? Are not these my brave men, brave shoemakers, all gentlemen of the gentle craft ? Prince am I none, yet am I nobly born, as being the sole son of a shoemaker. Away, rubbish ! vanish, melt; melt like kitchen-stuff.

Marg. Yea, yea, 'tis well; I must be called rubbish, kitchen-stuff, for a sort of knaves.

Firk. Nay, dame, you shall not weep and wail in woe for me. Master, I'll stay no longer ; here's an inventory of my shop-tools. Adieu, master ; Hodge, farewell.

Hodge. Nay, stay, Firk ; thou shalt not go alone.

Marg. I pray, let them go; there be more maids than Mawkin, more men than Hodge, and more fools than Firk.

Firk. Fools ? Nails ! if I tarry now, I would my guts might be turned to shoe-thread.

Hodge. And if I stay, I pray God I may be turned to a Turk, and set in Finsbury [1] for boys to shoot at.— Come, Firk.

Eyre. Stay, my fine knaves, you arms of my trade, you pillars of my profession. What, shall a tittle-tattle's words make you forsake Simon Eyre ?—Avaunt, kitchen-stuff ! Rip, you brown-bread Tannikin ; [2] out of my sight ! Move me not ! Have not I ta'en you from selling tripes in Eastcheap, and set you in my shop, and made you hail-fellow with Simon Eyre, the shoemaker ? And now do you deal thus with my journeymen ? Look, you powder-beef-quean, on the face of Hodge, here's a face for a lord.

Firk. And here's a face for any lady in Christendom.

Eyre. Rip, you chitterling, avaunt ! Boy, bid the

---

[1] Finsbury was a famous practising ground for archery at this time.

[2] A name given to Dutchwomen.

tapster of the Boar's Head fill me a dozen cans of beer for my journeymen.

Firk. A dozen cans? O, brave! Hodge, now I'll stay.

Eyre. (*In a low voice to the* Boy). An the knave fills any more than two, he pays for them. (*Exit* Boy. *Aloud.*) A dozen cans of beer for my journeymen. (*Re-enter* Boy.) Here, you mad Mesopotamians, wash your livers with this liquor. Where be the odd ten? No more, Madge, no more.—Well said. Drink and to work! —What work dost thou, Hodge? what work?

Hodge. I am a making a pair of shoes for my lord mayor's daughter, Mistress Rose.

Firk. And I a pair of shoes for Sybil, my lord's maid. I deal with her.

Eyre. Sybil? Fie, defile not thy fine workmanly fingers with the feet of kitchenstuff and basting-ladles. Ladies of the court, fine ladies, my lads, commit their feet to our apparelling; put gross work to Hans. Yark and seam, yark and seam!

Firk. For yarking and seaming let me alone, an I come to't.

Hodge. Well, master, all this is from the bias.[1] Do you remember the ship my fellow Hans told you of? The skipper and he are both drinking at the Swan. Here be the Portuguese to give earnest. If you go through with it, you cannot choose but be a lord at least.

Firk. Nay, dame, if my master prove not a lord, and you a lady, hang me.

Marg. Yea, like enough, if you may loiter and tipple thus.

Firk. Tipple, dame? No, we have been bargaining with Skellum Skanderbag:[2] can you Dutch spreaken for a ship of silk Cyprus, laden with sugar-candy.

---

[1] By the way, beside the question.

[2] German: Schelm, a scoundrel. Skanderbag, or Scander Beg (*i.e.* Lord Alexander), a Turkish name for John Kastriota, the Albanian hero, who freed his country from the yoke of the Turks (1443—1467).

Enter Boy *with a velvet coat and an Alderman's gown.*
EYRE *puts them on.*

Eyre. Peace, Firk ; silence, Tittle-tattle ! Hodge, I'll
go through with it. Here's a seal-ring, and I have sent
for a guarded gown [1] and a damask cassock. See where
it comes ; look here, Maggy ; help me, Firk ; apparel me,
Hodge ; silk and satin, you mad Philistines, silk and
satin.

Firk. Ha, ha, my master will be as proud as a dog in
a doublet, all in beaten [2] damask and velvet.

Eyre. Softly, Firk, for rearing [3] of the nap, and wearing threadbare my garments. How dost thou like me,
Firk ? How do I look, my fine Hodge ?

Hodge. Why, now you look like yourself, master. I
warrant you, there's few in the city, but will give you the
wall, and come upon you with the right worshipful.

Firk. Nails, my master looks like a threadbare cloak
new turned and dressed. Lord, Lord, to see what good
raiment doth ! Dame, dame, are you not enamoured ?

Eyre. How say'st thou, Maggy, am I not brisk ? Am
I not fine ?

Marg. Fine ? By my troth, sweetheart, very fine ! By
my troth, I never liked thee so well in my life, sweetheart ;
but let that pass. I warrant, there be many women in the
city have not such handsome husbands, but only for their
apparel ; but let that pass too.

Re-enter HANS *and* Skipper.

*Hans. Godden day, mester. Dis be de skipper dat heb
de skip van marchandice ; de commodity ben good ; nempt
it, master, nempt it.* [4]

Eyre. Godamercy, Hans ; welcome, skipper. Where
lies this ship of merchandise ?

---

[1] A robe ornamented with guards or facings.
[2] Stamped.   [3] Raising up, ruffling.
[4] Good day, master. This is the skipper that has the ship of
merchandise ; the commodity is good ; take it, master, take it.

Skip. *De skip ben in revere; dor be van Sugar, cyvet, almonds, cambrick, and a towsand towsand tings, gotz sacrament; nempt it, mester: ye sal heb good copen.*[1]

Firk. To him, master! O sweet master! O sweet wares! Prunes, almonds, sugar-candy, carrot-roots, turnips, O brave fatting meat! Let not a man buy a nutmeg but yourself.

Eyre. Peace, Firk! Come, skipper, I'll go aboard with you.—Hans, have you made him drink?

Skip. *Yaw, yaw, ic heb veale gedrunck.*[2]

Eyre. Come, Hans, follow me. Skipper, thou shalt have my countenance in the city. [*Exeunt.*

Firk. *Yaw, heb veale gedrunck,* quoth a. They may well be called butter-boxes, when they drink fat veal and thick beer too. But come, dame, I hope you'll chide us no more.

Marg. No, faith, Firk; no, perdy,[3] Hodge. I do feel honour creep upon me, and which is more, a certain rising in my flesh; but let that pass.

Firk. Rising in your flesh do you feel, say you? Ay, you may be with child, but why should not my master feel a rising in his flesh, having a gown and a gold ring on? But you are such a shrew, you'll soon pull him down.

Marg. Ha, ha! prithee, peace! Thou mak'st my worship laugh; but let that pass. Come, I'll go in; Hodge, prithee, go before me; Firk, follow me.

Firk. Firk doth follow: Hodge, pass out in state.

[*Exeunt.*

---

[1] The ship lies in the river; there are sugar, civet, almonds, cambric, and a thousand thousand things, by God's sacrament, take it, master; you shall have a good bargain.

[2] Yes, yes, I have drunk well.

[3] Fr. *Par Dieu.* The word here means "truly."

SCENE II.—*London : a Room in* LINCOLN'S *House.*

Enter the EARL OF LINCOLN *and* DODGER.

Lincoln. How now, good Dodger, what's the news in
    France ?

Dodger. My lord, upon the eighteenth day of May
The French and English were prepared to fight ;
Each side with eager fury gave the sign
Of a most hot encounter.   Five long hours
Both armies fought together ; at the length
The lot of victory fell on our side.
Twelve thousand of the Frenchmen that day died,
Four thousand English, and no man of name
But Captain Hyam and young Ardington,
Two gallant gentlemen, I knew them well.

Lincoln. But Dodger, prithee, tell me, in this fight
How did my cousin Lacy bear himself ?

Dodger. My lord, your cousin Lacy was not there.

Lincoln. Not there ?

Dodger.   No, my good lord.

Lincoln.   Sure, thou mistakest.
I saw him shipped, and a thousand eyes beside
Were witnesses of the farewells which he gave,
When I, with weeping eyes, bid him adieu.
Dodger, take heed.

Dodger.   My lord, I am advised,
That what I spake is true : to prove it so,
His cousin Askew, that supplied his place,
Sent me for him from France, that secretly
He might convey himself thither.

Lincoln.   Is't even so ?
Dares he so carelessly venture his life
Upon the indignation of a king ?
Has he despised my love, and spurned those favours
Which I with prodigal hand poured on his head ?
He shall repent his rashness with his soul ;

Since of my love he makes no estimate,
I'll make him wish he had not known my hate.
Thou hast no other news?
    Dodger.   None else, my lord.
    Lincoln. None worse I know thou hast.—Procure the
        king
To crown his giddy brows with ample honours,
Send him chief colonel, and all my hope
Thus to be dashed!   But 'tis in vain to grieve,
One evil cannot a worse relieve.
Upon my life, I have found out his plot;
That old dog, Love, that fawned upon him so,
Love to that puling girl, his fair-cheeked Rose,
The lord mayor's daughter, hath distracted him,
And in the fire of that love's lunacy
Hath he burnt up himself, consumed his credit,
Lost the king's love, yea, and I fear, his life,
Only to get a wanton to his wife,
Dodger, it is so.
    Dodger.   I fear so, my good lord.
    Lincoln. It is so—nay, sure it cannot be!
I am at my wits' end.   Dodger!
    Dodger.   Yea, my lord.
    Lincoln. Thou art acquainted with my nephew's
        haunts;
Spend this gold for thy pains; go seek him out;
Watch at my lord mayor's—there if he live,
Dodger, thou shalt be sure to meet with him.
Prithee, be diligent.—Lacy, thy name
Lived once in honour, now 'tis dead in shame.—
Be circumspect.   [*Exit.*
    Dodger.   I warrant you, my lord.   [*Exit.*

SCENE III.—*London: a Room in the* LORD MAYOR'S *House.*

Enter the LORD MAYOR *and* MASTER SCOTT.

L. Mayor.   Good Master Scott, I have been bold with
    you,
To be a witness to a wedding-knot
Betwixt young Master Hammon and my daughter.
O, stand aside ; see where the lovers come.

Enter MASTER HAMMON *and* ROSE.

Rose. Can it be possible you love me so ?
No, no, within those eyeballs I espy
Apparent likelihoods of flattery.
Pray now, let go my hand.
    Ham.   Sweet Mistress Rose,
Misconstrue not my words, nor misconceive
Of my affection, whose devoted soul
Swears that I love thee dearer than my heart.
    Rose. As dear as your own heart ?   I judge it right,
Men love their hearts best when th'are out of sight.
    Ham. I love you, by this hand.
    Rose.   Yet hands off now !
If flesh be frail, how weak and frail's your vow !
    Ham. Then by my life I swear.
    Rose.   Then do not brawl ;
One quarrel loseth wife and life and all.
Is not your meaning thus ?
    Ham.   In faith, you jest.
    Rose. Love loves to sport ; therefore leave love, y'are
        best.
    L. Mayor. What ? square they, Master Scott ?
    Scott.   Sir, never doubt,
Lovers are quickly in, and quickly out.
    Ham. Sweet Rose, be not so strange in fancying me.
Nay, never turn aside, shun not my sight :
I am not grown so fond, to fond [1] my love

---

[1] Found, set ; a play upon fond.

On any that shall quit it with disdain ;
If you will love me, so—if not, farewell.

 L. Mayor. Why, how now, lovers, are you both agreed ?

 Ham. Yes, faith, my lord.

 L. Mayor.   'Tis well, give me your hand.
Give me yours, daughter.—How now, both pull back !
What means this, girl ?

 Rose.   I mean to live a maid.

 Ham. But not to die one ; pause, ere that be said.

              [*Aside.*

 L. Mayor. Will you still cross me, still be obstinate ?

 Ham. Nay, chide her not, my lord, for doing well ;
If she can live an happy virgin's life,
'Tis far more blessed than to be a wife.

 Rose. Say, sir, I cannot : I have made a vow,
Whoever be my husband, 'tis not you.

 L. Mayor. Your tongue is quick ; but Master Hammon,
   know,
I bade you welcome to another end.

 Ham. What, would you have me pule and pine and
    pray,
  With ' lovely lady,' ' mistress of my heart,'
 ' Pardon your servant,' and the rhymer play,
  Railing on Cupid and his tyrant's-dart ;
Or shall I undertake some martial spoil,
Wearing your glove at tourney and at tilt,
And tell how many gallants I unhorsed—
Sweet, will this pleasure you ?

 Rose.   Yea, when wilt begin ?
What, love rhymes, man ?   Fie on that deadly sin !

 L. Mayor. If you will have her, I'll make her agree.

 Ham. Enforced love is worse than hate to me.
(*Aside.*)   There is a wench keeps shop in the Old Change,
To her will I ; it is not wealth I seek,
I have enough, and will prefer her love
Before the world.—(*Aloud.*) My good lord mayor, adieu.
Old love for me, I have no luck with new. [*Exit.*

L. Mayor. Now, mammet,[1] you have well behaved
 yourself,
But you shall curse your coyness if I live.—
Who's within there? See you convey your mistress
Straight to th'Old Ford! I'll keep you straight enough,
Fore God, I would have sworn the puling girl
Would willingly accepted Hammon's love ;
But banish him, my thoughts ! — Go, minion, in !
          [*Exit* ROSE.
Now tell me, Master Scott, would you have thought
That Master Simon Eyre, the shoemaker,
Had been of wealth to buy such merchandise ?
 Scott. 'Twas well, my lord, your honour and myself
Grew partners with him ; for your bills of lading
Shew that Eyre's gains in one commodity
Rise at the least to full three thousand pound
Besides like gain in other merchandise.
 L. Mayor. Well, he shall spend some of his thousands
 now,
For I have sent for him to the Guildhall.

Enter EYRE.

See, where he comes.—Good morrow, Master Eyre.
 Eyre. Poor Simon Eyre, my lord, your shoemaker.
 L. Mayor. Well, well, it likes yourself to term you so.

Enter DODGER.

Now, Master Dodger, what's the news with you ?
 Dodger. I'd gladly speak in private to your honour.
 L. Mayor. You shall, you shall.—Master Eyre and
 Master Scott,
I have some business with this gentleman ;
I pray, let me entreat you to walk before
To the Guildhall; I'll follow presently.
Master Eyre, I hope ere noon to call you sheriff.

---

[1] Puppet ; derived from Mahomet,

Eyre. I would not care, my lord, if you might call me King of Spain.—Come, Master Scott.

[Exeunt EYRE *and* SCOTT.

L. Mayor. Now, Master Dodger, what's the news you bring?

Dodger. The Earl of Lincoln by me greets your lordship, And earnestly requests you, if you can, Inform him, where his nephew Lacy keeps.

L. Mayor. Is not his nephew Lacy now in France?

Dodger. No, I assure your lordship, but disguised Lurks here in London.

L. Mayor.   London? is't even so? It may be; but upon my faith and soul, I know not where he lives, or whether he lives : So tell my Lord of Lincoln.—Lurks in London? Well, Master Dodger, you perhaps may start him; Be but the means to rid him into France, I'll give you a dozen angels [1] for your pains : So much I love his honour, hate his nephew. And, prithee, so inform thy lord from me.

Dodger. I take my leave.   [*Exit* DODGER.

L. Mayor.   Farewell, good Master Dodger. Lacy in London? I dare pawn my life, My daughter knows thereof, and for that cause Denied young Master Hammon in his love. Well, I am glad I sent her to Old Ford. Gods Lord, 'tis late; to Guildhall I must hie; I know my brethren stay my company.   [*Exit.*

SCENE IV.—*London : a Room in* EYRE'S *House.*

Enter FIRK, MARGERY, HANS, *and* ROGER.

Marg. Thou goest too fast for me, Roger. O, Firk !

---

[1] Coins worth about 10*s.* each.

Firk. Ay, forsooth.

Marg. I pray thee, run—do you hear?—run to Guild-hall, and learn if my husband, Master Eyre, will take that worshipful vocation of Master Sheriff upon him. Hie thee, good Firk.

Firk. Take it? Well, I go; an' he should not take it, Firk swears to forswear him. Yes, forsooth, I go to Guildhall.

Marg. Nay, when? thou art too compendious and tedious.

Firk. O rare, your excellence is full of eloquence; how like a new cart-wheel my dame speaks, and she looks like an old musty ale-bottle [1] going to scalding.

Marg. Nay, when? thou wilt make me melancholy.

Firk. God forbid your worship should fall into that humour;—I run.   [*Exit.*

Marg. Let me see now, Roger and Hans.

Hodge. Ay, forsooth, dame—mistress I should say, but the old term so sticks to the roof of my mouth, I can hardly lick it off.

Marg. Even what thou wilt, good Roger; dame is a fair name for any honest Christian; but let that pass. How dost thou, Hans?

Hans. Mee tanck you, vro. [2]

Marg. Well, Hans and Roger, you see, God hath blest your master, and, perdy, if ever he comes to be Master Sheriff of London—as we are all mortal—you shall see, I will have some odd thing or other in a corner for you: I will not be your back-friend; but let that pass. Hans, pray thee, tie my shoe.

Hans. Yaw, ic sal, vro. [3]

Marg. Roger, thou know'st the size of my foot; as it is none of the biggest, so I thank God, it is handsome

---

[1] Ale-kegs, made of wood; hence the need for scalding.

[2] I thank you, mistress!

[3] Yes, I shall, mistress!

enough ; prithee, let me have a pair of shoes made, cork, good Roger, wooden heel too.[1]

Hodge. You shall.

Marg. Art thou acquainted with never a farthingale-maker, nor a French hood-maker ? I must enlarge my bum, ha, ha ! How shall I look in a hood, I wonder ! Perdy,[2] oddly, I think.

Hodge. As a cat out of a pillory :[3] very well, I warrant you, mistress.

Marg. Indeed, all flesh is grass ; and, Roger, canst thou tell where I may buy a good hair ?

Hodge. Yes, forsooth, at the poulterer's in Gracious Street.[4]

Marg. Thou art an ungracious wag ; perdy, I mean a false hair for my periwig.

Hodge. Why, mistress, the next time I cut my beard, you shall have the shavings of it ; but they are all true hairs.

Marg. It is very hot, I must get me a fan or else a mask.

Hodge. So you had need to hide your wicked face.

Marg. Fie, upon it, how costly this world's calling is ; perdy, but that it is one of the wonderful works of God, I would not deal with it. Is not Firk come yet ? Hans, be not so sad, let it pass and vanish, as my husband's worship says.

Hans. Ick bin vrolicke, lot see yow soo.[5]

Hodge. Mistress, will you drink a pipe of tobacco?

Marg. Oh, fie upon it, Roger, perdy ! These filthy tobacco-pipes are the most idle slavering baubles that ever I felt. Out upon it ! God bless us, men look not like men that use them.

---

[1] High-heeled cork shoes were in fashion for ladies at this time.   [2] Truly ; see *ante*, p. 33.

[3] A comparison suggested by the likeness of the flaps of the hood to the boards of a pillory, between which the head of the prisoner was fastened.

[4] The old name for Gracechurch Street before the fire of London.

[5] I am merry ; let's see you so too !

Enter RALPH, *lame.*

Roger. What, fellow Ralph? Mistress, look here, Jane's husband! Why, how now, lame? Hans, make much of him, he's a brother of our trade, a good workman, and a tall soldier.

Hans. You be welcome, broder.

Marg. Perdy, I knew him not. How dost thou, good Ralph? I am glad to see thee well.

Ralph. I would to God you saw me, dame, as well
As when I went from London into France.

Marg. Trust me, I am sorry, Ralph, to see thee impotent. Lord, how the wars have made him sunburnt! The left leg is not well; 'twas a fair gift of God the infirmity took not hold a little higher, considering thou camest from France; but let that pass.

Ralph. I am glad to see you well, and I rejoice
To hear that God hath blest my master so
Since my departure.

Marg. Yea, truly, Ralph, I thank my Maker; but let that pass.

Hodge. And, sirrah Ralph, what news, what news in France?

Ralph. Tell me, good Roger, first, what news in England? How does my Jane? When didst thou see my wife?
Where lives my poor heart? She'll be poor indeed,
Now I want limbs to get whereon to feed.

Hodge. Limbs? Hast thou not hands, man? Thou shalt never see a shoemaker want bread, though he have but three fingers on a hand.

Ralph. Yet all this while I hear not of my Jane.

Marg. O Ralph, your wife,—perdy, we know not what's become of her. She was here a while, and because she was married, grew more stately than became her; I checked her, and so forth; away she flung, never returned, nor said bye nor bah; and, Ralph, you know,

" ka me, ka thee."[1]   And so, as I tell ye——Roger, is
not Firk come yet?

Hodge. No, forsooth.

Marg. And so, indeed, we heard not of her, but I hear
she lives in London; but let that pass.   If she had
wanted, she might have opened her case to me or my
husband, or to any of my men; I am sure, there's not
any of them, perdy, but would have done her good to
his power.   Hans, look if Firk be come.

Hans. Yaw, ik sal, vro.[2]   [*Exit* HANS.

Marg. And so, as I said——but, Ralph, why dost thou
weep? Thou knowest that naked we came out of our
mother's womb, and naked we must return; and, therefore, thank God for all things.

Hodge. No, faith, Jane is a stranger here; but, Ralph,
pull up a good heart, I know thou hast one. Thy wife,
man, is in London; one told me, he saw her a while ago
very brave and neat; we'll ferret her out, an' London hold
her.

Marg. Alas, poor soul, he's overcome with sorrow; he
does but as I do, weep for the loss of any good thing.
But, Ralph, get thee in, call for some meat and drink,
thou shalt find me worshipful towards thee.

Ralph. I thank you, dame; since I want limbs and
        lands,

I'll trust to God, my good friends, and my hands. [*Exit.*

Enter HANS *and* FIRK *running.*

Firk. Run, good Hans! O Hodge, O mistress!
Hodge, heave up thine ears; mistress, smug up[3] your
looks; on with your best apparel; my master is chosen,
my master is called, nay, condemned by the cry of the
country to be sheriff of the city for this famous year now
to come. And time now being, a great many men in
black gowns were asked for their voices and their hands'

---

[1] Serve me, and I'll serve thee.   [2] Yes, I shall, dame !
            [3] Brighten up.

and my master had all their fists about his ears presently,
and they cried ' Ay, ay, ay, ay,'—and so I came away—
> Wherefore without all other grieve
> I do salute you, Mistress Shrieve.[1]

Hans. *Yaw, my mester is de groot man, de shrieve.*

Hodge. Did not I tell you, mistress? Now I may
boldly say : Good-morrow to your worship.

Marg. Good-morrow, good Roger. I thank you, my
good people all.—Firk, hold up thy hand : here's a three-
penny piece for thy tidings.

Firk. 'Tis but three-half-pence, I think. Yes, 'tis
three-pence, I smell the rose.[2]

Hodge. But, mistress, be ruled by me, and do not speak
so pulingly.

Firk. 'Tis her worship speaks so, and not she. No,
faith, mistress, speak me in the old key : ' To it, Firk,'
' there, good Firk,' ' ply your business, Hodge,' ' Hodge,
with a full mouth,' ' I'll fill your bellies with good cheer,
till they cry twang.'

Enter EYRE *wearing a gold chain.*

Hans. *See, myn liever broder, heer compt my meester.*

Marg. Welcome home, Master Shrieve ; I pray God
continue you in health and wealth.

Eyre. See here, my Maggy, a chain, a gold chain for
Simon Eyre. I shall make thee a lady ; here's a French
hood for thee ; on with it, on with it ! dress thy brows
with this flap of a shoulder of mutton,[3] to make thee look
lovely. Where be my fine men ? Roger, I'll make over my
shop and tools to thee ; Firk, thou shalt be the foreman ;
Hans, thou shalt have an hundred for twenty.[4] Be as

---

[1] Sheriff.

[2] " The three-farthing silver pieces of Queen Elizabeth had the
profile of the sovereign with a rose at the back of her head."—*Dyce*
(Note to *King John.*)

[3] The flap of a hood trimmed with fur or sheep's wool.

[4] *i.e.* For the twenty Portuguese previously lent.

mad knaves as your master Sim Eyre hath been, and you
shall live to be Sheriffs of London.—How dost thou like
me, Margery? Prince am I none, yet am I princely born.
Firk, Hodge, and Hans!

All three. Ay forsooth, what says your worship, Master
Sheriff?

Eyre. Worship and honour, you Babylonian knaves,
for the gentle craft. But I forgot myself, I am bidden
by my lord mayor to dinner to Old Ford; he's gone before, I must after. Come, Madge, on with your trinkets!
Now, my true Trojans, my fine Firk, my dapper Hodge,
my honest Hans, some device, some odd crotchets, some
morris, or such like, for the honour of the gentlemen
shoemakers. Meet me at Old Ford, you know my mind.
Come, Madge, away. Shut up the shop, knaves, and
make holiday.   [*Exeunt.*

Firk. O rare! O brave! Come, Hodge; follow me,
  Hans;
We'll be with them for a morris-dance.   [*Exeunt.*

SCENE V.—*A Room at Old Ford.*

Enter the LORD MAYOR, ROSE, EYRE, MARGERY *in a
French hood,* SYBIL, *and other* Servants.

L. Mayor. Trust me, you are as welcome to Old Ford
As I myself.

Marg. Truly, I thank your lordship.

L. Mayor. Would our bad cheer were worth the
  thanks you give.

Eyre. Good cheer, my lord mayor, fine cheer! A fine
  house, fine walls, all fine and neat.

L. Mayor. Now, by my troth, I'll tell thee, Master Eyre,
It does me good, and all my brethren,
That such a madcap fellow as thyself
Is entered into our society.

Marg. Ay, but, my lord, he must learn now to put on gravity.

Eyre. Peace, Maggy, a fig for gravity ! When I go to Guildhall in my scarlet gown, I'll look as demurely as a saint, and speak as gravely as a justice of peace ; but now I am here at Old Ford, at my good lord mayor's house, let it go by, vanish, Maggy, I'll be merry ; away with flip-flap, these fooleries, these gulleries. What, honey? Prince am I none, yet am I princely born. What says my lord mayor ?

L. Mayor. Ha, ha, ha ! I had rather than a thousand pound, I had an heart but half so light as yours.

Eyre. Why, what should I do, my lord? A pound of care pays not a dram of debt. Hum, let's be merry, whiles we are young ; old age, sack and sugar will steal upon us, ere we be aware.[1]

THE FIRST THREE-MEN'S SONG.[2]

O the month of May, the merry month of May,
  So frolick, so gay, and so green, so green, so green !
O, and then did I unto my true love say :
  "Sweet Peg, thou shalt be my summer's queen !

" Now the nightingale, the pretty nightingale,
  The sweetest singer in all the forest's choir,
Entreats thee, sweet Peggy, to hear thy true love's tale ;
  Lo, yonder she sitteth, her breast against a brier.

---

[1] Herrick, who was a goldsmith's apprentice in London during the time when this play was performed, seems to have appropriated these words of Eyre's, and turned them into rhyme in these lines :—
  " Let's now take our time,
    While we're in our prime,
      And old, old age is afar off ;
    For the evil, evil days,
    Will come on apace,
      Before we can be aware of."

[2] A song or catch for three voices. In the original, the two Three-Men's Songs are printed separately from the rest of the play, and the place for their insertion is only very uncertainly indicated.

" But O, I spy the cuckoo, the cuckoo, the cuckoo ;
  See where she sitteth : come away, my joy ;
Come away, I prithee : I do not like the cuckoo
  Should sing where my Peggy and I kiss and toy."

O the month of May, the merry month of May,
  So frolick, so gay, and so green, so green, so green !
And then did I unto my true love say :
  " Sweet Peg, thou shalt be my summer's queen ! "

L. Mayor. It's well done ; Mistress Eyre, pray, give
        good counsel
To my daughter.

Marg. I hope, Mistress Rose will have the grace to
take nothing that's bad.

L. Mayor. Pray God she do ; for i' faith, Mistress Eyre,
I would bestow upon that peevish girl
A thousand marks more than I mean to give her,
Upon condition she'd be ruled by me ;
The ape still crosseth me.   There came of late
A proper gentleman of fair revenues,
Whom gladly I would call son-in-law :
But my fine cockney would have none of him.
You'll prove a coxcomb for it, ere you die :
A courtier, or no man must please your eye.

Eyre. Be ruled, sweet Rose : th'art ripe for a man.
Marry not with a boy that has no more hair on his face
than thou hast on thy cheeks.   A courtier, wash, go by,
stand not upon pishery-pashery : those silken fellows are
but painted images, outsides, outsides, Rose ; their inner
linings are torn.   No, my fine mouse, marry me with a
gentleman grocer like my lord mayor, your father ; a
grocer is a sweet trade : plums, plums.   Had I a son or
daughter should marry out of the generation and blood
of the shoemakers, he should pack ; what, the gentle
trade is a living for a man through Europe, through the
world.   [*A noise within of a tabor and a pipe.*

L. Mayor. What noise is this?

Eyre. O my lord mayor, a crew of good fellows that for love to your honour are come hither with a morris-dance. Come in, my Mesopotamians, cheerily.

Enter HODGE, HANS, RALPH, FIRK, *and other* Shoe-makers, *in a morris; after a little dancing the* LORD MAYOR *speaks.*

L. Mayor. Master Eyre, are all these shoemakers?

Eyre. All cordwainers, my good lord mayor.

Rose. (*Aside.*) How like my Lacy looks yond' shoe-maker!

Hans. (*Aside.*) O that I durst but speak unto my love!

L. Mayor. Sybil, go fetch some wine to make these drink. You are all welcome.

All. We thank your lordship.

[ROSE *takes a cup of wine and goes to* HANS.

Rose. For his sake whose fair shape thou represent'st, Good friend, I drink to thee.

Hans. Ic bedancke, good frister.[1]

Marg. I see, Mistress Rose, you do not want judgment; you have drunk to the properest man I keep.

Firk. Here be some have done their parts to be as proper as he.

L. Mayor. Well, urgent business calls me back to London :

Good fellows, first go in and taste our cheer ;

And to make merry as you homeward go,

Spend these two angels [2] in beer at Stratford-Bow.

Eyre. To these two, my mad lads, Sim Eyre adds an-other ; then cheerily, Firk ; tickle it, Hans, and all for the honour of shoemakers.   [*All go dancing out.*

L. Mayor. Come, Master Eyre, let's have your company.   [*Exeunt.*

---

[1] I thank you, good maid !

[2] See note *ante*, p. 39.

Rose. Sybil, what shall I do?

Sybil. Why, what's the matter?

Rose. That Hans the shoemaker is my love Lacy, Disguised in that attire to find me out.
How should I find the means to speak with him?

Sybil. What, mistress, never fear; I dare venture my maidenhead to nothing, and that's great odds, that Hans the Dutchman, when we come to London, shall not only see and speak with you, but in spite of all your father's policies steal you away and marry you. Will not this please you?

Rose. Do this, and ever be assured of my love.

Sybil. Away, then, and follow your father to London, lest your absence cause him to suspect something:

To morrow, if my counsel be obeyed,
I'll bind you prentice to the gentle trade. [*Exeunt.*

ACT THE FOURTH.

SCENE I.—*A Street in London.*

JANE *in a Seamster's shop, working; enter* Master HAMMON, *muffled; he stands aloof.*

HAM. Yonder's the shop, and there my
fair love sits.
She's fair and lovely, but she is not
mine.
O, would she were ! Thrice have I
courted her,
Thrice hath my hand been moistened with her hand,
Whilst my poor famished eyes do feed on that
Which made them famish. I am unfortunate :
I still love one, yet nobody loves me.
I muse, in other men what women see,
That I so want ! Fine Mistress Rose was coy,
And this too curious ! Oh, no, she is chaste,
And for she thinks me wanton, she denies
To cheer my cold heart with her sunny eyes.
How prettily she works, oh pretty hand !
Oh happy work ! It doth me good to stand
Unseen to see her. Thus I oft have stood
In frosty evenings, a light burning by her,
Enduring biting cold, only to eye her.
One only look hath seemed as rich to me
As a king's crown ; such is love's lunacy.

Muffled I'll pass along, and by that try
Whether she know me.

 Jane.   Sir, what is't you buy?
What is't you lack, sir, calico, or lawn,
Fine cambric shirts, or bands, what will you buy?

 Ham. (*Aside.*) That which thou wilt not sell. Faith,
  yet I'll try:
How do you sell this handkerchief?

 Jane.   Good cheap.

 Ham. And how these ruffs?

 Jane.   Cheap too.

 Ham.   And how this band?

 Jane. Cheap too.

 Ham. All cheap; how sell you then this hand?

 Jane. My hands are not to be sold.

 Ham.   To be given then!
Nay, faith, I come to buy.

 Jane.   But none knows when.

 Ham. Good sweet, leave work a little while; let's play.

 Jane. I cannot live by keeping holiday.

 Ham. I'll pay you for the time which shall be lost.

 Jane. With me you shall not be at so much cost.

 Ham. Look, how you wound this cloth, so you wound
me.

 Jane. It may be so.

 Ham.   'Tis so.

 Jane.   What remedy?

 Ham. Nay, faith, you are too coy.

 Jane.   Let go my hand.

 Ham. I will do any task at your command,
I would let go this beauty, were I not
In mind to disobey you by a power
That controls kings: I love you!

 Jane.   So, now part.

 Ham. With hands I may, but never with my heart.
In faith, I love you.

 Jane.   I believe you do.

Ham. Shall a true love in me breed hate in you?
Jane. I hate you not.
Ham.   Then you must love?
Jane.   I do.
What are you better now?   I love not you.
   Ham. All this, I hope, is but a woman's fray,
That means : come to me, when she cries : away !
In earnest, mistress, I do not jest,
A true chaste love hath entered in my breast.
I love you dearly, as I love my life,
I love you as a husband loves a wife ;
That, and no other love, my love requires,
Thy wealth, I know, is little ; my desires
Thirst not for gold.   Sweet, beauteous Jane, what's mine
Shall, if thou make myself thine, all be thine.
Say, judge, what is thy sentence, life or death?
Mercy or cruelty lies in thy breath.
   Jane. Good sir, I do believe you love me well ;
For 'tis a silly conquest, silly pride
For one like you—I mean a gentleman—
To boast that by his love-tricks he hath brought
Such and such women to his amorous lure ;
I think you do not so, yet many do,
And make it even a very trade to woo.
I could be coy, as many women be,
Feed you with sunshine smiles and wanton looks,
But I detest witchcraft ; say that I
Do constantly believe, you constant have——
   Ham. Why dost thou not believe me?
   Jane.   I believe you ;
But yet, good sir, because I will not grieve you
With hopes to taste fruit which will never fall,
In simple truth this is the sum of all :
My husband lives, at least, I hope he lives.
Pressed was he to these bitter wars in France ;
Bitter they are to me by wanting him.
I have but one heart, and that heart's his due.

How can I then bestow the same on you?
Whilst he lives, his I live, be it ne'er so poor,
And rather be his wife than a king's whore.

Ham. Chaste and dear woman, I will not abuse thee,
Although it cost my life, if thou refuse me.
Thy husband, pressed for France, what was his name?

Jane. Ralph Damport.

Ham. Damport?—Here's a letter sent
From France to me, from a dear friend of mine,
A gentleman of place; here he doth write
Their names that have been slain in every fight.

Jane. I hope death's scroll contains not my love's
name.

Ham. Cannot you read?

Jane. I can.

Ham. Peruse the same.
To my remembrance such a name I read
Amongst the rest. See here.

Jane. Ay me, he's dead!
He's dead! if this be true, my dear heart's slain!

Ham. Have patience, dear love.

Jane. Hence, hence!

Ham. Nay, sweet Jane,
Make not poor sorrow proud with these rich tears.
I mourn thy husband's death, because thou mourn'st.

Jane. That bill is forged; 'tis signed by forgery.

Ham. I'll bring thee letters sent besides to many,
Carrying the like report: Jane, 'tis too true.
Come, weep not: mourning, though it rise from love,
Helps not the mourned, yet hurts them that mourn.

Jane. For God's sake, leave me.

Ham. Whither dost thou turn?
Forget the dead, love them that are alive;
His love is faded, try how mine will thrive.

Jane. 'Tis now no time for me to think on love.

Ham. 'Tis now best time for you to think on love,
Because your love lives not.

Jane.   Though he be dead,
My love to him shall not be buried;
For God's sake, leave me to myself alone.

 Ham. 'Twould kill my soul, to leave thee drowned in
   moan.
Answer me to my suit, and I am gone;
Say to me yea or no.

 Jane.   No.

 Ham.   Then farewell!
One farewell will not serve, I come again;
Come, dry these wet cheeks; tell me, faith, sweet Jane,
Yea or no, once more.

 Jane.   Once more I say: no;
Once more be gone, I pray; else will I go.

 Ham. Nay, then I will grow rude, by this white hand,
Until you change that cold " no "; here I'll stand
Till by your hard heart——

 Jane.   Nay, for God's love, peace!
My sorrows by your presence more increase.
Not that you thus are present, but all grief
Desires to be alone; therefore in brief
Thus much I say, and saying bid adieu:
If ever I wed man, it shall be you.

 Ham. O blessed voice! Dear Jane, I'll urge no more,
Thy breath hath made me rich.

 Jane.   Death makes me poor.
           [*Exeunt.*

SCENE II.—*London: a Street before* HODGE'S *Shop.*

HODGE, *at his shop-board*, RALPH, FIRK, HANS, *and
a* Boy *at work.*

 All. Hey, down a down, down derry.
 Hodge. Well said, my hearts; ply your work to-day,

we loitered yesterday ; to it pell-mell, that we may live to be lord mayors, or aldermen at least.

Firk. Hey, down a down, derry.

Hodge. Well said, i' faith ! How say'st thou, Hans, doth not Firk tickle it ?

Hans. Yaw, mester.

Firk. Not so neither, my organ-pipe squeaks this morning for want of liquoring. Hey, down a down, derry !

Hans. Forward, Firk, tow best un jolly yongster. Hort, I, mester, ic bid yo, cut me un pair vampres vor Mester Jeffre's boots.[1]

Hodge. Thou shalt, Hans.

Firk. Master !

Hodge. How now, boy ?

Firk. Pray, now you are in the cutting vein, cut me out a pair of counterfeits,[2] or else my work will not pass current ; hey, down a down !

Hodge. Tell me, sirs, are my cousin Mrs. Priscilla's shoes done ?

Firk. Your cousin ? No, master ; one of your aunts, hang her ; let them alone.

Ralph. I am in hand with them ; she gave charge that none but I should do them for her.

Firk. Thou do for her ? then 'twill be a lame doing, and that she loves not. Ralph, thou might'st have sent her to me, in faith, I would have yearked and firked your Priscilla. Hey, down a down, derry. This gear will not hold.

Hodge. How say'st thou, Firk, were we not merry at Old Ford ?

Firk. How, merry ? why, our buttocks went jiggy-joggy like a quagmire. Well, Sir Roger Oatmeal, if I thought

---

[1] " Forward, Firk, thou art a jolly youngster. Hark, ay, master, I bid you cut me a pair of vamps for Master Jeffrey's boots." Vamps ; upper leathers of a shoe.

[2] A play upon " vamps," which sometimes has this meaning.

all meal of that nature, I would eat nothing but bagpud-
dings.

Ralph. Of all good fortunes my fellow Hans had the
best.

Firk. 'Tis true, because Mistress Rose drank to him.

Hodge. Well, well, work apace. They say, seven of the
aldermen be dead, or very sick.

Firk. I care not, I'll be none.

Ralph. No, nor I; but then my Master Eyre will come
quickly to be lord mayor.

Enter SYBIL.

Firk. Whoop, yonder comes Sybil.

Hodge. Sybil, welcome, i'faith; and how dost thou, mad
wench?

Firk. Syb-whore, welcome to London.

Sybil. Godamercy, sweet Firk; good lord, Hodge, what
a delicious shop you have got! You tickle it, i'faith.

Ralph. Godamercy, Sybil, for our good cheer at Old
Ford.

Sybil. That you shall have, Ralph.

Firk. Nay, by the mass, we had tickling cheer, Sybil;
and how the plague dost thou and Mistress Rose and my
lord mayor? I put the women in first.

Sybil. Well, Godamercy; but God's me, I forget myself, where's Hans the Fleming?

Firk. Hark, butter-box, now you must yelp out some
spreken.

Hans. Wat begaie you? Vat vod you, Frister? [1]

Sybil. Marry, you must come to my young mistress, to
pull on her shoes you made last.

Hans. Vare ben your egle fro, vare ben your mistris? [2]

Sybil. Marry, here at our London house in Cornhill.

Firk. Will nobody serve her turn but Hans?

Sybil. No, sir. Come, Hans, I stand upon needles.

[1] What do you want (was begehrt ihr), what would you, girl?
[2] Where is your noble lady, where is your mistress?

Hodge. Why then, Sybil, take heed of pricking.

Sybil. For that let me alone. I have a trick in my budget. Come, Hans.

Hans. Yaw, yaw, ic sall meete yo gane.[1]

[*Exit* HANS *and* SYBIL.

Hodge. Go, Hans, make haste again. Come, who lacks work ?

Firk. I, master, for I lack my breakfast ; 'tis munching-time, and past.

Hodge. Is't so ? why, then leave work, Ralph. To breakfast ! Boy, look to the tools. Come, Ralph ; come, Firk.   [*Exeunt.*

SCENE III.—*The Same.*

Enter a Serving-man.

Serv. Let me see now, the sign of the Last in Tower Street. Mass, yonder's the house. What, haw ! Who's within ?

Enter RALPH.

Ralph. Who calls there ? What want you, sir ?

Serv. Marry, I would have a pair of shoes made for a gentlewoman against to-morrow morning. What, can you do them ?

Ralph. Yes, sir, you shall have them. But what length's her foot?

Serv. Why, you must make them in all parts like this shoe ; but, at any hand, fail not to do them, for the gentlewoman is to be married very early in the morning.

Ralph. How ? by this shoe must it be made ? by this ? Are you sure, sir, by this?

Serv. How, by this ? Am I sure, by this ? Art thou in thy wits ? I tell thee, I must have a pair of shoes

---

[1] Yes, yes, I shall go with you.

dost thou mark me? a pair of shoes, two shoes, made by this very shoe, this same shoe, against to-morrow morning by four a clock. Dost understand me? Canst thou do't?

Ralph. Yes, sir, yes—I—I—I can do't. By this shoe, you say? I should know this shoe. Yes, sir, yes, by this shoe, I can do't. Four a clock, well. Whither shall I bring them?

Serv. To the sign of the Golden Ball in Watling Street; enquire for one Master Hammon, a gentleman, my master.

Ralph. Yea, sir; by this shoe, you say?

Serv. I say, Master Hammon at the Golden Ball; he's the bridegroom, and those shoes are for his bride.

Ralph. They shall be done by this shoe; well, well, Master Hammon at the Golden Shoe—I would say, the Golden Ball; very well, very well. But I pray you, sir, where must Master Hammon be married?

Serv. At Saint Faith's Church, under Paul's.[1] But what's that to thee? Prithee, dispatch those shoes, and so farewell.   [*Exit.*

Ralph. By this shoe, said he. How am I amazed
At this strange accident! Upon my life,
This was the very shoe I gave my wife,
When I was pressed for France; since when, alas!
I never could hear of her: it is the same,
And Hammon's bride no other but my Jane.

Enter FIRK.

Firk. 'Snails,[2] Ralph, thou hast lost thy part of three pots, a countryman of mine gave me to breakfast.

Ralph. I care not; I have found a better thing.

Firk. A thing? away! Is it a man's thing, or a woman's thing?

[1] "At the west end of this Jesus chapel, under the choir of Paul's, also was a parish church of St. Faith, commonly called St. Faith under Paul's."—*Stow.*
[2] A corruption of "God's nails."

Ralph. Firk, dost thou know this shoe?

Firk. No, by my troth; neither doth that know me! I have no acquaintance with it, 'tis a mere stranger to me.

Ralph. Why, then I do; this shoe, I durst be sworn,
Once covered the instep of my Jane.
This is her size, her breadth, thus trod my love;
These true-love knots I pricked; I hold my life,
By this old shoe I shall find out my wife.

Firk. Ha, ha! Old shoe, that wert new! How a murrain came this ague-fit of foolishness upon thee?

Ralph. Thus, Firk: even now here came a serving-
      man;
By this shoe would he have a new pair made
Against to-morrow morning for his mistress,
That's to be married to a gentleman.
And why may not this be my sweet Jane?

Firk. And why may'st not thou be my sweet ass? Ha, ha!

Ralph. Well, laugh and spare not! But the truth is
      this:
Against to-morrow morning I'll provide
A lusty crew of honest shoemakers,
To watch the going of the bride to church.
If she prove Jane, I'll take her in despite
From Hammon and the devil, were he by.
If it be not my Jane, what remedy?
Hereof I am sure, I shall live till I die,
Although I never with a woman lie.   [*Exit.*

Firk. Thou lie with a woman to build nothing but Cripple-gates! Well, God sends fools fortune, and it may be, he may light upon his matrimony by such a device; for wedding and hanging goes by destiny. [*Exit.*

SCENE IV.—*London : a Room in the* LORD MAYOR'S
House.

Enter HANS *and* ROSE, *arm in arm.*

Hans. How happy am I by embracing thee !
Oh, I did fear such cross mishaps did reign,
That I should never see my Rose again.

Rose. Sweet Lacy, since fair opportunity
Offers herself to further our escape,
Let not too over-fond esteem of me
Hinder that happy hour.   Invent the means,
And Rose will follow thee through all the world.

Hans. Oh, how I surfeit with excess of joy,
Made happy by thy rich perfection !
But since thou pay'st sweet interest to my hopes,
Redoubling love on love, let me once more
Like to a bold-faced debtor crave of thee,
This night to steal abroad, and at Eyre's house,
Who now by death of certain aldermen
Is mayor of London, and my master once,
Meet thou thy Lacy, where in spite of change,
Your father's anger, and mine uncle's hate,
Our happy nuptials will we consummate.

Enter SYBIL.

Sybil. Oh God, what will you do, mistress ?   Shift for
yourself, your father is at hand !   He's coming, he's
coming !   Master Lacy, hide yourself in my mistress !
For God's sake, shift for yourselves !

Hans. Your father come, sweet Rose—what shall I do ?
Where shall I hide me ?   How shall I escape ?

Rose. A man, and want wit in extremity ?
Come, come, be Hans still, play the shoemaker,
Pull on my shoe.

Enter the LORD MAYOR.

Hans. Mass, and that's well remembered.

Sybil. Here comes your father.

Hans. Forware, metresse, 'tis un good skow, it sal vel dute, or ye sal neit betallen.[1]

Rose. Oh God, it pincheth me ; what will you do ?

Hans. (*Aside.*) Your father's presence pincheth, not the shoe.

L. Mayor. Well done ; fit my daughter well, and she shall please thee well.

Hans. Yaw, yaw, ick weit dat well; forware, 'tis un good skoo, 'tis gimait van neits leither; se euer, mine here.[2]

Enter a Prentice.

L. Mayor. I do believe it.—What's the news with you ?

Prentice. Please you, the Earl of Lincoln at the gate
Is newly 'lighted, and would speak with you.

L. Mayor. The Earl of Lincoln come to speak with me ?
Well, well, I know his errand.   Daughter Rose,
Send hence your shoemaker, dispatch, have done !
Syb, make things handsome !   Sir boy, follow me.

[*Exit.*

Hans. Mine uncle come !   Oh, what may this portend ?
Sweet Rose, this of our love threatens an end.

Rose. Be not dismayed at this ; whate'er befall,
Rose is thine own.   To witness I speak truth,
Where thou appoint'st the place, I'll meet with thee.
I will not fix a day to follow thee,
But presently steal hence.   Do not reply :
Love which gave strength to bear my father's hate,
Shall now add wings to further our escape.   [*Exeunt.*

[1] Indeed, mistress, 'tis a good shoe, it shall fit well, or you shall not pay.

[2] Yes, yes, I know that well ; indeed, 'tis a good shoe, 'tis made of neat's leather, see here, good sir !

SCENE V.—*Another Room in the same House.*

Enter the LORD MAYOR *and the* EARL OF LINCOLN.

L. Mayor. Believe me, on my credit, I speak
    truth :
Since first your nephew Lacy went to France,
I have not seen him.   It seemed strange to me,
When Dodger told me that he stayed behind,
Neglecting the high charge the king imposed.

Lincoln. Trust me, Sir Roger Oateley, I did think
Your counsel had given head to this attempt,
Drawn to it by the love he bears your child.
Here I did hope to find him in your house ;
But now I see mine error, and confess,
My judgment wronged you by conceiving so.

L. Mayor. Lodge in my house, say you ?   Trust me,
    my lord,
I love your nephew Lacy too too dearly,
So much to wrong his honour ; and he hath done so,
That first gave him advice to stay from France.
To witness I speak truth, I let you know,
How careful I have been to keep my daughter
Free from all conference or speech of him ;
Not that I scorn your nephew, but in love
I bear your honour, lest your noble blood
Should by my mean worth be dishonoured.

Lincoln. [*Aside.*] How far the churl's tongue wanders
    from his heart !
Well, well, Sir Roger Oateley, I believe you,
With more than many thanks for the kind love,
So much you seem to bear me.   But, my lord,
Let me request your help to seek my nephew,
Whom if I find, I'll straight embark for France.
So shall your Rose be free, my thoughts at rest,
And much care die which now lies in my breast.

Enter SYBIL.

Sybil. Oh Lord! Help, for God's sake! my mistress; oh, my young mistress!

L. Mayor. Where is thy mistress? What's become of her?

Sybil. She's gone, she's fled!

L. Mayor. Gone! Whither is she fled?

Sybil. I know not, forsooth; she's fled out of doors with Hans the shoemaker; I saw them scud, scud, scud, apace, apace!

L. Mayor. Which way? What, John! Where be my men? Which way?

Sybil. I know not, an it please your worship.

L. Mayor. Fled with a shoemaker? Can this be true?

Sybil. Oh Lord, sir, as true as God's in Heaven.

Lincoln. Her love turned shoemaker? I am glad of this.

L. Mayor. A Fleming butter-box, a shoemaker!
Will she forget her birth, requite my care
With such ingratitude? Scorned she young Hammon
To love a honniken,[1] a needy knave?
Well, let her fly, I'll not fly after her,
Let her starve, if she will; she's none of mine.

Lincoln. Be not so cruel, sir.

Enter FIRK *with shoes.*

Sybil.   I am glad, she's 'scaped.

L. Mayor. I'll not account of her as of my child.
Was there no better object for her eyes
But a foul drunken lubber, swill-belly,
A shoemaker? That's brave!

Firk. Yea, forsooth; 'tis a very brave shoe, and as fit as a pudding.   •

L. Mayor. How now, what knave is this? From whence comest thou?

---

[1] Honeykin (?); poor honey, poor creature.

Firk. No knave, sir. I am Firk the shoemaker, lusty
Roger's chief lusty journeyman, and I have come hither
to take up the pretty leg of sweet Mistress Rose, and
thus hoping your worship is in as good health, as I was
at the making hereof, I bid you farewell, yours, Firk.

L. Mayor. Stay, stay, Sir Knave!

Lincoln. Come hither, shoemaker!

Firk. 'Tis happy the knave is put before the shoemaker, or else I would not have vouchsafed to come
back to you. I am moved, for I stir.

L. Mayor. My lord, this villain calls us knaves by
craft.

Firk. Then 'tis by the gentle craft, and to call one
knave gently, is no harm. Sit your worship merry![1] Syb,
your young mistress—I'll so bob them, now my Master
Eyre is lord mayor of London.

L. Mayor. Tell me, sirrah, who's man are you?

Firk. I am glad to see your worship so merry. I have
no maw to this gear, no stomach as yet to a red petticoat.
                                        [*Pointing to* SYBIL.

Lincoln. He means not, sir, to woo you to his maid,
But only doth demand who's man you are.

Firk. I sing now to the tune of Rogero. Roger, my
fellow, is now my master.

Lincoln. Sirrah, know'st thou one Hans, a shoemaker?

Firk. Hans, shoemaker? Oh yes, stay, yes, I have
him. I tell you what, I speak it in secret: Mistress
Rose and he are by this time—no, not so, but shortly are
to come over one another with "Can you dance the
shaking of the sheets?" It is that Hans—(*Aside.*) I'll
so gull these diggers![2]

L. Mayor. Know'st thou, then, where he is?

Firk. Yes, forsooth; yea, marry!

Lincoln. Canst thou, in sadness——

---

[1] " Rest you merry."—*Shak.*, Romeo and Juliet, Act I, Sc. 2.
[2] *i.e.* Diggers for information.

Firk. No, forsooth ; no, marry !

L. Mayor. Tell me, good honest fellow, where he is,
And thou shalt see what I'll bestow on thee.

Firk. Honest fellow ? No, sir ; not so, sir ; my profession is the gentle craft; I care not for seeing, I love
feeling ; let me feel it here ; *aurium tenus*, ten pieces of
gold ; *genuum tenus*, ten pieces of silver ; and then Firk
is your man in a new pair of stretchers.[1]

L. Mayor. Here is an angel, part of thy reward,
Which I will give thee ; tell me where he is.

Firk. No point ! Shall I betray my brother ? no !
Shall I prove Judas to Hans ? no ! Shall I cry treason to
my corporation ? no, I shall be firked and yerked then.
But give me your angel ; your angel shall tell you.

Lincoln. Do so, good fellow ; 'tis no hurt to thee.

Firk. Send simpering Syb away.

L. Mayor. Huswife, get you in.   [*Exit* SYBIL.

Firk. Pitchers have ears, and maids have wide mouths ;
but for Hans Prauns, upon my word, to-morrow morning
he and young Mistress Rose go to this gear, they shall be
married together, by this rush, or else turn Firk to a
firkin of butter, to tan leather withal.

L. Mayor. But art thou sure of this ?

Firk. Am I sure that Paul's steeple is a handful higher
than London Stone,[2] or that the Pissing-Conduit [3] leaks
nothing but pure Mother Bunch ? Am I sure I am lusty
Firk ? God's nails, do you think I am so base to gull
you ?

Lincoln. Where are they married ? Dost thou know the
church.

Firk. I never go to church, but I know the name of
it ; it is a swearing church—stay a while, 'tis--ay, by the
mass, no, no,—'tis—ay, by my troth, no, nor that ; 'tis

[1] *i.e.* Stretchers of the truth, fibs.
[2] A stone in St. Swithin's (now cased in the wall of the church),
which marked the centre from which the old Roman-roads radiated.
[3] A small conduit near the Royal Exchange.

—ay, by my faith, that, that, 'tis, ay, by my Faith's Church under Paul's Cross. There they shall be knit like a pair of stockings in matrimony; there they'll be inconie.[1]

Lincoln. Upon my life, my nephew Lacy walks
In the disguise of this Dutch shoemaker.

Firk. Yes, forsooth.

Lincoln. Doth he not, honest fellow?

Firk. No, forsooth; I think Hans is nobody but Hans, no spirit.

L. Mayor. My mind misgives me now, 'tis so, indeed.

Lincoln. My cousin speaks the language, knows the trade.

L. Mayor. Let me request your company, my lord;
Your honourable presence may, no doubt,
Refrain their headstrong rashness, when myself
Going alone perchance may be o'erborne.
Shall I request this favour?

Lincoln.   This, or what else.

Firk. Then you must rise betimes, for they mean to fall to their hey-pass and repass, pindy-pandy, which hand will you have,[2] very early.

L. Mayor. My care shall every way equal their haste.
This night accept your lodging in my house,
The earlier shall we stir, and at Saint Faith's
Prevent this giddy hare-brained nuptial.
This traffic of hot love shall yield cold gains:
They ban our loves, and we'll forbid their banns. [*Exit.*

Lincoln. At Saint Faith's Church thou say'st?

Firk. Yes, by their troth.

Lincoln. Be secret, on thy life.   [*Exit.*

Firk. Yes, when I kiss your wife! Ha, ha, here's no craft in the gentle craft. I came hither of purpose with

---

[1] A pretty sight. See p, 74, l. 1. Compare Shakespeare's "Love's Labour's Lost," Act III., Sc. 1, 136, and Act IV., Sc. 1, 144.

[2] Terms used in a common children's game, the point being to discover in which of the two hands some small object was hidden.

shoes to Sir Roger's worship, whilst Rose, his daughter, be cony-catched by Hans. Soft now; these two gulls will be at Saint Faith's Church to-morrow morning, to take Master Bridegroom and Mistress Bride napping, and they, in the mean time, shall chop up the matter at the Savoy. But the best sport is, Sir Roger Oateley will find my fellow lame Ralph's wife going to marry a gentleman, and then he'll stop her instead of his daughter. Oh brave! there will be fine tickling sport. Soft now, what have I to do? Oh, I know; now a mess of shoemakers meet at the Woolsack in Ivy Lane, to cozen my gentleman of lame Ralph's wife, that's true.

> Alack, alack!
> Girls, hold out tack!
> For now smocks for this jumbling
> Shall go to wrack.   [*Exit.*

ACT THE FIFTH.

SCENE I.—*A Room in* EYRE'S *House.*

Enter EYRE, MARGERY, HANS, *and* ROSE.

YRE. This is the morning, then; stay, my bully, my honest Hans, is it not?

Hans. This is the morning that must make us two happy or miserable; therefore, if you——

Eyre. Away with these ifs and ands, Hans, and these et caeteras! By mine honour, Rowland Lacy, none but the king shall wrong thee. Come, fear nothing, am not I Sim Eyre? Is not Sim Eyre lord mayor of London? Fear nothing, Rose: let them all say what they can; dainty, come thou to me—laughest thou?

Marg. Good my lord, stand her friend in what thing you may.

Eyre. Why, my sweet Lady Madgy, think you Simon Eyre can forget his fine Dutch journeyman? No, vah! Fie, I scorn it, it shall never be cast in my teeth, that I was unthankful. Lady Madgy, thou had'st never covered thy Saracen's head with this French flap, nor loaden thy bum with this farthingale, ('tis trash, trumpery, vanity); Simon Eyre had never walked in a red petticoat, nor wore a chain of gold, but for my fine journeyman's Portuguese.—And shall I leave him? No! Prince am I none, yet bear a princely mind.

Hans. My lord, 'tis time for us to part from hence.

Eyre. Lady Madgy, Lady Madgy, take two or three of my pie crust-eaters, my buff-jerkin varlets, that do walk in black gowns at Simon Eyre's heels ; take them, good Lady Madgy; trip and go, my brown queen of periwigs, with my delicate Rose and my jolly Rowland to the Savoy ; see them linked, countenance the marriage; and when it is done, cling, cling together, you Hamborow turtle-doves. I'll bear you out, come to Simon Eyre ; come, dwell with me, Hans, thou shalt eat minced-pies and marchpane.[1] Rose, away, cricket ; trip and go, my Lady Madgy, to the Savoy ; Hans, wed, and to bed ; kiss, and away ! Go, vanish !

Marg. Farewell, my lord.

Rose. Make haste, sweet love.

Marg.   She'd fain the deed were done.

Hans. Come, my sweet Rose ; faster than deer we'll run.   [*Exeunt* HANS, ROSE, *and* MARGERY.

Eyre. Go, vanish, vanish ! Avaunt, I say ! By the Lord of Ludgate, it's a mad life to be a lord mayor ; it's a stirring life, a fine life, a velvet life, a careful life. Well, Simon Eyre, yet set a good face on it, in the honour of Saint Hugh. Soft, the king this day comes to dine with me, to see my new buildings ; his majesty is welcome, he shall have good cheer, delicate cheer, princely cheer. This day, my fellow prentices of London come to dine with me too, they shall have fine cheer, gentlemanlike cheer. I promised the mad Cappadocians, when we all served at the Conduit together, that if ever I came to be mayor of London, I would feast them all, and I'll do't, I'll do't, by the life of Pharaoh ; by this beard, Sim Eyre will be no flincher. Besides, I have procured that upon every Shrove-Tuesday, at the sound of the pancake bell, my fine dapper Assyrian lads shall clap up their shop windows, and away. This is the day, and this day they shall do't, they shall do't.

---

[1] A sweet biscuit, similar to a macaroon.—*Nares.*

Boys, that day are you free, let masters care,
And prentices shall pray for Simon Eyre.   [*Exit.*

SCENE II.—*A Street near St. Faith's Church.*

Enter HODGE, FIRK, RALPH, *and five or six* Shoemakers,
all with cudgels or such weapons.

Hodge. Come, Ralph; stand to it, Firk.   My masters,
as we are the brave bloods of the shoemakers, heirs apparent to Saint Hugh, and perpetual benefactors to all
good fellows, thou shalt have no wrong; were Hammon
a king of spades, he should not delve in thy close without thy sufferance.   But tell me, Ralph, art thou sure 'tis
thy wife?

Ralph. Am I sure this is Firk?   This morning, when
I stroked[1] on her shoes, I looked upon her, and she upon
me, and sighed, asked me if ever I knew one Ralph.
Yes, said I.   For his sake, said she—tears standing in
her eyes—and for thou art somewhat like him, spend this
piece of gold.   I took it; my lame leg and my travel beyond sea made me unknown.   All is one for that: I
know she's mine.

Firk. Did she give thee this gold?   O glorious glittering gold!   She's thine own, 'tis thy wife, and she loves
thee; for I'll stand to't, there's no woman will give gold
to any man, but she thinks better of him, than she thinks
of them she gives silver to.   And for Hammon, neither
Hammon nor hangman shall wrong thee in London.   Is
not our old master Eyre, lord mayor?   Speak, my hearts.

All. Yes, and Hammon shall know it to his cost.

Enter HAMMON, *his* Serving-man, JANE *and* Others.

Hodge. Peace, my bullies; yonder they come.

Ralph. Stand to't, my hearts.   Firk, let me speak first.

[1] Fitted.

Hodge. No, Ralph, let me.—Hammon, whither away so early ?

Ham. Unmannerly, rude slave, what's that to thee ?

Firk. To him, sir ? Yes, sir, and to me, and others. Good-morrow, Jane, how dost thou ? Good Lord, how the world is changed with you ! God be thanked !

Ham. Villains, hands off ! How dare you touch my love ?

All. Villains ? Down with them ! Cry clubs for prentices ! [1]

Hodge. Hold, my hearts ! Touch her, Hammon ? Yea, and more than that : we'll carry her away with us. My masters and gentlemen, never draw your bird-spits ; shoemakers are steel to the back, men every inch of them, all spirit.

Those of Hammon's side. Well, and what of all this ?

Hodge. I'll show you.—Jane, dost thou know this man ? 'Tis Ralph, I can tell thee ; nay, 'tis he in faith, though he be lamed by the wars. Yet look not strange, but run to him, fold him about the neck and kiss him.

Jane. Lives then my husband ? Oh God, let me go, Let me embrace my Ralph.

Ham. What means my Jane ?

Jane. Nay, what meant you, to tell me, he was slain ?

Ham. Pardon me, dear love, for being misled.
(*To* RALPH.) 'Twas rumoured here in London, thou wert dead.

Firk. Thou seest he lives. Lass, go, pack home with him. Now, Master Hammon, where's your mistress, your wife ?

Serv. 'Swounds, master, fight for her ! Will you thus lose her ?

All. Down with that creature ! Clubs ! Down with him !

Hodge. Hold, hold !

---

[1] In any public affray, the cry was " Clubs, Clubs !" by way of calling for help (particularly by the London 'prentices). —*Nares.*

Ham. Hold, fool! Sirs, he shall do no wrong.
Will my Jane leave me thus, and break her faith?

Firk. Yea, sir! She must, sir! She shall, sir! What
then? Mend it!

Hodge. Hark, fellow Ralph, follow my counsel: set the
wench in the midst, and let her choose her man, and let
her be his woman.

Jane. Whom should I choose? Whom should my
    thoughts affect
But him whom Heaven hath made to be my love?
Thou art my husband, and these humble weeds
Makes thee more beautiful than all his wealth.
Therefore, I will but put off his attire,
Returning it into the owner's hand,
And after ever be thy constant wife.

Hodge. Not a rag, Jane! The law's on our side; he
that sows in another man's ground, forfeits his harvest.
Get thee home, Ralph; follow him, Jane; he shall not
have so much as a busk-point [1] from thee.

Firk. Stand to that, Ralph; the appurtenances are
thine own. Hammon, look not at her!

Serv. O, swounds, no!

Firk. Blue coat, be quiet, we'll give you a new livery
else; we'll make Shrove Tuesday Saint George's Day for
you. Look not, Hammon, leer not! I'll firk you! For
thy head now, one glance, one sheep's eye, anything, at
her! Touch not a rag, lest I and my brethren beat you
to clouts.

Serv. Come, Master Hammon, there's no striving here.

Ham. Good fellows, hear me speak; and, honest Ralph,
Whom I have injured most by loving Jane,
Mark what I offer thee: here in fair gold
Is twenty pound, I'll give it for thy Jane;
If this content thee not, thou shalt have more.

Hodge. Sell not thy wife, Ralph; make her not a whore.

---

[1] A piece of lace with a tag, which fastened the busk, or piece of
whalebone, used to keep the stays in position.

Ham. Say, wilt thou freely cease thy claim in her,
And let her be my wife?

All.   No, do not, Ralph.

Ralph. Sirrah Hammon, Hammon, dost thou think a
shoemaker is so base to be a bawd to his own wife for
commodity? Take thy gold, choke with it! Were I not
lame, I would make thee eat thy words.

Firk. A shoemaker sell his flesh and blood? Oh
indignity!

Hodge. Sirrah, take up your pelf, and be packing.

Ham. I will not touch one penny, but in lieu
Of that great wrong I offered thy Jane,
To Jane and thee I give that twenty pound.
Since I have failed of her, during my life,
I vow, no woman else shall be my wife.
Farewell, good fellows of the gentle trade:
Your morning mirth my mourning day hath made. [*Exit.*

Firk. (*To the* Serving-man.) Touch the gold, creature,
if you dare! Y'are best be trudging. Here, Jane, take
thou it. Now let's home, my hearts.

Hodge. Stay! Who comes here? Jane, on again with
thy mask!

Enter the EARL OF LINCOLN, *the* LORD MAYOR *and*
Servants.

Lincoln. Yonder's the lying varlet mocked us so.

L. Mayor. Come hither, sirrah!

Firk. I, sir? I am sirrah? You mean me, do you not?

Lincoln. Where is my nephew married?

Firk. Is he married? God give him joy, I am glad of
it. They have a fair day, and the sign is in a good planet,
Mars in Venus.

L. Mayor. Villain, thou toldst me that my daughter
Rose
This morning should be married at Saint Faith's;
We have watched there these three hours at the least,
Yet see we no such thing.

Firk. Truly, I am sorry for't ; a bride's a pretty thing.

Hodge. Come to the purpose. Yonder's the bride and bridegroom you look for, I hope. Though you be lords, you are not to bar by your authority men from women, are you ?

L. Mayor. See, see, my daughter's masked.

Lincoln.   True, and my nephew, To hide his guilt, counterfeits him lame.

Firk. Yea, truly ; God help the poor couple, they are lame and blind.

L. Mayor. I'll ease her blindness.

Lincoln.   I'll his lameness cure.

Firk. Lie down, sirs, and laugh ! My fellow Ralph is taken for Rowland Lacy, and Jane for Mistress Damask Rose. This is all my knavery.

L. Mayor. What, have I found you, minion ?

Lincoln.   O base wretch
Nay, hide thy face, the horror of thy guilt
Can hardly be washed off. Where are thy powers ?
What battles have you made ? O yes, I see,
Thou fought'st with Shame, and Shame hath conquered
        thee.
This lameness will not serve.

L. Mayor.   Unmask yourself.

Lincoln. Lead home your daughter.

L. Mayor.   Take your nephew hence.

Ralph. Hence ! Swounds, what mean you ? Are you mad ? I hope you cannot enforce my wife from me. Where's Hammon ?

L. Mayor. Your wife ?

Lincoln. What, Hammon ?

Ralph. Yea, my wife ; and, therefore, the proudest of you that lays hands on her first, I'll lay my crutch 'cross his pate.

Firk. To him, lame Ralph ! Here's brave sport !

Ralph. Rose call you her ? Why, her name is Jane. Look here else; do you know her now ? [*Unmasking* JANE.

Lincoln. Is this your daughter ?

L. Mayor.   No, nor this your nephew.
My Lord of Lincoln, we are both abused
By this base, crafty varlet.

Firk. Yea, forsooth, no varlet ; forsooth, no base ;
forsooth, I am but mean ; no crafty neither, but of the
gentle craft.

L. Mayor. Where is my daughter Rose ?   Where is my
    child ?

Lincoln. Where is my nephew Lacy married ?

Firk. Why, here is good laced mutton, as I promised
you.

Lincoln. Villain, I'll have thee punished for this wrong.

Firk. Punish the journeyman villain, but not the
journeyman shoemaker.

Enter DODGER.

Dodger. My lord, I come to bring unwelcome news.
Your nephew Lacy and your daughter Rose
Early this morning wedded at the Savoy,
None being present but the lady mayoress.
Besides, I learnt among the officers,
The lord mayor vows to stand in their defence
'Gainst any that shall seek to cross the match.

Lincoln. Dares Eyre the shoemaker uphold the deed ?

Firk. Yes, sir, shoemakers dare stand in a woman's
quarrel, I warrant you, as deep as another, and deeper
too.

Dodger. Besides, his grace to-day dines with the
    mayor ;
Who on his knees humbly intends to fall
And beg a pardon for your nephew's fault.

Lincoln. But I'll prevent him !   Come, Sir Roger
    Oateley ;
The king will do us justice in this cause.
Howe'er their hands have made them man and wife,
I will disjoin the match, or lose my life.   [*Exeunt.*

Firk. Adieu, Monsieur Dodger! Farewell, fools! Ha, ha! Oh, if they had stayed, I would have so lambed [1] them with flouts! O heart, my codpiece-point is ready to fly in pieces every time I think upon Mistress Rose; but let that pass, as my lady mayoress says.

Hodge. This matter is answered. Come, Ralph; home with thy wife. Come, my fine shoemakers, let's to our master's, the new lord mayor, and there swagger this Shrove-Tuesday. I'll promise you wine enough, for Madge keeps the cellar.

All. O rare! Madge is a good wench.

Firk. And I'll promise you meat enough, for simp'ring Susan keeps the larder. I'll lead you to victuals, my brave soldiers; follow your captain. O brave! Hark, hark!   [*Bell rings.*

All. The pancake-bell rings, the pancake-bell! Tri-lill, my hearts!

Firk. Oh brave! Oh sweet bell! O delicate pan-cakes! Open the doors, my hearts, and shut up the windows! keep in the house, let out the pancakes! Oh rare, my hearts! Let's march together for the honour of Saint Hugh to the great new hall [2] in Gracious Street-corner, which our master, the new lord mayor, hath built.

Ralph. O the crew of good fellows that will dine at my lord mayor's cost to-day!

Hodge. By the Lord, my lord mayor is a most brave man. How shall prentices be bound to pray for him and the honour of the gentlemen shoemakers! Let's feed and be fat with my lord's bounty.

Firk. O musical bell, still! O Hodge, O my brethren! There's cheer for the heavens: venison-pasties walk up and down piping hot, like sergeants; beef and brewess [3] comes marching in dry-vats,[4] fritters and pancakes comes

---

[1] Whipped.   [2] Leadenhall.   [See note *post*, p. 85.]
    [3] See note *ante*, p. 19.   [4] Barrels.

trowling in in wheel-barrows; hens and oranges hopping in porters'-baskets, collops and eggs in scuttles, and tarts and custards comes quavering in in malt-shovels.

Enter more Prentices.

All. Whoop, look here, look here!

Hodge. How now, mad lads, whither away so fast?

1st Prentice. Whither? Why, to the great new hall, know you not why? The lord mayor hath bidden all the prentices in London to breakfast this morning.

All. Oh brave shoemaker, oh brave lord of incomprehensible good-fellowship! Whoo! Hark you! The pancake-bell rings.   [*Cast up caps.*

Firk. Nay, more, my hearts! Every Shrove-Tuesday is our year of jubilee; and when the pancake-bell rings, we are as free as my lord mayor; we may shut up our shops, and make holiday. I'll have it called Saint Hugh's Holiday.

All. Agreed, agreed! Saint Hugh's Holiday.

Hodge. And this shall continue for ever.

All. Oh brave! Come, come, my hearts! Away, away!

Firk. O eternal credit to us of the gentle craft! March fair, my hearts! Oh rare!   [*Exeunt.*

SCENE III.—*A Street in London.*

Enter the KING *and his* Train *across the stage.*

King. Is our lord mayor of London such a gallant?

Nobleman. One of the merriest madcaps in your land.
Your grace will think, when you behold the man,
He's rather a wild ruffian than a mayor.
Yet thus much I'll ensure your majesty.
In all his actions that concern his state,
He is as serious, provident, and wise,

As full of gravity amongst the grave,
As any mayor hath been these many years.

    King. I am with child,[1] till I behold this huff-cap.[2]
But all my doubt is, when we come in presence,
His madness will be dashed clean out of countenance.

    Nobleman. It may be so, my liege.

    King.   Which to prevent,
Let some one give him notice, 'tis our pleasure
That he put on his wonted merriment.
Set forward!

    All. On afore!   *[Exeunt.*

SCENE IV.—*A Great Hall.*

    Enter EYRE, HODGE, FIRK, RALPH, *and other* Shoe-
makers, *all with napkins on their shoulders.*

    Eyre. Come, my fine Hodge, my jolly gentlemen shoe-
makers; soft, where be these cannibals, these varlets,
my officers? Let them all walk and wait upon my
brethren; for my meaning is, that none but shoemakers,
none but the livery of my company shall in their satin
hoods wait upon the trencher of my sovereign.

    Firk. O my lord, it will be rare!

    Eyre. No more, Firk; come, lively! Let your fellow-
prentices want no cheer; let wine be plentiful as beer,
and beer as water. Hang these penny-pinching fathers,
that cram wealth in innocent lamb-skins. Rip, knaves,
avaunt! Look to my guests!

    Hodge. My lord, we are at our wits' end for room;
those hundred tables will not feast the fourth part of them.

    Eyre. Then cover me those hundred tables again,
and again, till all my jolly prentices be feasted. Avoid,
Hodge! Run, Ralph! Frisk about, my nimble Firk!
Carouse me fathom-healths to the honour of the shoe-

----

    [1] In suspense.   [2] *i.e.* Swaggerer.

makers. Do they drink lively, Hodge? Do they tickle it, Firk?

Firk. Tickle it? Some of them have taken their liquor standing so long that they can stand no longer; but for meat, they would eat it, an they had it.

Eyre. Want they meat? Where's this swag-belly, this greasy kitchenstuff cook? Call the varlet to me! Want meat? Firk, Hodge, lame Ralph, run, my tall men, beleaguer the shambles, beggar all Eastcheap, serve me whole oxen in chargers, and let sheep whine upon the tables like pigs for want of good fellows to eat them. Want meat? Vanish, Firk! Avaunt, Hodge!

Hodge. Your lordship mistakes my man Firk; he means, their bellies want meat, not the boards; for they have drunk so much, they can eat nothing.

THE SECOND THREE MEN'S SONG.[1]

Cold's the wind, and wet's the rain,
    Saint Hugh be our good speed:
Ill is the weather that bringeth no gain,
    Nor helps good hearts in need.

Trowl[2] the bowl, the jolly nut-brown bowl,
    And here, kind mate, to thee:
Let's sing a dirge for Saint Hugh's soul,
    And down it merrily.

Down a down heydown a down,
    Hey derry derry, down a down!
        (*Close with the tenor boy*)
Ho, well done; to me let come!
    Ring, compass, gentle joy.

Trowl the bowl, the nut-brown bowl,
    And here, kind mate, to thee: etc.
        [*Repeat as often as there be men to drink; and
            at last when all have drunk, this verse:*

---

[1] See note to First Three Men's Song, p. 46.
[2] Pass, push about from one to the other, in drinking.

Cold's the wind, and wet's the rain,
    Saint Hugh be our good speed :
Ill is the weather that bringeth no gain,
    Nor helps good hearts in need.

Enter HANS, ROSE, *and* MARGERY.

Marg. Where is my lord ?

Eyre. How now, Lady Madgy ?

Marg. The king's most excellent majesty is new come ;
he sends me for thy honour ; one of his most worshipful peers bade me tell thou must be merry, and so
forth ; but let that pass.

Eyre. Is my sovereign come ?   Vanish, my tall shoemakers, my nimble brethren ; look to my guests, the
prentices.   Yet stay a little !   How now, Hans ?   How
looks my little Rose ?

Hans. Let me request you to remember me.
I know, your honour easily may obtain
Free pardon of the king for me and Rose,
And reconcile me to my uncle's grace.

Eyre. Have done, my good Hans, my honest journeyman ; look cheerily !   I'll fall upon both my knees, till
they be as hard as horn, but I'll get thy pardon.

Marg. Good my lord, have a care what you speak to
his grace.

Eyre. Away, you Islington whitepot ! [1] hence, you
hopperarse ! you barley-pudding, full of maggots ! you
broiled carbonado ! [2] avaunt, avaunt, avoid, Mephis-
tophiles !   Shall Sim Eyre learn to speak of you, Lady
Madgy ?   Vanish, Mother Miniver-cap ; vanish, go, trip
and go ; meddle with your partlets [3] and your pishery-
pashery, your flewes [4] and your whirligigs ; go, rub, out of
mine alley !   Sim Eyre knows how to speak to a Pope, to

---

[1] " A dish, made of milk, eggs and sugar, baked in a pot."—
Webster.
[2] A steak cut crossways for broiling.
[3] Bands or collars for the neck.
[4] Flaps ; as resembling the hanging chaps of a hound,

Sultan Soliman, to Tamburlaine,[1] an he were here ; and shall I melt, shall I droop before my sovereign? No, come, my Lady Madgy! Follow me, Hans! About your business, my frolic free-booters! Firk, frisk about, and about, and about, for the honour of mad Simon Eyre, lord mayor of London.

Firk. Hey, for the honour of the shoemakers.

[*Exeunt.*

SCENE V.—*An Open Yard before the Hall.*

A long flourish, or two.   Enter the KING, *Nobles,* EYRE, MARGERY, LACY, ROSE.   LACY *and* ROSE *kneel.*

King. Well, Lacy, though the fact was very foul
Of your revolting from our kingly love
And your own duty, yet we pardon you.
Rise both, and, Mistress Lacy, thank my lord mayor
For your young bridegroom here.

Eyre. So, my dear liege, Sim Eyre and my brethren, the gentlemen shoemakers, shall set your sweet majesty's image cheek by jowl by Saint Hugh for this honour you have done poor Simon Eyre. I beseech your grace, pardon my rude behaviour ; I am a handicraftsman, yet my heart is without craft ; I would be sorry at my soul, that my boldness should offend my king.

King. Nay, I pray thee, good lord mayor, be even as merry
As if thou wert among thy shoemakers ;
It does me good to see thee in this humour.

Eyre. Say'st thou me so, my sweet Dioclesian? Then, humph! Prince am I none, yet am I princely born. By the Lord of Ludgate, my liege, I'll be as merry as a pie.[2]

---

[1] The allusion is, no doubt, to Kyd's *Soliman and Perseda*, and to Marlowe's *Tamburlaine*, though these were long after Eyre's time.

[2] Magpie.

King. Tell me, in faith, mad Eyre, how old thou art.

Eyre. My liege, a very boy, a stripling, a younker; you see not a white hair on my head, not a gray in this beard. Every hair, I assure thy majesty, that sticks in this beard, Sim Eyre values at the King of Babylon's ransom, Tamar Cham's [1] beard was a rubbing brush to't : yet I'll shave it off, and stuff tennis-balls with it, to please my bully king.

King. But all this while I do not know your age.

Eyre. My liege, I am six and fifty year old, yet I can cry humph ! with a sound heart for the honour of Saint Hugh. Mark this old wench, my king : I danced the shaking of the sheets with her six and thirty years ago, and yet I hope to get two or three young lord mayors, ere I die. I am lusty still, Sim Eyre still. Care and cold lodging brings white hairs. My sweet Majesty, let care vanish, cast it upon thy nobles, it will make thee look always young like Apollo, and cry humph ! Prince am I none, yet am I princely born.

King. Ha, ha !
Say, Cornwall, didst thou ever see his like?

Cornwall. Not I, my lord.

Enter the EARL OF LINCOLN *and the* LORD MAYOR.

King.   Lincoln, what news with you?

Lincoln. My gracious lord, have care unto yourself, For there are traitors here.

All. Traitors? Where? Who?

Eyre. Traitors in my house ? God forbid ! Where be my officers ? I'll spend my soul, ere my king feel harm.

King. Where is the traitor, Lincoln ?

Lincoln.   Here he stands.

[1] Tamerlane (Tamburlaine), Cham, or Khan of Tartary. Compare Shakespeare's *Much Ado about Nothing*, Act II. Sc. i.

King. Cornwall, lay hold on Lacy !—Lincoln, speak,
What canst thou lay unto thy nephew's charge ?

    Lincoln. This, my dear liege : your Grace, to do me
        honour,
Heaped on the head of this degenerate boy
Desertless favours; you made choice of him,
To be commander over powers in France.
But he——

    King. Good Lincoln, prithee, pause a while !
Even in thine eyes I read what thou wouldst speak.
I know how Lacy did neglect our love,
Ran himself deeply, in the highest degree,
Into vile treason——

    Lincoln.   Is he not a traitor?

    King. Lincoln, he was ; now have we pardoned him.
'Twas not a base want of true valour's fire,
That held him out of France, but love's desire.

    Lincoln. I will not bear his shame upon my back.

    King. Nor shalt thou, Lincoln ; I forgive you both.

    Lincoln. Then, good my liege, forbid the boy to wed
One whose mean birth will much disgrace his bed.

    King. Are they not married ?

    Lincoln.   No, my liege.

    Both.   We are.

    King. Shall I divorce them then ? O be it far,
That any hand on earth should dare untie
The sacred knot, knit by God's majesty ;
I would not for my crown disjoin their hands,
That are conjoined in holy nuptial bands.
How say'st thou, Lacy, wouldst thou lose thy Rose ?

    Lacy. Not for all India's wealth, my sovereign.

    King. But Rose, I am sure, her Lacy would forego ?

    Rose. If Rose were asked that question, she'd say no.

    King. You hear them, Lincoln ?

    Lincoln.   Yea, my liege, I do.

    King. Yet canst thou find i'th' heart to part these two ?
Who seeks, besides you, to divorce these lovers ?

L. Mayor. I do, my gracious lord, I am her father.

King. Sir Roger Oateley, our last mayor, I think?

Nobleman. The same, my liege.

King.   Would you offend Love's laws?
Well, you shall have your wills, you sue to me,
To prohibit the match. Soft, let me see—
You both are married, Lacy, art thou not?

Lacy. I am, dread sovereign.

King.   Then, upon thy life,
I charge thee, not to call this woman wife.

L. Mayor. I thank your grace.

Rose.   O my most gracious lord!
                                        [*Kneels.*

King. Nay, Rose, never woo me; I tell you true,
Although as yet I am a bachelor,
Yet I believe, I shall not marry you.

Rose. Can you divide the body from the soul,
Yet make the body live?

King.   Yea, so profound?
I cannot, Rose, but you I must divide.
This fair maid, bridegroom, cannot be your bride.
Are you pleased, Lincoln? Oateley, are you pleased?

Both. Yes, my lord.

King.   Then must my heart be eased;
For, credit me, my conscience lives in pain,
Till these whom I divorced, be joined again.
Lacy, give me thy hand; Rose, lend me thine!
Be what you would be! Kiss now! So, that's fine.
At night, lovers, to bed!—Now, let me see,
Which of you all mislikes this harmony.

L. Mayor. Will you then take from me my child per-
    force?

King. Why, tell me, Oateley: shines not Lacy's
    name
As bright in the world's eye as the gay beams
Of any citizen?

Lincoln.   Yea, but, my gracious lord,

I do mislike the match far more than he ;
Her blood is too too base.

 King.   Lincoln, no more.
Dost thou not know that love respects no blood,
Cares not for difference of birth or state ?
The maid is young, well born, fair, virtuous,
A worthy bride for any gentleman.
Besides, your nephew for her sake did stoop
To bare necessity, and, as I hear,
Forgetting honours and all courtly pleasures,
To gain her love, became a shoemaker.
As for the honour which he lost in France,
Thus I redeem it : Lacy, kneel thee down !—
Arise, Sir Rowland Lacy ! Tell me now,
Tell me in earnest, Oateley, canst thou chide,
Seeing thy Rose a lady and a bride ?

 L. Mayor. I am content with what your grace hath done.

 Lincoln. And I, my liege, since there's no remedy.

 King. Come on, then, all shake hands : I'll have you
   friends ;
Where there is much love, all discord ends.
What says my mad lord mayor to all this love ?

 Eyre. O my liege, this honour you have done to my
fine journeyman here, Rowland Lacy, and all these
favours which you have shown to me this day in my poor
house, will make Simon Eyre live longer by one dozen of
warm summers more than he should.

 King. Nay, my mad lord mayor, that shall be thy
   name,
If any grace of mine can length thy life,
One honour more Ill do thee : that new building,[1]
Which at thy cost in Cornhill is erected,
Shall take a name from us ; we'll have it called

---

[1] "A.D. 1419. This year Sir Symon Eyre built Leadenhall, at
his proper expense, as it now appears, and gave the same to the City
to be employed as a public granary for laying up corn against a time
of scarcity."—*Maitland*, ii., p. 187.

The Leadenhall, because in digging it
You found the lead that covereth the same.

Eyre. I thank your majesty.

Marg. God bless your grace !

King. Lincoln, a word with you !

Enter HODGE, FIRK, RALPH, *and more* Shoemakers.

Eyre. How now, my mad knaves? Peace, speak softly, yonder is the king.

King. With the old troop which there we keep in pay,
We will incorporate a new supply.
Before one summer more pass o'er my head,
France shall repent, England was injured.
What are all those?

Lacy.   All shoemakers, my liege,
Sometime my fellows ; in their companies
I lived as merry as an emperor.

King. My mad lord mayor, are all these shoemakers ?

Eyre. All shoemakers, my liege ; all gentlemen of the gentle craft, true Trojans, courageous cordwainers ; they all kneel to the shrine of holy Saint Hugh.

All the Shoemakers. God save your majesty !

King. Mad Simon, would they anything with us ?

Eyre. Mum, mad knaves ! Not a word ! I'll do't ; I warrant you. They are all beggars, my liege ; all for themselves, and I for them all on both my knees do entreat, that for the honour of poor Simon Eyre and the good of his brethren, these mad knaves, your grace would vouchsafe some privilege to my new Leadenhall, that it may be lawful for us to buy and sell leather there two days a week.

King. Mad Sim, I grant your suit, you shall have patent
To hold two market-days in Leadenhall,
Mondays and Fridays, those shall be the times.
Will this content you?

All. Jesus bless your grace !

Eyre. In the name of these my poor brethren shoe-makers, I most humbly thank your grace. But before I rise, seeing you are in the giving vein and we in the begging, grant Sim Eyre one boon more.

King. What is it, my lord mayor?

Eyre. Vouchsafe to taste of a poor banquet that stands sweetly waiting for your sweet presence.

King. I shall undo thee, Eyre, only with feasts;
Already have I been too troublesome;
Say, have I not?

Eyre. O my dear king, Sim Eyre was taken unawares upon a day of shroving,[1] which I promised long ago to the prentices of London.

> For, an't please your highness, in time past,
> I bare the water-tankard, and my coat
> Sits not a whit the worse upon my back;
> And then, upon a morning, some mad boys,
> It was Shrove Tuesday, even as 'tis now,

Gave me my breakfast, and I swore then by the stopple of my tankard, if ever I came to be lord mayor of London, I would feast all the prentices. This day, my liege, I did it, and the slaves had an hundred tables five times covered; they are gone home and vanished;

> Yet add more honour to the gentle trade,
> Taste of Eyre's banquet, Simon's happy made.

King. Eyre, I will taste of thy banquet, and will say,
I have not met more pleasure on a day.
Friends of the gentle craft, thanks to you all,
Thanks, my kind lady mayoress, for our cheer.—
Come, lords, a while let's revel it at home!
When all our sports and banquetings are done,
Wars must right wrongs which Frenchmen have begun.

[*Exeunt.*

[1] Merry-making.

THE HONEST WHORE.

IN TWO PARTS.

———∞•§•∞———

PART THE FIRST.

DRAMATIS PERSONÆ.

GASPARO TREBAZZI, Duke of Milan.
HIPPOLITO, a Count.
CASTRUCHIO.
SINEZI.
PIORATTO.
FLUELLO.
MATHEO.
BENEDICT, a Doctor.
ANSELMO, a Friar.
FUSTIGO, Brother of VIOLA.
CANDIDO, a Linen-draper.
GEORGE, his Servant.
First Prentice.
Second Prentice.
CRAMBO.
POH.
ROGER, Servant of BELLAFRONT.
Porter,
Sweeper.
Madmen, Servants, &c.

INFELICE, Daughter of the Duke.
BELLAFRONT, a Harlot.
VIOLA, Wife of Candido.
Mistress FINGERLOCK, a Bawd.

SCENE—MILAN and the Neighbourhood.

Was laid out 'fore her body; and the worms
That now must feast with her, were even bespoke,
And solemnly invited like strange guests.

Mat. Strange feeders they are indeed, my lord, and,
like your jester, or young courtier, will enter upon any
man's trencher without bidding.

Hip. Curst be that day for ever that robbed her
Of breath, and me, of bliss ! henceforth let it stand
Within the wizard's book (the calendar)
Marked with a marginal finger, to be chosen
By thieves, by villains, and black murderers,
As the best day for them to labour in.
If henceforth this adulterous bawdy world
Be got with child with treason, sacrilege,
Atheism, rapes, treacherous friendship, perjury,
Slander (the beggar's sin), lies (sin of fools),
Or any other damned impieties,
On Monday let 'em be delivered :
I swear to thee, Matheo, by my soul,
Hereafter weekly on that day I'll glue
Mine eye-lids down, because they shall not gaze
On any female cheek.   And being locked up
In my close chamber, there I'll meditate
On nothing but my Infelice's end,
Or on a dead man's skull draw out mine own.

Mat. You'll do all these good works now every Monday, because it is so bad : but I hope upon Tuesday
morning I shall take you with a wench.

Hip. If ever, whilst frail blood through my veins run,
On woman's beams I throw affection,
Save her that's dead : or that I loosely fly
To th' shore of any other wafting eye,
Let me not prosper, Heaven !   I will be true,
Even to her dust and ashes : could her tomb
Stand whilst I lived, so long that it might rot,
That should fall down, but she be ne'er forgot.

Mat. If you have this strange monster, honesty, in

Dekker.   H your belly, why so jig-makers [1] and chroniclers shall pick something out of you ; but an I smell not you and a bawdy house out within these ten days, let my nose be as big as an English bag-pudding : I'll follow your lordship, though it be to the place aforenamed.   [*Exeunt.*

SCENE II.—*Another Street.*

Enter Fustigo *in some fantastic Sea-suit, meeting a* Porter.

Fus. How now, porter, will she come ?

Por. If I may trust a woman, sir, she will come.

Fus. There's for thy pains [*Gives money*]. Godamercy, if ever I stand in need of a wench that will come with a wet finger,[2] porter, thou shalt earn my money before any clarissimo [3] in Milan ; yet, so God sa' me, she's mine own sister body and soul, as I am a Christian gentleman ; farewell ; I'll ponder till she come : thou hast been no bawd in fetching this woman, I assure thee.

Por. No matter if I had, sir, better men than porters are bawds.

Fus. O God, sir, many that have borne offices. But, porter, art sure thou went'st into a true house ?

Por. I think so, for I met with no thieves.

Fus. Nay, but art sure it was my sister, Viola.

Por. I am sure, by all superscriptions, it was the party you ciphered.

Fus. Not very tall ?

Por. Nor very low ; a middling woman.

Fus. 'Twas she, 'faith, 'twas she, a pretty plump cheek, like mine ?

Por. At a blush a little, very much like you.

---

[1] Ballad-makers.
[2] *i.e.* Readily. Compare *Gull's Horn Book*, Notts Ed. p. 160.
[3] Grandee.

Fus. Godso, I would not for a ducat she had kicked up her heels, for I ha' spent an abomination this voyage, marry, I did it amongst sailors and gentlemen. There's a little modicum more, porter, for making thee stay [*Gives money*]; farewell, honest porter.

Por. I am in your debt, sir; God preserve you.

Fus. Not so, neither, good porter. [*Exit* Porter.] God's lid, yonder she comes. [*Enter* VIOLA.] Sister Viola, I am glad to see you stirring: it's news to have me here, is't not, sister?

Vio. Yes, trust me; I wondered who should be so bold to send for me: you are welcome to Milan, brother.

Fus. Troth, sister, I heard you were married to a very rich chuff,[1] and I was very sorry for it, that I had no better clothes, and that made me send; for you know we Milaners love to strut upon Spanish leather. And how do all our friends?

Vio. Very well; you ha' travelled enough now, I trow, to sow your wild oats.

Fus. A pox on 'em! wild oats? I ha' not an oat to throw at a horse. Troth, sister, I ha' sowed my oats, and reaped two hundred ducats if I had 'em here. Marry, I must entreat you to lend me some thirty or forty till the ship come: by this hand, I'll discharge at my day, by this hand.

Vio. These are your old oaths.

Fus. Why, sister, do you think I'll forswear my hand?

Vio. Well, well, you shall have them: put yourself into better fashion, because I must employ you in a serious matter.

Fus. I'll sweat like a horse if I like the matter.

Vio. You ha' cast off all your old swaggering humours?

Fus. I had not sailed a league in that great fishpond, the sea, but I cast up my very gall.

---

[1] A contemptuous term for an old man of means.

Vio. I am the more sorry, for I must employ a true swaggerer.

Fus. Nay by this iron, sister, they shall find I am powder and touch-box, if they put fire once into me.

Vio. Then lend me your ears.

Fus. Mine ears are yours, dear sister.

Vio. I am married to a man that has wealth enough, and wit enough.

Fus. A linen-draper, I was told, sister.

Vio. Very true, a grave citizen, I want nothing that a wife can wish from a husband : but here's the spite, he has not all the things belonging to a man.

Fus. God's my life, he's a very mandrake,[1] or else (God bless us) one a' these whiblins,[2] and that's worse, and then all the children that he gets lawfully of your body, sister, are bastards by a statute.

Vio. O, you run over me too fast, brother ; I have heard it often said, that he who cannot be angry is no man. I am sure my husband is a man in print, for all things else save only in this, no tempest can move him.

Fus. 'Slid, would he had been at sea with us ! he should ha' been moved, and moved again, for I'll be sworn, la, our drunken ship reeled like a Dutchman.

Vio. No loss of goods can increase in him a wrinkle, no crabbed language make his countenance sour, the stubbornness of no servant shake him ; he has no more gall in him than a dove, no more sting than an ant ; musician will he never be, yet I find much music in him, but he loves no frets, and is so free from anger, that many times I am ready to bite off my tongue, because it wants that virtue which all women's tongues have, to anger their husbands : brother, mine can by no thunder, turn him into a sharpness.

Fus. Belike his blood, sister, is well brewed then.

---

[1] The superstitions about this plant, its fancied resemblance to the human figure, led to its being frequently alluded to in this way.

[2] Query Whimlings—idiots.

Vio. I protest to thee, Fustigo, I love him most affectionately ; but I know not—I ha' such a tickling within me—such a strange longing; nay, verily I do long.

Fus. Then you're with child, sister, by all signs and tokens ; nay, I am partly a physician, and partly something else.   I ha' read Albertus Magnus, and Aristotle's Problems.

Vio. You're wide a' th' bow hand[1] still, brother : my longings are not wanton, but wayward : I long to have my patient husband eat up a whole porcupine, to the intent, the bristling quills may stick about his lips like a Flemish mustachio, and be shot at me : I shall be leaner the new moon, unless I can make him horn-mad.

Fus. 'Sfoot, half a quarter of an hour does that ; make him a cuckold.

Vio. Pooh, he would count such a cut no unkindness.

Fus. The honester citizen he ; then make him drunk and cut off his beard.

Vio. Fie, fie, idle, idle ! he's no Frenchman, to fret at the loss of a little scald[2] hair.   No, brother, thus it shall be—you must be secret.

Fus. As your mid-wife, I protest, sister, or a barber-surgeon.

Vio. Repair to the Tortoise here in St. Christopher's Street ; I will send you money ; turn yourself into a brave man : instead of the arms of your mistress, let your sword and your military scarf hang about your neck.

Fus. I must have a great horseman's French feather too, sister.

Vio. O, by any means, to show your light head, else your hat will sit like a coxcomb : to be brief, you must be in all points a most terrible wide-mouthed swaggerer.

Fus. Nay, for swaggering points let me alone.

Vio. Resort then to our shop, and, in my husband's presence, kiss me, snatch rings, jewels, or any thing, so you give it back again, brother, in secret.

---

[1] Wide of the mark.   [2] Scurfy.

Fus. By this hand, sister.

Vio. Swear as if you came but new from knighting.

Fus. Nay, I'll swear after four-hundred a year.

Vio. Swagger worse than a lieutenant among fresh-water soldiers, call me your love, your ingle,[1] your cousin, or so ; but sister at no hand.

Fus. No, no, it shall be cousin, or rather coz ; that's the gulling word between the citizens' wives and their mad-caps that man 'em to the garden ; to call you one a' mine aunts'[2] sister, were as good as call you arrant whore ; no, no, let me alone to cousin you rarely.

Vio. H'as heard I have a brother, but never saw him, therefore put on a good face.

Fus. The best in Milan, I warrant.

Vio. Take up wares, but pay nothing, rifle my bosom, my pocket, my purse, the boxes for money to dice with ; but, brother, you must give all back again in secret.

Fus. By this welkin that here roars I will, or else let me never know what a secret is : why, sister, do you think I'll cony-catch[3] you, when you are my cousin ? God's my life, then I were a stark ass. If I fret not his guts, beg me for a fool.[4]

Vio. Be circumspect, and do so then. Farewell.

Fus. The Tortoise, sister ! I'll stay there ; forty ducats.

Vio. Thither I'll send.—[*Exit* FUSTIGO.]—This law can none deny,

Women must have their longings, or they die.   [*Exit.*

---

[1] Bosom friend.

[2] " Aunt " was a cant term both for a prostitute and a bawd.— *Dyce.*

[3] Cheat.

[4] *i.e.* An idiot. The phrase had its origin in the practice of the crown granting the custody of idiots and their possessions to persons who had interest enough to secure the appointments.

SCENE III.—*A Chamber in the Duke's Palace.*

Enter the Duke, Doctor BENEDICT, *and two* Servants.

Duke. Give charge that none do enter, lock the
    doors—   -   [*Speaking as he enters.*
And fellows, what your eyes and ears receive,
Upon your lives trust not the gadding air
To carry the least part of it.   The glass, the hour-glass !
    Doct. Here, my lord.   [*Brings hour-glass.*
    Duke. Ah, 'tis near spent !
But, Doctor Benedict, does your art speak truth ?
Art sure the soporiferous stream will ebb,
And leave the crystal banks of her white body
Pure as they were at first, just at the hour ?
    Doct. Just at the hour, my lord.
    Duke. Uncurtain her :
            [*A curtain is drawn back and* INFELICE *dis-
               covered lying on a couch.*
Softly !—See, doctor, what a coldish heat
Spreads over all her body !
    Doct. Now it works :
The vital spirits that by a sleepy charm
Were bound up fast, and threw an icy rust
On her exterior parts, now 'gin to break ;
Trouble her not, my lord.
    Duke. Some stools ! [*Servants set stools.*] You called
For music, did you not? Oh ho, it speaks,   [*Music.*
It speaks ! Watch, sirs, her waking, note those sands.
Doctor, sit down : A dukedom that should weigh
Mine own down twice, being put into one scale,
And that fond [1] desperate boy, Hippolito,
Making the weight up, should not at my hands
Buy her i'th'other, were her state more light
Than her's, who makes a dowry up with alms.
Doctor, I'll starve her on the Apennine

Foolish,

Ere he shall marry her.   I must confess,
Hippolito is nobly born ; a man—
Did not mine enemies' blood boil in his veins—
Whom I would court to be my son-in-law;
But princes, whose high spleens for empery swell,
Are not with easy art made parallel.

 Servants. She wakes, my lord.

 Duke. Look, Doctor Benedict—
I charge you on your lives, maintain for truth,
What e'er the doctor or myself aver,
For you shall bear her hence to Bergamo.

 Inf. O God, what fearful dreams ! [*Wakening.*

 Doct. Lady.

 Inf. Ha !

 Duke. Girl.
Why, Infelice, how is't now, ha, speak ?

 Inf. I'm well—what makes this doctor here ?—I'm
  well.

 Duke. Thou wert not so even now, sickness' pale
  hand
Laid hold on thee even in the midst of feasting ;
And when a cup crowned with thy lover's health
Had touched thy lips, a sensible cold dew
Stood on thy cheeks, as if that death had wept
To see such beauty alter.

 Inf. I remember
I sate at banquet, but felt no such change.

 Duke. Thou hast forgot, then, how a messenger
Came wildly in, with this unsavory news,
That he was dead ?

 Inf. What messenger ? who's dead ?

 Duke. Hippolito.   Alack ! wring not thy hands.

 Inf. I saw no messenger, heard no such news.

 Doct. Trust me you did, sweet lady.

 Duke. La, you now !

 1st Ser. Yes, indeed, madam.

 Duke. La, you now.—'Tis well, good knaves !

Inf. You ha' slain him, and now you'll murder me.

Duke. Good Infelice, vex not thus thyself,
Of this the bad report before did strike
So coldly to thy heart, that the swift currents
Of life were all frozen up——

Inf. It is untrue,
Tis most untrue, O most unnatural father !

Duke. And we had much to do by art's best cunning,
To fetch life back again.

Doct. Most certain, lady.

Duke. Why, la, you now, you'll not believe me.
         Friends,
Swear we not all ? had we not much to do ?

Servants. Yes, indeed, my lord, much.

Duke. Death drew such fearful pictures in thy face,
That were Hippolite alive again,
I'd kneel and woo the noble gentleman
To be thy husband : now I sore repent
My sharpness to him, and his family ;
Nay, do not weep for him ; we all must die——
Doctor, this place where she so oft hath seen
His lively presence, hurts her, does it not ?

Doct. Doubtless, my lord, it does.

Duke. It does, it does :
Therefore, sweet girl, thou shalt to Bergamo.

Inf. Even where you will ; in any place there's woe.

Duke. A coach is ready, Bergamo doth stand
In a most wholesome air, sweet walks ; there's deer,
Ay, thou shalt hunt and send us venison,
Which like some goddess in the Cyprian groves,
Thine own fair hand shall strike ;—Sirs, you shall teach
         her
To stand, and how to shoot ; ay, she shall hunt :
Cast off this sorrow.   In, girl, and prepare
This night to ride away to Bergamo.

Inf. O most unhappy maid !   [*Exit.*

Duke. Follow her close.

and their teeth deluded, and, if anger could have seized a man, there was matter enough i'faith to vex any citizen in the world, if he were not too much made a fool by his wife.

Flu. Ay, I'll swear for't : 'sfoot, had it been my case, I should ha' played mad tricks with my wife and family : first, I would ha' spitted the men, stewed the maids, and baked the mistress, and so served them in.

Pio. Why 'twould ha' tempted any blood but his,
And thou to vex him? thou to anger him
With some poor shallow jest?

Cas. 'Sblood, Signor Pioratto, you that disparage my conceit, I'll wage a hundred ducats upon the head on't, that it moves him, frets him, and galls him.

Pio. Done, 'tis a lay,[1] join golls[2] on't : witness Signor Fluello.

Cas. Witness : 'tis done :
Come, follow me : the house is not far off,
I'll thrust him from his humour, vex his breast,
And win a hundred ducats by one jest.   [*Exeunt.*

SCENE V.—Candido's *Shop*.

GEORGE *and two* Prentices *discovered : enter* VIOLA.

Vio. Come, you put up your wares in good order here, do you not, think you? one piece cast this way, another that way ! you had need have a patient master indeed.

Geo. Ay, I'll be sworn, for we have a curst mistress.
        [*Aside.*

Vio. You mumble, do you? mumble? I would your master or I could be a note more angry ! for two patient

---

¹ Bet.   ² Hands.

folks in a house spoil all the servants that ever shall come under them.

1st Pren. You patient! ay, so is the devil when he is horn-mad. [*Aside.*

Enter CASTRUCHIO, FLUELLO, *and* PIORATTO.

Geo. Gentlemen, what do you lack? [1]

1st. Pren. What is't you buy?

2nd Pren. See fine hollands, fine cambrics, fine lawns.

Geo. What is't you lack?

2nd Pren. What is't you buy?

Cas. Where's Signor Candido, thy master?

Geo. Faith, signor, he's a little negotiated, he'll appear presently.

Cas. Fellow, let's see a lawn, a choice one, sirrah.

Geo. The best in all Milan, gentlemen, and this is the piece. I can fit you gentlemen with fine calicoes too for doublets, the only sweet fashion now, most delicate and courtly, a meek gentle calico, cut upon two double affable taffetas,—ah, most neat, feat, and unmatchable!

Flu. A notable voluble-tongued villain.

Pio. I warrant this fellow was never begot without much prating.

Cas. What, and is this she, sayest thou?

Geo. Ay, and the purest she that ever you fingered since you were a gentleman : look how even she is, look how clean she is, ha! as even as the brow of Cynthia, and as clean as your sons and heirs when they ha' spent all.

Cas. Pooh, thou talkest—pox on't, 'tis rough.

Geo. How? is she rough? but if you bid pox on't, sir, 'twill take away the roughness presently.

Flu. Ha, signor; has he fitted your French curse?

Geo. Look you, gentlemen, here's another, compare them I pray, *compara Virgilium cum Homero*, compare virgins with harlots.

---

[1] The shopkeeper's common cry at this period.

Cand. Look you, gentlemen, there's your ware, I thank you, I have your money here ; pray know my shop, pray let me have your custom.

Vio. Custom quoth'a.

Cand. Let me take more of your money.

Vio. You had need so.

Pio. Hark in thine ear, thou'st lost an hundred ducats.

Cas. Well, well, I know't : is't possible that *homo*
Should be nor man, nor woman : not once moved ;
No not at such an injury, not at all !
Sure he's a pigeon, for he has no gall.

Flu. Come, come, you're angry though you smother it :
You're vexed i'faith ; confess.

Cand. Why, gentlemen,
Should you conceit me to be vexed or moved ?
He has my ware, I have his money for't,
And that's no argument I'm angry : no :
The best logician cannot prove me so.

Flu. Oh, but the hateful name of a penn'orth of lawn,
And then cut out i'th' middle of the piece :
Pah, I guess it by myself, 'twould move a lamb
Were he a linen-draper, 'twould, i'faith.

Cand. Well, give me leave to answer you for that :
We are set here to please all customers,
Their humours and their fancies ;—offend none :
We get by many, if we lose by one.
May be his mind stood to no more than that,
A penn'orth serves him, and 'mongst trades 'tis found,
Deny a penn'orth, it may cross a pound.
Oh, he that means to thrive, with patient eye
Must please the devil if he come to buy !

Flu. O wondrous man, patient 'bove wrong or woe,
How blessed were men, if women could be so !

Cand. And to express how well my breast is pleased,
And satisfied in all :—George fill a beaker.

[*Exit* GEORGE.

I'll drink unto that gentleman, who lately
Bestowed his money with me.
 Vio. God's my life,
We shall have all our gains drunk out in beakers,
To make amends for pennyworths of lawn !

Re-enter GEORGE *with beaker.*

 Cand. Here wife, begin you to the gentleman.
 Vio. I begin to him !   [*Spills the wine.*
 Cand. George, fill't up again :
'Twas my fault, my hand shook. [*Exit* GEORGE.
 Pio. How strangely this doth show !
A patient man linked with a waspish shrew.
 Flu. A silver and gilt beaker : I've a trick
To work upon that beaker, sure 'twill fret him ;
It cannot choose but vex him. [*Aside.*] Signor Castruchio,
In pity to thee I have a conceit,
Will save thy hundred ducats yet ; 'twill do't,
And work him to impatience.
 Cas. Sweet Fluello, I should be bountiful to that
conceit.
 Flu. Well, 'tis enough.

Re-enter GEORGE *with beaker.*

 Cand. Here gentlemen to you,
I wish your custom, you are exceeding welcome.
          [*Drinks.*
 Cas. I pledge you, Signor Candido—[*Drinks.*]—here
you that must receive a hundred ducats.
 Pio. I'll pledge them deep, i'faith, Castruchio.—
Signor Fluello.   [*Drinks.*
 Flu. Come : play't off to me ;
I am your last man.
 Cand. George supply the cup.
   [*Exit* GEORGE *who returns with beaker filled.*

Flu. So, so, good honest George,—
Here Signor Candido, all this to you.

Cand. O, you must pardon me, I use it not.

Flu. Will you not pledge me then?

Cand. Yes, but not that:
Great love is shown in little.

Flu. Blurt[1] on your sentences!
'Sfoot, you shall pledge me all.

Cand. Indeed I shall not.

Flu. Not pledge me? 'Sblood, I'll carry away the beaker then.

Cand. The beaker? Oh! that at your pleasure, sir.

Flu. Now by this drink I will.   [*Drinks.*

Cas. Pledge him, he'll do't else.

Flu. So: I ha' done you right on my thumb-nail,
What, will you pledge me now?

Cand. You know me, sir, I am not of that sin.

Flu. Why then farewell:
I'll bear away the beaker by this light.

Cand. That's as you please; 'tis very good.

Flu. Nay, it doth please me, and as you say, 'tis a very good one. Farewell Signor Candido.

Pio. Farewell Candido.

Cand. You're welcome gentlemen.

Cas. Art not moved yet?
I think his patience is above our wit.

> [*Exeunt* CASTRUCHIO, FLUELLO *carrying
> off the beaker, and* PIORATTO.

Geo. I told you before, mistress, they were all cheaters.

Vio. Why fool! why husband! why madman! I hope you will not let 'em sneak away so with a silver and gilt beaker, the best in the house too.—Go, fellows, make hue and cry after them.

Cand. Pray let your tongue lie still, all will be well.—
Come hither, George, hie to the constable,

---

[1] An exclamation of contempt, equivalent to "a fig for."—*Dyce.*

And in calm order wish him to attach them ;
Make no great stir, because they're gentlemen,
And a thing partly done in merriment.
'Tis but a size above a jest thou knowest,
Therefore pursue it mildly. Go begone,
The constable's hard by, bring him along,—make haste
       again.   [*Exit* GEORGE.

Vio. O you're a goodly patient woodcock,[1] are you
not now? See what your patience comes to : every one
saddles you, and rides you ; you'll be shortly the common
stone-horse of Milan : a woman's well holped up with
such a meacock[2]; I had rather have a husband that
would swaddle[3] me thrice a day, than such a one, that
will be gulled twice in half-an-hour : Oh, I could burn
all the wares in my shop for anger.

Cand. Pray wear a peaceful temper ; be my wife,
That is, be patient ; for a wife and husband
Share but one soul between them : this being known,
Why should not one soul then agree in one ?

Vio. Hang your agreements ! but if my beaker be
gone.—   [*Exit.*

Re-enter CASTRUCHIO, FLUELLO, PIORATTO, *and* GEORGE.

Cand. Oh, here they come.

Geo. The constable, sir, let 'em come along with me,
because there should be no wondering : he stays at door.

Cas. Constable, Goodman Abra'm.[4]

Flu. Now Signor Candido, 'sblood why do you attach us?

Cas. 'Sheart ! attach us !

Cand. Nay swear not, gallants,
Your oaths may move your souls, but not move me ;
You have a silver beaker of my wife's.

Flu. You say not true : 'tis gilt.

---

[1] Proverbial term for a simpleton.   [2] Milksop.   [3] Beat.
[4] Thieves' slang for a man who shams madness to gain his ends.
Compare Dekker's *Bellman of London*, Grosart, sc. III., p. 101.

Cand. Then you say true ;
And being gilt, the guilt lies more on you.

Cas. I hope y'are not angry, sir.

Cand. Then you hope right ; for I'm not angry.

Flu. No, but a little moved.

Cand. I moved ! 'twas you were moved, you were
brought hither.

Cas. But you, out of your anger and impatience,
Caused us to be attached.

Cand. Nay, you misplace it :
Out of my quiet sufferance I did that,
And not of any wrath.   Had I shown anger,
I should have then pursued you with the law,
And hunted you to shame, as many worldlings
Do build their anger upon feebler grounds ;
The more's the pity ; many lose their lives
For scarce so much coin as will hide their palm :
Which is most cruel ; those have vexèd spirits
That pursue lives ; in this opinion rest,
The loss of millions could not move my breast.

Flu. Thou art a blest man, and with peace dost deal,
Such a meek spirit can bless a commonweal.

Cand. Gentlemen, now 'tis upon eating-time,
Pray part not hence, but dine with me to-day.

Cas. I never heard a carter yet say nay
To such a motion.   I'll not be the first.

Pio. Nor I.

Flu. Nor I.

Cand. The constable shall bear you company.
George, call him in : let the world say what it can,
Nothing can drive me from a patient man.   [*Exeunt.*

ACT THE SECOND.

SCENE I.—*A Room in* BELLAFRONT'S *House.*

Enter ROGER *with a stool, cushion, looking-glass and chafing-dish; these being set down, he pulls out of his pocket a phial with white colour in it, and two boxes, one with white, another with red paint; he places all things in order, and a candle by them, singing the ends of old ballads as he does it. At last* BELLAFRONT, *as he rubs his cheek with the colours, whistles within.*

OG. Anon, forsooth.

    Bell. [*Within.*] What are you playing the rogue about?

    Rog. About you, forsooth; I'm drawing up a hole in your white silk stocking.

    Bell. Is my glass there? and my boxes of complexion?

    Rog. Yes, forsooth: your boxes of complexion are here, I think: yes, 'tis here: here's your two complexions, and if I had all the four complexions, I should ne'er set a good face upon't. Some men I see, are born, under hard-favoured planets as well as women. Zounds, I look worse now than I did before! and it makes her face glister most damnably. There's knavery in daubing, I hold my life; or else this is only female pomatum.

Enter BELLAFRONT *not full ready ;*[1] *she sits down ; curls her hair with her bodkin ; and colours her lips.*

Bell. Where's my ruff and poker,[2] you blockhead ?

Rog. Your ruff, your poker, are engendering together upon the cupboard of the court, or the court cupboard.[3]

Bell. Fetch 'em : is the pox in your hams, you can go no faster ?   [*Strikes him.*

Rog. Would the pox were in your fingers, unless you could leave flinging ! catch—   [*Exit.*

Bell. I'll catch you, you dog, by and by : do you grumble ?   [*Sings.*

    Cupid is a God, as naked as my nail,
    I'll whip him with a rod, if he my true love fail.

    Re-enter ROGER *with ruff and poker.*

Rog. There's your ruff, shall I poke it ?

Bell. Yes, honest Roger—no, stay ; prithee, good boy, hold here. [*Sings.*]   [ROGER *holds the glass and candle.*] Down, down, down, down, I fall down and arise,—down—I never shall arise.

Rog. Troth mistress, then leave the trade if you shall

Bell. What trade, Goodman Abra'm ?[4]   [never rise.

Rog. Why that of down and arise or the falling trade.

Bell. I'll fall with you by and by.

Rog. If you do I know who shall smart for't : Troth, mistress, what do I look like now ?

Bell. Like as you are ; a panderly sixpenny rascal.

Rog. I may thank you for that : in faith I look like an old proverb, " Hold the candle before the devil."

Bell. Ud's life, I'll stick my knife in your guts an you prate to me so !—What ?   [*Sings.*
Well met, pug, the pearl of beauty : umh, umh.

How now, Sir Knave ? you forget your duty, umh, umh,
Marry muff,[5] sir, are you grown so dainty ; fa, la, la, leera, la.
Is it you, sir ? the worst of twenty, fa, la, la, leera, la.

---

[1] *i.e.* Not fully dressed.   [2] A stick used for plaiting ruffs.
[3] Sideboard.   [4] See note, *ante,* p. 115.
         [5] A common ejaculation of contempt.

Pox on you, how dost thou hold my glass?

Rog. Why, as I hold your door : with my fingers.

Bell. Nay, pray thee, sweet honey Roger, hold up handsomely.   [*Sings.*

Pretty wantons warble, &c.

We shall ha' guests to day, I lay my little maidenhead ; my nose itches so.

Rog. I said so too last night, when our fleas twinged me.

Bell. So, poke my ruff now, my gown, my gown! have I my fall? where's my fall, Roger?

Rog. Your fall, forsooth, is behind.   [*Knocking within.*

Bell. God's my pittikins![1] some fool or other knocks.

Rog. Shall I open to the fool, mistress?

Bell. And all these baubles lying thus? Away with it quickly.—Ay, ay, knock, and be damned, whosoever you be!—So : give the fresh salmon line now : let him come ashore. [*Exit* ROGER.] He shall serve for my breakfast, though he go against my stomach.

Enter FLUELLO, CASTRUCHIO, *and* PIORATTO, *with* ROGER.

Flu. Morrow, coz.

Cas. How does my sweet acquaintance?

Pio. Save thee, little marmoset : how dost thou, good, pretty rogue?

Bell. Well, God-a-mercy, good, pretty rascal.

Flu. Roger, some light, I prithee.

Rog. You shall, signor, for we that live here in this vale of misery are as dark as hell.   [*Exit for a candle.*

Cas. Good tobacco, Fluello?

Flu. Smell.

Pio. It may be tickling gear : for it plays with my nose already.   [*Re-enter* ROGER *with candle.*

Rog. Here's another light angel,[2] signor.   [neighing?

Bell. What? you pied curtal,[3] what's that you are

---

[1] A corruption of "God's my pity."—*Dyce.*

[2] A gold coin worth about ten shillings. The play upon the word was one of the commonest puns of the time.

[3] A docked horse.

Rog. I say God send us the light of Heaven, or some more angels.

Bell. Go fetch some wine, and drink half of it.

Rog. I must fetch some wine, gentlemen, and drink half of it.

Flu. Here Roger.

Cas. No, let me send, prithee.

Flu. Hold, you cankerworm.

Rog. You shall send both, if you please, signors.

Pio. Stay, what's best to drink a' mornings?

Rog. Hippocras,[1] sir, for my mistress, if I fetch it, is most dear to her.

Flu. Hippocras? there then, here's a teston for you, you snake.   [*They give money.*

Rog. Right sir, here's three shillings and sixpence for a pottle[2] and a manchet.[3]   [*Exit.*

Cas. Here's most Herculanean tobacco; ha' some, acquaintance?

Bell. Faugh, not I, makes your breath stink like the piss of a fox. Acquaintance, where supped you last night?

Cas. At a place, sweet acquaintance, where your health danced the canaries,[4] i'faith : you should ha' been there.

Bell. I there among your punks![5] marry, faugh, hang'em; I scorn't : will you never leave sucking of eggs in other folk's hens' nests?

Cas. Why, in good troth, if you'll trust me, acquaintance, there was not one hen at the board ; ask Fluello.

Flu. No, faith, coz, none but cocks ; Signor Malavella drunk to thee.

Bell. O, a pure beagle; that horse-leech there?

Flu. And the knight, Sir Oliver Lollio, swore he would bestow a taffeta petticoat on thee, but to break his fast with thee.

Bell. With me? I'll choke him then, hang him, mole-catcher! it's the dreamingest snotty-nose.

---

[1] Spiced and sweetened wine.   [2] Half a gallon.
[3] A roll of fine bread.   [4] A sprightly dance.   [5] Prostitutes.

Pio. Well, many took that Lollio for a fool, but he's a subtle fool.

Bell. Ay, and he has fellows : of all filthy, dry-fisted knights, I cannot abide that he should touch me.

Cas. Why, wench ? is he scabbed ?

Bell. Hang him, he'll not live to be so honest, nor to the credit to have scabs about him ; his betters have 'em : but I hate to wear out any of his coarse knight-hood, because he's made like an alderman's night-gown, faced all with cony [1] before, and within nothing but fox : this sweet Oliver will eat mutton till he be ready to burst, but the lean-jawed slave will not pay for the scraping of his trencher.

Pio. Plague him ; set him beneath the salt, and let him not touch a bit, till every one has had his full cut.

Flu. Lord Ello, the gentleman-usher, came into us too ; marry 'twas in our cheese, for he had been to borrow money for his lord, of a citizen.

Cas. What an ass is that lord, to borrow money of a citizen !

Bell. Nay, God's my pity, what an ass is that citizen to lend money to a lord !

Enter MATHEO *and* HIPPOLITO ; HIPPOLITO *saluting the company, as a stranger, walks off.* [2] ROGER *comes in sadly behind them, with a pottle pot, and stands aloof off.*

Mat. Save you, gallants. Signor Fluello, exceedingly well met, as I may say.

Flu. Signor Matheo, exceedingly well met too, as I may say.

Mat. And how fares my little pretty mistress ?

Bell. Ee'n as my little pretty servant ; sees three court dishes before her, and not one good bit in them :—How now ? why the devil standest thou so ? Art in a trance ?

Rog. Yes, forsooth.

Bell. Why dost not fill out their wine ?

---

[1] Rabbit-skin.   [2] *i.e.* Retires to the background.

Hip. Perhaps I shall.

Mat. Perhaps? faugh! I know you can swear to me you will.

Hip. Since you will press me, on my word, I will.

[*Exit.*

Bell. What sullen picture is this, servant?

Mat. It's Count Hippolito, the brave count.

Pio. As gallant a spirit as any in Milan, you sweet Jew.

Flu. Oh! he's a most essential gentleman, coz.

Cas. Did you never hear of Count Hippolito, acquaintance?

Bell. Marry muff,[1] a' your counts, and be no more life in 'em.

Mat. He's so malcontent! sirrah[2] Bellafront—An you be honest gallants, let's sup together, and have the count with us :—thou shalt sit at the upper end, punk.[3]

Bell. Punk? you soused gurnet!

Mat. King's truce: come, I'll bestow the supper to have him but laugh.

Cas. He betrays his youth too grossly to that tyrant melancholy.

Mat. All this is for a woman.

Bell. A woman? some whore! what sweet jewel is't?

Pio. Would she heard you!

Flu. Troth, so would I.

Cas. And I, by Heaven.

Bell. Nay, good servant, what woman?

Mat. Pah!

Bell. Prithee, tell me; a buss, and tell me: I warrant he's an honest fellow, if he take on thus for a wench: good rogue, who?

Mat. By th' Lord I will not, must not, faith' mistress. Is't a match, sirs? this night, at th' Antelope: ay, for there's best wine, and good boys.

---

[1] See note, *ante*, p. 118.
[2] The term sirrah was applied often to women as well as to men.
[3] Prostitute.

Flu., Cas., Pio. It's done; at th' Antelope.

Bell. I cannot be there to night.

Mat. Cannot? by th' Lord you shall.

Bell. By the Lady I will not : shall !

Flu. Why, then, put it off till Friday; wu't come then, coz ?

Bell. Well.

Re-enter ROGER.

Mat. You're the waspishest ape. Roger, put your mistress in mind to sup with us on Friday next. You're best come like a madwoman, without a band, in your waistcoat, and the linings of your kirtle outward, like every common hackney that steals out at the back gate of her sweet knight's lodging.

Bell. Go, go, hang yourself!

Cas. It's dinner-time, Matheo; shall's hence?

All. Yes, yes.—Farewell, wench.

Bell. Farewell, boys.—[*Exeunt all except* BELLAFRONT *and* ROGER.]—Roger, what wine sent they for?

Rog. Bastard wine,[1] for if it had been truly begotten, it would ha' been ashamed to come in. Here's six shillings to pay for nursing the bastard.

Bell. A company of rooks! O good sweet Roger, run to the poulter's, and buy me some fine larks!

Rog. No woodcocks?[2]

Bell. Yes, faith, a couple, if they be not dear.

Rog. I'll buy but one, there's one already here.

[*Exit.*

Enter HIPPOLITO.

Hip. Is the gentleman, my friend, departed, mistress?

Bell. His back is but new turned, sir.

Hip. Fare you well.

Bell. I can direct you to him.

Hip. Can you, pray?

Bell. If you please, stay, he'll not be absent long.

Hip. I care not much.

---

[1] A sweet Spanish wine.   [2] Simpletons.

Abuse his coin, conveying it to your lover,
And in the end you show him a French trick,
And so you leave him, that a coach may run
Between his legs for breadth.

Bell. Oh, by my soul,
Not I! therein I'll prove an honest whore,
In being true to one, and to no more.

Hip. If any be disposed to trust your oath,
Let him: I'll not be he; I know you feign
All that you speak; ay, for a mingled harlot
Is true in nothing but in being false.
What! shall I teach you how to loath yourself?
And mildly too, not without sense or reason.

Bell. I am content; I would feign loath myself
If you not love me.

Hip. Then if your gracious blood
Be not all wasted, I shall assay to do't.
Lend me your silence, and attention.
You have no soul, that makes you weigh so light;
Heaven's treasure bought it:
And half-a-crown hath sold it:—for your body
Is like the common-shore, that still receives
All the town's filth.   The sin of many men
Is within you; and thus much I suppose,
That if all your committers stood in rank,
They'd make a lane, in which your shame might
          dwell,
And with their spaces reach from hence to hell.
Nay, shall I urge it more? there has been known
As many by one harlot, maimed and dismembered,
As would ha' stuffed an hospital: this I might
Apply to you, and perhaps do you right:
O you're as base as any beast that bears,—
Your body is e'en hired, and so are theirs.
For gold and sparkling jewels, if he can,
You'll let a Jew get you with Christian:
Be he a Moor, a Tartar, though his face

Look uglier than a dead man's skull.
Could the devil put on a human shape,
If his purse shake out crowns, up then he gets;
Whores will be rid to hell with golden bits.
So that you're crueller than Turks, for they
Sell Christians only, you sell yourselves away.
Why, those that love you, hate you : and will term you
Liquorish damnation ; with themselves half-sunk
After the sin is laid out, and e'en curse
Their fruitless riot ; for what one begets
Another poisons ; lust and murder hit :
A tree being often shook, what fruit can knit?

    Bell. O me unhappy !

    Hip. I can vex you more :
A harlot is like Dunkirk, true to none,
Swallows both English, Spanish, fulsome Dutch,
Back-doored Italian, last of all, the French,
And he sticks to you, faith, gives you your diet,
Brings you acquainted, first with Monsieur Doctor
And then you know what follows.

    Bell. Misery.
Rank, stinking, and most loathsome misery.

    Hip. Methinks a toad is happier than a whore ;
That with one poison swells, with thousands more
The other stocks her veins : harlot? fie, fie !
You are the miserablest creatures breathing,
The very slaves of nature ; mark me else :
You put on rich attires, others' eyes wear them,
You eat, but to supply your blood with sin :
And this strange curse e'en haunts you to your graves.
From fools you get, and spend it upon slaves :
Like bears and apes, you're baited and show tricks
For money ; but your bawd the sweetness licks.
Indeed, you are their journey-women, and do
All base and damned works they list set you to :
So that you ne'er are rich ; for do but show me,
In present memory, or in ages past,

    Dekker.   K

The fairest and most famous courtesan,
Whose flesh was dear'st : that raised the price of sin,
And held it up ; to whose intemperate bosom,
Princes, earls, lords, the worst has been a knight,
The mean'st a gentleman, have offered up
Whole hecatombs of sighs, and rained in showers
Handfuls of gold ; yet, for all this, at last
Diseases sucked her marrow, then grew so poor,
That she has begged e'en at a beggar's door.
And (wherein Heaven has a finger) when this idol,
From coast to coast, has leapt on foreign shores,
And had more worship than th' outlandish whores:
When several nations have gone over her,
When for each several city she has seen,
Her maidenhead has been new, and been sold dear :
Did live well there, and might have died unknown,
And undefamed ; back comes she to her own,
And there both miserably lives and dies,
Scorned even of those that once adored her eyes,
As if her fatal circled life thus ran,
Her pride should end there, where it first began.
What do you weep to hear your story read?
Nay, if you spoil your cheeks, I'll read no more.

    Bell. O yes, I pray, proceed :
Indeed, 'twill do me good to weep, indeed.

    Hip. To give those tears a relish, this I add,
You're like the Jews, scattered, in no place certain,
Your days are tedious, your hours burdensome :
And were't not for full suppers, midnight revels,
Dancing, wine, riotous meetings, which do drown,
And bury quite in you all virtuous thoughts,
And on your eyelids hang so heavily,
They have no power to look so high as Heaven,—
You'd sit and muse on nothing but despair,
Curse that devil Lust, that so burns up your blood,
And in ten thousand shivers break your glass
For his temptation.   Say you taste delight,

To have a golden gull from rise to set,
To mete[1] you in his hot luxurious arms,
Yet your nights pay for all : I know you dream
Of warrants, whips, and beadles, and then start
At a door's windy creak : think every weasel
To be a constable, and every rat
A long-tailed officer : Are you now not slaves?
Oh, you've damnation without pleasure for it !
Such is the state of harlots.   To conclude :
When you are old and can well paint no more,
You turn bawd, and are then worse than before :
Make use of this : farewell.

    Bell. Oh, I pray, stay.

    Hip. I see Matheo comes not : time hath barred me ;
Would all the harlots in the town had heard me.   [*Exit.*

    Bell. Stay yet a little longer !   No ? quite gone !
Curst be that minute—for it was no more,
So soon a maid is changed into a whore—
Wherein I first fell ! be it for ever black !
Yet why should sweet Hippolito shun mine eyes?
For whose true love I would become pure, honest,
Hate the world's mixtures, and the smiles of gold.
Am I not fair? why should he fly me then ?
Fair creatures are desired, not scorned of men.
How many gallants have drunk healths to me,
Out of their daggered arms, and thought them blest,
Enjoying but mine eyes at prodigal feasts !
And does Hippolito detest my love?
Oh, sure their heedless lusts but flattered me,
I am not pleasing, beautiful, nor young.
Hippolito hath spied some ugly blemish,
Eclipsing all my beauties : I am foul :
Harlot !   Ay, that's the spot that taints my soul.
What ! has he left his weapon here behind him
And gone forgetful?   O fit instrument
To let forth all the poison of my flesh !

             [1] Measure.

                              K 2

Thy master hates me, 'cause my blood hath ranged:
But when 'tis forth, then he'll believe I'm changed.

As she is about to stab herself re-enter HIPPOLITO.

Hip. Mad woman, what art doing?
Bell. Either love me,
Or split my heart upon thy rapier's point:
Yet do not neither; for thou then destroy'st
That which I love thee for—thy virtues.   Here, here;
                    [*Gives sword to* HIPPOLITO.
Th'art crueller, and kill'st me with disdain:
To die so, sheds no blood, yet 'tis worse pain.
                         [*Exit* HIPPOLITO.
Not speak to me!   Not bid farewell? a scorn?
Hated! this must not be; some means I'll try.
Would all whores were as honest now as I!   [*Exit.*

ACT THE THIRD.

SCENE I.—CANDIDO'S *Shop.*

CANDIDO, VIOLA, GEORGE, *and two* Prentices *discovered :*
FUSTIGO *enters, walking by.*

Geo. See, gentlemen, what you lack ; a fine holland, a fine cambric : see what you buy.

1st Pren. Holland for shirts, cambric for bands ; what is't you lack ?

Fus. 'Sfoot, I lack 'em all ; nay, more, I lack money to buy 'em. Let me see, let me look again : mass, this is the shop. [*Aside.*] What coz ! sweet coz ! how dost, i'faith, since last night after candlelight ? we had good sport, i'faith, had we not ? and when shall's laugh again ?

Vio. When you will, cousin.

Fus. Spoke like a kind Lacedemonian : I see yonder's thy husband.

Vio. Ay, there's the sweet youth, God bless him !

Fus. And how is't, cousin ? and how, how is't, thou squall ?[1]

Vio. Well, cousin, how fare you ?

Fus. How fare I ? for sixpence a-meal, wench, as well as heart can wish, with calves' chaldrons,[2] and chitterlings ;[3] besides, I have a punk after supper, as good as a roasted apple.

---

[1] Wench.   [2] Calves' Fry.   [3] Tripe.

Cand. Are you my wife's cousin?

Fus. I am, sir; what hast thou to do with that?

Cand. O, nothing, but you're welcome.

Fus. The devil's dung in thy teeth! I'll be welcome whether thou wilt or no, I.—What ring's this, coz? very pretty and fantastical, i'faith! let's see it.

Vio. Pooh! nay, you wrench my finger.

Fus. I ha' sworn I'll ha't, and I hope you will not let my oaths be cracked in the ring, will you? [*Seizes the ring.*] I hope, sir, you are not malicholly [1] at this, for all your great looks: are you angry?

Cand. Angry? not I, sir, nay if she can part
So easily with her ring, 'tis with my heart.

Geo. Suffer this, sir, and suffer all, a whoreson gull, to—

Cand. Peace George, when she has reaped what I have
     sown,
She'll say, one grain tastes better of her own,
Than whole sheaves gathered from another's land:
Wit's never good, till bought at a dear hand.

Geo. But in the mean-time she makes an ass of some body.

2nd Pren. See, see, see, sir, as you turn your back they do nothing but kiss.

Cand. No matter, let 'em: when I touch her lip,
I shall not feel his kisses, no, nor miss
Any of her lip: no harm in kissing is.
Look to your business, pray, make up your wares.

Fus. Troth, coz, and well remembered, I would thou wouldst give me five yards of lawn, to make my punk some falling bands a' the fashion; three falling one upon another, for that's the new edition now: she's out of linen horribly, too; troth, sh' as never a good smock to her back neither, but one that has a great many patches in't, and that I'm fain to wear myself for want of shift, too: prithee, put me into wholesome napery, and bestow some clean commodities upon us.

---

[1] A corruption of the word "melancholy."

Vio. Reach me those cambrics, and the lawns hither.

Cand. What to do, wife? to lavish out my goods upon a fool?

Fus. Fool? Snails, eat the fool, or I'll so batter your crown, that it shall scarce go for five shillings.

2nd Pren. Do you hear, sir? you're best be quiet, and say a fool tells you so.

Fus. Nails, I think so, for thou tellest me.

Cand. Are you angry, sir, because I named the fool?
Trust me, you are not wise in my own house,
And to my face to play the antic thus :
If you needs play the madman, choose a stage
Of lesser compass, where few eyes may note
Your action's error : but if still you miss,
As here you do, for one clap, ten will hiss.

Fus. Zounds, cousin, he talks to me, as if I were a scurvy tragedian.

2nd Pren. Sirrah George, I ha' thought upon a device, how to break his pate, beat him soundly, and ship him away.

Geo. Do't.

2nd Pren. I'll go in, pass through the house, give some of our fellow-prentices the watch-word when they shall enter ; then come and fetch my master in by a wile, and place one in the hall to hold him in conference, whilst we cudgel the gull out of his coxcomb.

[*Exit* 2nd Prentice.

Geo. Do't : away, do't.

Vio. Must I call twice for these cambrics and lawns?

Cand. Nay see, you anger her, George, prithee despatch.

1st Pren. Two of the choicest pieces are in the warehouse, sir.

Cand. Go fetch them presently.

Fus. Ay, do, make haste, sirrah.   [*Exit* 1st Prentice.

Cand. Why were you such a stranger all this while, being my wife's cousin?

Fus. Stranger? no sir, I'm a natural Milaner born.

Cand. I perceive still it is your natural guise to mistake me, but you are welcome, sir; I much wish your acquaintance.

Fus. My acquaintance? I scorn that, i'faith; I hope my acquaintance goes in chains of gold three and fifty times double:—you know who I mean, coz; the posts of his gate are a-painting too.[1]

Re-enter the 2nd Prentice.

2nd Pren. Signor Pandulfo the merchant desires conference with you.

Cand. Signor Pandulfo? I'll be with him straight, Attend your mistress and the gentleman.   [*Exit.*

Vio. When do you show those pieces?

Fus. Ay, when do you show those pieces?

Prentices. [*Within.*] Presently, sir, presently: we are but charging them.

Fus. Come, sirrah: you flat-cap,[2] where be these whites?

Re-enter 1st Prentice *with pieces.*

Geo. Flat-cap? hark in your ear, sir, you're a flat fool, an ass, a gull, and I'll thrum [3] you:—do you see this cambric, sir?

Fus. 'Sfoot coz, a good jest, did you hear him? he told me in my ears, I was. a " flat fool, an ass, a gull, and I'll thrum you:—do you see this cambric sir? "

Vio. What, not my men, I hope?

Fus. No, not your men, but one of your men i'faith.

1st Pren. I pray, sir, come hither, what say you to this? here's an excellent good one.

Fus. Ay, marry, this likes [4] me well; cut me·off some half-score yards.

---

[1] In allusion to the painting of a citizen's gateposts on his promotion to be sheriff, so as to display official notices the better.

[2] A slang term applied to citizens in allusion to their head gear.

[3] Beat.   [4] Pleases.

2nd Pren. Let your whores cut; you're an impudent coxcomb; you get none, and yet I'll thrum you :—a very good cambric, sir.

Fus. Again, again, as God judge me! 'Sfoot, coz, they stand thrumming here with me all day, and yet I get nothing.

1st Pren. A word, I pray, sir, you must not be angry. Prentices have hot bloods, young fellows,—what say you to this piece? Look you, 'tis so delicate, so soft, so even, so fine a thread, that a lady may wear it.

Fus. 'Sfoot, I think so, if a knight marry my punk, a lady shall wear it : cut me off twenty yards : thou'rt an honest lad.

1st Pren. Not without money, gull, and I'll thrum you too.

Prentices. [*Within.*] Gull, we'll thrum you.

Fus. O Lord, sister, did you not hear something cry thrum? zounds, your men here make a plain ass of me.

Vio. What, to my face so impudent?

Geo. Ay, in a cause so honest, we'll not suffer
Our master's goods to vanish moneyless.

Vio. You will not suffer them?

2nd Pren. No, and you may blush,
In going about to vex so mild a breast,
As is our master's.

Vio. Take away those pieces.
Cousin, I give them freely.

Fus. Mass, and I'll take 'em as freely.

Geo., 1st and 2nd Pren., and other prentices, rushing in.
We'll make you lay 'em down again more freely.

[*They all attack* FUSTIGO *with their clubs.*
Vio. Help, help! my brother will be murdered.

Re-enter CANDIDO.

Cand. How now, what coil is here? forbear I say.

[*Exeunt all the* Prentices *except the* 1st *and* 2nd.
Geo. He calls us flat-caps, and abuses us.

Cand. Why, sirs, do such examples flow from me?

Vio. They're of your keeping, sir.   Alas, poor brother.

Fus. I 'faith they ha' peppered me, sister; look, dost not spin? call you these prentices? I'll ne'er play at cards more when clubs is trump : I have a goodly coxcomb, sister, have I not?

Cand. Sister and brother? brother to my wife?

Fus. If you have any skill in heraldry, you may soon know that; break but her pate, and you shall see her blood and mine is all one.

Cand. A surgeon! run, a surgeon! [*Exit* 1st Prentice.]   Why then wore you that forged name of cousin?

Fus. Because it's a common thing to call coz, and ningle[1] now-a-days all the world over.

Cand. Cousin! A name of much deceit, folly, and sin,
For under that common abused word,
Many an honest-tempered citizen
Is made a monster, and his wife trained out
To foul adulterous action, full of fraud.
I may well call that word, a city's bawd.

Fus. Troth, brother, my sister would needs ha' me take upon me to gull your patience a little : but it has made double gules[2] on my coxcomb.

Vio. What, playing the woman? blabbing now, you fool?

Cand. Oh, my wife did but exercise a jest upon your wit.

Fus. 'Sfoot, my wit bleeds for't, methinks.

Cand. Then let this warning more of sense afford;
The name of cousin is a bloody word.

Fus. I'll ne'er call coz again whilst I live, to have such a coil about it; this should be a coronation day; for my head runs claret lustily.   [*Exit.*

Cand. Go, wish[3] the surgeon to have great respect —
    [*Exit* 2nd Prentice.

---

[1] A contraction of "mine ingle," *i.e.* my favourite or friend.
[2] The heraldic term for *red*.   [3] Desire.

Enter an Officer.

How now, my friend? what, do they sit to day?

 Offi. Yes, sir, they expect you at the senate-house.

 Cand. I thank your pains; I'll not be last man there.—

           [*Exit* Officer.

My gown, George, go, my gown. [*Exit* GEORGE.] A
 happy land,

Where grave men meet each cause to understand;

Whose consciences are not cut out in bribes

To gull the poor man's right; but in even scales,

Peize[1] rich and poor, without corruption's vails.[2]

Re-enter GEORGE.

Come, where's the gown?

 Geo. I cannot find the key, sir.

 Cand. Request it of your mistress.

 Vio. Come not to me for any key;

I'll not be troubled to deliver it.

 Cand. Good wife, kind wife, it is a needful trouble, but
for my gown!

 Vio. Moths swallow down your gown!

You set my teeth on edge with talking on't.

 Cand. Nay, prithee, sweet,—I cannot meet without it,

I should have a great fine set on my head.

 Vio. Set on your coxcomb; tush, fine me no fines.

 Cand. Believe me, sweet, none greets the senate-
 house,

Without his robe of reverence,—that's his gown.

 Vio. Well, then, you're like to cross that custom once;

You get no key, nor gown; and so depart.—

This trick will vex him sure, and fret his heart.

           [*Aside and Exit.*

 Cand. Stay, let me see, I must have some device,—

My cloak's too short: fie, fie, no cloak will do't;

It must be something fashioned like a gown,

---

[1] Weigh.   [2] Perquisites.

With my arms out.   Oh George, come hither, George :
I prithee, lend me thine advice.

  Geo. Troth, sir, were't any but you, they would break
open chest.

  Cand. O no ! break open chest ! that's a thief's office ;
Therein you counsel me against my blood :
'Twould show impatience that : any meek means
I would be glad to embrace.   Mass, I have got it.
Go, step up, fetch me down one of the carpets,[1]
The saddest-coloured carpet, honest George,
Cut thou a hole i'th' middle for my neck,
Two for mine arms.   Nay, prithee, look not strange.

  Geo. I hope you do not think, sir, as you mean.

  Cand. Prithee, about it quickly, the hour chides me :
Warily, George, softly, take heed of eyes, [*Exit* GEORGE.
Out of two evils he's accounted wise,
That can pick out the least ; the fine imposed
For an un-gowned senator, is about
Forty crusadoes,[2] the carpet not 'bove four.
Thus have I chosen the lesser evil yet,
Preserved my patience, foiled her desperate wit.

Re-enter GEORGE *with carpet.*

  Geo. Here, sir, here's the carpet.

  Cand. O well done, George, we'll cut it just i'th' midst.
                              [*They cut the carpet.*
'Tis very well ; I thank thee : help it on.

  Geo. It must come over your head, sir, like a wench's
    petticoat.

  Cand. Thou'rt in the right, good George ; it must
    indeed.

Fetch me a night-cap : for I'll gird it close,
As if my health were queasy : 'twill show well
For a rude, careless night-gown, will't not, think'st ?

---

  [1] Table covers.
  [2] Portuguese coins, worth about 2*s.* 10*d.* each, but varying in value.

Geo. Indifferent well, sir, for a night-gown, being girt
and pleated.

Cand. Ay, and a night-cap on my head.

Geo. That's true sir, I'll run and fetch one, and a staff.
                                              [*Exit.*

Cand. For thus they cannot choose but conster [1] it,
One that is out of health, takes no delight,
Wears his apparel without appetite,
And puts on heedless raiment without form.—

Re-enter GEORGE, *with nightcap and staff.*

So, so, kind George, [*Puts on nightcap.*]—be secret now:
and, prithee, do not laugh at me till I'm out of sight.

Geo. I laugh? not I, sir.

Cand. Now to the senate-house:
Methinks, I'd rather wear, without a frown,
A patient carpet, than an angry gown.   [*Exit.*

Geo. Now, looks my master just like one of our carpet
knights, [2] only he's somewhat the honester of the two.

Re-enter VIOLA.

Vio. What, is your master gone?

Geo. Yes, forsooth, his back is but new turned.

Vio. And in his cloak? did he not vex and swear?

Geo. No, but he'll make you swear anon.—   [*Aside.*]
No, indeed, he went away like a lamb.

Vio. Key, sink to hell! still patient, patient still?
I am with child [3] to vex him: prithee, George,
If e'er thou look'st for favour at my hands,
Uphold one jest for me.

Geo. Against my master?

Vio. 'Tis a mere jest in faith: say, wilt thou do't?

Geo. Well, what is't?

Vio. Here, take this key; thou know'st where all
     things lie.

[1] Construe.
[2] *i.e.* Bourgeois knights dubbed for civil, not for martial, honours.
[3] *i.e.* I long.

Mis. F. Marry come up, with a pox, have you nobody to rail against, but your bawd now?

Bell. And you, knave pander, kinsman to a bawd.

Rog. You and I, madonna, are cousins.

Bell. Of the same blood and making, near allied;
Thou, that art slave to sixpence, base metalled villain!

Rog. Sixpence? nay, that's not so: I never took under two shillings four-pence; I hope I know my fee.

Bell. I know not against which most to inveigh:
For both of you are damned so equally.
Thou never spar'st for oaths, swear'st any thing,
As if thy soul were made of shoe-leather:
"God damn me, gentleman, if she be within!"
When in the next room she's found dallying.

Rog. If it be my vocation to swear, every man in his vocation: I hope my betters swear and damn themselves, and why should not I?

Bell. Roger, you cheat kind gentlemen.

Rog. The more gulls they.

Bell. Slave, I cashier thee.

Mis. F. An you do cashier him, he shall be entertained.

Rog. Shall I? then blurt[1] a' your service.

Bell. As hell would have it, entertained by you!
I dare the devil himself to match those two.   [*Exit.*

Mis. F. Marry gup, are you grown so holy, so pure, so honest with a pox?

Rog. Scurvy honest punk! but stay, madonna, how must our agreement be now? for, you know, I am to have all the comings-in at the hall-door, and you at the chamber-door.

Mis. F. True Roger except my vails.

Rog. Vails? what vails?

Mis. F. Why as thus; if a couple come in a coach, and light to lie down a little, then, Roger, that's my fee, and you may walk abroad; for the coachman himself is their pander.

[1] See note *ante,* p. 114.

Rog. Is 'a so? in truth I have almost forgot, for want of exercise.   But how if I fetch this citizen's wife to that gull, and that madonna to that gallant, how then?

Mis. F. Why then, Roger, you are to have sixpence a lane; so many lanes, so many sixpences.

Rog. Is't so? then I see we two shall agree, and live together.

Mis. F. Ay, Roger, so long as there be any taverns and bawdy-houses in Milan.   [*Exeunt.*

SCENE III.—*A Chamber in* BELLAFRONT'S *House.*

BELLAFRONT *discovered sitting with a lute ; pen, ink, and paper on a table before her.*

Bell. [*Sings.*]

> The courtier's flattering jewels,
> Temptations only fuels,
> The lawyer's ill-got moneys,
> That suck up poor bees' honeys:
> The citizen's sons riot,
> The gallant's costly diet :
> Silks and velvets, pearls and ambers,
> Shall not draw me to their chambers.
>   Silks and velvets, &c.   [*She writes.*

Oh, 'tis in vain to write! it will not please;
Ink on this paper would ha' but presented
The foul black spots that stick upon my soul,
And rather made me loathsomer, than wrought
My love's impression in Hippolito's thought:
No, I must turn the chaste leaves of my breast,
And pick out some sweet means to breed my rest.
Hippolito, believe me I will be
As true unto thy heart, as thy heart to thee,
And hate all men, their gifts and company!

Dekker.   L

Enter MATHEO, CASTRUCHIO, FLUELLO, *and* PIORATTO.

Mat. You, goody punk, *subaudi* cockatrice, oh you're
a sweet whore of your promise, are you not, think you?
how well you came to supper to us last night; mew, a
whore, and break her word! nay, you may blush, and
hold down your head at it well enough. 'Sfoot, ask
these gallants if we stayed not till we were as hungry as
sergeants.

Flu. Ay, and their yeomen too.

Cas. Nay, faith, acquaintance, let me tell you, you
forgat yourself too much: we had excellent cheer, rare
vintage, and were drunk after supper.

Pio. And when we were in, our woodcocks,[1] sweet
rogue, a brace of gulls, dwelling here in the city, came
in, and paid all the shot.

Mat. Pox on her! let her alone.

Bell. Oh, I pray do, if you be gentlemen:
I pray, depart the house: beshrew the door
For being so easily entreated! faith,
I lent but little ear unto your talk;
My mind was busied otherwise, in troth,
And so your words did unregarded pass:
Let this suffice,—I am not as I was.

Flu. I am not what I was? no, I'll be sworn thou
art not: for thou wert honest at five, and now thou'rt
a punk at fifteen: thou wert yesterday a simple whore,
and now thou'rt a cunning, cony-catching baggage to
day.

Bell. I'll say I'm worse; I pray, forsake me then:
I do desire you leave me, gentlemen.
And leave yourselves: O be not what you are,
Spendthrifts of soul and body!
Let me persuade you to forsake all harlots,
Worse than the deadliest poisons, they are worse:
For o'er their souls hangs an eternal curse.

---

[1] Simpletons.

In being slaves to slaves, their labours perish ;
They're seldom blest with fruit ; for ere it blossoms,
Many a worm confounds it.
They have no issue but foul ugly ones,
That run along with them, e'en to their graves :
For, 'stead of children, they breed rank diseases,
And all you gallants can bestow on them,
Is that French infant, which ne'er acts, but speaks :
What shallow son and heir, then, foolish gallants,
Would waste all his inheritance, to purchase
A filthy, loathed disease ? and pawn his body
To a dry evil : that usury's worst of all,
When th' interest will eat out the principal.

Mat. 'Sfoot, she gulls 'em the best ! this is always her fashion, when she would be rid of any company that she cares not for, to enjoy mine alone. [*Aside.*

Flu. What's here ? instructions, admonitions, and caveats ? Come out, you scabbard of vengeance.

Mat. Fluello, spurn your hounds when they fist, you shall not spurn my punk, I can tell you : my blood is vexed.

Flu. Pox a' your blood : make it a quarrel.

Mat. You're a slave ! will that serve turn ?

Pio. 'Sblood, hold, hold !

Cas. Matheo, Fluello, for shame, put up !

Mat. Spurn my sweet varlet ?

Bel. O how many thus
Moved with a little folly, have let out
Their souls in brothel-houses ! fell down and died
Just at their harlot's foot, as 'twere in pride.

Flu. Matheo, we shall meet.

Mat. Ay, ay ; any where, saving at church :
Pray take heed we meet not there.

Flu. Adieu, damnation !

Cas. Cockatrice, farewell !

Pio. There's more deceit in women, than in hell.

   [*Exeunt* CASTRUCHIO, FLUELLO *and* PIORATTO.

Mat. Ha, ha, thou dost gull 'em so rarely, so naturally !
If I did not think thou hadst been in earnest : thou art a
sweet rogue for't i'faith.

Bell. Why are not you gone too, Signor Matheo ?
I pray depart my house : you may believe me,
In troth, I have no part of harlot in me.

Mat. How's this ?

Bell. Indeed, I love you not : but hate you worse
Than any man, because you were the first
Gave money for my soul : you brake the ice,
Which after turned a puddle ; I was led
By your temptation to be miserable :
I pray, seek out some other that will fall,
Or rather, I pray seek out none at all.

Mat. Is't possible to be impossible ! an honest whore !
I have heard many honest wenches turn strumpets with a
wet finger,[1] but for a harlot to turn honest is one of
Hercules' labours. It was more easy for him in one
night to make fifty queans, than to make one of them
honest again in fifty years. Come, I hope thou dost but
jest.

Bell. 'Tis time to leave off jesting, I had almost
Jested away salvation : I shall love you,
If you will soon forsake me.

Mat. God be with thee !

Bell. O tempt no more women ! shun their weighty
       curse ;
Women, at best, are bad, make them not worse.
You gladly seek our sex's overthrow :
But not to raise our states. For all your wrongs,
Will you vouchsafe me but due recompense,
To marry with me ?

Mat. How ! marry with a punk, a cockatrice, a harlot ?
maarr, faugh, I'll be burnt through the nose first.

Bell. Why, la, these are your oaths ! you love to undo
us,

[1] Easily, readily.

To put Heaven from us, whilst our best hours waste;
You love to make us lewd, but never chaste.

    Mat. I'll hear no more of this, this ground upon,
Thou'rt damned for altering thy religion.   [*Exit.*

    Bell. Thy lust and sin speak so much : go thou, my
        ruin,
The first fall my soul took ! By my example
I hope few maidens now will put their heads
Under men's girdles ; who least trusts is most wise :
Men's oaths do cast a mist before our eyes.
My best of wit, be ready ! Now I go,
By some device to greet Hippolito.

ACT THE FOURTH.

SCENE I.—*A Chamber in* HIPPOLITO'S *House.*

Enter a Servant.

ER. So, this is Monday morning, and now must I to my huswifery.—[*Sets out a table, on which he places a skull, a picture of* INFELICE, *a book, and a taper.*] —Would I had been created a shoe-maker, for all the gentle-craft are gen-tlemen every Monday by their copy, and scorn then to work one true stitch. My master means sure to turn me into a student, for here's my book, here my desk, here my light, this my close chamber, and here my punk : so that this dull drowzy first day of the week, makes me half a priest, half a chandler, half a painter, half a sexton, ay, and half a bawd ; for all this day my office is to do nothing but keep the door. To prove it, look you, this good face and yonder gentleman, so soon as ever my back is turned, will be naught together.

Enter HIPPOLITO.

Hip. Are all the windows shut ?

Ser. Close, sir, as the fist of a courtier that hath stood in three reigns.

Hip. Thou art a faithful servant, and observ'st

The calendar, both of my solemn vows,
And ceremonious sorrow.   Get thee gone ;
I charge thee on thy life, let not the sound
Of any woman's voice pierce through that door.

Ser. If they do, my lord, I'll pierce some of them ;
What will your lordship have to breakfast ?

Hip. Sighs.

Ser. What to dinner?

Hip. Tears.

Ser. The one of them, my lord, will fill you too full of
wind, the other wet you too much.   What to supper ?

Hip. That which now thou canst not get me, the constancy of a woman.

Ser. Indeed that's harder to come by than ever was
Ostend.[1]

Hip. Prithee, away.

Ser. I'll make away myself presently, which few
servants will do for their lords ; but rather help to make
them away : Now to my door-keeping ; I hope to pick
something out of it.   [*Aside and exit.*

Hip. [*Taking up* INFELICE'S *picture.*] My Infelice's
            face, her brow, her eye,
The dimple on her cheek ! and such sweet skill,
Hath from the cunning workman's pencil flown,
These lips look fresh and lively as her own,
Seeming to move and speak.   'Las ! now I see,
The reason why fond [2] women love to buy
Adulterate complexion !   Here 'tis read :
False colours last after the true be dead.
Of all the roses grafted on her cheeks,
Of all the graces dancing in her eyes,
Of all the music set upon her tongue,
Of all that was past woman's excellence,

---

[1] The siege of Ostend was protracted for three years and ten
weeks.—The place was eventually captured by the Marquis of
Spinola on Sep. 8, 1604.

[2] Foolish.

In her white bosom,—look! a painted board
Circumscribes all : Earth can no bliss afford,
Nothing of her but this.   This cannot speak,
It has no lap for me to rest upon,
No lip worth tasting : here the worms will feed,
As in her coffin : hence, then, idle art !
True love's best pictured in a true-love's heart :
Here art thou drawn, sweet maid, till this be dead ;
So that thou liv'st twice, twice art buried :
Thou figure of my friend, lie there.   What's here ?

                          [Takes up the skull.

Perhaps this shrewd pate was mine enemy's :
'Las ! say it were : I need not fear him now !
For all his braves, his contumelious breath,
His frowns, though dagger-pointed, all his plots,
Though ne'er so mischievous, his Italian pills,
His quarrels, and that common fence, his law,
See, see, they're all eaten out ! here's not left one :
How clean they're picked away to the bare bone !
How mad are mortals, then, to rear great names
On tops of swelling houses ! or to wear out
Their fingers' ends in dirt, to scrape up gold !
Not caring, so that sumpter-horse, the back,
Be hung with gaudy trappings, with what coarse—
Yea, rags most beggarly, they clothe the soul :
Yet, after all, their gayness looks thus foul.
What fools are men to build a garish tomb,
Only to save the carcase whilst it rots,
To maintain't long in stinking, make good carrion,
But leave no good deeds to preserve them sound !
For good deeds keep men sweet, long above ground.
And must all come to this ? fools, wife, all hither ?
Must all heads thus at last be laid together ?
Draw me my picture then, thou grave neat workman,
After this fashion, not like this ; these colours,
In time, kissing but air, will be kissed off :
But here's a fellow ; that which he lays on

Till doomsday alters not complexion :
Death's the best painter then : They that draw shapes,
And live by wicked faces, are but God's apes.
They come but near the life, and there they stay ;
This fellow draws life too : his art is fuller,
The pictures which he makes are without colour.

Re-enter Servant.

Ser. Here's a parson [1] would speak with you, sir.

Hip. Hah !

Ser. A parson, sir, would speak with you.

Hip. Vicar ?

Ser. Vicar ! no sir, has too good a face to be a vicar yet, a youth, a very youth.

Hip. What youth ? of man or woman ? lock the doors.

Ser. If it be a woman, marrow-bones and potato pies keep me from meddling with her, for the thing has got the breeches ! 'tis a male-varlet sure, my lord, for a woman's tailor ne'er measured him.

Hip. Let him give thee his message and be gone.

Ser. He says he's Signor Matheo's man, but I know he lies.

Hip How dost thou know it ?

Ser. 'Cause he has ne'er a beard : 'tis his boy, I think, sir, whosoe'er paid for his nursing.

Hip. Send him and keep the door.   [*Exit* Servant.
[*Reads.*] " *Fata si liceat mihi,*
Fingere arbitrio meo,
Temperem zephyro levi
Vela." [2]
I'd sail were I to choose, not in the ocean,
Cedars are shaken, when shrubs do feel no bruise.

Enter BELLAFRONT, *dressed as a* Page, *with a letter.*

How ? from Matheo ?

[1] *i.e.* A person,—thus spelt to mark the servant's mispronunciation.
[2] From Seneca's *Oedipus.*

Bell. Yes, my lord.

Hip. Art sick?

Bell. Not all in health, my lord.

Hip. Keep off.

Bell. I do.—

Hard fate when women are compelled to woo.   [*Aside.*

Hip. This paper does speak nothing.

Bell. Yes, my lord,

Matter of life it speaks, and therefore writ
In hidden character : to me instruction
My master gives, and, 'less you please to stay
Till you both meet, I can the text display.

Hip. Do so ; read out.

Bell. I am already out :

Look on my face, and read the strangest story!

Hip. What, villain, ho?——

Re-enter Servant.

Ser. Call you, my lord?

Hip. Thou slave, thou hast let in the devil !

Ser. Lord bless us, where? he's not cloven, my lord,
that I can see : besides the devil goes more like a
gentleman than a page ; good my lord, *Buon coraggio !* [1]

Hip. Thou hast let in a woman in man's shape.
And thou art damned for't.

Ser. Not damned I hope for putting in a woman to a
lord.

Hip. Fetch me my rapier,—do not ; I shall kill thee.
Purge this infected chamber of that plague,
That runs upon me thus : Slave, thrust her hence.

Ser. Alas, my lord, I shall never be able to thrust her
hence without help ! Come, mermaid, you must to sea
again.

Bell. Hear me but speak, my words shall be all
          music ;

Hear me but speak.   [*Knocking within.*

---

[1] Ital. Good courage.

Hip. Another beats the door,
T'other she-devil ! look.

Ser. Why, then, hell's broke loose.

Hip. Hence ; guard the chamber : let no more come
     on,   [*Exit* Servant.
One woman serves for man's damnation—
Beshrew thee, thou dost make me violate
The chastest and most sanctimonious vow,
That e'er was entered in the court of Heaven !
I was, on meditation's spotless wings,
Upon my journey thither ; like a storm
Thou beat'st my ripened cogitations,
Flat to the ground : and like a thief dost stand,
To steal devotion from the holy land.

Bell. If woman were thy mother—if thy heart,
Be not all marble, or if't marble be,
Let my tears soften it, to pity me—
I do beseech thee, do not thus with scorn
Destroy a woman !

Hip. Woman, I beseech thee,
Get thee some other suit, this fits thee not :
I would not grant it to a kneeling queen,
I cannot love thee, nor I must not : see
                          [*Points to* INFELICE'S *picture.*
The copy of that obligation,
Where my soul's bound in heavy penalties.

Bell. She's dead, you told me, she'll let fall her suit.

Hip. My vows to her, fled after her to Heaven :
Were thine eyes clear as mine, thou might'st behold her,
Watching upon yon battlements of stars,
How I observe them.   Should I break my bond,
This board would rive in twain, these wooden lips
Call me most perjured villain.   Let it suffice,
I ha' set thee in the path ; is't not a sign
I love thee, when with one so most most dear,
I'll have thee fellow ?   All are fellows there.

Bell. Be greater than a king ; save not a body,

But from eternal shipwreck keep a soul,
If not, and that again, sin's path I tread,
The grief be mine, the guilt fall on thy head !

    Hip. Stay, and take physic for it ; read this book,
Ask counsel of this head, what's to be done ;
He'll strike it dead, that 'tis damnation
If you turn Turk again. Oh, do it not !
Though Heaven cannot allure you to do well,
From doing ill let hell fright you : and learn this,
The soul whose bosom lust did never touch,
Is God's fair bride, and maidens' souls are such :
The soul that leaving chastity's white shore,
Swims in hot sensual streams, is the devil's whore.—

Re-enter Servant *with letter.*

How now, who comes ?

    Ser. No more knaves, my lord, that wear smocks :
here's a letter from Doctor Benedict ; I would not enter
his man, though he had hairs at his mouth, for fear he
should be a woman, for some women have beards ; marry,
they are half-witches. 'Slid !¹ you are a sweet youth to
wear a cod-piece, and have no pins to stick upon't.

    Hip. I'll meet the doctor, tell him ; yet to-night
I cannot : but at morrow rising sun
I will not fail.—[*Exit* Servant.]—Go, woman ; fare thee
    well.   [*Exit.*

    Bell. The lowest fall can be but into hell :
It does not move him I must therefore fly
From this undoing city, and with tears
Wash off all anger from my father's brow ;
He cannot sure but joy, seeing me new born.
A woman honest first, and then turn whore,
Is, as with me, common to thousands more :
But from a strumpet to turn chaste, that sound
Has oft been heard, that woman hardly found.   [*Exit.*

---

¹ " Slid " according to Halliwell is a north country oath.

SCENE II.—*A Street.*

Enter FUSTIGO, CRAMBO, *and* POH.

Fus. Hold up your hands, gentlemen, here's one, two, three [*Giving money*]—nay, I warrant they are sound pistoles, and without flaws ; I had them of my sister and I know she uses to put up nothing that's cracked—four, five, six, seven, eight and nine ; by this hand bring me but a piece of his blood, and you shall have nine more. I'll lurk in a tavern not far off, and provide supper to close up the end of the tragedy : the linen-draper's, remember. Stand to't, I beseech you, and play your parts perfectly.

Cram. Look you, signor, 'tis not your gold that we weigh—

Fus. Nay, nay, weigh it and spare not ; if it lack one grain of corn, I'll give you a bushel of wheat to make it up.

Cram. But by your favour, signor, which of the servants is it ? because we'll punish justly.

Fus. Marry 'tis the head man ; you shall taste him by his tongue ; a pretty, tall, prating fellow, with a Tuscalonian beard.

Poh. Tuscalonian ? very good.

Fus. God's life, I was ne'er so thrummed since I was a gentleman : my coxcomb was dry beaten, as if my hair had been hemp.

Cram. We'll dry-beat some of them.

Fus. Nay, it grew so high, that my sister cried out murder, very manfully : I have her consent, in a manner, to have him peppered : else I'll not do't, to win more than ten cheaters do at a rifling : break but his pate, or so, only his mazer,[1] because I'll have his head in a cloth as well as mine ; he's a linen-draper, and may take enough. I could enter mine action of battery against him, but we

---

[1] A corruption of "mazzard," the head.

Geo. Troth, mistress, nothing : not so much as a bee, he did not hum : not so much as a bawd, he did not hem : not so much as a cuckold, he did not ha : neither hum, hem, nor ha ; only stared me in the face, passed along, and made haste in, as if my looks had worked with him, to give him a stool.

Vio. Sure he's vexed now, this trick has moved his
       spleen,
He's angered now, because he uttered nothing :
And wordless wrath breaks out more violent,
May be he'll strive for place, when he comes down,
But if thou lov'st me, George, afford him none.

Geo. Nay, let me alone to play my master's prize,[1] as long as my mistress warrants me : I'm sure I have his best clothes on, and I scorn to give place to any that is inferior in apparel to me, that's an axiom, a principle, and is observed as much as the fashion ; let that persuade you then, that I'll shoulder with him for the upper hand in the shop, as long as this chain will maintain it.

Vio. Spoke with the spirit of a master, though with the tongue of a prentice.

Re-enter CANDIDO *dressed as a* Prentice.

Why how now, madman ? what in your tricksi-coats ?
    Cand. O peace, good mistress.

Enter CRAMBO *and* POH.

See, what you lack ? what is't you buy ? pure calicoes, fine hollands, choice cambrics, neat lawns : see what you buy ? pray come near, my master will use you well, he can afford you a penny-worth.

Vio. Ay, that he can, out of a whole piece of lawn i'faith.

Cand. Pray see your choice here, gentlemen.

Vio. O fine fool ! what, a madman ! a patient mad-

---

[1] A quibble. A master's was one of the three degrees in fencing, for each of which a " prize " was publicly played.

man ! who ever heard of the like ?   Well, sir, I'll fit you
and your humour presently : what, cross-points ? I'll untie 'em all in a trice : I'll vex you i'faith : boy, take your
cloak, quick, come.   [*Exit with* 1st Prentice.

Cand. Be covered, George, this chain and welted gown
Bare to this coat ? then the world's upside down.

Geo. Umh, umh, hum.

Cram. That's the shop, and there's the fellow.

Poh. Ay, but the master is walking in there.

Cram. No matter, we'll in.

Poh. 'Sblood, dost long to lie in limbo ?

Cram. An limbo be in hell, I care not.

Cand. Look you, gentlemen, your choice : cambrics ?

Cram. No, sir, some shirting.

Cand. You shall.

Cram. Have you none of this striped canvas for
doublets ?

Cand. None striped, sir, but plain.

2nd Pren. I think there be one piece striped within.

Geo. Step, sirrah, and fetch it, hum, hum, hum.

                    [*Exit* 2nd Pren., *and returns with the piece.*

Cand. Look you, gentleman, I'll make but one spread-
ing, here's a piece of cloth, fine, yet shall wear like iron,
'tis without fault ; take this upon my word, 'tis without
fault.

Cram. Then 'tis better than you, sirrah.

Cand. Ay, and a number more : Oh, that each soul
Were but as spotless as this innocent white,
And had as few breaks in it !

Cram. 'Twould have some then :   •
There was a fray here last day in this shop.

Cand. There was, indeed, a little flea-biting.

Poh. A gentleman had his pate broke ; call you that
but a flea-biting ?

Cand. He had so.

Cram. Zounds, do you stand to it ? [*Strikes* CANDIDO.

Geo. 'Sfoot, clubs, clubs ! prentices, down with 'em !

Enter several Prentices *with clubs, who disarm* CRAMBO
and POH.

Ah, you rogues, strike a citizen in's shop?

Cand. None of you stir, I pray; forbear, good George.

Cram. I beseech you, sir, we mistook our marks; deliver us our weapons.

Geo. Your head bleeds, sir; cry clubs!

Cand. I say you shall not; pray be patient,
Give them their weapons: sirs, you'd best be gone,
I tell you here are boys more tough than bears:
Hence, lest more fists do walk about your ears.

Cram., Poh. We thank you, sir.   *[Exeunt.*

Cand. You shall not follow them;
Let them alone, pray; this did me no harm;
Troth, I was cold, and the blow made me warm,
I thank 'em for't: besides, I had decreed
To have a vein pricked, I did mean to bleed:
So that there's money saved: they're honest men,
Pray use 'em well, when they appear again.

Geo. Yes, sir, we'll use 'em like honest men.

Cand. Ay, well said, George, like honest men, though they be arrant knaves, for that's the phrase of the city; help to lay up these wares.

Re-enter VIOLA *and* 1st Prentice *with* Officers.

Vio. Yonder he stands.

1st Off. What in a prentice-coat?

Vio. Ay, ay; mad, mad; pray take heed.

Cand. How now! what news with them?
What make they with my wife?
Officers, is she attached?—Look to your wares.

Vio. He talks to himself: oh, he's much gone indeed.

1st Off. Pray, pluck up a good heart, be not so fearful:
Sirs, hark, we'll gather to him by degrees.

Vio. Ay, ay, by degrees I pray: Oh me! What makes he with the lawn in his hand? He'll tear all the ware in my shop.

1st Off. Fear not, we'll catch him on a sudden.

Vio. Oh! you had need do so ; pray take heed of your warrant.

1st Off. I warrant, mistress.   Now, Signor Candido.

Cand. Now, sir, what news with you, sir ?

Vio. What news with you ? he says : oh, he's far gone !

1st Off. I pray, fear nothing ; let's alone with him,
Signor, you look not like yourself, methinks,—
Steal you a' t'other side ; you're changed, you're altered.

Cand. Changed, sir, why true, sir.   Is change strange ?
        'Tis not
The fashion unless it alter ! monarchs turn
To beggars, beggars creep into the nests
Of princes, masters serve their prentices,
Ladies their serving-men, men turn to women.

1st Off. And women turn to men.

Cand. Ay, and women turn to men, you say true : ha,
ha, a mad world, a mad world.   [Officers *seize* CANDIDO.

1st Off. Have we caught you, sir ?

Cand. Caught me ? well, well, you have caught me.

Vio. He laughs in your faces.

Geo. A rescue, prentices ! my master's catchpolled.

1st Off. I charge you, keep the peace, or have your legs
Gartered with irons ! we have from the duke
A warrant strong enough for what we do.

Cand. I pray, rest quiet, I desire no rescue.

Vio. La, he desires no rescue, 'las poor heart,
He talks against himself.

Cand. Well, what's the matter ?

1st Off. Look to that arm,   [Officers *bind* CANDIDO.
Pray, make sure work, double the cord.

Cand. Why, why ?

Vio. Look how his head goes, should he get but loose,
Oh 'twere as much as all our lives were worth !

1st Off. Fear not, we'll make all sure for our own safety.

Cand. Are you at leisure now ? well, what's the matter ?
Why do I enter into bonds thus, ha ?

1st Off. Because you're mad, put fear upon your wife.

Vio. Oh ay, I went in danger of my life every minute.

Cand. What, am I mad, say you, and I not know it?

1st Off. That proves you mad, because you know it not.

Vio. Pray talk to him as little as you can,
You see he's too far spent.

Cand. Bound, with strong cord!
A sister's thread, i'faith, had been enough,
To lead me anywhere.—Wife, do you long?
You are mad too, or else you do me wrong.

Geo. But are you mad indeed, master?

Cand. My wife says so,
And what she says, George, is all truth, you know.—
And whither now, to Bethlem Monastery?
Ha! whither?

1st Off. Faith, e'en to the madmen's pound.

Cand. A' God's name! still I feel my patience sound.
                    [*Exeunt* Officers *with* CANDIDO.

Geo. Come, we'll see whither he goes; if the master be
mad, we are his servants, and must follow his steps; we'll
be mad-caps too.   Farewell, mistress, you shall have us
all in Bedlam.   [*Exeunt* GEORGE *and* Prentices.

Vio. I think I ha' fitted you now, you and your clothes,
If this move not his patience, nothing can;
I'll swear then I've a saint, and not a man.   [*Exit.*

SCENE IV.—*Grounds near the* DUKE'S *Palace.*

Enter DUKE, Doctor BENEDICT, FLUELLO,
            CASTRUCHIO, *and* PIORATTO.

Duke. Give us a little leave.
            [*Exeunt* FLUELLO, CASTRUCHIO, *and* PIORATTO.
                        Doctor, your news.

Doct. I sent for him my lord, at last he came,

And did receive all speech that went from me,
As gilded pills made to prolong his health.
My credit with him wrought it ; for some men
Swallow even empty hooks, like fools that fear
No drowning where 'tis deepest, 'cause 'tis clear :
In th'end we sat and eat : a health I drank
To Infelice's sweet departed soul.
This train I knew would take.

   Duke. 'Twas excellent.

   Doct. He fell with such devotion on his knees,
To pledge the fame—

   Duke. Fond, superstitious fool !

   Doct. That had he been inflamed with zeal of prayer,
He could not pour't out with more reverence :
About my neck he hung, wept on my cheek,
Kissed it, and swore he would adore my lips,
Because they brought forth Infelice's name.

   Duke. Ha, ha ! alack, alack.

   Doct. The cup he lifts up high, and thus he said ;
Here noble maid !—drinks, and was poisonèd.

   Duke. And died ?

   Doct. And died, my lord.

   Duke. Thou in that word
Hast pieced mine aged hours out with more years,
Than thou hast taken from Hippolito.
A noble youth he was, but lesser branches
Hindering the greater's growth, must be lopt off,
And feed the fire.   Doctor, we're now all thine,
And use us so : be bold.

   Doct. Thanks, gracious lord—
My honoured lord :—

   Duke. Hum.

   Doct. I do beseech your grace to bury deep,
This bloody act of mine.

   Duke. Nay, nay, for that,
Doctor, look you to it, me it shall not move ;
They're cursed that ill do, not that ill do love.

Doct. You throw an angry forehead on my face :
But be you pleased backward thus far to look,
That for your good, this evil I undertook—

Duke. Ay, ay, we conster [1] so.

Doct. And only for your love.

Duke. Confessed : 'tis true.

Doct. Nor let it stand against me as a bar,
To thrust me from your presence ; nor believe
As princes have quick thoughts, that now my finger
Being dipt in blood, I will not spare the hand,
But that for gold,—as what can gold not do ?—
I may be hired to work the like on you.

Duke. Which to prevent—

Doct. 'Tis from my heart as far.

Duke. No matter, doctor ; 'cause I'll fearless sleep,
And that you shall stand clear of that suspicion,
I banish thee for ever from my court.
This principle is old, but true as fate,
Kings may love treason, but the traitor hate.   [*Exit.*

Doct. Is't so ? nay then, duke, your stale principle,
With one as stale, the doctor thus shall quit—
He falls himself that digs another's pit.

Enter the Doctor's Servant.

How now ! where is he ? will he meet me ?

Ser. Meet you, sir ? he might have met with three
fencers in this time, and have received less hurt than by
meeting one doctor of physic : Why, sir, he has walked
under the old abbey-wall yonder this hour, till he's more
cold than a citizen's country house in Janivery. You may
smell him behind, sir : la, you, yonder he comes.

Doct. Leave me.

Ser. I'th' lurch, if you will.   [*Exit.*

Enter HIPPOLITO.

Doct. O my most noble friend !

----
[1] Construe.

Hip. Few but yourself,
Could have enticed me thus, to trust the air
With my close sighs.   You sent for me ; what news ?
   Doct. Come, you must doff this black, dye that pale
       cheek
Into his own colour, go, attire yourself
Fresh as a bridegroom when he meets his bride.
The duke has done much treason to thy love ;
Tis now revealed, 'tis now to be revenged :
Be merry, honoured friend, thy lady lives.
   Hip. What lady?
   Doct. Infelice, she's revived ;
Revived?   Alack ! death never had the heart,
To take breath from her.
   Hip. Umh : I thank you, sir,
Physic prolongs life, when it cannot save ;
This helps not my hopes, mine are in their grave,
You do some wrong to mock me.
   Doct. By that love
Which I have ever borne you, what I speak
Is truth : the maiden lives ; that funeral,
Duke's tears, the mourning, was all counterfeit ;
A sleepy draught cozened the world and you :
I was his minister, and then chambered up,
To stop discovery.
   Hip. O treacherous duke !
   Doct. He cannot hope so certainly for bliss,
As he believes that I have poisoned you :
He wooed me to't ; I yielded, and confirmed him
In his most bloody thoughts.
   Hip. A very devil !
   Doct. Her did he closely coach to Bergamo,
And thither—
   Hip. Will I ride : stood Bergamo
In the low countries of black hell, I'll to her.
   Doct. You shall to her, but not to Bergamo :
How passion makes you fly beyond yourself.

Much of that weary journey I ha' cut off;
For she by letters hath intelligence
Of your supposed death, her own interment,
And all those plots, which that false duke, her father,
Has wrought against you; and she'll meet you—

    Hip. Oh, when?

    Doct. Nay, see; how covetous are your desires!
Early to-morrow morn.

    Hip. Oh where, good father?

    Doct. At Bethlem Monastery: are you pleased now?

    Hip. At Bethlem Monastery! the place well fits,
It is the school where those that lose their wits,
Practise again to get them: I am sick
Of that disease; all love is lunatic.

    Doct. We'll steal away this night in some disguise:
Father Anselmo, a most reverend friar,
Expects our coming; before whom we lay
Reasons so strong, that he shall yield in bands
Of holy wedlock to tie both your hands.

    Hip. This is such happiness,
That to believe it, 'tis impossible.

    Doct. Let all your joys then die in misbelief;
I will reveal no more.

    Hip. O yes, good father,
I am so well acquainted with despair,
I know not how to hope: I believe all.

    Doct. We'll hence this night, much must be done,
        much said:
But if the doctor fail not in his charms,
Your lady shall ere morning fill these arms.

    Hip. Heavenly physician! for thy fame shall spread,
That mak'st two lovers speak when they be dead. [*Exeunt.*

ACT THE FIFTH.

SCENE I.—*A Hall in the* Duke's *Palace.*

Enter Viola, *with a petition and* George.

IO. Oh watch, good George, watch which way the duke comes.

Geo. Here comes one of the butterflies; ask him.

Enter Pioratto.

Vio. Pray, sir, comes the duke this [way?

Pio. He's upon coming, mistress.

Vio. I thank you, sir. [*Exit* Pioratto.] George, are there many mad folks where thy master lies?

Geo. Oh yes, of all countries some; but especially mad Greeks, they swarm. Troth mistress, the world is altered with you; you had not wont to stand thus with a paper humbly complaining: but you're well enough served: provender pricked you, as it does many of our city wives besides.

Vio. Dost think, George, we shall get him forth?

Geo. Truly, mistress, I cannot tell; I think you'll hardly get him forth. Why, 'tis strange! 'Sfoot, I have known many women that have had mad rascals to their husbands, whom they would belabour by all means possible to keep 'em in their right wits, but of a woman to long to turn a tame man into a madman, why the devil himself was never used so by his dam.

Vio. How does he talk, George ! ha ! good George, tell me.

Geo. Why you're best go see.

Vio. Alas, I am afraid !

Geo. Afraid ! you had more need be ashamed, he may rather be afraid of you.

Vio. But, George, he's not stark mad, is he ? he does not rave, he is not horn-mad, George, is he ?

Geo. Nay I know not that, but he talks like a justice of peace, of a thousand matters, and to no purpose.

Vio. I'll to the monastery : I shall be mad till I enjoy him, I shall be sick until I see him ; yet when I do see him, I shall weep out mine eyes.

Geo. I'd fain see a woman weep out her eyes, that's as true as to say, a man's cloak burns, when it hangs in the water : I know you'll weep, mistress, but what says the painted cloth ?[1]

> Trust not a woman when she cries,
> For she'll pump water from her eyes
> With a wet finger,[2] and in faster showers,
> Than April when he rains down flowers.

Vio. Ay, but George, that painted cloth is worthy to be hanged up for lying ; all women have not tears at will, unless they have good cause.

Geo. Ay, but mistress, how easily will they find a cause, and as one of our cheese-trenchers[3] says very learnedly,

> As out of wormwood bees suck honey,
> As from poor clients lawyers firk money,
> As parsley from a roasted cony :
> So, though the day be ne'er so funny,
> If wives will have it rain, down then it drives,
> The calmest husbands make the stormiest wives—

---

[1] A cheap substitute for tapestry and very frequently having verses inscribed on it as in the present instance.

[2] Readily. Possibly the above use of the term points to its derivation.

[3] Cheese-trenchers used to be inscribed with proverbial phrases.

Vio. —Tame, George.   But I ha' done storming now.

Geo. Why that's well done : good mistress, throw
aside this fashion of your humour, be not so fantastical
in wearing it : storm no more, long no more.   This
longing has made you come short of many a good thing
that you might have had from my master : Here comes
the duke.

Enter DUKE, FLUELLO, PIORATTO, *and* SINEZI.

Vio. O, I beseech you, pardon my offence,
In that I durst abuse your grace's warrant ;
Deliver forth my husband, good my lord.

Duke. Who is her husband ?

Flu. Candido, my lord.

Duke. Where is he ?

Vio. He's among the lunatics ;
He was a man made up without a gall ;
Nothing could move him, nothing could convert
His meek blood into fury ; yet like a monster,
I often beat at the most constant rock
Of his unshaken patience, and did long
To vex him.

Duke. Did you so ?

Vio. And for that purpose,
Had warrant from your grace, to carry him
To Bethlem Monastery, whence they will not free him,
Without your grace's hand that sent him in.

Duke. You have longed fair ; 'tis you are mad, I fear ;
It's fit to fetch him thence, and keep you there :
If he be mad, why would you have him forth ?

Geo. An please your grace, he's not stark mad, but
only talks like a young gentleman, somewhat fantastically,
that's all : there's a thousand about your court, city, and
country madder than he.

Duke. Provide a warrant, you shall have our hand.

Geo. Here's a warrant ready drawn, my lord.

Duke. Get pen and ink, get pen and ink.   [*Exit* GEO.

Enter CASTRUCHIO.

Cas. Where is my lord the duke?

Duke. How now! more madmen?

Cas. I have strange news, my lord.

Duke. Of what? of whom?

Cas. Of Infelice, and a marriage.

Duke. Ha! where? with whom?

Cas. Hippolito.

Re-enter GEORGE, *with pen and ink.*

Geo. Here, my lord.

Duke. Hence, with that woman! void the room!

Flu. Away! the duke's vexed.

Geo. Whoop, come, mistress, the duke's mad too.

[*Exeunt* VIOLA *and* GEORGE.

Duke. Who told me that Hippolito was dead?

Cas. He that can make any man dead, the doctor:
but, my lord, he's as full of life as wild-fire, and as quick.
Hippolito, the doctor, and one more rid hence this
evening; the inn at which they light is Bethlem Monastery;
Infelice comes from Bergamo and meets them there.
Hippolito is mad, for he means this day to be married;
the afternoon is the hour, and Friar Anselmo is the
knitter.

Duke. From Bergamo? is't possible? it cannot be.
It cannot be.

Cas. I will not swear, my lord;
But this intelligence I took from one
Whose brains work in the plot.

Duke. What's he?

Cas. Matheo.

Flu. Matheo knows all.

Pior. He's Hippolito's bosom.

Duke. How far stands Bethlem hence?

Cas., Flu., &c. Six or seven miles.

Duke, Is't so? not married till the afternoon:

Stay, stay, let's work out some prevention. How !
This is most strange ; can none but mad men serve
To dress their wedding dinner ? All of you
Get presently to horse, disguise yourselves
Like country-gentlemen,
Or riding citizens, or so : and take
Each man a several path, but let us meet
At Bethlem Monastery, some space of time
Being spent between the arrival each of other,
As if we came to see the lunatics.
To horse, away ! be secret on your lives.
Love must be punished that unjustly thrives.

[*Exeunt all but* FLUELLO.

Flu. Be secret on your lives ! Castruchio,
You're but a scurvy spaniel ; honest lord,
Good lady : zounds, their love is just, 'tis good,
And I'll prevent you, though I swim in blood.   [*Exit.*

SCENE II.—*An Apartment in Bethlem Monastery.*

Enter Friar ANSELMO, HIPPOLITO, MATHEO, *and*
INFELICE.

Hip. Nay, nay, resolve,[1] good father, or deny.
Ans. You press me to an act, both full of danger,
And full of happiness ; for I behold
Your father's frowns, his threats, nay, perhaps death
To him that dare do this : yet, noble lord,
Such comfortable beams break through these clouds
By this blest marriage, that your honoured word
Being pawned in my defence, I will tie fast
The holy wedding-knot.
Hip. Tush, fear not the duke.

---

[1] Consent.

Ans. O son ! wisely to fear, is to be free from fear.

Hip. You have our words, and you shall have our lives,

To guard you safe from all ensuing danger.

Mat. Ay, ay, chop 'em up, and away.

Ans. Stay, when is't fit for me, and safest for you,

To entertain this business ?

Hip. Not till the evening.

Ans. Be't so, there is a chapel stands hard by,

Upon the west end of the abbey wall ;

Thither convey yourselves, and when the sun

Hath turned his back upon this upper world,

I'll marry you ; that done, no thundering voice

Can break the sacred bond : yet, lady, here

You are most safe.

Inf. Father, your love's most dear.

Mat. Ay, well said, lock us into some little room by ourselves, that we may be mad for an hour or two.

Hip. O, good Matheo, no, let's make no noise.

Mat. How ! no noise ! do you know where you are ? 'sfoot, amongst all the mad-caps in Milan : so that to throw the house out at window will be the better, and no man will suspect that we lurk here to steal mutton [1]: the more sober we are, the more scurvy 'tis.   And though the friar tell us, that here we are safest, I am not of his mind, for if those lay here that had lost their money, none would ever look after them, but here are none but those that have lost their wits, so that if hue and cry be made, hither they'll come ; and my reason is, because none goes to be married till he be stark mad.

Hip. Muffle yourselves, yonder's Fluello.

Enter FLUELLO.

Mat. Zounds !

Flu. O my lord, these cloaks are not for this rain ! the

---

[1] *i.e.* To steal a wench.

tempest is too great : I come sweating to tell you of it,
that you may get out of it.

Mat. Why, what's the matter?

Flu. What's the matter? you have mattered it fair :
the duke's at hand.

All. The duke?

Flu. The very duke.

Hip. Then all our plots
Are turned upon our heads ; and we're blown up
With our own underminings.   'Sfoot, how comes he?
What villain durst betray our being here?

Flu. Castruchio! Castruchio told the duke, and
Matheo here told Castruchio.

Hip. Would you betray me to Castruchio?

Mat. 'Sfoot, he damned himself to the pit of hell, if he
spake on't again.

Hip. So did you swear to me : so were you damned.

Mat. Pox on 'em, and there be no faith in men, if a
man shall not believe oaths : he took bread and salt,[1] by
this light, that he would never open his lips.

Hip. O God, O God !

Ans. Son, be not desperate,
Have patience, you shall trip your enemy
Down by his own slights.[2]   How far is the duke hence?

Flu. He's but new set out : Castruchio, Pioratto and
Sinezi come along with him ; you have time enough yet
to prevent[3] them, if you have but courage.

Ans. Ye shall steal secretly into the chapel,
And presently be married.   If the duke
Abide here still, spite of ten thousand eyes,
You shall 'scape hence like friars.

Hip. O blest disguise ! O happy man !

Ans. Talk not of happiness till your closed hand
Have her by th' forehead, like the lock of Time :

---

[1] It was the ancient practice when persons were sworn for them to
eat bread and salt.
[2] Artifices.   [3] Anticipate.

Be nor too slow, nor hasty, now you climb
Up to the tower of bliss ; only be wary
And patient, that's all : If you like my plot,
Build and despatch ; if not, farewell, then not.

    Hip. O yes, we do applaud it ! we'll dispute
No longer, but will hence and execute.
Fluello, you'll stay here : let us be gone ;
The ground that frighted lovers tread upon
Is stuck with thorns.

    Ans. Come, then, away, 'tis meet,
To escape those thorns, to put on wingèd feet.

        [*Exeunt* ANSELMO, HIPPOLITO *and* INFELICE.

    Mat. No words, I pray, Fluello, for't stands us upon.

    Flu. Oh, sir, let that be your lesson ! [*Exit* MATHEO.
Alas, poor lovers ! On what hopes and fears
Men toss themselves for women ! When she's got,
The best has in her that which pleaseth not.

    Enter the DUKE, CASTRUCHIO, PIORATTO, *and* SINEZI
        from different doors, muffled.

    Duke. Who's there ?

    Cas. My lord.

    Duke. Peace ; send that lord away.
A lordship will spoil all ; let's be all fellows.
What's he ?

    Cas. Fluello, or else Sinezi, by his little legs.

    Cas., Flu., Pio. All friends, all friends.

    Duke. What ? met upon the very point of time ?
Is this the place ?

    Pio. This is the place, my lord.

    Duke. Dream you on lordships ? come no more lords,
      I pray :
You have not seen these lovers yet ?

    All. Not yet.

    Duke. Castruchio, art thou sure this wedding feast
Is not till afternoon ?

    Cas. So't is given out, my lord.

Duke. Nay, nay, 'tis like ; thieves must observe their
     hours ;
Lovers watch minutes like astronomers ;
How shall the interim hours by us be spent ?

Flu. Let's all go see the madmen.

Cas., Pio., Sin. Mass, content.

Enter a Sweeper.

Duke. Oh, here comes one ; question him, question him,

Flu. Now, honest fellow ? dost thou belong to the
house ?

Sweep. Yes, forsooth, I am one of the implements, I
sweep the madmen's rooms, and fetch straw for 'em, and
buy chains to tie 'em, and rods to whip 'em. I was a
mad wag myself here, once, but I thank Father Anselmo,
he lashed me into my right mind again.

Duke. Anselmo is the friar must marry them ;
Question him where he is.

Cas. And where is Father Anselmo now ?

Sweep. Marry, he's gone but e'en now.

Duke. Ay, well done.—Tell me, whither is he gone ?

Sweep. Why, to God a'mighty.

Flu. Ha, ha ! this fellow's a fool, talks idly.

Pio. Sirrah, are all the mad folks in Milan brought
hither ?

Sweep. How, all ? there's a question indeed : why if
all the mad folks in Milan should come hither, there
would not be left ten men in the city.

Duke. Few gentlemen or courtiers here, ha ?

Sweep. O yes, abundance, abundance ! lands no sooner
fall into their hands, but straight they run out a' their
wits : citizens' sons and heirs are free of the house by
their fathers' copy. Farmers' sons come hither like
geese, in flocks, and when they ha' sold all their corn-
fields, here they sit and pick the straws.

Sin. Methinks you should have women here as well as
men.

Dekker.   N

Sweep. Oh, ay, a plague on 'em, there's no ho![1] with 'em; they're madder than March hares.

Flu. Are there no lawyers amongst you?

Sweep. Oh no, not one; never any lawyer, we dare not let a lawyer come in, for he'll make 'em mad faster than we can recover 'em.

Duke. And how long is't ere you recover any of these?

Sweep. Why, according to the quantity of the moon that's got into 'em. An alderman's son will be mad a great while, a very great while, especially if his friends left him well; a whore will hardly come to her wits again: a puritan, there's no hope of him, unless he may pull down the steeple, and hang himself i' th' bell-ropes.

Flu. I perceive all sorts of fish come to your net.

Sweep. Yes, in truth, we have blocks[2] for all heads; we have good store of wild-oats here: for the courtier is mad at the citizen, the citizen is mad at the countryman; the shoemaker is mad at the cobbler, the cobbler at the car-man; the punk is mad that the merchant's wife is no whore, the merchant's wife is mad that the punk is so common a whore. Gods so, here's Father Anselmo; pray say nothing that I tell tales out of the school.

[*Exit.*

Re-enter ANSELMO *and* Servants.

All. God bless you, father.

Ans. I thank you, gentlemen.

Cas. Pray, may we see some of those wretched souls, That here are in your keeping?

Ans. Yes, you shall.
But gentlemen, I must disarm you then:
There are of mad men, as there are of tame,
All humoured not alike: we have here some,
So apish and fantastic, play with a feather,
And, though 'twould grieve a soul to see God's image

---

[1] *i.e.* They are not to be restrained by being called to.
[2] Hats.

So blemished and defaced, yet do they act
Such antic and such pretty lunacies,
That spite of sorrow they will make you smile :
Others again we have like hungry lions,
Fierce as wild-bulls, untameable as flies,
And these have oftentimes from strangers' sides
Snatched rapiers suddenly, and done much harm,
Whom if you'll see, you must be weaponless.

    All. With all our hearts.

                     [*Giving their weapons to* ANSELMO.

    Ans. Here, take these weapons in,—

                     [*Exit* Servant *with weapons.*

Stand off a little, pray ; so, so, 'tis well :
I'll show you here a man that was sometimes
A very grave and wealthy citizen ;
Has served a prenticeship to this misfortune,
Been here seven years, and dwelt in Bergamo.

    Duke. How fell he from his wits ?

    Ans. By loss at sea ;
I'll stand aside, question him you alone,
For if he spy me, he'll not speak a word,
Unless he's throughly vexed.

        [*Opens a door and then retires : enter* 1st Mad-
              man, *wrapt in a net.*

    Flu. Alas, poor soul !

    Cas. A very old man.

    Duke. God speed, father !

    1*st Mad.* God speed the plough, thou shalt not speed
me.

    Pio. We see you, old man, for all you dance in a net.

    1*st Mad.* True, but thou wilt dance in a halter, and I
shall not see thee.

    Ans. Oh do not vex him, pray.

    Cas. Are you a fisherman, father ?

    1*st Mad.* No, I am neither fish nor flesh.

    Flu. What do you with that net then ?

    1*st Mad.* Dost not see, fool ? there's a fresh salmon

                          N 2

in't ; if you step one foot further, you'll be over shoes, for you see I'm over head and ears in the salt-water : and if you fall into this whirl-pool where I am, you're drowned : you're a drowned rat. I am fishing here for five ships, but I cannot have a good draught, for my net breaks still, and breaks ; but I'll break some of your necks an I catch you in my clutches. Stay, stay, stay, stay, stay, where's the wind ? where's the wind ? where's the wind ? where's the wind ? Out you gulls, you goose-caps, you gudgeon-eaters ! do you look for the wind in the heavens ? ha, ha, ha, ha ! no, no ! look there, look there, look there ! the wind is always at that door : hark how it blows, puff, puff, puff !

All. Ha, ha, ha !

1st Mad. Do you laugh at God's creatures ? Do you mock old age, you rogues ? Is this gray beard and head counterfeit that you cry, ha, ha, ha ? Sirrah, art not thou my eldest son ?

Pio. Yes indeed, father.

1st Mad. Then thou'rt a fool, for my eldest son had a polt-foot,[1] crooked legs, a verjuice face, and a pear-coloured beard : I made him a scholar, and he made himself a fool.—Sirrah, thou there : hold out thy hand.

Duke. My hand ? well, here 'tis.

1st Mad. Look, look, look, look ! has he not long nails, and short hair ?

Flu. Yes, monstrous short hair, and abominable long nails.

1st Mad. Ten-penny nails, are they not ?

Flu. Yes, ten-penny nails.

1st Mad. Such nails had my second boy. Kneel down, thou varlet, and ask thy father's blessing. Such nails had my middlemost son, and I made him a promoter :[2] and he scraped, and scraped, and scraped, till he got the devil and all : but he scraped thus, and thus, and thus, and it went under his legs, till at length a

---

[1] Club foot.   [2] Informer.

company of kites, taking him for carrion, swept up all, all, all, all, all, all, all. If you love your lives, look to yourselves : see, see, see, see, the Turks' galleys are fighting with my ships ! Bounce go the guns ! Oooh ! cry the men ! Rumble, rumble, go the waters ! Alas, there ; 'tis sunk, 'tis sunk : I am undone, I am undone ! You are the damned pirates have undone me : you are, by the Lord, you are, you are ! Stop 'em—you are !

Ans. Why, how now sirrah ! must I fall to tame you ?

1st Mad. Tame me ! no, I'll be madder than a roasted cat. See, see, I am burnt with gunpowder,—these are our close fights !

Ans. I'll whip you, if you grow unruly thus.

1st Mad. Whip me ?   Out you toad ! Whip me ? What justice is this, to whip me because I am a beggar ? Alas ! I am a poor man : a very poor man ! I am starved, and have had no meat by this light, ever since the great flood ; I am a poor man.

Ans. Well, well, be quiet, and you shall have meat.

1st Mad. Ay, ay, pray do ; for look you, here be my guts : these are my ribs—you may look through my ribs —see how my guts come out ! These are my red guts, my very guts, oh, oh !

Ans. Take him in there.

[*Servants* remove 1st Madman.

Flu., Pio., &c. A very piteous sight.

Cas. Father, I see you have a busy charge.

Ans. They must be used like children, pleased with toys,
And anon whipped for their unruliness :
I'll show you now a pair quite different
From him that's gone : he was all words ; and these
Unless you urge 'em, seldom spend their speech,
But save their tongues.

[*Opens another door, from which enter* 2nd *and*
3rd Madmen.

La, you ; this hithermost

Fell from the happy quietness of mind,
About a maiden that he loved, and died :
He followed her to church, being full of tears,
And as her body went into the ground,
He fell stark mad.   This is a married man,
Was jealous of a fair, but, as some say,
A very virtuous wife ; and that spoiled him.

3rd Mad. All these are whoremongers, and lay with my wife : whore, whore, whore, whore, whore !

Flu. Observe him.

3rd Mad. Gaffer shoemaker, you pulled on my wife's pumps, and then crept into her pantofles :[1] lie there, lie there !—This was her tailor.   You cut out her loose-bodied gown, and put in a yard more than I allowed her ; lie there by the shoemaker.   O master doctor ! are you here? you gave me a purgation, and then crept into my wife's chamber, to feel her pulses, and you said, and she said, and her maid said, that they went pit-a-pat, pit-a-pat, pit-a-pat.   Doctor, I'll put you anon into my wife's urinal.   Heigh, come aloft, Jack : this was her schoolmaster, and taught her to play upon the virginals, and still his jacks leapt up, up.[2]   You pricked her out nothing but bawdy lessons, but I'll prick you all, fiddler—doctor—tailor — shoemaker — shoemaker — fiddler—doctor—tailor !   So ! lie with my wife again, now.

Cas. See how he notes the other, now he feeds.

3rd Mad. Give me some porridge.

2nd Mad. I'll give thee none.

3rd Mad. Give me some porridge.

2nd Mad. I'll not give thee a bit.

3rd Mad. Give me that flap-dragon.[3]

2nd Mad. I'll not give thee a spoonful: thou liest, it's

---

[1] Slippers.   Fr. *pantoufles.*
[2] In playing the virginal the sound ceased whenever the jack fell and touched the string.
[3] A flap-dragon was a raisin floating on lighted spirit in a dish or glass and had to be snatched out with the mouth and swallowed. Gallants used to toast their mistresses in flap-dragons.

no dragon, 'tis a parrot, that I bought for my sweetheart, and I'll keep it.

3rd Mad. Here's an almond for parrot.

2nd. Mad. Hang thyself!

3rd Mad. Here's a rope for parrot.[1]

2nd Mad. Eat it, for I'll eat this.

3rd Mad. I'll shoot at thee, an thou't give me none.

2nd Mad. Wu't thou?

3rd Mad. I'll run a tilt at thee, an thou't give me none.

2nd Mad. Wu't thou? do an thou darest.

3rd Mad. Bounce! [*Strikes him.*

2nd Mad. O—oh! I am slain! murder, murder, murder! I am slain; my brains are beaten out.

Ans. How now, you villains! Bring me whips: I'll whip you.

2nd Mad. I am dead! I am slain! ring out the bell, for I am dead.

Duke. How will you do now, sirrah? you ha' killed him.

3rd Mad. I'll answer't at sessions: he was eating of almond-butter, and I longed for't: the child had never been delivered out of my belly, if I had not killed him. I'll answer't at sessions, so my wife may be burnt i' th' hand, too.

Ans. Take 'em in both: bury him, for he's dead.

2nd Mad. Indeed, I am dead; put me, I pray, into a good pit-hole.

3rd Mad. I'll answer't at sessions.

[*Servants remove* 2nd *and* 3rd Madmen.

Enter BELLAFRONT.

Ans. How now, huswife, whither gad you?

Bell. A-nutting, forsooth: how do you, gaffer? how do you, gaffer? there's a French curtsey for you, too.

---

[1] "An almond for parrot," and "a rope for parrot," were common phrases at the time.

Flu. 'Tis Bellafront!

Pio. 'Tis the punk, by th' Lord!

Duke. Father, what's she, I pray?

Ans. As yet I know not,
She came in but this day; talks little idly,
And therefore has the freedom of the house.

Bell. Do not you know me?—nor you?—nor you?—
nor you?

All. No, indeed.

Bell. Then you are an ass,—and you an ass,—and you
are an ass,—for I know you.

Ans. Why, what are they? come, tell me, what are
they?

Bell. They're fish-wives, will you buy any gudgeons?
God's santy![1] yonder come friars, I know them too—

Enter HIPPOLITO, MATHEO, *and* INFELICE, *disguised
as* Friars.

How do you, friar?

Ans. Nay, nay, away, you must not trouble friars.—
The duke is here, speak nothing.

Bell. Nay, indeed, you shall not go: we'll run at
barley-break first, and you shall be in hell.[2]

Mat. My punk turned mad whore, as all her fellows
are!

Hip. Say nothing; but steal hence, when you spy time.

Ans. I'll lock you up, if you're unruly: fie!

Bell. Fie? marry, soh! they shall not go indeed, till I
ha' told 'em their fortunes.

Duke. Good father, give her leave.

Bell. Ay, pray, good father, and I'll give you my
blessing.

Ans. Well then, be brief, but if you're thus unruly,
I'll have you locked up fast.

---

[1] A corruption of God's sanctity or God's saints.—*Steevens.*

[2] In the game of barley-break the ground was divided into three
compartments, the middle one of which was called "hell."

Pio. Come, to their fortunes.

Bell. Let me see, one, two, three, and four.   I'll begin
with the little friar [1] first.   Here's a fine hand, indeed ! I
never saw friar have such a dainty hand : here's a hand
for a lady !   Here's your fortune :—

You love a friar better than a nun ;

Yet long you'll love no friar, nor no friar's son.

Bow a little, the line of life is out, yet I'm afraid,

For all you're holy, you'll not die a maid.

God give you joy !

Now to you, Friar Tuck.

Mat. God send me good luck !

Bell. You love one, and one loves you :

You're a false knave, and she's a Jew,

Here is a dial that false ever goes—

Mat. O your wit drops !

Bell. Troth, so does your nose—

Nay lets shake hands with you too; pray open, here's a
        fine hand !

Ho friar, ho ! God be here,

So he had need : you'll keep good cheer,

Here's a free table,[2] but a frozen breast,

For you'll starve those that love you best ;

Yet you have good fortune, for if I'm no liar,

Then you are no friar, nor you, nor you no friar,

Haha, haha !   [*Discovers them.*

Duke. Are holy habits cloaks for villany ?

Draw all your weapons !

Hip. Do; draw all your weapons.

Duke. Where are your weapons? draw !

Cas., Pio., &c. The friar has gulled us of 'em.

Mat. O rare trick !

You ha' learnt one mad point of arithmetic.

Hip. Why swells your spleen so high? against what
        bosom

---

[1] *i.e.* Infelice.

[2] A quibble. " Table " also meant the palm of the hand. —*Dyce.*

Would you your weapons draw? her's? 'tis your daughter's:
Mine? 'tis your son's.

Duke. Son?

Mat. Son, by yonder sun.

Hip. You cannot shed blood here but 'tis your own;
To spill your own blood were damnation:
Lay smooth that wrinkled brow, and I will throw
Myself beneath your feet:
Let it be ruggèd still and flinted ore,
What can come forth but sparkles, that will burn
Yourself and us? She's mine; my claim's most good;
She's mine by marriage, though she's yours by blood.

Ans. [*Kneeling.*] I have a hand, dear lord, deep in
this act,
For I foresaw this storm, yet willingly
Put forth to meet it. Oft have I seen a father
Washing the wounds of his dear son in tears,
A son to curse the sword that struck his father,
Both slain i' th' quarrel of your families.
Those scars are now ta'en off; and I beseech you
To seal our pardon! All was to this end,
To turn the ancient hates of your two houses
To fresh green friendship, that your loves might look
Like the spring's forehead, comfortably sweet:
And your vexed souls in peaceful union meet,
Their blood will now be yours, yours will be their's,
And happiness shall crown your silver hairs.

Flu. You see, my lord, there's now no remedy.

Cas., Pio., &c. Beseech your lordship!

Duke. You beseech fair, you have me in place fit
To bridle me—Rise friar, you may be glad
You can make madmen tame, and tame men mad,
Since Fate hath conquered, I must rest content,
To strive now, would but add new punishment:
I yield unto your happiness; be blest,
Our families shall henceforth breathe in rest.

All. Oh, happy change!

Duke. Your's now is my content,
I throw upon your joys my full consent.

Bell. Am not I a good girl, for finding the friar in the well ? God's-so, you are a brave man : will not you buy me some sugar-plums, because I am so good a fortune-teller ?

Duke. Would thou hadst wit, thou pretty soul, to ask,
As I have will to give.

Bell. Pretty soul? a pretty soul is better than a pretty body : do not you know my pretty soul ? I know you : Is not your name Matheo ?

Mat. Yes, lamb.

Bell. Baa lamb ! there you lie, for I am mutton.[1]— Look, fine man ! he was mad for me once, and I was mad for him once, and he was mad for her once, and were you never mad? Yes, I warrant; I had a fine jewel once, a very fine jewel, and that naughty man stole it away from me,—a very fine and a rich jewel.

Duke. What jewel, pretty maid?

Bell. Maid? nay, that's a lie : O, 'twas a very rich jewel, called a maidenhead, and had not you it, leerer ?

Mat. Out, you mad ass ! away.

Duke. Had he thy maidenhead ?
He shall make thee amends, and marry thee.

Bell. Shall he? O brave Arthur of Bradley [2] then?

Duke. And if he bear the mind of a gentleman,
I know he will.

Mat. I think I rifled her of some such paltry jewel.

Duke. Did you ? Then marry her ; you see the wrong
Has led her spirits into a lunacy.

Mat. How? marry her, my lord? 'Sfoot, marry a madwoman? Let a man get the tamest wife he can come by, she'll be mad enough afterward, do what he can.

Duke. Nay then, Father Anselmo here shall do his best,
To bring her to her wits ; and will you then ?

---

[1] *i.e.* A wench, a prostitute.
[2] An allusion to a ballad of that name.

Mat. I cannot tell, I may choose.

Duke. Nay, then, law shall compel : I tell you, sir,
So much her hard fate moves me, you should not breathe
Under this air, unless you married her.

Mat. Well, then, when her wits stand in their right
　　　place,
I'll marry her.

Bell. I thank your grace.—Matheo, thou art mine :
I am not mad, but put on this disguise,
Only for you, my lord ; for you can tell
Much wonder of me, but you are gone : farewell.
Matheo, thou didst first turn my soul black,
Now make it white again : I do protest,
I'm pure as fire now, chaste as Cynthia's breast.

Hip. I durst be sworn, Matheo, she's indeed.

Mat. Cony-catched, gulled, must I sail in your fly-
　　　boat,
Because I helped to rear your main-mast first ?
Plague 'found [1] you for't, 'tis well.
The cuckold's stamp goes current in all nations,
Some men ha' horns giv'n them at their creations,
If I be one of those, why so : 'tis better
To take a common wench, and make her good,
Than one that simpers, and at first will scarce
Be tempted forth over the threshold door,
Yet in one se'nnight, zounds, turns arrant whore !
Come wench, thou shalt be mine, give me thy golls, [2]
We'll talk of legs hereafter.—See, my lord,
God give us joy !

All. God give you joy !

Enter Viola *and* George.

Geo. Come mistress, we are in Bedlam now ; mass and
see, we come in pudding-time, for here's the duke.

Vio. My husband, good my lord.

Duke. Have I thy husband ?

---

[1] *i.e.* Confound.　　　　　　　　　[2] Hands.

THE HONEST WHORE.

PART THE SECOND.

ACT THE FIRST.

SCENE I.—*A Hall in* HIPPOLITO'S *House.*

On one side enter BERALDO, CAROLO, FONTINELL, *and* ASTOLFO, *with* Serving-men, *or* Pages, *attending on them ; on the other side enter* LODOVICO.

OD. Good day, gallants.

All. Good morrow, sweet Lodovico.

Lod. How dost thou, Carolo?

Car. Faith, as the physicians do in a plague, see the world sick, and am well myself.

Fon. Here's a sweet morning, gentlemen.

Lod. Oh, a morning to tempt Jove from his ningle,[1] Ganymede; which is but to give dairy-wenches green gowns as they are going a-milking. What, is thy lord stirring yet?

[1] Favourite.

Ast. Yes, he will not be horsed this hour, sure.

Ber. My lady swears he shall, for she longs to be at court.

Car. Oh, we shall ride switch and spur ; would we were there once.

Enter BRYAN.

Lod. How now, is thy lord ready ?

Bry. No, so crees sa' me, my lady will have some little ting in her pelly first.

Car. Oh, then they'll to breakfast.

Lod. Footman, does my lord ride i'th' coach with my lady, or on horseback ?

Bry. No, foot, la, my lady will have me lord sheet wid her, my lord will sheet in de one side, and my lady sheet in de toder side.   [*Exit.*

Lod. My lady sheet in de toder side ! Did you ever hear a rascal talk so like a pagan ? Is't not strange that a fellow of his star, should be seen here so long in Italy, yet speak so from a Christian ?

Enter ANTONIO, *with a book.*

Ast. An Irishman in Italy ! that so strange ! why, the nation have running heads.   [*They walk up and down.*

Lod. Nay, Carolo, this is more strange, I ha' been in France, there's few of them. Marry, England they count a warm chimney corner, and there they swarm like crickets to the crevice of a brew-house ; but sir, in England I have noted one thing.

Ast., Ber., &c. What's that, what's that of England ?

Lod. Marry this, sir,—what's he yonder ?

Ber. A poor fellow would speak with my lord.

Lod. In England, sir,—troth, I ever laugh when I think on't : to see a whole nation should be marked i'th' forehead, as a man may say, with one iron : why, sir, there all costermongers are Irishmen.

Car. Oh, that's to show their antiquity, as coming from Eve, who was an apple-wife, and they take after the mother.

Ast., Ber., &c. Good, good! ha, ha!

Lod. Why, then, should all your chimney-sweepers likewise be Irishmen? answer that now; come, your wit.

Car. Faith, that's soon answered, for St. Patrick, you know, keeps purgatory; he makes the fire, and his countrymen could do nothing, if they cannot sweep the chimneys.

Ast., Ber., &c. Good again.

Lod. Then, sir, have you many of them, like this fellow, especially those of his hair, footmen to noblemen and others,[1] and the knaves are very faithful where they love. By my faith, very proper men many of them, and as active as the clouds,—whirr, hah!

Ast., Ber., &c. Are they so?

Lod. And stout! exceeding stout; why, I warrant, this precious wild villain, if he were put to't, would fight more desperately than sixteen Dunkirks.[2]

Ast. The women, they say, are very fair.

Lod. No, no, our country *buona-robas,*[3] oh! are the sugarest, delicious rogues!

Ast. Oh, look, he has a feeling of them!

Lod. Not I, I protest. There's a saying when they commend nations. It goes, the Irishman for his hand, the Welshman for a leg, the Englishman for a face, the Dutchman for a beard.

Fon. I'faith, they may make swabbers of them.

Lod. The Spaniard,—let me see,—for a little foot, I take it; the Frenchman,—what a pox hath he? and so of the rest. Are they at breakfast yet? come walk.

Ast. This Lodovico is a notable tongued fellow.

---

[1] The running footmen of those days were generally Irishmen.
[2] Meaning Dunkirk privateers.
[3] *Buona roba* is an Italian phrase for a courtesan.

Fon. Discourses well.

Ber. And a very honest gentleman.

Ast. Oh! he's well valued by my lord.

Enter BELLAFRONT, *with a petition.*

Fon. How now, how now, what's she?

Ber. Let's make towards her.

Bell. Will it be long, sir, ere my lord come forth?

Ast. Would you speak with my lord?

Lod. How now, what's this, a nurse's bill? hath any here got thee with child and now will not keep it?

Bell. No, sir, my business is unto my lord.

Lod. He's about his own wife's now, he'll hardly dispatch two causes in a morning.

Ast. No matter what he says, fair lady; he's a knight, there's no hold to be taken at his words.

Fon. My lord will pass this way presently.

Ber. A pretty, plump rogue.

Ast. A good lusty, bouncing baggage.

Ber. Do you know her?

Lod. A pox on her, I was sure her name was in my table-book once; I know not of what cut her die is now, but she has been more common than tobacco: this is she that had the name of the Honest Whore.

Ast., Ber., &c. Is this she?

Lod. This is the blackamoor that by washing was turned white: this is the birding-piece new scoured: this is she that, if any of her religion can be saved, was saved by my lord Hippolito.

Ast. She has been a goodly creature.

Lod. She has been! that's the epitaph of all whores. I'm well acquainted with the poor gentleman her husband. Lord! what fortunes that man has overreached! She knows not me, yet I have been in her company; I scarce know her, for the beauty of her cheek hath, like the moon, suffered strange eclipses since I beheld it: but women are like medlars,—no sooner ripe but rotten:

A woman last was made, but is spent first.
Yet man is oft proved in performance worst.

Ast., Ber., &c. My lord is come.

Enter HIPPOLITO, INFELICE, *and two* Waiting-women.

Hip. We ha' wasted half this morning. Morrow,
Lodovico.

Lod. Morrow, madam.

Hip. Let's away to horse.

Lod., Ast., &c. Ay, ay, to horse, to horse.

Bell. I do beseech your lordship, let your eye read o'er
this wretched paper.

Hip. I'm in haste, pray thee, good woman, take some
apter time.

Inf. Good woman, do.

Bell. Oh 'las ! it does concern a poor man's life.

Hip. Life ! sweetheart ?—Seat yourself, I'll but read
this and come.

Lod. What stockings have you put on this morning,
madam ? if they be not yellow,[1] change them ; that paper
is a letter from some wench to your husband.

Inf. Oh sir, that cannot make me jealous.

> [*Exeunt all except* HIPPOLITO, BELLAFRONT,
> *and* ANTONIO.

Hip. Your business, sir ? to me ?

Ant. Yes, my good lord.

Hip. Presently, sir.—Are you Matheo's wife ?

Bell. That most unfortunate woman.

Hip. I'm sorry these storms are fallen on him ; I love
        Matheo,
And any good shall do him ; he and I
Have sealed two bonds of friendship, which are strong
In me, however fortune does him wrong.
He speaks here he's condemned.   Is't so ?

Bell. Too true.   [here ;

Hip. What was he whom he killed ? Oh, his name's

---

[1] Yellow was typical of jealousy.

Old Giacomo, son to the Florentine ;
Giacomo, a dog, that to meet profit,
Would to the very eyelids wade in blood
Of his own children.   Tell Matheo,
The duke, my father, hardly shall deny
His signèd pardon ; 'twas fair fight, yes,
If rumour's tongue go true ; so writes he here.—
To-morrow morning I return from court,
Pray be you here then.—I'll have done, sir, straight :—

[To ANTONIO.

But in troth say, are you Matheo's wife?
You have forgot me.

   Bell. No, my lord.

   Hip. Your turner,
That made you smooth to run an even bias,
You know I loved you when your very soul
Was full of discord : art not a good wench still?

   Bell. Umph, when I had lost my way to Heaven, you
      showed it :
I was new born that day.

Re-enter LODOVICO.

   Lod. 'Sfoot, my lord, your lady asks if you have not
left your wench yet?   When you get in once, you never
have done.   Come, come, come, pay your old score, and
send her packing ; come.

   Hip. Ride softly on before, I'll o'ertake you.

   Lod. Your lady swears she'll have no riding on before,
without ye.

   Hip. Prithee, good Lodovico.

   Lod. My lord, pray hasten.

   Hip. I come.   [*Exit* LODOVICO.
To-morrow let me see you, fare you well ;
Commend me to Matheo.   Pray one word more :
Does not your father live about the court?

   Bell. I think he does, but such rude spots of shame
Stick on my cheek, that he scarce knows my name.

Hip. Orlando Friscobaldo, is't not?

Bell. Yes, my lord.

Hip. What does he for you?

Bell. All he should: when children
From duty start, parents from love may swerve;
He nothing does: for nothing I deserve.

Hip. Shall I join him unto you, and restore you to
wonted grace?

Bell. It is impossible.

Hip. It shall be put to trial: fare you well.

[*Exit* BELLAFRONT.

The face I would not look on! Sure then 'twas rare,
When in despite of grief, 'tis still thus fair.
Now, sir, your business with me.

Ant. I am bold
T'express my love and duty to your lordship
In these few leaves.

Hip. A book!

Ant. Yes, my good lord.

Hip. Are you a scholar?

Ant. Yes, my lord, a poor one.

Hip. Sir, you honour me.
Kings may be scholars' patrons, but, faith, tell me,
To how many hands besides hath this bird flown,
How many partners share with me?

Ant. Not one,
In troth, not one: your name I held more dear;
I'm not, my lord, of that low character.

Hip. Your name I pray?

Ant. Antonio Georgio.

Hip. Of Milan?

Ant. Yes, my lord.

Hip. I'll borrow leave
To read you o'er, and then we'll talk: till then
Drink up this gold; good wits should love good wine;
This of your loves, the earnest that of mine.—

[*Gives money.*

Re-enter BRYAN.

How now, sir, where's your lady? not gone yet?

Bry. I fart di lady is run away from dee, a mighty deal of ground, she sent me back for dine own sweet face, I pray dee come, my lord, away, wu't tow go now?

Hip. Is the coach gone? Saddle my horse, the sorrel.

Bry. A pox a' de horse's nose, he is a lousy rascally fellow, when I came to gird his belly, his scurvy guts rumbled; di horse farted in my face, and dow knowest, an Irishman cannot abide a fart. But I have saddled de hobby-horse, di fine hobby is ready, I pray dee my good sweet lord, wi't tow go now, and I will run to de devil before dee?

Hip. Well, sir,—I pray let's see you, master scholar.

Bry. Come, I pray dee, wu't come, sweet face? Go.

[*Exeunt.*

SCENE II. —*An Apartment in the* DUKE'S *Palace.*

Enter LODOVICO, CAROLO, ASTOLFO, *and* BERALDO.

Lod. Godso', gentlemen, what do we forget?

Car., Ast., Ber. What?

Lod. Are not we all enjoined as this day.—Thursday is't not? Ay, as this day to be at the linen-draper's house at dinner?

Car. Signor Candido, the patient man.

Ast. Afore Jove, true, upon this day he's married.

Ber. I wonder, that being so stung with a wasp before, he dares venture again to come about the eaves amongst bees.

Lod. Oh 'tis rare sucking a sweet honey comb! pray

Heaven his old wife be buried deep enough, that she rise not up to call for her dance ! The poor fiddlers' instruments would crack for it, she'd tickle them. At any hand let's try what mettle is in his new bride ; if there be none, we'll put in some. Troth, it's a very noble citizen, I pity he should marry again ; I'll walk along, for it is a good old fellow.

Car. I warrant the wives of Milan would give any fellow twenty thousand ducats, that could but have the face to beg of the duke, that all the citizens in Milan might be bound to the peace of patience, as the linendraper is.

Lod. Oh, fie upon't ! 'twould undo all us that are courtiers, we should have no whoop ! with the wenches then.

Enter HIPPOLITO.

Car., Ast., Ber. My lord's come.

Hip. How now, what news ?

Car., Ast., Ber. None.

Lod. Your lady is with the duke, her father.

Hip. And we'll to them both presently—

Enter ORLANDO FRISCOBALDO.

Who's that !

Car., Ast., Ber. Signor Friscobaldo.

Hip. Friscobaldo, oh ! pray call him, and leave me, we two have business.

Car. Ho Signor ! Signor Friscobaldo ! The Lord Hippolito. [*Exeunt all but* HIPPOLITO *and* FRISCOBALDO.

Orl. My noble lord : my Lord Hippolito ! the duke's son ! his brave daughter's brave husband ! how does your honoured lordship ! does your nobility remember so poor a gentleman as Signor Orlando Friscobaldo ! old mad Orlando !

Hip. Oh, sir, our friends ! they ought to be unto us as our jewels, as dearly valued, being locked up, and unseen, as when we wear them in our hands. I see,

Friscobaldo, age hath not command of your blood, for all Time's sickle has gone over you, you are Orlando still.

Orl. Why, my lord, are not the fields mown and cut down, and stripped bare, and yet wear they not pied coats again? Though my head be like a leek, white, may not my heart be like the blade, green?

Hip. Scarce can I read the stories on your brow, Which age hath writ there; you look youthful still.

Orl. I eat snakes,[1] my lord, I eat snakes. My heart shall never have a wrinkle in it, so long as I can cry "Hem," with a clear voice.

Hip. You are the happier man, sir.

Orl. Happy man? I'll give you, my lord, the true picture of a happy man; I was turning leaves over this morning, and found it; an excellent Italian painter drew it; if I have it in the right colours, I'll bestow it on your lordship.

Hip. I stay for it.

Orl. He that makes gold his wife, but not his whore, He that at noon-day walks by a prison door, He that i'th' sun is neither beam nor mote, He that's not mad after a petticoat, He for whom poor men's curses dig no grave, He that is neither lord's nor lawyer's slave, He that makes this his sea, and that his shore, He that in's coffin is richer than before, He that counts youth his sword, and age his staff, He whose right hand carves his own epitaph, He that upon his deathbed is a swan, And dead, no crow—he is a happy man.

Hip. It's very well; I thank you for this picture.

Orl. After this picture, my lord, do I strive to have my face drawn: for I am not covetous, am not in debt; sit neither at the duke's side, nor lie at his feet. Wenching and I have done; no man I wrong, no man I fear, no man I fee; I take heed how far I walk, because I know

---

[1] A supposed recipe for restoring youth.—*Dyce.*

yonder's my home ; I would not die like a rich man, to carry nothing away save a winding sheet : but like a good man, to leave Orlando behind me. I sowed leaves in my youth, and I reap now books in my age. I fill this hand, and empty this ; and when the bell shall toll for me, if I prove a swan, and go singing to my nest, why so ! If a crow ! throw me out for carrion, and pick out mine eyes. May not old Friscobaldo, my lord, be merry now ! ha ?

Hip. You may ; would I were partner in your mirth.

Orl. I have a little, have all things. I have nothing ; I have no wife, I have no child, have no chick ; and why should not I be in my jocundare ?

Hip. Is your wife then departed ?

Orl. She's an old dweller in those high countries, yet not from me. Here, she's here : but before me, when a knave and a quean are married, they commonly walk like serjeants together : but a good couple are seldom parted.

Hip. You had a daughter too, sir, had you not ?

Orl. O my lord ! this old tree had one branch, and but one branch growing out of it. It was young, it was fair, it was straight ; I pruned it daily, dressed it carefully, kept it from the wind, helped it to the sun, yet for all my skill in planting, it grew crooked, it bore crabs ; I hewed it down ; what's become of it, I neither know, nor care.

Hip. Then I can tell you what's become of it ;
That branch is withered.

Orl. So 'twas long ago.

Hip. Her name I think was Bellafront, she's dead.

Orl. Ha ? dead ?

Hip. Yes ; what of her was left, not worth the keeping, Even in my sight was thrown into a grave.

Orl. Dead ! my last and best peace go with her ! I see Death's a good trencherman, he can eat coarse homely meat, as well as the daintiest.

Hip. Why, Friscobaldo, was she homely ?

Orl. O my lord ! a strumpet is one of the devil's vines ; all the sins, like so many poles, are stuck upright out of

hell, to be her props, that she may spread upon them.
And when she's ripe, every slave has a pull at her, then
must she be pressed. The young beautiful grape sets the
teeth of lust on edge, yet to taste that liquorish wine, is to
drink a man's own damnation. Is she dead?

Hip. She's turned to earth.

Orl. Would she were turned to Heaven! Umph, is she
dead? I am glad the world has lost one of his idols; no
whoremonger will at midnight beat at the doors. In her
grave sleep all my shame, and her own; and all my
sorrows, and all her sins!

Hip. I'm glad you're wax, not marble; you are made
Of man's best temper; there are now good hopes
That all these heaps of ice about your heart,
By which a father's love was frozen up,
Are thawed in these sweet showers, fetched from your
We are ne'er like angels till our passion dies. [eyes;
She is not dead, but lives under worse fate;
I think she's poor; and more to clip her wings,
Her husband at this hour lies in the jail,
For killing of a man. To save his blood,
Join all your force with mine : mine shall be shown :
The getting of his life preserves your own.

Orl. In my daughter, you will say! does she live then?
I am sorry I wasted tears upon a harlot; but the best is
I have a handkercher to drink them up, soap can wash
them all out again. Is she poor?

Hip. Trust me, I think she is.

Orl. Then she's a right strumpet; I ne'er knew any of
their trade rich two years together; sieves can hold no
water, nor harlots hoard up money; they have too many
vents, too many sluices to let it out; taverns, tailors,
bawds, panders, fiddlers, swaggerers, fools and knaves do
all wait upon a common harlot's trencher : she is the galli-
pot to which these drones fly, not for love to the pot,
but for the sweet sucket[1] within it, her money, her money.

___
[1] Preserve.

Hip. I almost dare pawn my word, her bosom
Gives warmth to no such snakes. When did you see her?

Orl. Not seventeen summers.

Hip. Is your hate so old?

Orl. Older; it has a white head, and shall never die
till she be buried: her wrongs shall be my bedfellow.

Hip. Work yet his life, since in it lives her fame.

Orl. No, let him hang, and half her infamy departs
out of the world: I hate him for her; he taught her first
to taste poison; I hate her for herself, because she
refused my physic.

Hip. Nay, but Friscobaldo!—

Orl. I detest her, I defy [1] both, she's not mine,
she's—

Hip. Hear her but speak.

Orl. I love no mermaids, I'll not be caught with a
quail-pipe. [2]

Hip. You're now beyond all reason.

Orl. I am then a beast. Sir, I had rather be a beast,
and not dishonour my creation, than be a doting father,
and like Time, be the destruction of mine own
brood.

Hip. Is't dotage to relieve your child, being poor?

Orl. Is't fit for an old man to keep a whore?

Hip. 'Tis charity too.

Orl. 'Tis foolery; relieve her!
Were her cold limbs stretched out upon a bier,
I would not sell this dirt under my nails
To buy her an hour's breath, nor give this hair,
Unless it were to choke her.

Hip. Fare you well, for I'll trouble you no more.

Orl. And fare you well, sir. [*Exit* HIPPOLITO.] Go
thy ways; we have few lords of thy making, that love
wenches for their honesty. 'Las my girl! art thou
poor? poverty dwells next door to despair, there's
but a wall between them; despair is one of hell's

---

[1] Renounce.   [2] Made use of by fowlers to allure quails.

Cand. Oh, peace, I pray thee, thus far off I stand,
I spied the error of my servants;
She called for claret, and you filled out sack;
That cup give me, 'tis for an old man's back,
And not for hers.   Indeed, 'twas but mistaken;
Ask all these else.

Guests. No faith, 'twas but mistaken.

1st Pren. Nay, she took it right enough.

Cand. Good Luke, reach her that glass of claret.
Here mistress bride, pledge me there.

Bride. Now I'll none.   [*Exit.*

Cand. How now?

Lod. Look what your mistress ails.

1st Pren. Nothing, sir, but about filling a wrong glass,
—a scurvy trick.

Cand. I pray you, hold your tongue.—My servant there
tells me she is not well.

Guests. Step to her, step to her.

Lod. A word with you : do ye hear?   This wench,
your new wife, will take you down in your wedding shoes,
unless you hang her up in her wedding garters.

Cand. How, hang her in her garters?

Lod. Will you be a tame pigeon still?   Shall your back
be like a tortoise shell, to let carts go over it, yet not to
break?   This she-cat will have more lives than your last
puss had, and will scratch worse, and mouse you worse :
look to't.

Cand. What would you have me do, sir?

Lod. What would I have you do?   Swear, swagger,
brawl, fling! for fighting it's no matter, we ha' had knocking pusses enow already; you know, that a woman was
made of the rib of a man, and that rib was crooked.   The
moral of which is, that a man must, from his beginning
be crooked to his wife; be you like an orange to her, let
her cut you never so fair, be you sour as vinegar.   Will
you be ruled by me?

Cand. In any thing that's civil, honest, and just.

Lod. Have you ever a prentice's suit will fit me?

Cand. I have the very same which myself wore.

Lod. I'll send my man for't within this half hour, and within this two hour I'll be your prentice. The hen shall not overcrow the cock; I'll sharpen your spurs.

Cand. It will be but some jest, sir?

Lod. Only a jest: farewell, come, Carolo.

        [*Exeunt* LODOVICO, CAROLO, *and* ASTOLFO.

Guests. We'll take our leaves, sir, too.

Cand. Pray conceit not ill
Of my wife's sudden rising. This young knight,
Sir Lodovico, is deep seen in physic,
And he tells me, the disease called the mother,[1]
Hangs on my wife, it is a vehement heaving
And beating of the stomach, and that swelling
Did with the pain thereof cramp up her arm,
That hit his lips, and brake the glass,—no harm,
It was no harm!

Guests. No, signor, none at all.

Cand. The straightest arrow may fly wide by chance.
But come, we'll close this brawl up in some dance.

                      [*Exeunt.*

[1] Hysteria.

ACT THE SECOND.

SCENE I.—*A Room in* Matheo's *House.*

Enter Bellafront *and* Matheo.

ELL. O my sweet husband! wert thou in thy grave and art alive again? Oh welcome, welcome!

Mat. Dost know me? my cloak, prithee, lay't up. Yes, faith, my winding-sheet was taken out of lavender, to be stuck with rosemary[1]: I lacked but the knot here, or here; yet if I had had it, I should ha' made a wry mouth at the world like a plaice[2]: but sweetest villain, I am here now and I will talk with thee soon.

Bell. And glad am I thou art here.

Mat. Did these heels caper in shackles? Ah! my little plump rogue, I'll bear up for all this, and fly high. *Catso catso.*[3]

Bell. Matheo?

Mat. What sayest, what sayest? O brave fresh air! a pox on these grates and gingling of keys, and rattling of iron. I'll bear up, I'll fly high, wench, hang toff.

Bell. Matheo, prithee, make thy prison thy glass,
And in it view the wrinkles, and the scars,
By which thou wert disfigured; viewing them, mend them.

---

[1] Rosemary was used as an emblem of remembrance at both funerals and weddings.
[2] A favourite simile with the writers of the time.
[3] *Ital.* A term of abuse or contempt.

Mat. I'll go visit all the mad rogues now, and the good roaring boys.[1]

Bell. Thou dost not hear me?

Mat. Yes, faith, do I.

Bell. Thou has been in the hands of misery, and ta'en strong physic; prithee now be sound.

Mat. Yes. 'Sfoot, I wonder how the inside of a tavern looks now. Oh, when shall I bizzle, bizzle?[2]

Bell. Nay, see, thou'rt thirsty still for poison! Come, I will not have thee swagger.

Mat. Honest ape's face!

Bell. 'Tis that sharpened an axe to cut thy throat.
Good love, I would not have thee sell thy substance
And time, worth all, in those damned shops of hell;
Those dicing houses, that stand never well,
But when they stand most ill; that four-squared sin
Has almost lodged us in the beggar's inn.
Besides, to speak which even my soul does grieve,
A sort of ravens have hung upon thy sleeve,
And fed upon thee: good Mat, if you please,
Scorn to spread wing amongst so base as these;
By them thy fame is speckled, yet it shows
Clear amongst them; so crows are fair with crows.
Custom in sin, gives sin a lovely dye;
Blackness in Moors is no deformity.

Mat. Bellafront, Bellafront, I protest to thee, I swear, as I hope for my soul, I will turn over a new leaf.   The prison I confess has bit me; the best man that sails in such a ship, may be lousy.   [*Knocking within.*

Bell. One knocks at door.

Mat. I'll be the porter: they shall see a jail cannot hold a brave spirit, I'll fly high.   [*Exit.*

Bell. How wild is his behaviour! Oh, I fear

---

[1] Roystering young gallants.   A highly favourable female version of the type is given in Dekker and Middleton's comedy, *The Roaring Girl.*
[2] *i.e.* Get a chance of drinking to excess.

He's spoiled by prison, he's half damned comes there,
But I must sit all storms : when a full sail
His fortunes spread, he loved me : being now poor,
I'll beg for him, and no wife can do more.

Re-enter MATHEO, *with* ORLANDO *disguised as a*
Serving-man.

Mat. Come in, pray ! would you speak with me, sir?
Orl. Is your name Signor Matheo ?
Mat. My name is Signor Matheo.
Orl. Is this gentlewoman your wife, sir ?
Mat. This gentlewoman is my wife, sir.
Orl. The Destinies spin a strong and even thread of
both your loves !—The mother's own face, I ha' not
forgot that. [*Aside.*] I'm an old man, sir, and am troubled
with a whoreson salt rheum, that I cannot hold my water.
—Gentlewoman, the last man I served was your father.
Bell. My father? any tongue that sounds his name,
Speaks music to me ; welcome, good old man !
How does my father ? lives he ? has he health ?
How does my father ?—I so much do shame him,
So much do wound him, that I scarce dare name him.

                                                    [*Aside.*

Orl. I can speak no more.
Mat. How now, old lad, what dost cry ?
Orl. The rheum still, sir, nothing else ; I should be
well seasoned, for mine eyes lie in brine. Look you, sir,
I have a suit to you.
Mat. What is't, my little white-pate ?
Orl. Troth, sir, I have a mind to serve your worship.
Mat. To serve me ? Troth, my friend, my fortunes
are, as a man may say—
Orl. Nay, look you, sir, I know, when all sins are old
in us, and go upon crutches, that covetousness does but
then lie in her cradle ; 'tis not so with me. Lechery loves
to dwell in the fairest lodging, and covetousness in the
oldest buildings, that are ready to fall : but my white

head, sir, is no inn for such a gossip.   If a serving-man at
my years, that has sailed about the world, be not stored
with biscuit enough to serve him the voyage out of his
life, and to bring him East home, ill pity but all his days
should be fasting days.   I care not so much for wages, for
I have scraped a handful of gold together.   I have a
little money, sir, which I would put into your worship's
hands, not so much to make it more—

Mat. No, no, you say well, thou sayest well; but I
must tell you,—how much is the money, sayest thou ?

Orl. About twenty pound, sir.

Mat. Twenty pound ?   Let me see : that shall bring
thee in, after ten *per centum per annum.*

Orl. No, no, no, sir, no : I cannot abide to have
money engender : fie upon this silver lechery, fie ; if I may
have meat to my mouth, and rags to my back, and a flock-
bed to snort upon when I die, the longer liver take all.

Mat. A good old boy, i'faith !   If thou servest me,
thou shalt eat as *I* eat, drink as *I* drink, lie as *I* lie, and
ride as *I* ride.

Orl. That's if you have money to hire horses.   [*Aside.*

Mat. Front, what dost thou think on't ?   This good
old lad here shall serve me.

Bell. Alas, Matheo, wilt thou load a back
That is already broke ?

Mat. Peace, pox on you, peace.   There's a trick in't,
I fly high, it shall be so, Front, as I tell you : give me
thy hand, thou shalt serve me i'faith : welcome : as for
your money—

Orl. Nay, look you, sir, I have it here.

Mat. Pish, keep it thyself, man, and then thou'rt sure
'tis safe.

Orl. Safe ! an' twere ten thousand ducats, your worship
should be my cash-keeper ; I have heard what your
worship is, an excellent dunghill cock, to scatter all
abroad ; but I'll venture twenty pounds on's head.

[*Gives money to* MATHEO.

Mat. And didst thou serve my worshipful father-in-law, Signor Orlando Friscobaldo, that madman, once?

Orl. I served him so long, till he turned me out of doors.

Mat. It's a notable chuff[1] : I ha' not seen him many a day.

Orl. No matter an you ne'er see him; it's an arrant grandee, a churl, and as damned a cut-throat.

Bell. Thou villain, curb thy tongue! thou art a Judas, To sell thy master's name to slander thus.

Mat. Away, ass! He speaks but truth, thy father is a—

Bell. Gentleman.

Mat. And an old knave. There's more deceit in him than in sixteen 'pothecaries : it's a devil; thou mayest beg, starve, hang, damn! does he send thee so much as a cheese?

Orl. Or so much as a gammon of bacon, He'll give it his dogs first.

Mat. A jail, a jail.

Orl. A Jew, a Jew, sir.

Mat. A dog!

Orl. An English mastiff, sir.

Mat. Pox rot out his old stinking garbage!

Bell. Art not ashamed to strike an absent man thus? Art not ashamed to let this vile dog bark, And bite my father thus? I'll not endure it. Out of my doors, base slave!

Mat. Your doors? a vengeance! I shall live to cut that old rogue's throat, for all you take his part thus.

Orl. He shall live to see thee hanged first. [*Aside.*

Enter HIPPOLITO.

Mat. God's-so, my lord, your lordship is most welcome, I'm proud of this, my lord.

Hip. Was bold to see you. Is that your wife?

[1] See note *ante*, p. 99.

Mat. Yes, sir.

Hip. I'll borrow her lip.   [*Kisses* BELLAFRONT.

Mat. With all my heart, my lord.

Orl. Who's this, I pray, sir.

Mat. My Lord Hippolito : what's thy name ?

Orl. Pacheco.

Mat. Pacheco, fine name ; thou seest, Pacheco, I keep
company with no scoundrels, nor base fellows.

Hip. Came not my footman to you ?

Bell. Yes, my lord.

Hip. I sent by him a diamond and a letter,
Did you receive them ?

Bell. Yes, my lord, I did.

Hip. Read you the letter ?

Bell. O'er and o'er tis read.

Hip. And, faith, your answer ?

Bell. Now the time's not fit,
You see, my husband's here.

Hip. I'll now then leave you,
And choose mine hour ; but ere I part away,
Hark you, remember I must have no nay—
Matheo, I will leave you.

Mat. A glass of wine.

Hip. Not now, I'll visit you at other times.
You're come off well, then ?

Mat. Excellent well.   I thank your lordship : I owe
you my life, my lord ; and will pay my best blood in any
service of yours.

Hip. I'll take no such dear payment.   Hark you,
Matheo, I know the prison is a gulf.   If money run low
with you, my purse is your's : call for it.

Mat. Faith, my lord, I thank my stars, they send me
down some ; I cannot sink, so long these bladders
hold.

Hip. I will not see your fortunes ebb, pray, try.
To starve in full barns were fond[1] modesty.

[1] Foolish.

Bell. 'Tis all gold.

Orl. 'Tis like so : it may be, he thinks you want money, and therefore bestows his alms bravely, like a lord.

Bell. He thinks a silver net can catch the poor;
Here's bait to choke a nun, and turn her whore.
Wilt thou be honest to me ?

Orl. As your nails to your fingers, which I think never deceived you.

Bell. Thou to this lord shalt go, commend me to him,
And tell him this, the town has held out long,
Because within 'twas rather true than strong.
To sell it now were base ; Say 'tis no hold
Built of weak stuff, to be blown up with gold.
He shall believe thee by this token, or this ;
If not, by this.   [*Giving purse, ring and letters.*

Orl. Is this all ?

Bell. This is all.

Orl. Mine own girl still !   [*Aside.*

Bell. A star may shoot, not fall.   [*Exit.*

Orl. A star ? nay, thou art more than the moon, for thou hast neither changing quarters, nor a man standing in thy circle with a bush of thorns. Is't possible the Lord Hippolito, whose face is as civil as the outside of a dedicatory book, should be a muttonmonger ?[1] A poor man has but one ewe, and this grandee sheep-biter leaves whole flocks of fat wethers, whom he may knock down, to devour this. I'll trust neither lord nor butcher with quick flesh for this trick ; the cuckoo, I see now, sings all the year, though every man cannot hear him ; but I'll spoil his notes. Can neither love-letters, nor the devil's common pick-locks, gold, nor precious stones make my girl draw up her percullis ?[2] Hold out still, wench.
All are not bawds, I see now, that keep doors,
Nor all good wenches that are marked for whores. [*Exit.*

---

[1] Whoremonger.   [2] Portcullis.

SCENE II.—*Before* CANDIDO'S *Shop.*

Enter CANDIDO, *and* LODOVICO *disguised as a* Prentice.

Lod. Come, come, come, what do ye lack, sir? what do ye lack, sir? what is't ye lack, sir? Is not my worship well suited? did you ever see a gentleman better disguised?

Cand. Never, believe me, signor.

Lod. Yes, but when he has been drunk. There be prentices would make mad gallants, for they would spend all, and drink, and whore, and so forth; and I see we gallants could make mad prentices. How does thy wife like me? Nay, I must not be so saucy, then I spoil all: pray you how does my mistress like me?

Cand. Well; for she takes you for a very simple fellow.

Lod. And they that are taken for such are commonly the arrantest knaves: but to our comedy, come.

Cand. I shall not act it; chide, you say, and fret,
And grow impatient: I shall never do't.

Lod. 'Sblood, cannot you do as all the world does, counterfeit?

Cand. Were I a painter, that should live by drawing
Nothing but pictures of an angry man,
I should not earn my colours; I cannot do't.

Lod. Remember you're a linen-draper, and that if you give your wife a yard, she'll take an ell: give her not therefore a quarter of your yard, not a nail.

Cand. Say I should turn to ice, and nip her love
Now 'tis but in the bud.

Lod. Well, say she's nipt.

Cand. It will so overcharge her heart with grief,
That like a cannon, when her sighs go off,
She in her duty either will recoil,
Or break in pieces and so die: her death,
By my unkindness might be counted murder.

Lod. Die? never, never. I do not bid you beat her, nor give her black eyes, nor pinch her sides; but cross

Keep the laws of the noble science, sir, and measure
weapons with her; your yard is a plain heathenish
weapon; 'tis too short, she may give you a handful, and
yet you'll not reach her.

 Cand. Yet I ha' the longer arm.—Come fall to't roundly,
And spare not me, wife, for I'll lay't on soundly:
If o'er husbands their wives will needs be masters,
We men will have a law to win't at wasters.[1]

 Lod. 'Tis for the breeches, is't not?

 Cand. For the breeches!

 Bride. Husband, I'm for you, I'll not strike in jest.

 Cand. Nor I.

 Bride. But will you sign to one request?

 Cand. What's that?

 Bride. Let me give the first blow,

 Cand. The first blow, wife? shall I?

 Lod. Let her ha't:
If she strike hard, in to her, and break her pate.

 Cand. A bargain: strike!

 Bride. Then guard you from this blow,
For I play all at legs, but 'tis thus low.   [*Kneels.*
Behold, I'm such a cunning fencer grown,
I keep my ground, yet down I will be thrown
With the least blow you give me: I disdain
The wife that is her husband's sovereign.
She that upon your pillow first did rest,
They say, the breeches wore, which I detest:
The tax which she imposed on you, I abate you;
If me you make your master, I shall hate you.
The world shall judge who offers fairest play;
You win the breeches, but I win the day.

 Cand. Thou win'st the day indeed, give me thy hand;
I'll challenge thee no more: my patient breast
Played thus the rebel, only for a jest:
Here's the rank rider, that breaks colts; 'tis he
Can tame the mad folks, and curst wives easily.

---

[1] Cudgels.

Bride. Who? your man?

Cand. My man? my master, though his head be bare,
But he's so courteous, he'll put off his hair.

Lod. Nay, if your service be so hot a man cannot keep
his hair on, I'll serve you no longer.

　　　　　　　　　　　　　　[Takes off his false hair.

Bride. Is this your schoolmaster?

Lod. Yes, faith, wench, I taught him to take thee
down: I hope thou canst take him down without
teaching;

You ha' got the conquest, and you both are friends.

Cand. Bear witness else.

Lod. My prenticeship then ends.

Cand. For the good service you to me have done,
I give you all your years.

Lod. I thank you, master.
I'll kiss my mistress now, that she may say,
My man was bound, and free all in one day.　　*[Exeunt.*

ACT THE THIRD.

SCENE I.—*An Apartment in* HIPPOLITO'S *House.*

Enter INFELICE, *and* ORLANDO *disguised as a* Serving-man.

NF. From whom sayst thou?

Orl. From a poor gentlewoman, madam, whom I serve.

Inf. And what's your business?

Orl. This madam: my poor mistress has a waste piece of ground, which is her own by inheritance, and left to her by her mother. There's a lord now that goes about not to take it clean from her, but to enclose it to himself, and to join it to a piece of his lordship's.

Inf. What would she have me do in this?

Orl. No more, madam, but what one woman should do for another in such a case. My honourable lord your husband, would do any thing in her behalf, but she had rather put herself into your hands, because you, a woman, may do more with the duke, your father.

Inf. Where lies this land?

Orl. Within a stone's cast of this place; my mistress, I think, would be content to let him enjoy it after her decease, if that would serve his turn, so my master would yield too; but she cannot abide to hear that the lord should meddle with it in her lifetime.

Inf. Is she then married? why stirs not her husband in it?

Orl. Her husband stirs in it underhand : but because the other is a great rich man, my master is loath to be seen in it too much.

Inf. Let her in writing draw the cause at large :
And I will move the duke.

Orl. 'Tis set down, madam, here in black and white already : work it so madam, that she may keep her own without disturbance, grievance, molestation, or meddling of any other; and she bestows this purse of gold on your ladyship.

Inf. Old man, I'll plead for her, but take no fees :
Give lawyers them, I swim not in that flood ;
I'll touch no gold, till I have done her good.

Orl. I would all proctors' clerks were of your mind, I should law more amongst them than I do then ; here, madam, is the survey, not only of the manor itself, but of the grange-house, with every meadow, pasture, plough-land, cony-burrow, fish-pond, hedge, ditch, and bush, that stands in it. *[Gives a letter.*

Inf. My husband's name, and hand and seal at arms
To a love letter? Where hadst thou this writing?

Orl. From the foresaid party, madam, that would keep the foresaid land out of the foresaid lord's fingers.

Inf. My lord turned ranger now?

Orl. You're a good huntress, lady ; you ha' found your game already : your lord would fain be a ranger, but my mistress requests you to let him run a course in your own park. If you'll not do't for love, then do't for money ! she has no white money, but there's gold ; or else she prays you to ring him by this token, and so you shall be sure his nose will not be rooting other men's pastures.

[Gives purse and ring.

Inf. This very purse was woven with mine own hands ;
This diamond on that very night, when he
Untied my virgin girdle, gave I him :

And must a common harlot share in mine?
Old man, to quit thy pains, take thou the gold.

Orl. Not I, madam, old serving-men want no money.

Inf. Cupid himself was sure his secretary;
These lines are even the arrows love let flies,
The very ink dropt out of Venus' eyes.

Orl. I do not think, madam, but he fetched off some
poet or other for those lines, for they are parlous hawks
to fly at wenches.

Inf. Here's honied poison! To me he ne'er thus writ;
But lust can set a double edge on wit.

Orl. Nay, that's true, madam, a wench will whet any
thing, if it be not too dull.

Inf. Oaths, promises, preferments, jewels, gold,
What snares should break, if all these cannot hold?
What creature is thy mistress?

Orl. One of those creatures that are contrary to man;
a woman.

Inf. What manner of woman?

Orl. A little tiny woman, lower than your ladyship by
head and shoulders, but as mad a wench as ever unlaced
a petticoat: these things should I indeed have delivered
to my lord, your husband.

Inf. They are delivered better: why should she
Send back these things?

Orl. 'Ware, 'ware, there's knavery.

Inf. Strumpets, like cheating gamesters, will not win
At first: these are but baits to draw him in.
How might I learn his hunting hours?

Orl. The Irish footman can tell you all his hunting
hours, the park he hunts in, the doe he would strike;
that Irish shackatory[1] beats the bush for him, and knows
all; he brought that letter, and that ring; he is the carrier.

Inf. Knowest thou what other gifts have passed between them?

Orl. Little Saint Patrick knows all.

---

[1] A hound,—derived from "Shake a Tory."

Inf. Him I'll examine presently.

Orl. Not whilst I am here, sweet madam.

Inf. Be gone then, and what lies in me command.

[*Exit* ORLANDO.

Enter BRYAN.

Inf. How much cost those satins,
And cloth of silver, which my husband sent by you
To a low gentlewoman yonder?

Bry. Faat satins? faat silvers, faat low gentlefolks?
dow pratest dow knowest not what, i'faat, la.

Inf. She there, to whom you carried letters.

Bry. By dis hand and bod dow saist true, if I did so,
oh how? I know not a letter a' de book i'faat, la.

Inf. Did your lord never send you with a ring, sir,
Set with a diamond?

Bry. Never, sa *crees*[1] fa' me, never! he may run at a
towsand rings i'faat, and I never hold his stirrup, till he
leap into de saddle. By Saint Patrick, madam, I never
touch my lord's diamond, nor ever had to do, i'faat, la,
with any of his precious stones.

Enter HIPPOLITO.

Inf. Are you so close, you bawd, you pandering slave?

[*Strikes* BRYAN.

Hip. How now? why, Infelice; what's your quarrel?

Inf. Out of my sight, base varlet! get thee gone.

Hip. Away, you rogue!

Bry. *Slawne loot*,[2] fare de well, fare de well. *Ah
marragh frofat boddah breen!*[3]   [*Exit.*

Hip. What, grown a fighter? prithee, what's the matter?

Inf. If you'll needs know, it was about the clock:
How works the day, my lord, pray, by your watch?

Hip. Lest you cuff me, I'll tell you presently: I am
near two.

---

[1] *Críosd*—Christ.
[2] Irish : *Slán lúitheach*—A joyous farewell (?).
[3] Irish : *As a márach frómhadh bodach bréan*—On the morrow of
a feast, a clown is a beast.

Inf. How, two ?   I'm scarce at one.

Hip. One of us then goes false.

Inf. Then sure 'tis you,

Mine goes by heaven's dial, the sun, and it goes true.

    Hip. I think, indeed, mine runs somewhat too fast.

    Inf. Set it to mine at one then.

    Hip. One ? 'tis past :

'Tis past one by the sun.

    Inf. Faith, then, belike,

Neither your clock nor mine does truly strike ;

And since it is uncertain which goes true,

Better be false at one, than false at two.

    Hip. You're very pleasant, madam.

    Inf. Yet not merry.

    Hip. Why, Infelice, what should make you sad ?

    Inf. Nothing, my lord, but my false watch : pray, tell

You see, my clock or yours is out of frame,   [me,—

Must we upon the workmen lay the blame,

Or on ourselves that keep them ?

    Hip. Faith on both.

He may by knavery spoil them, we by sloth.

But why talk you all riddle thus ? I read

Strange comments in those margins of your looks :

Your cheeks of late are like bad printed books,

So dimly charactered, I scarce can spell

One line of love in them.   Sure all's not well.

    Inf. All is not well indeed, my dearest lord ;

Lock up thy gates of hearing, that no sound

Of what I speak may enter.

    Hip. What means this ?

    Inf. Or if my own tongue must myself betray,

Count it a dream, or turn thine eyes away,

And think me not thy wife.   [*Kneels.*

    Hip. Why do you kneel ?

    Inf. Earth is sin's cushion : when the sick soul feels

Herself growing poor, then she turns beggar, cries,

And kneels for help : Hippolito, for husband

I dare not call thee, I have stolen that jewel
Of my chaste honour, which was only thine,
And given it to a slave.
   Hip. Ha?
   Inf. On thy pillow
Adultery and lust have slept, thy groom
Hath climbed the unlawful tree, and plucked the sweets,
A villain hath usurped a husband's sheets.
   Hip. S'death, who?—a cuckold!—who?
   Inf. This Irish footman.
   Hip. Worse than damnation! a wild kerne,[1] a frog,
A dog: whom I'll scarce spurn.   Longed you for sham-
      rock?
Were it my father's father, heart, I'll kill him,
Although I take him on his death-bed gasping
'Twixt Heaven and hell! a shag-haired cur! Bold strum-
Why hang'st thou on me? think'st I'll be a bawd   [pet,
To a whore, because she's noble?
   Inf. I beg but this,
Set not my shame out to the world's broad eye,
Yet let thy vengeance, like my fault, soar high,
So it be in darkened clouds.
   Hip. Darkened! my horns
Cannot be darkened, nor shall my revenge.
A harlot to my slave? the act is base,
Common, but foul, so shall not thy disgrace.
Could not I feed your appetite? O women
You were created angels, pure and fair;
But since the first fell, tempting devils you are,
You should be men's bliss, but you prove their rods:
Were there no women, men might live like gods;
You ha' been too much down already; rise,
Get from my sight, and henceforth shun my bed;
I'll with no strumpet's breath be poisonèd.
As for your Irish lubrican, that spirit
Whom by preposterous charms thy lust hath raised

---

[1] A rough sturdy fellow.   Irish: *Ceithearneach*—A soldier.

In a wrong circle, him I'll damn more black
Then any tyrant's soul.

   Inf. Hippolito !

   Hip. Tell me, didst thou bait hooks to draw him to
Or did he bewitch.thee ?   [thee,

   Inf. The slave did woo me.

   Hip. Tu-whoos in that screech-owl's language Oh,
       who'd trust

Your cork-heeled sex ?   I think to sate your lust,
You'd love a horse, a bear, a croaking toad,
So your hot itching veins might have their bound :
Then the wild Irish dart[1] was thrown ?   Come, how ?
The manner of this fight ?

   Inf. 'Twas thus, he gave me this battery first.—Oh, I
Mistake—believe me, all this in beaten gold ;
Yet I held out, but at length thus was charmed.

                  [*Gives letter, purse and ring.*

What ? change your diamond, wench, the act is base,
Common, but foul, so shall not your disgrace :
Could not I feed your appetite ?   O men,
You were created angels, pure and fair,
But since the first fell, worse than devils you are.
You should our shields be, but you prove our rods.
Were there no men, women might live like gods.
Guilty, my lord ?

   Hip. Yes, guilty my good lady.

   Inf. Nay, you may laugh, but henceforth shun my
       bed,

With no whore's leavings I'll be poisonèd.   [*Exit.*

   Hip. O'er-reached so finely ?   'Tis the very diamond
And letter which I sent : this villany
Some spider closely weaves, whose poisonèd bulk
I must let forth.   Who's there without ?

   Ser. [*Within.*] My lord calls ?

   Hip. Send me the footman.

   [1] An allusion to the darts carried by the Irish running footmen.—
Dyce.

Ser. [*Within.*] Call the footman to my lord,—Bryan, Bryan!

Hip. It can be no man else, that Irish Judas,
Bred in a country where no venom prospers
But in the nation's blood, hath thus betrayed me.

Re-enter BRYAN.

Slave, get you from your service.

Bry. Faat meanest thou by this now?

Hip. Question me not, nor tempt my fury, villain
Couldst thou turn all the mountains in the land,
To hills of gold, and give me : here thou stayest not.

Bry. I'faat, I care not.

Hip. Prate not, but get thee gone, I shall send else.

Bry. Ay, do predy, I had rather have thee make a scabbard of my guts, and let out all de Irish puddings in my poor belly, den to be a false knave to de, i'faat! I will never see dine own sweet face more. *A mawhid deer a gra,*[1] fare dee well, fare dee well; I will go steal cows again in Ireland.   [*Exit.*

Hip. He's damned that raised this whirlwind, which
hath blown
Into her eyes this jealousy : yet I'll on,
I'll on, stood armed devils staring in my face,
To be pursued in flight, quickens the race,
Shall my blood-streams by a wife's lust be barred?
Fond[2] woman, no : iron grows by strokes more hard ;
Lawless desires are seas scorning all bounds,
Or sulphur, which being rammed up, more confounds,
Struggling with madmen madness nothing tames,
Winds wrestling with great fires incense the flames.
                [*Exit.*

[1] Irish : *Maighisdir mo grádh*—Master of my love.   [2] Foolish.

Bell. I care not for gay feathers, I.

Mat. What dost care for then? why dost grieve?

Bell. Why do I grieve? A thousand sorrows strike
At one poor heart, and yet it lives. Matheo,
Thou art a gamester, prithee, throw at all,
Set all upon one cast. We kneel and pray,
And struggle for life, yet must be cast away.
Meet misery quickly then, split all, sell all,
And when thou'st sold all, spend it; but I beseech thee
Build not thy mind on me to coin thee more,
To get it wouldst thou have me play the whore?

Mat. 'Twas your profession before I married you.

Bell. Umh? it was indeed : if all men should be branded
For sins long since laid up, who could be saved?
The quarter-day's at hand, how will you do
To pay the rent, Matheo?

Mat. Why? do as all of our occupation do against
quarter-days : break up house, remove, shift your lodgings : pox a' your quarters!

Enter LODOVICO.

Lod. Where's this gallant?

Mat. Signor Lodovico? how does my little Mirror of
Knighthood?[1] this is kindly done i'faith : welcome, by
my troth.

Lod. And how dost, frolic?—Save you fair lady.—
Thou lookest smug and bravely, noble Mat.

Mat. Drink and feed, laugh and lie warm.

Lod. Is this thy wife?

Mat. A poor gentlewoman, sir, whom I make use of
a'nights.

Lod. Pay custom to your lips, sweet lady. [*Kisses her.*

Mat. Borrow some shells[2] of him—some wine, sweet-

Lod. I'll send for't then, i'faith. [heart.

---

[1] An allusion to the well-known romance of this name, from the
Spanish.

[2] A cant term for money.

Mat. You send for't?—Some wine, I prithee.

Bell. I ha' no money.

Mat. 'Sblood, nor I.—What wine love you, signor?

Lod. Here! (*Offering money,*) or I'll not stay, I protest; trouble the gentlewoman too much?

> [*Gives money to* BELLAFRONT, *who goes out.*

And what news flies abroad, Matheo?

Mat. Troth, none. Oh signor, we ha' been merry in our days.

Lod. And no doubt shall again.
The divine powers never shoot darts at men
Mortal, to kill them.

Mat. You say true.

Lod. Why should we grieve at want? Say the world
        made thee
Her minion, that thy head lay in her lap,
And that she danced thee on her wanton knee,
She could but give thee a whole world: that's all,
And that all's nothing; the world's greatest part
Cannot fill up one corner of thy heart.
Say three corners were all filled, alas!
Of what art thou possessed, a thin blown glass:
Such as is by boys puffed into the air.
Were twenty kingdoms thine, thou'dst live in care:
Thou couldst not sleep the better, nor live longer,
Nor merrier be, nor healthfuller, nor stronger.
If, then, thou want'st, thus make that want thy pleasure,
No man wants all things, nor has all in measure.

Mat. I am the most wretched fellow: sure some left-handed priest hath christened me, I am so unlucky; I am never out of one puddle or another; still falling.

Re-enter BELLAFRONT *with wine.*

             Fill out wine to my little finger.
With my heart, i'faith.   [*Drinks.*

Lod. Thanks, good Matheo.
To your own sweet self.   [*Drinks.*

there's few good i' th' city ; I am as well furnished as any, and, though I say it, as well customed.

Bots. We have meats of all sorts of dressing ; we have stewed meat for your Frenchman, pretty light picking meat for your Italian, and that which is rotten roasted for Don Spaniardo.

Lod. A pox on't.

Bots. We have poulterer's ware for your sweet bloods, as dove, chicken, duck, teal, woodcock, and so forth ; and butcher's meat for the citizen : yet muttons [1] fall very bad this year.

Lod. Stay, is not that my patient linen-draper yonder, and my fine young smug mistress, his wife ?

Car. Sirrah,[2] grannam, I'll give thee for thy fee twenty crowns, if thou canst but procure me the wearing of yon velvet cap.

Mis. H. You'd wear another thing besides the cap. You're a wag.

Bots. Twenty crowns ? we'll share, and I'll be your pully to draw her on.

Lod. Do't presently ; we'll ha' some sport.

Mis. H. Wheel you about, sweet men : do you see ? I'll cheapen wares of the man, whilst Bots is doing with his wife.

Lod. To't : if we come into the shop to do you grace, we'll call you madam.

Bots. Pox a' your old face, give it the badge of all scurvy faces, a mask.

                    [MISTRESS HORSELEECH *puts on a mask.*

Cand. What is't you lack, gentlewoman ? Cambric or lawns, or fine hollands ? Pray draw near, I can sell you a pennyworth.

Bots. Some cambric for my old lady.

Cand. Cambric ? you shall, the purest thread in Milan.

---

[1] Prostitutes.   [2] See note *ante,* p. 124.

Car. Save you, Signor Candido.

Lod. How does my noble master? how my fair mistress?

Cand. My worshipful good servant.—View it well, for 'tis both fine and even.   [*Shows cambric.*

Car. Cry you mercy, madam; though masked, I thought it should be you by your man.—Pray, signor, show her the best, for she commonly deals for good ware.

Cand. Then this shall fit her.—This is for your ladyship.

Bots. A word, I pray; there is a waiting gentlewoman of my lady's: her name is Ruyna, says she's your kinswoman, and that you should be one of her aunts.

Bride. One of her aunts? troth, sir, I know her not.

Bots. If it please you to bestow the poor labour of your legs at any time, I will be your convoy thither?

Bride. I am a snail, sir, seldom leave my house. If't please her to visit me, she shall be welcome.

Bots. Do you hear? the naked truth is; my lady hath a young knight, her son, who loves you, you're made, if you lay hold upon't; this jewel he sends you. [*Offers jewel.*

Bride. Sir, I return his love and jewel with scorn; let go my hand, or I shall call my husband. You are an arrant knave.   [*Exit.*

Lod. What will she do?

Bots. Do? They shall all do if Bots sets upon them once: she was as if she had professed the trade, squeamish at first; at last I showed her this jewel, said a knight sent it her.

Lod. Is't gold, and right stones?

Bots. Copper, copper, I go a fishing with these baits. She nibbled, but would not swallow the hook, because the conger-head, her husband, was by; but she bids the gentleman name any afternoon, and she'll meet him at her garden house,[1] which I know.

---

[1] Gardens with summer-houses were very common in the suburbs of London at the time, and were often used as places of intrigue.—*Dyce.*

Lod. Is this no lie now?

Bots. Damme, if—

Lod. Oh, prithee stay there.

Bots. The twenty crowns, sir.

Lod. Before he has his work done? but on my knightly word he shall pay't thee.

Enter ASTOLFO, BERALDO, FONTINELL, *and* BRYAN.

Ast. I thought thou hadst been gone into thine own country.

Bry. No, faat, la, I cannot go dis four or tree days.

Ber. Look thee, yonder's the shop, and that's the man himself.

Fon. Thou shalt but cheapen, and do as we told thee, to put a jest upon him, to abuse his patience.

Bry. I'faat, I doubt my pate shall be knocked: but, sa crees sa' me, for your shakes, I will run to any linen-draper in hell: come predee.

Ast., Ber., Fon. Save you, gallants.

Lod., Car. Oh, well met!

Cand. You'll give no more, you say? I cannot take it.

Mis. H. Truly I'll give no more.

Cand. It must not fetch it.

What would you have, sweet gentlemen.

Ast. Nay, here's the customer.

[*Exeunt* BOTS *and* Mistress HORSELEECH.

Lod. The garden-house, you say? we'll bolt[1] out your roguery.

Cand. I will but lay these parcels by—my men
Are all at the custom house unloading wares,
If cambric you would deal in, there's the best,
All Milan cannot sample it.

Lod. Do your hear it? one, two, three,—'Sfoot, there came in four gallants! Sure your wife is slipt up, and the fourth man, I hold my life, is grafting your warden tree.[2]

---

[1] Sift.   [2] Pear-tree.

Cand. Ha, ha, ha! you gentlemen are full of jest.
If she be up, she's gone some wares to show;
I have above as good wares as below.

Lod. Have you so? nay, then—

Cand. Now, gentlemen, is't cambrics?

Bry. I predee now let me have de best waures.

Cand. What's that he says, pray, gentlemen?

Lod. Marry, he says we are like to have the best
wars.

Cand. The best wars? all are bad, yet wars do good,
And, like to surgeons, let sick kingdom's blood.

Bry. Faat a devil pratest tow so? a pox on dee! I
preddee, let me see some hollen, to make linen shirts, for
fear my body be lousy.

Cand. Indeed, I understand no word he speaks.

Car. Marry, he says that at the siege in Holland
There was much bawdry used among the soldiers,
Though they were lousy.

Cand. It may be so, that likely; true, indeed,
In every garden, sir, does grow that weed.

Bry. Pox on de gardens, and de weeds, and de fool's
cap dere, and de clouts! hear? dost make a hobby-horse
of me?   [*Tearing the cambric.*

All. Oh, fie! he has torn the cambric.

Cand. 'Tis no matter.

Ast. It frets me to the soul.

Cand. So does 't not me.
My customers do oft for remnants call,
These are two remnants, now, no loss at all.
But let me tell you, were my servants here,
It would ha' cost more.—Thank you, gentlemen,
I use you well, pray know my shop again.

All. Ha, ha, ha! come, come, let's go, let's go.
                                        [*Exeunt.*

ACT THE FOURTH.

SCENE I.—*A Room in* MATHEO'S *House.*

Enter MATHEO *brave*,[1] *and* BELLAFRONT.

AT. How am I suited, Front? am I not gallant, ha?

Bell. Yes, sir, you are suited well.

Mat. Exceeding passing well, and to the time.

Bell. The tailor has played his part with you.

Mat. And I have played a gentleman's part with my tailor, for I owe him for the making of it.

Bell. And why did you so, sir?

Mat. To keep the fashion; it's your only fashion now, of your best rank of gallants, to make their tailors wait for their money; neither were it wisdom indeed to pay them upon the first edition of a new suit; for commonly the suit is owing for, when the linings are worn out, and there's no reason, then, that the tailor should be paid before the mercer.

Bell. Is this the suit the knight bestowed upon you?

Mat. This is the suit, and I need not shame to wear it, for better men than I would be glad to have suits bestowed on them. It's a generous fellow,—but— pox on him—we whose pericranions are the very limbecks and stillatories of good wit and fly high, must drive liquor

---

[1] Finely attired.

out of stale gaping oysters—shallow knight, poor squire
Tinacheo : I'll make a wild Cataian[1] of forty such : hang
him, he's an ass, he's always sober.

Bell. This is your fault to wound your friends still.

Mat. No, faith, Front, Lodovico is a noble Slavonian :
it's more rare to see him in a woman's company, than for
a Spaniard to go into England, and to challenge the
English fencers there.—[*Knocking within.*] One knocks,
—see.—[*Exit* BELLAFRONT.]—La, fa, fol, la, fa, la, [*Sings*]
rustle in silks and satins ! there's music in this, and a
taffeta petticoat, it makes both fly high. *Catso.*

Re-enter BELLAFRONT *with* ORLANDO *in his own dress,
and four* Servants.

Bell. Matheo ! 'tis my father.

Mat. Ha ! father ? It's no matter, he finds no tattered
prodigals here.

Orl. Is not the door good enough to hold your blue
coats ?[2] away, knaves, Wear not your clothes thread-
bare at knees for me ; beg Heaven's blessing, not mine.
—[*Exeunt* Servants.]—Oh cry your worship mercy, sir ;
was somewhat bold to talk to this gentlewoman, your wife
here.

Mat. A poor gentlewoman, sir.

Orl. Stand not, sir, bare to me ; I ha' read oft
That serpents who creep low, belch ranker poison
Than wingèd dragons do that fly aloft.

Mat. If it offend you, sir, 'tis for my pleasure.

Orl. Your pleasure be't, sir. Umh, is this your palace?

Bell. Yes, and our kingdom, for 'tis our content.

Orl. It's a very poor kingdom then ; what, are all your
subjects gone a sheep-shearing ? not a maid ? not a man?
not so much as a cat ? You keep a good house belike,
just like one of your profession, every room with bare

---

[1] A Cataian came to signify a sharper because the people of Cataia
(China) were famous for their thieving propensities.—*Dyce.*

[2] Serving-men's livery at this time was usually blue.

walls, and a half-headed bed to vault upon, as all your bawdy-houses are. Pray who are your upholsters? Oh, the spiders, I see, they bestow hangings upon you.

Mat. Bawdy-house? Zounds, sir—

Bell. Oh sweet Matheo, peace. Upon my knees
I do beseech you, sir, not to arraign me
For sins, which Heaven, I hope, long since hath pardoned!
Those flames, like lightning flashes, are so spent,
The heat no more remains, than where ships went,
Or where birds cut the air, the print remains.

Mat. Pox on him, kneel to a dog.

Bell. She that's a whore,
Lives gallant, fares well, is not, like me, poor.
I ha' now as small acquaintance with that sin,
As if I had never known't, t' had never been.

Orl. No acquaintance with it? what maintains thee then? how dost live then? Has thy husband any lands? any rents coming in, any stock going, any ploughs jogging, any ships sailing? hast thou any wares to turn, so much as to get a single penny by?
Yes thou hast ware to sell,
Knaves are thy chapmen, and thy shop is hell.

Mat. Do you hear, sir?

Orl. So, sir, I do hear, sir, more of you than you dream I do.

Mat. You fly a little too high, sir.

Orl. Why, sir, too high?

Mat. I ha' suffered your tongue, like a bard cater-tray,[1] to run all this while, and ha' not stopt it.

Orl. Well, sir, you talk like a gamester.

Mat. If you come to bark at her, because she's a poor rogue, look you, here's a fine path, sir, and there, there's the door.

Bell. Matheo?

Mat. Your blue coats stay for you, sir. I love a good honest roaring boy, and so—

---

[1] A kind of false dice.

Orl. That's the devil.

Mat. Sir, sir, I'll ha' no Joves in my house to thunder avaunt : she shall live and be maintained when you, like a keg of musty sturgeon, shall stink ; where ? in your coffin—how ? be a musty fellow, and lousy.

Orl. I know she shall be maintained, but how ? she like a quean, thou like a knave ; she like a whore, thou like a thief.

Mat. Thief ? Zounds ! Thief ?

Bell. Good, dearest Mat !—Father !

Mat. Pox on you both ! I'll not be braved. New satin scorns to be put down with bare bawdy velvet. Thief ?

Orl. Ay, thief, th'art a murderer, a cheater, a whore-monger, a pot-hunter, a borrower a beggar—

Bell. Dear father—

Mat. An old ass, a dog, a churl, a chuff, an usurer, a villain, a moth, a mangy mule, with an old velvet foot-cloth on his back, sir.

Bell. Oh me !

Orl. Varlet, for this I'll hang thee.

Mat. Ha, ha, alas !

Orl. Thou keepest a man of mine here, under my nose—

Mat. Under thy beard.

Orl. As arrant a smell-smock, for an old mutton-monger [1] as thyself.

Mat. No, as yourself.

Orl. As arrant a purse-taker as ever cried, Stand ! yet a good fellow I confess, and valiant ; but he'll bring thee to th' gallows ; you both have robbed of late two poor country pedlars.

Mat. How's this ? how's this ? dost thou fly high ? rob pedlars ?—bear witness, Front—rob pedlars ? my man and I a thief ?

Bell. Oh, sir, no more.

---

[1] Whoremonger.

Orl. Ay, knave, two pedlars; hue and cry is up; warrants are out, and I shall see thee climb a ladder.

Mat. And come down again as well as a bricklayer or a tiler. How the vengeance knows he this? If I be hanged, I'll tell the people I married old Friscobaldo's daughter; I'll frisco you, and your old carcass.

Orl. Tell what you canst; if I stay here longer, I shall be hanged too, for being in thy company; therefore, as I found you, I leave you—

Mat. Kneel, and get money of him.

Orl. A knave and a quean, a thief and a strumpet, a couple of beggars, a brace of baggages.

Mat. Hang upon him—Ay, ay, sir, farewell; we are— follow close—we are beggars—in satin—to him.

Bell. Is this your comfort, when so many years
You ha' left me frozen to death?

Orl. Freeze still, starve still!

Bell. Yes, so I shall: I must: I must and will.
If as you say I'm poor, relieve me then,
Let me not sell my body to base men.
You call me strumpet, Heaven knows I am none:
Your cruelty may drive me to be one:
Let not that sin be yours; let not the shame
Of common whore live longer than my name.
That cunning bawd, necessity, night and day
Plots to undo me; drive that hag away,
Lest being at lowest ebb, as now I am,
I sink for ever.

Orl. Lowest ebb, what ebb?

Bell. So poor, that, though to tell it be my shame,
I am not worth a dish to hold my meat;
I am yet poorer, I want bread to eat.

Orl. It's not seen by your cheeks.

Mat. I think she has read an homily to tickle the old rogue.   [*Aside.*

Orl. Want bread! there's satin: bake that,

Mat. 'Sblood, make pasties of my clothes?

Orl. A fair new cloak, stew that; an excellent gilt rapier.

Mat. Will you eat that, sir?

Orl. I could feast ten good fellows with these hangers.[1]

Mat. The pox, you shall!

Orl. I shall not, till thou begg'st, think thou art poor;
And when thou begg'st I'll feed thee at my door,
As I feed dogs, with bones; till then beg, borrow,
Pawn, steal, and hang, turn bawd, when th'art whore.—
My heart-strings sure would crack, were they strained
            more.   [*Aside, and exit.*

Mat. This is your father, your damned—Confusion
light upon all the generation of you; he can come bragging hither with four white herrings at's tail in blue coats,
without roes in their bellies, but I may starve ere he give
me so much as a cob.[2]

Bell. What tell you me of this? alas!

Mat. Go, trot after your dad, do you capitulate; I'll
pawn not for you; I'll not steal to be hanged for such an
hypocritical, close, common harlot: away, you dog!—
Brave i'faith! Udsfoot, give me some meat.

Bell. Yes, sir.   [*Exit.*

Mat. Goodman slave, my man too, is galloped to the
devil a' t'other side : Pacheco, I'll checo you. Is this
your dad's day? England, they say, is the only hell for
horses, and only paradise for women : pray get you to
that paradise, because you're called an honest whore;
there they live none but honest whores with a pox.
Marry here in our city, all your sex are but foot-cloth
nags,[3] the master no sooner lights but the man leaps
into the saddle.

Re-enter BELLAFRONT *with meat and drink.*

Bell. Will you sit down I pray, sir?

Mat. [*Sitting down.*] I could tear, by th' Lord, his

---

[1] The loops or straps appended to the girdle in which the dagger
or small sword usually hung.—*Halliwell.*

[2] Means both a herring and a piece of money

[3] Horses with long housings.

If rescue come not : like a man of war
I'll therefore bravely out ; somewhat I'll do,
And either save them both, or perish too. [*Exit.*

    Hip. 'Tis my fate to be bewitched by those eyes.

    Bell. Fate ? your folly.

Why should my face thus mad you ? 'Las, those colours
Are wound up long ago, which beauty spread ;
The flowers that once grew here, are witherèd.
You turned my black soul white, made it look new,
And should I sin, it ne'er should be with you.

    Hip. Your hand, I'll offer you fair play :   When
       first
We met i'th 'lists together, you remember
You were a common rebel ; with one parley
I won you to come in.

    Bell. You did.

    Hip I'll try
If now I can beat down this chastity
With the same ordnance ; will you yield this fort,
If the power of argument now, as then,
I get of you the conquest : as before
I turned you honest, now to turn you whore,
By force of strong persuasion ?

    Bell. If you can,
I yield.

    Hip. The alarum's struck up ; I'm your man.

    Bell. A woman gives defiance.

    Hip. Sit.   [*They seat themselves.*

    Bell. Begin :
'Tis a brave battle to encounter sin.

    Hip. You men that are to fight in the same war
To which I'm prest, and plead at the same bar,
To win a woman, if you'd have me speed,
Send all your wishes !

    Bell. No doubt you're heard ; proceed.

    Hip. To be a harlot, that you stand upon,
The very name's a charm to make you one.

Harlotta was a dame of so divine
And ravishing touch, that she was concubine
To an English king ; [1] her sweet bewitching eye
Did the king's heart-strings in such love-knots tie,
That even the coyest was proud when she could hear
Men say, " behold, another harlot there ! "
And after her all women that were fair
Were harlots called as to this day some are :
Besides, her dalliance she so well does mix,
That she's in Latin called the *Meretrix*.
Thus for the name ; for the profession, this,
Who lives in bondage, lives laced ; the chief bliss
This world below can yield, is liberty :
And who, than whores, with looser wings dare fly ?
As Juno's proud bird spreads the fairest tail,
So does a strumpet hoist the loftiest sail,
She's no man's slave ; men are her slaves ; her eye
Moves not on wheels screwed up with jealousy.
She, horsed or coached, does merry journeys make,
Free as the sun in his gilt zodiac :
As bravely does she shine, as fast she's driven,
But stays not long in any house of heaven ;
But shifts from sign to sign, her amorous prizes
More rich being when she's down, than when she
        rises.
In brief, gentlemen hunt them, soldiers fight for them,
Few men but know them, few or none abhor them :
Thus for sport's sake speak I, as to a woman,
Whom, as the worst ground, I would turn to common :
But you I would enclose for mine own bed.

   Bell. So should a husband be dishonourèd.

   Hip. Dishonoured ? not a whit : to fall to one
Besides your husband is to fall to none,
For one no number is.

---

   [1] Steevens pointed out that Arlotte was not the concubine of an English king but was the mistress of the father of William the Conqueror.

Two of one trade ne'er love : no more do you.
Why are you sharp 'gainst that you once professed ?

 Bell. Why dote you on that, which you did once
  detest ?
I cannot, seeing she's woven of such bad stuff,
Set colours on a harlot base enough.
Nothing did make me, when I loved them best,
To loathe them more than this : when in the street
A fair young modest damsel I did meet,
She seemed to all a dove, when I passed by,
And I to all a raven : every eye
That followed her went with a bashful glance,
At me each bold and jeering countenance
Darted forth scorn ; to her as if she had been
Some tower unvanquished, would they vail,
'Gainst me swoln rumour hoisted every sail.
She, crowned with reverend praises, passed by them,
I, though with face masked, could not 'scape the hem,
For, as if Heaven had set strange marks on whores,
Because they should be pointing stocks to man,
Drest up in civilest shape, a courtesan—
Let her walk saint-like, noteless, and unknown,
Yet she's betrayed by some trick of her own.
Were harlots therefore wise, they'd be sold dear :
For men account them good but for one year,
And then like almanacs whose dates are gone,
They are thrown by, and no more looked upon.
Who'll therefore backward fall, who will launch forth
In seas so foul, for ventures no more worth ?
Lust's voyage hath, if not this course, this cross,
Buy ne'er so cheap, your ware comes home with loss.
What, shall I sound retreat ? the battle's done :
Let the world judge which of us two have won.

 Hip. I !

 Bell. You ? nay then as cowards do in fight,
What by blows cannot, shall be saved by flight. [*Exit.*

 Hip. Fly to earth's fixèd centre : to the caves

Of everlasting horror, I'll pursue thee,
Though loaden with sins, even to hell's brazen doors.
Thus wisest men turn fools, doting on whores.   [*Exit.*

SCENE II.—*An Apartment in the* DUKE'S *Palace.*

Enter the DUKE, LODOVICO, *and* ORLANDO, *disguised as
a* Serving-man ; *after them* INFELICE, CAROLO,
ASTOLFO, BERALDO, *and* FONTINELL.

Orl. I beseech your grace, though your eye be so
piercing as under a poor blue coat to cull out an honest
father from an old serving-man, yet, good my lord, discover not the plot to any, but only this gentleman that is
now to be an actor in our ensuing comedy.

Duke. Thou hast thy wish, Orlando, pass unknown,
Sforza shall only go along with thee,
To see that warrant served upon thy son.

Lod. To attach him upon felony, for two pedlars : is't
not so ?

Orl. Right, my noble knight : those pedlars were two
knaves of mine ; he fleeced the men before, and now he
purposes to flay the master. He will rob me ; his teeth
water to be nibbling at my gold, but this shall hang him
by th' gills, till I pull him on shore.

Duke. Away : ply you the business.

Orl. Thanks to your grace : but, my good lord, for my
daughter—

Duke. You know what I have said.

Orl. And remember what I have sworn. She's more
honest, on my soul, than one of the Turks' wenches,
watched by a hundred eunuchs.

Lod. So she had need, for the Turks make them whores.

Orl. He's a Turk that makes any woman a whore ;
he's no true Christian, I'm sure. I commit your grace.

Duke. Infelice.

Dekker.   8

Inf. Here, sir.

Lod. Signor Friscobaldo.

Orl. Frisking again? Pacheco.

Lod. Uds so, Pacheco? we'll have some sport with this warrant: 'tis to apprehend all suspected persons in the house. Besides, there's one Bots a pander, and one Madam Horseleech a bawd, that have abused my friend; those two conies will we ferret into the purse-net.[1]

Orl. Let me alone for dabbing them o'th' neck: come. come.

Lod. Do ye hear, gallants? meet me anon at Matheo's, *Car.*, *Ast.*, *&c.* Enough.

                [*Exeunt* LODOVICO *and* ORLANDO.

Duke. Th' old fellow sings that note thou didst before
Only his tunes are, that she is no whore,
But that she sent his letters and his gifts,
Out of a noble triumph o'er his lust,
To show she trampled his assaults in dust.

Inf. 'Tis a good honest servant, that old man.

Duke. I doubt no less.

Inf. And it may be my husband,
Because when once this woman was unmasked,
He levelled all her thoughts, and made them fit,
Now he'd mar all again, to try his wit.

Duke. It may be so too, for to turn a harlot
Honest, it must be by strong antidotes;
'Tis rare, as to see panthers change their spots.
And when she's once a star fixed and shines bright,
Though 'twere impiety then to dim her light,
Because we see such tapers seldom burn,
Yet 'tis the pride and glory of some men,
To change her to a blazing star again,
And it may be, Hippolito does no more.
It cannot be but you're acquainted all
With that same madness of our son-in law,
That dotes so on a courtesan.

---

[1] A net, the mouth of which was drawn together with a string

All. Yes, my lord.

Car. All the city thinks he's a whoremonger.

Ast. Yet I warrant he'll swear no man marks him.

Ber. 'Tis like so, for when a man goes a wenching, it is as if he had a strong stinking breath, every one smells him out, yet he feels it not, though it be ranker than the sweat of sixteen bear warders.

Duke. I doubt then you have all those stinking breaths, You might be all smelt out.

Car. Troth, my lord, I think we are all as you ha' been in your youth when you went a-maying, we all love to hear the cuckoo sing upon other men's trees.

Duke. It's well ; yet you confess.   But, girl, thy bed
Shall not be parted with a courtesan.
'Tis strange,
No frown of mine, no frown of the poor lady,
My abused child, his wife, no care of fame,
Of honour, heaven, or hell, no not that name
Of common strumpet, can affright, or woo him
To abandon her ; the harlot does undo him ;
She has bewitched him, robbed him of his shape,
Turned him into a beast, his reason's lost ;
You see he looks wild, does he not ?

Car. I ha' noted new moons
In's face, my lord, all full of change.

Duke. He's no more like unto Hippolito,
Than dead men are to living—never sleeps,
Or if he do, it's dreams : and in those dreams
His arms work, and then cries, Sweet—what's her name,
What's the drab's name ?

Ast. In troth, my lord, I know not,
I know no drabs, not I.

Duke. Oh, Bellafront !—
And, catching her fast, cries, My Bellafront !

Car. A drench that's able to kill a horse, cannot kill this disease of smock-smelling, my lord, if it have once eaten deep.

Duke. I'll try all physic, and this medicine first :
I have directed warrants strong and peremptory
To purge our city Milan, and to cure
The outward parts, the suburbs, for the attaching
Of all those women, who like gold want weight,
Cities, like ships, should have no idle freight.

Car. No, my lord, and light wenches are no idle
freight ; but what's your grace's reach in this ?

Duke. This, Carolo.   If she whom my son doats on,
Be in that muster-book enrolled, he'll shame
Ever t'approach one of such noted name.

Car. But say she be not ?

Duke. Yet on harlots' heads
New laws shall fall so heavy, and such blows shall
Give to those that haunt them, that Hippolito
If not for fear of law, for love to her,
If he love truly, shall her bed forbear.

Car. Attach all the light heels i'th' city, and clap 'em
up ? why, my lord, you dive into a well unsearchable : all
the whores within the walls, and without the walls ?   I
would not be he should meddle with them for ten such
dukedoms ; the army that you speak on is able to fill all
the prisons within this city, and to leave not a drinking
room in any tavern besides.

Duke. Those only shall be caught that are of note ;
Harlots in each street flow :
The fish being thus i'th net, ourself will sit,
And with eye most severe dispose of it.
Come, girl.   [*Exeunt* DUKE *and* INFELICE.

Car. Arraign the poor whores !

Ast. I'll not miss that sessions.

Font. Nor I.

Ber. Nor I, though I hold up my hand there myself.
                                        [*Exeunt.*

SCENE III.—*A Room in* MATHEO'S *House.*

Enter MATHEO, LODOVICO, *and* ORLANDO *disguised as*
a Serving-man.

Mat. Let who will come, my noble chevalier, I can
but play the kind host, and bid 'em welcome.

Lod. We'll trouble your house, Matheo, but as Dutchmen do in taverns, drink, be merry, and be gone.

Orl. Indeed, if you be right Dutchmen, if you fall to
drinking, you must be gone.

Mat. The worst is, my wife is not at home; but we'll
fly high, my generous knight, for all that: there's no music
when a woman is in the concert.

Orl. No; for she's like a pair of virginals,
Always with jacks at her tail.

Enter ASTOLFO, CAROLO, BERALDO *and* FONTINELL.

Lod. See, the covey is sprung.

Ast., Car., &c. Save you, gallants.

Mat. Happily encountered, sweet bloods.

Lod. Gentlemen, you all know Signor Candido, the
linen-draper, he that's more patient than a brown baker,
upon the day when he heats his oven, and has forty scolds
about him.

Ast., Car., &c. Yes, we know him all, what of him?

Lod. Would it not be a good fit of mirth, to make a
piece of English cloth of him, and to stretch him on the
tenters, till the threads of his own natural humour crack,
by making him drink healths, tobacco,[1] dance, sing bawdy
songs, or to run any bias according as we think good to
cast him?

Car. 'Twere a morris-dance worth the seeing.

Ast. But the old fox is so crafty, we shall hardly hunt
him out of his den.

Mat. To that train I ha' given fire already; and the
hook to draw him hither, is to see certain pieces of lawn,

---

[1] To drink tobacco was a common phrase for smoking it.—*Reed.*

which I told him I have to sell, and indeed have such ;
fetch them down, Pacheco.

Orl. Yes, sir, I'm your water-spaniel, and will fetch any
thing—but I'll fetch one dish of meat anon shall turn
your stomach, and that's a constable.   [*Aside and exit.*

Enter Bots *ushering in* Mistress Horseleech.

Ast., Ber., Fon. How now ? how now ?

Car. What gally-foist [1] is this ?

Lod. Peace, two dishes of stewed prunes,[2] a bawd and
a pander.   My worthy lieutenant Bots ; why, now I see
thou'rt a man of thy word, welcome.—Welcome Mistress
Horseleech : pray, gentlemen, salute this reverend matron.

Mis. H. Thanks to all your worships.

Lod. I bade a drawer send in wine, too : did none
come along with thee, grannam, but the lieutenant ?

Mis. H. None came along with me but Bots, if it like
your worship.

Bots. Who the pox should come along with you but
Bots.

Enter two Vintners *with wine.*

Ast., Car., &c. Oh brave ! march fair.

Lod. Are you come ? that's well.

Mat. Here's ordnance able to sack a city.

Lod. Come, repeat, read this inventory.

1st Vint. *Imprimis,* a pottle of Greek wine, a pottle of
Peter-sameene,[3] a pottle of Charnico,[4] and a pottle of
Leatica.[5]

Lod. You're paid ?

2nd Vint. Yes, Sir.   [*Exeunt* Vintners.

Mat. So shall some of us be anon, I fear.

---

[1] A long barge with oars.

[2] A common dish in the brothels of the time.

[3] A corruption of Pedro Ximenes, a sweet Spanish wine, so called
from the grape of that name.

[4] A sweet Portuguese wine from the neighbourhood of Lisbon.

[5] *i.e.* Aleatico, a red Italian muscatel wine with a rich aromatic
avour.

Bots. Here's a hot day towards : but zounds, this is the life out of which a soldier sucks sweetness ! when this artillery goes off roundly, some must drop to the ground : cannon, demi-cannon, saker, and basilisk.[1]

Lod. Give fire, lieutenant.

Bots. So, so :   Must I venture first upon the breach ? to you all, gallants : Bots sets upon you all.   [*Drinks.*

Ast., Car., &c. It's hard, Bots, if we pepper not you, as well as you pepper us.

Enter CANDIDO.

Lod. My noble linen-draper !—some wine !—Welcome old lad !

Mat. You're welcome, signor.

Cand. These lawns, sir ?

Mat. Presently ; my man is gone for them : we ha' rigged a fleet, you see here, to sail about the world.

Cand. A dangerous voyage, sailing in such ships.

Bots. There's no casting over board yet.

Lod. Because you are an old lady, I will have you be acquainted with this grave citizen, pray bestow your lips upon him, and bid him welcome.

Mis. H. Any citizen shall be most welcome to me : —I have used to buy ware at your shop.

Cand. It may be so, good madam.

Mis. H. Your prentices know my dealings well ; I trust your good wife be in good case : if it please you, bear her a token from my lips, by word of mouth.

                                          [*Kisses him.*

Cand. I pray no more ; forsooth, 'tis very well,
Indeed I love no sweetmeats :—Sh'as a breath
Stinks worse than fifty polecats. [*Aside.*] Sir, a word,
Is she a lady ?

Lod. A woman of a good house, and an ancient, she's a bawd.

---

[1] The saker and basilisk were both pieces of ordnance.

Cand. A bawd? Sir, I'll steal hence, and see your lawns
Some other time.

Mat. Steal out of such company? Pacheco, my man
is but gone for''em: Lieutenant Bots, drink to this worthy
old fellow, and teach him to fly high.

Lod., Ast., &c. Swagger: and make him do't on his
knees.

Cand. How, Bots? now bless me, what do I with Bots?
No wine in sooth, no wine, good Master Bots.

Bots. Gray-beard, goat's pizzle: 'tis a health, have
this in your guts, or this, there [*Touching his sword.*] I
will sing a bawdy song, sir, because your verjuice face is
melancholy, to make liquor go down glib. Will you fall
on your marrowbones, and pledge this health? 'Tis to
my mistress, a whore.

Cand. Here's ratsbane upon ratsbane, Master Bots;
I pray, sir, pardon me: you are a soldier,
Press me not to this service, I am old,
And shoot not in such pot-guns.[1]

Bots. Cap, I'll teach you.

Cand. To drink healths, is to drink sickness—gentlemen,
Pray rescue me.

Bots. Zounds, who dare?

Lod., Ast., &c. We shall ha' stabbing then?

Cand. I ha' reckonings to cast up, good Master Bots.

Bots. This will make you cast 'em up better.

Lod. Why does your hand shake so?

Cand. The palsy, signor, danceth in my blood.

Bots. Pipe with a pox, sir, then, or I'll make your
blood dance—

Cand. Hold, hold, good Master Bots, I drink. [*Kneels.*[2]

Ast., Lod., &c. To whom?

Cand. To the old countess there.   [*Drinks.*

---

[1] A play upon "pop-guns."
[2] It was a common custom to kneel when drinking a health,
especially the health of a superior.

Mis. H. To me, old boy? this is he that never drunk
wine! Once again to't.

Cand. With much ado the poison is got down,
Though I can scarce get up ; never before
Drank I a whore's health, nor will never more.

Re-enter ORLANDO *with lawns.*

Mat. Hast been at gallows?

Orl. Yes, sir, for I make account to suffer to day.

Mat. Look, signor ; here's the commodity.

Cand. Your price?

Mat. Thus.[1]

Cand. No : too dear : thus.

Mat. No : O fie, you must fly higher : yet take 'em
home, trifles shall not make us quarrel, we'll agree, you
shall have them, and a pennyworth ; I'll fetch money at
your shop.

Cand. Be it so, good signor, send me going.

Mat. Going? a deep bowl of wine for Signor Candido.

Orl. He would be going.

Cand. I'll rather stay than go so : stop your bowl.

Enter Constable *and* Billmen.

Lod. How now?

Bots. Is't Shrove-Tuesday, that these ghosts walk ?[2]

Mat. What's your business, sir?

Const. From the duke : you are the man we look for,
signor. I have warrant here from the duke, to apprehend
you upon felony for robbing two pedlars : I charge you
i'th' duke's name go quickly.

Mat. Is the wind turned? Well : this is that old wolf,
my father-in-law :—seek out your mistress, sirrah.

---

[1] The price was here probably indicated by displaying the fingers.

[2] On Shrove Tuesday the authorities made a search for brothel-
keepers, and on the same day the London apprentices went about
wrecking houses of ill-fame.

ACT THE FIFTH.

SCENE I.—*A Street.*

Enter at one side HIPPOLITO ; *at the other,* LODOVICO, ASTOLFO, CAROLO, BERALDO *and* FONTINELL.

OD. Yonder's the Lord Hippolito ; by any means leave him and me to-gether ; now will I turn him to a madman.

Ast., Car., &c. Save you my lord.

[*Exeunt all except* HIPPOLITO *and* LODOVICO.

Lod. I ha' strange news to tell you.

Hip. What are they ?

Lod. Your mare's i'th' pound.

Hip. How's this ?

Lod. Your nightingale is in a limebush.

Hip. Ha ?

Lod. Your puritanical honest whore sits in a blue gown.[1]

Hip. Blue gown !

Lod. She'll chalk out your way to her now : she beats chalk.

Hip. Where ? who dares ?—

Lod. Do you know the brick-house of castigation, by the river side[2] that runs by Milan,—the school where they pronounce no letter well but O ?

---

[1] It was in a blue gown that strumpets had to do penance.
[2] Meaning Bridewell, where loose women were whipped.

Hip. I know it not.

Lod. Any man that has borne office of constable, or any woman that has fallen from a horse-load to a cart-load,[1] or like an old hen that has had none but rotten eggs in her nest, can direct you to her : there you shall see your punk amongst her back-friends.

There you may have her at your will,

For there she beats chalk, or grinds in the mill[2]

With a whip deedle, deedle, deedle, deedle ;

Ah little monkey.

Hip. What rogue durst serve that warrant, knowing I loved her ?

Lod. Some worshipful rascal, I lay my life.

Hip. I'll beat the lodgings down about their ears That are her keepers.

Lod. So you may bring an old house over her head.

Hip. I'll to her—

I'll to her, stood armed fiends to guard the doors. [*Exit.*

Lod. Oh me ! what monsters are men made by whores ! If this false fire do kindle him, there's one faggot More to the bonfire.   Now to my Bridewell birds ; What song will they sing ?   [*Exit.*

SCENE II.—*An Apartment in Bridewell.*

Enter DUKE, INFELICE, CAROLO, ASTOLFO, BERALDO, FONTINELL, *and several* Masters of Bridewell.

Duke. Your Bridewell ? that the name ? for beauty, strength,

Capacity and form of ancient building,

---

[1] An allusion to the carting of prostitutes, who were at the same time pelted by the populace with rotten eggs.

[2] Breaking chalk, grinding in mills, raising sand and gravel and making of lime were among the employments assigned to vagrants and others committed to Bridewell —*Reed.*

Bell. In this house.

        [*Exeunt* BELLAFRONT *and* 2nd Master.

Duke. Fetch you him hither—·

Is this the party?

Orl. This is the hen, my lord, that the cock with the lordly comb, your son-in-law, would crow over, and tread.

Duke. Are your two servants ready?

Orl. My two pedlars are packed together, my good
    lord.

Duke. 'Tis well: this day in judgment shall be
    spent:

Vice, like a wound lanced, mends by punishment.

Inf. Let me be gone, my lord, or stand unseen;

'Tis rare when a judge strikes, and that none die,

And 'tis unfit then women should be by.

    1st Mast. We'll place you, lady, in some private
    room.

Inf. Pray do so.

        [*Exit with* 1st Master, *who returns
        alone.*

Orl. Thus nice dames swear, it is unfit their eyes

Should view men carved up for anatomies,[1]

Yet they'll see all, so they may stand unseen;

Many women sure will sin behind a screen.

Enter LODOVICO.

Lod. Your son, the Lord Hippolito, is entered.

Duke. Tell him we wish his presence. A word,
    Sforza;

On what wings flew he hither?

  Lod. These—I told him his lark whom he loved, was a Bridewell-bird; he's mad that this cage should hold her, and is come to let her out.

Duke. 'Tis excellent: away, go call him hither.

        [*Exit* LODOVICO.

        [1] *i.e.* Skeletons

Cast. It's Candido, my lord, he's here among the
lunatics : Father Anselmo, pray fetch him forth. [*Exit*
ANSELMO.] This mad woman is his wife, and though she
were not with child, yet did she long most spitefully to
have her husband mad : and because she would be sure
he should turn Jew, she placed him here in Bethlem.
Yonder he comes.

Enter ANSELMO *with* CANDIDO.

Duke. Come hither, signor ; are you mad ?
Cand. You are not mad.
Duke. Why, I know that.
Cand. Then may you know I am not mad, that know
You are not mad, and that you are the duke :
None is mad here but one.—How do you, wife ?
What do you long for now ?— Pardon, my lord :
She had lost her child's nose else : I did cut out
Pennyworths of lawn, the lawn was yet mine own :
A carpet was my gown, yet 'twas mine own :
I wore my man's coat, yet the cloth mine own :
Had a cracked crown, the crown was yet mine own.
She says for this I'm mad : were her words true,
I should be mad indeed : O foolish skill ! [1]
Is patience madness ?   I'll be a madman still.
   Vio. Forgive me, and I'll vex your spirit no more.
                                                    [*Kneels.*
   Duke. Come, come, we'll have you friends ; join
hearts, join hands.
   Cand. See, my lord, we are even,—
Nay rise, for ill deeds kneel unto none but Heaven.
   Duke. Signor, methinks patience has laid on you
Such heavy weight, that you should loathe it——
   Cand. Loathe it !
   Duke. For he whose breast is tender, blood so cool,
That no wrongs heat it, is a patient fool :
What comfort do you find in being so calm ?

   [1] *i.e.* Reason.

DRAMATIS PERSONÆ.

GASPARO TREBAZZI, Duk of Milan.
HIPPOLITO, a Count, Husband of INFELICE.
ORLANDO FRISCOBALDO, Father of BELLAFRONT.
MATHEO, Husband of BELLAFRONT.
CANDIDO, a Linen Draper.
LODOVICO SFORZA.
BERALDO.
CAROLO.
FONTINELL.
ASTOLFO.
ANTONIO GEORGIO, a poor Scholar.
BRYAN, an Irish Footman.
BOTS, a Pander.
Masters of Bridewell, Prentices, Servants, &c.

INFELICE, Wife of HIPPOLITO.
BELLAFRONT, Wife of MATHEO.
CANDIDO'S Bride.
Mistress HORSELEECH, a Bawd.
DOROTHEA TARGET,   }
PENELOPE WHOREHOUND, }   Harlots.
CATHARINA BOUNTINALL, }

SCENE—MILAN.

Re-enter on one side 2nd Master *and* BELLAFRONT *with*
    MATHEO, *and* Constable ; *on the other,* LODOVICO
    with HIPPOLITO. ORLANDO *goes out, and returns
    with two of his* Servants *disguised as* Pedlars.

Duke. You are to us a stranger, worthy lord,
'Tis strange to see you here.

Hip. It is most fit,
That where the sun goes, atomies [1] follow it.

Duke. Atomies neither shape, nor honour bear :
Be you yourself, a sunbeam to shine clear.—
Is this the gentleman ?   Stand forth and hear
Your accusation.

Mat. I'll hear none : I fly high in that : rather than
kites shall seize upon me, and pick out mine eyes to my
face, I'll strike my talons through mine own heart first,
and spit my blood in theirs.   I am here for shriving
those two fools of their sinful pack : when those jackdaws
have cawed over me, then must I cry guilty, or not guilty ;
the law has work enough already and therefore I'll
put no work of mine into his hands ; the hangman shall
ha't first ; I did pluck those ganders, did rob them.

Duke. 'Tis well done to confess.

Mat. Confess and be hanged, and then I fly high, is't
not so ?   That for that ; a gallows is the worst rub that a
good bowler can meet with ; I stumbled against such a
post, else this night I had played the part of a true son
in these days, undone my father-in-law ; with him would
I ha' run at leap-frog, and come over his gold, though I
had broke his neck for't : but the poor salmon-trout is
now in the net.

Hip. And now the law must teach you to fly high.

Mat. Right, my lord, and then may you fly low ; no
more words :—a mouse, mum, you are stopped.

Bell. Be good to my poor husband, dear my lords.

Mat. Ass !

_____

[1] Atoms.

Why shouldst thou pray them to be good to me,
When no man here is good to one another?

Duke. Did any hand work in this theft but yours?

Mat. O, yes, my lord, yes :—the hangman has never one son at a birth, his children always come by couples : though I cannot give the old dog, my father, a bone to gnaw, the daughter shall be sure of a choke-pear.[1] Yes, my lord, there was one more that fiddled my fine pedlars, and that was my wife.

Bell. Alas, I?

Orl. O everlasting, supernatural superlative villain !
　　　　　　　　　　　　　　　　　　　　[*Aside.*

Duke, Lod., &c. Your wife, Matheo?

Hip. Sure it cannot be.

Mat. Oh, sir, you love no quarters of mutton that hang up, you love none but whole mutton. She set the robbery, I performed it ; she spurred me on, I galloped away.

Orl. My lords,—

Bell. My lords,—fellow, give me speech,—if my poor life

May ransom thine, I yield it to the law,
Thou hurt'st thy soul, yet wip'st off no offence,
By casting blots upon my innocence :
Let not these spare me, but tell truth : no, see
Who slips his neck out of the misery,
Though not out of the mischief : let thy servant
That shared in this base act, accuse me here,
Why should my husband perish, he go clear?

Orl. A good child, hang thine own father !　　[*Aside.*

Duke. Old fellow, was thy hand in too?

Orl. My hand was in the pie, my lord, I confess it : my mistress, I see, will bring me to the gallows, and so leave me ; but I'll not leave her so : I had rather hang in a woman's company, than in a man's ; because if we should go to hell together, I should scarce be letten in,

---

[1] Slang term for a small copper coin.

for all the devils are afraid to have any women come amongst them. As I am true thief, she neither consented to this felony, nor knew of it.

Duke. What fury prompts thee on to kill thy wife?

Mat. It is my humour, sir, 'tis a foolish bag-pipe that I make myself merry with : why should I eat hemp-seed at the hangman's thirteen-pence halfpenny[1] ordinary, and have this whore laugh at me, as I swing, as I totter?

Duke. Is she a whore?

Mat. A six-penny mutton pasty, for any to cut up.

Orl. Ah, toad, toad, toad.

Mat. A barber's cittern[2] for every serving-man to play upon ; that lord, your son, knows it.

Hip. I, sir? Am I her bawd then?

Mat. No, sir, but she's your whore then.

Orl. Yea, spider ; dost catch at great flies? [*Aside.*

Hip. My whore?

Mat. I cannot talk, sir, and tell of your rems and your rees and your whirligigs and devices : but, my lord, I found 'em like sparrows in one nest, billing together, and bulling of me. I took 'em in bed, was ready to kill him, was up to stab her—

Hip. Close thy rank jaws :—pardon me, I am vexed ;
Thou art a villain, a malicious devil,
Deep as the place where thou art lost, thou liest,
Since I am thus far got into this storm,
I'll through, and thou shalt see I'll through untouched,
When thou shalt perish in it.

Re-enter INFELICE.

Inf. 'Tis my cue,
To enter now.—Room! let my prize[3] be played ;
I ha' lurked in clouds, yet heard what all have said ;
What jury more can prove sh'as wronged my bed,

---

[1] The amount of the hangman's fee.

[2] A cittern or lute was part of the appointments of a barber's shop of the period.

[3] A term in fencing. See note *ante*, p. 160.

Than her own husband ; she must be punishèd.
I challenge law, my lord ; letters and gold,
And jewels from my lord that woman took.

Hip. Against that black-mouthed devil, against letters
and gold,
And against a jealous wife, I do uphold
Thus far her reputation ; I could sooner
Shake th' Appenine, and crumble rocks to dust,
Than, though Jove's shower rained down, tempt her to
lust.

Bel. What shall I say ?

Orl. [*Throwing off his disguise.*] Say thou art not a
whore, and that's more than fifteen women amongst five
hundred dare swear without lying : this shalt thou say—
no, let me say't for thee—thy husband's a knave, this
lord's an honest man ; thou art no punk, this lady's a
right lady. Pacheco is a thief as his master is, but old
Orlando is as true a man as thy father is. I ha' seen you
fly high, sir, and I ha' seen you fly low, sir, and to keep
you from the gallows, sir, a blue coat have I worn, and a
thief did I turn. Mine own men are the pedlars, my
twenty pounds did fly high, sir, your wife's gown did fly
low, sir : whither fly you now, sir ? you ha' scaped the
gallows, to the devil you fly next, sir. Am I right, my
liege ?

Duke. Your father has the true physician played.

Mat. And I am now his patient.

Hip. And be so still ;
'Tis a good sign when our cheeks blush at ill.

Const. The linen-draper, Signor Candido,
He whom the city terms the patient man,
Is likewise here for buying of those lawns
The pedlars lost.

Inf. Alas, good Candido !

Duke. Fetch him [*Exit* Constable] and when these
payments up are cast,
Weigh out your light gold, but let's have them last.

Enter Candido *and* Constable, *who presently goes out.*

Duke. In Bridewell, Candido?

Cand. Yes, my good lord.

Duke. What make you here?

Cand. My lord, what make you here?

Duke. I'm here to save right, and to drive wrong
hence.

Cand. And I to bear wrong here with patience.

Duke. You ha' bought stol'n goods.

Cand. So they do say, my lord,

Yet bought I them upon a gentleman's word,

And I imagine now, as I thought then,

That there be thieves, but no thieves, gentlemen.

Hip. Your credit's cracked, being here.

Cand. No more than gold

Being cracked, which does his estimation hold.

I was in Bedlam once, but was I mad?

They made me pledge whores' healths, but am I bad

Because I'm with bad people?

Duke. Well, stand by;

If you take wrong, we'll cure the injury.

Re-enter Constable, *after him* Bots, *then two* Beadles, *one
with hemp, the other with a beetle.*[1]

Duke. Stay, stay, what's he? a prisoner?

Const. Yes, my lord.

Hip. He seems a soldier?

Bots. I am what I seem, sir, one of fortune's bastards,
a soldier and a gentleman, and am brought in here with
master constable's band of billmen, because they face me
down that I live, like those that keep bowling alleys, by
the sins of the people, in being a squire of the body.

Hip. Oh, an apple-squire.[2]

Bots. Yes, sir, that degree of scurvy squires; and that

---

[1] A heavy mallet.

[2] The term was applied both to a kept gallant and to a pander.

I am maintained by the best part that is commonly in a
woman, by the worst players of those parts; but I am
known to all this company.

Lod. My lord, 'tis true, we all know him, 'tis Lieutenant
Bots.

Duke. Bots, and where ha' you served, Bots?

Bots. In most of your hottest services in the Low-
countries : at the Groyne I was wounded in this thigh,
and halted upon't, but 'tis now sound. In Cleveland I
missed but little, having the bridge of my nose broken
down with two great stones, as I was scaling a fort. I
ha' been tried, sir, too, in Gelderland, and 'scaped hardly
there from being blown up at a breach : I was fired, and
lay i' th' surgeon's hands for't, till the fall of the leaf
following.

Hip. All this may be, and yet you no soldier.

Bots. No soldier, sir? I hope these are services that
your proudest commanders do venture upon, and never
come off sometimes.

Duke. Well, sir, because you say you are a soldier,
I'll use you like a gentleman.—Make room there,
Plant him amongst you ; we shall have anon
Strange hawks fly here before us : if none light
On you, you shall with freedom take your flight :
But if you prove a bird of baser wing,
We'll use you like such birds, here you shall sing.

Bots. I wish to be tried at no other weapon.

Duke. Why, is he furnished with those implements?

1st Master. The pander is more dangerous to a State,
Than is the common thief ; and though our laws
Lie heavier on the thief, yet that the pander
May know the hangman's ruff should fit him too,
Therefore he's set to beat hemp.

Duke. This does savour
Of justice ; basest slaves to basest labour.
Now pray, set open hell, and let us see
The she-devils that are here.

Inf. Methinks this place
Should make e'en Lais honest.

   1st Mast. Some it turns good,
But as some men, whose hands are once in blood,
Do in a pride spill more, so, some going hence,
Are, by being here, lost in more impudence.
Let it not to them, when they come, appear
That any one does as their judge sit here :
But that as gentlemen you come to see,
And then perhaps their tongues will walk more free.

   Duke. Let them be marshalled in.—[*Exeunt* 1st *and*
2nd Masters, Constable, *and* Beadles.]—Be covered all,
Fellows, now to make the scene more comical.

   Car. Will not you be smelt out, Bots?

   Bots. No, your bravest whores have the worse noses.

Re-enter 1st *and* 2nd Masters *and* Constable, *then*
    DOROTHEA TARGET, *brave*[1] *; after her two* Beadles,
    the one with a wheel, the other with a blue gown.

   Lod. Are not you a bride, forsooth?

   Dor. Say ye?

   Car. He would know if these be not your bridemen.

   Dor. Vuh! yes, sir: and look ye, do you see? the
bride-laces that I give at my wedding, will serve to tie
rosemary to both your coffins when you come from
hanging—Scab!

   Orl. Fie, punk, fie, fie, fie!

   Dor. Out, you stale, stinking head of garlic, foh, at my
heels.

   Orl. My head's cloven.

   Hip. O, let the gentlewoman alone, she's going to
shrift.

   Ast. Nay, to do penance.

   Car. Ay, ay, go, punk, go to the cross and be whipt.

   Dor. Marry mew, marry muff,[2] marry, hang you, goodman dog: whipt? do ye take me for a base spittle-

---

[1] Smartly attired.   [2] A term of contempt.

whore ? In troth, gentlemen, you wear the clothes of gentlemen, but you carry not the minds of gentlemen, to abuse a gentlewoman of my fashion.

Lod. Fashion ? pox a' your fashions ! art not a whore ?

Dor. Goodman slave.

Duke. O fie, abuse her not, let us two talk,
What might I call your name, pray ?

Dor. I'm not ashamed of my name, sir ; my name is Mistress Doll Target, a Western gentlewoman.

Lod. Her target against any pike in Milan.

Duke. Why is this wheel borne after her ?

1st Mast. She must spin.

Dor. A coarse thread it shall be, as all threads are.

Ast. If you spin, then you'll earn money here too ?

Dor. I had rather get half-a-crown abroad, than ten crowns here.

Orl. Abroad ? I think so.

Inf. Dost thou not weep now thou art here ?

Dor. Say ye ? weep ? yes, forsooth, as you did when you lost your maidenhead : do you not hear how I weep ?				[*Sings.*

Lod. Farewell, Doll.

Dor. Farewell, dog.					[*Exit.*

Duke. Past shame : past penitence ! Why is that blue gown ?

1st Mast. Being stript out of her wanton loose attire,
That garment she puts on, base to the eye,
Only to clothe her in humility.

Duke. Are all the rest like this ?

1st Mast. No, my good lord.
You see, this drab swells with a wanton rein,
The next that enters has a different strain.

Duke. Variety is good, let's see the rest.

				[*Exeunt* 1st *and* 2nd Masters *and* Constable.

Bots. Your grace sees I'm sound yet, and no bullets hit me.

Duke. Come off so, and 'tis well.

Lod., Ast., &c. Here's the second mess.

Re-enter 1st *and* 2nd Masters *and* Constable, *then* PENE-
LOPE WHOREHOUND, *dressed like a* Citizen's Wife ;
her two Beadles, *one with a blue gown, another with
chalk and a mallet.*

Pen. I ha' worn many a costly gown, but I was never
thus guarded[1] with blue coats, and beadles, and constables, and—

Car. Alas, fair mistress, spoil not thus your eyes.

Pen. Oh, sweet sir, I fear the spoiling of other places
about me that are dearer than my eyes ; if you be gentlemen, if you be men, or ever came of a woman, pity my
case ! stand to me, stick to me, good sir, you are an old
man.

Orl. Hang not on me, I prithee, old trees bear no
such fruit.

Pen. Will you bail me, gentlemen ?

Lod. Bail thee ? art in for debt ?

Pen. No ; God is my judge, sir, I am in for no debts ;
I paid my tailor for this gown, the last five shillings a-
week that was behind, yesterday.

Duke. What is your name, I pray ?

Pen. Penelope Whorehound, I come of the Whore-
hounds. How does Lieutenant Bots?

Lod., Ast., &c. Aha, Bots !

Bots. A very honest woman, as I'm a soldier—a pox
Bots ye.

Pen. I was never in this pickle before ; and yet if I go
amongst citizens' wives, they jeer at me ; if I go among
the loose-bodied gowns,[2] they cry a pox on me, because
I go civilly attired, and swear their trade was a good
trade, till such as I am took it out of their hands. Good
Lieutenant Bots, speak to these captains to bail me.

1st Mast. Begging for bail still ? you are a trim gossip ;

---

[1] A play upon the word, which also signifies "trimmed."
[2] Prostitutes.

Go give her the blue gown, set her to her chare.[1]
Work huswife, for your bread, away.

   Pen. Out, you dog!—a pox on you all!—women are
born to curse thee—but I shall live to see twenty such
flat-caps shaking dice for a penny-worth of pippins—out,
you blue-eyed rogue.   [*Exit.*

   Lod., Ast., &c. Ha, ha, ha.   [curse?

   Duke. Even now she wept, and prayed; now does she

   1st Mast. Seeing me; if still sh' had stayed, this had
been worse.

   Hip. Was she ever here before?

   1st Mast. Five times at least,
And thus if men come to her, have her eyes
Wrung, and wept out her bail.

   Lod., Ast., &c. Bots, you know her?

   Bots. Is there any gentleman here, that knows not a
whore, and is he a hair the worse for that?

   Duke. Is she a city-dame, she's so attired?

   1st Mast. No, my good lord, that's only but the veil
To her loose body, I have seen her here
In gayer masking suits, as several sauces
Give one dish several tastes, so change of habits
In whores is a bewitching art: to day
She's all in colours to besot gallants, then
In modest black, to catch the citizen,
And this from their examination's drawn.
Now shall you see a monster both in shape
And nature quite from these, that sheds no tear,
Nor yet is nice, 'tis a plain ramping bear;
Many such whales are cast upon this shore.

   Duke, Lod., &c. Let's see her.

   1st Mast. Then behold a swaggering whore.

            [*Exeunt* 1st *and* 2nd Masters *and* Constable.

   Orl. Keep your ground, Bots.

   Bots. I do but traverse to spy advantage how to arm
myself.

               [1] Task work.

Re-enter 1st *and* 2nd Masters *and* Constable ; *after them a*
  Beadle *beating a basin,*[1] *then* CATHERINA BOUNTINALL,
  with Mistress HORSELEECH ; *after them another*
  Beadle *with a blue head guarded*[2] *with yellow.*

Cat. Sirrah, when I cry hold your hands, hold, you
rogue-catcher, hold :—Bawd, are the French chilblains
in your heels, that you can come no faster? Are not
you, bawd, a whore's ancient,[3] and must not I follow my
colours ?

Mis. H. O Mistress Catherine, you do me wrong to
accuse me here as you do, before the right worshipful.
I am known for a motherly, honest woman, and no bawd.

Cat. Marry foh, honest? burnt[4] at fourteen, seven times
whipt, five times carted, nine times ducked, searched by
some hundred and fifty constables, and yet you are
honest ? Honest Mistress Horseleech, is this world a
world to keep bawds and whores honest ? How many
times hast thou given gentlemen a quart of wine in a
gallon pot? how many twelve-penny fees, nay two
shillings fees, nay, when any ambassadors ha' been here,
how many half-crown fees hast thou taken ? How many
carriers hast thou bribed for country wenches? how often
have I rinsed your lungs in *aqua vitæ*, and yet you are
honest ?

Duke. And what were you the whilst ?

Cat. Marry hang you, master slave, who made you an
examiner ?

Lod. Well said ! belike this devil spares no man.

Cat. What art thou, prithee ?   [*To* BOTS.

Bots. Nay, what art thou, prithee ?

Cat. A whore, art thou a thief ?

Bots. A thief, no, I defy[5] the calling ; I am a soldier,
have borne arms in the field, been in many a hot skirmish,
yet come off sound.

---

[1] At the carting of bawds and prostitutes they were preceded by
a mob beating basins and performing other rough music.
[2] Trimmed. [3] Ensign. [4] Branded. [5] Disdain.

Cat. Sound, with a pox to ye, ye abominable rogue! you a soldier? you in skirmishes? where? amongst pottle pots in a bawdy-house? Look, look here, you Madam Wormeaten, do you not know him?

Mis. H. Lieutenant Bots, where have ye been this many a day?

Bots. Old bawd, do not discredit me, seem not to know me.

Mis. H. Not to know ye, Master Bots? as long as I have breath, I cannot forget thy sweet face.

Duke. Why, do you know him? he says he is a soldier.

Cat. He a soldier? a pander, a dog that will lick up sixpence: do ye hear, you master swines'-snout, how long is't since you held the door for me, and cried to't again, No body comes! ye rogue, you?

Lod., Ast., &c. Ha, ha, ha! you're smelt out again, Bots.

Bots. Pox ruin her nose for't! an I be not revenged for this—um, ye bitch!

Lod. D'ye hear ye, madam? why does your ladyship swagger thus? you're very brave,[1] methinks.

Cat. Not at your cost, master cod's-head;
Is any man here blear-eyed to see me brave?

Ast. Yes, I am,
Because good clothes upon a whore's back
Is like fair painting upon a rotten wall.

Cat. Marry muff master whoremaster, you come upon me with sentences.

Ber. By this light, has small sense for't.

Lod. O fie, fie, do not vex her! And yet methinks a creature of more scurvy conditions should not know what a good petticoat were.

Cat. Marry come out, you're so busy about my petticoat, you'll creep up to my placket, an ye could but attain the honour: but an the outsides offend your rogueships, look o'the lining, 'tis silk.

Duke. Is't silk 'tis lined with, then?

---

[1] Finely dressed.

Cat. Silk? Ay, silk, master slave, you would be glad to wipe your nose with the skirt on't. This 'tis to come among a company of cod's-heads[1] that know not how to use a gentlewoman.

Duke. Tell her the duke is here.

1st Mast. Be modest, Kate, the duke is here.

Cat. If the devil were here, I care not: set forward, ye rogues, and give attendance according to your places! Let bawds and whores be sad, for I'll sing an the devil were a-dying.

[*Exit with* Mistress HORSELEECH *and* Beadles.

Duke. Why before her does the basin ring?

1st Mast. It is an emblem of their revelling,
The whips we use let forth their wanton blood,
Making them calm; and more to calm their pride,
Instead of coaches they in carts do ride.
Will your grace see more of this bad ware?

Duke. No, shut up shop, we'll now break up the fair,
Yet ere we part—you, sir, that take upon ye
The name of soldier, that true name of worth,
Which, action, not vain boasting, best sets forth,
To let you know how far a soldier's name
Stands from your title, and to let you see,
Soldiers must not be wronged where princes be:
This be your sentence.

All. Defend yourself, Bots.

Duke. First, all the private sufferance that the house
Inflicts upon offenders, you, as the basest,
Shall undergo it double, after which
You shall be whipt, sir, round about the city,
Then banished from the land.

Bots. Beseech, your grace!

Duke. Away with him, see it done, panders and whores
Are city-plagues which being kept alive,
Nothing that looks like goodness ere can thrive.
Now good Orlando, what say you to your bad son-in-law?

Orl. Marry this, my lord, he is my son-in-law, and in

law will I be his father : for if law can pepper him, he shall be so parboiled, that he shall stink no more i' th' nose of the common-wealth.

Bell. Be yet more kind and merciful, good father.

Orl. Dost thou beg for him, thou precious man's meat, thou ? has he not beaten thee, kicked thee, trod on thee, and dost thou fawn on him like his spaniel ? has he not pawned thee to thy petticoat, sold thee to thy smock, made ye leap at a crust, yet wouldst have me save him ?

Bell. Oh yes, good sir, women shall learn of me,
To love their husbands in greatest misery ;
Then show him pity, or you wreck myself.

Orl. Have ye eaten pigeons, that you're so kind-hearted to your mate ? Nay, you're a couple of wild bears, I'll have ye both baited at one stake : but as for this knave, the gallows is thy due, and the gallows thou shalt have, I'll have justice of the duke, the law shall have thy life—What, dost thou hold him ? let go, his hand. If thou dost not forsake him, a father's everlasting blessing fall upon both your heads ! Away, go, kiss out of my sight, play thou the whore no more, nor thou the thief again ; my house shall be thine, my meat shall be thine, and so shall my wine, but my money shall be mine, and yet when I die, so thou dost not fly high, take all ;
Yet, good Matheo, mend.
Thus for joy weeps Orlando, and doth end.

Duke. Then hear, Matheo : all your woes are stayed
By your good father-in-law : all your ills
Are clear purged from you by his working pills.—
Come, Signor Candido, these green young wits,
We see by circumstance, this plot have laid,
Still to provoke thy patience, which they find
A wall of brass ; no armour's like the mind.
Thou hast taught the city patience, now our court
Shall be thy sphere, where from thy good report,
Rumours this truth unto the world shall sing,
A patient man's a pattern for a king.   [*Exeunt omnes.*

THE PLEASANT COMEDY OF
OLD FORTUNATUS.

THE *Pleasant Comedy of Old Fortunatus* was first published in 1600, having been produced at Court on the Christmas before. The play as it stands is an amplification and a recast of an earlier play, *The First Part of Fortunatus*, which had been performed at Henslowe's Theatre about four years previously. This had long been laid aside, when the idea seems to have occurred to Henslowe to revive it in fuller form, and Dekker was commissioned to write a second part, with the result that he recast the whole in one play instead, adding the episode of the sons of Fortunatus to the original version. So far, the whole play was taken from the same source, the old *Volksbuch* of " Fortunatus," which, first published at Augsburg in 1509, was popular in various languages in the sixteenth century. An interesting account of this legend and of its connection with the play, is given in Professor Herford's "Studies in the Literary Relations of England and Germany in the Sixteenth Century," from which the present note on the play is largely drawn. When Dekker had completed his recast of the play, it was immediately ordered for performance at Court, and further scenes, in this case altogether extraneous to the original story— those, namely, in which Virtue and Vice are introduced as rivals to Fortune—were added with a special view to this end. Otherwise the play is pretty faithful to the story, even in its absurdities. It is worth mention that Hans Sachs had already dramatized the subject in 1553, which may have had something to do indirectly with the production of the first English version.

In the original quarto of 1600, *Old Fortunatus* is not divided into acts and scenes, and the division is here attempted for the first time. It has been necessary also in some instances to supply stage directions.

THE PROLOGUE AT COURT.[1]

Enter Two Old Men.

1st O. Man. Are you then travelling to the temple of Eliza?[2]

2nd O. Man. Even to her temple are my feeble limbs travelling. Some call her Pandora: some Gloriana, some Cynthia: some Delphœbe, some Astræa: all by several names to express several loves: yet all those names make but one celestial body, as all those loves meet to create but one soul.

1st O. Man. I am one of her own country, and we adore her by the name of Eliza.

2nd O. Man. Blessed name, happy country: your Eliza makes your land Elysium: but what do you offer?

1st O. Man. That which all true subjects should: when I was young, an armed hand; now I am crooked, an upright heart: but what offer you?

2nd O. Man. That which all strangers do: two eyes struck blind with admiration: two lips proud to sound her glory: two hands held up full of prayers and praises: what not, that may express love? what not, that may make her beloved?

1st O. Man. How long is't since you last beheld her?

2nd O. Man. A just year: yet that year hath seemed to me but one day, because her glory hath been my hourly contemplation, and yet that year hath seemed to me more than twice seven years, because so long I have been absent from her. Come therefore, good father, let's go faster, lest we come too late: for see, the tapers of the night are already lighted, and stand brightly burning in their starry candlesticks: see how gloriously the moon shines upon us.

[Both kneel.

[1] This Prologue and the Epilogue are specially devised for the performance of the play before the queen, hence "At Court."

[2] *i.e.* Queen Elizabeth, at this time in her sixty-eighth year.

Pandora is the only one of these poetic terms for Elizabeth peculiar to Dekker. The rest of them are used by others of the Elizabethan poets. He evidently here conceives Pandora on the side of her good fortune only, as receiving the gifts of the gods, and not in her more familiar association with the story of Pandora's Box and its evils.

1st O. Man. Peace, fool : tremble, and kneel : the moon
   say'st thou ?
Our eyes are dazzled by Eliza's beams,
See (if at least thou dare see) where she sits :
This is the great Pantheon of our goddess,
And all those faces which thine eyes thought stars,
Are nymphs attending on her deity.
Prithee begin, for I want power to speak.

2nd O. Man. No, no, speak thou, I want words to begin.
                                                          [*Weeps.*

1st O. Man. Alack, what shall I do ? com'st thou with me,
And weep'st now thou behold'st this majesty ?

2nd O. Man. Great landlady of hearts, pardon me.

1st O. Man. Blame not mine eyes, good father, in these
   tears.

2nd O. Man. My pure love shines, as thine doth in thy
   fears :
I weep for joy to see so many heads
Of prudent ladies, clothed in the livery
Of silver-handed age, for serving you,
Whilst in your eyes youth's glory doth renew :
I weep for joy to see the sun look old,
To see the moon mad at her often change,
To see the stars only by night to shine,
Whilst you are still bright, still one, still divine :
I weep for joy to see the world decay,
Yet see Eliza flourishing like May :
O pardon me your pilgrim, I have measured
Many a mile to find you : and have brought
Old Fortunatus and his family,
With other Cypriots, my poor countrymen,
To pay a whole year's tribute : O vouchsafe,
Dread Queen of Fairies, with your gracious eyes,
T'accept theirs and our humble sacrifice.

1st O. Man. Now I'll beg for thee too: and yet I need not :
Her sacred hand hath evermore been known,
As soon held out to strangers as her own.

2nd O. Man. Thou dost encourage me : I'll fetch them in,
They have no princely gifts, we are all poor,
Our offerings are true hearts, who can wish more ? [*Exeunt.*

PROLOGUE.

OF Love's sweet war our timorous Muse doth sing,
And to the bosom of each gentle dear,
Offers her artless tunes, borne on the wing
Of sacred poesy.   A benumbing fear,
That your nice souls, cloyed with delicious sounds,
Will loath her lowly notes, makes her pull in
Her fainting pinions, and her spirit confounds,
Before the weak voice of her song begin.
Yet since within the circle of each eye,
Being like so many suns in his round sphere,
No wrinkle yet is seen, she'll dare to fly,
Borne up with hopes, that as you oft do rear
With your fair hands, those who would else sink down,
So some will deign to smile, where all might frown :
And for this small circumference must stand,
For the imagined surface of much land,
Of many kingdoms, and since many a mile
Should here be measured out, our Muse entreats
Your thoughts to help poor art, and to allow
That I may serve as Chorus to her senses ;
She begs your pardon, for she'll send one forth,
Not when the laws of poesy do call,
But as the story needs ; your gracious eye
Gives life to Fortunatus' history.

                                           [*Exit.*

ATHELSTANE, King of England.

The Soldan of Egypt.

The Prince of Cyprus.

CORNWALL,
CHESTER, } English Nobles.
LINCOLN,

MONTROSE, } Scotch Nobles.
GALLOWAY,

ORLEANS, } French Nobles.
LONGAVILLE,

INSULTADO, a Spanish Lord.

FORTUNATUS.

AMPEDO, } Sons of FORTUNATUS.
ANDELOCIA,

SHADOW, Servant to AMPEDO and ANDELOCIA.

Kings, Nobles, Soldiers, Satyrs, a Carter, a Tailor, a Monk, a Shepherd, Chorus, Boys and other Attendants.

AGRIPYNE, Daughter of ATHELSTANE.

FORTUNE,
VIRTUE, } Goddesses.
VICE,

The Three Destinies.

Nymphs, Ladies, &c.

SCENE—CYPRUS, BABYLON, and ENGLAND.

OLD FORTUNATUS.

ACT THE FIRST.

SCENE I.—*A Wood in Cyprus.*

Enter FORTUNATUS *meanly attired; he walks about cracking nuts ere he speaks.*

ORT. So, ho, ho, ho, ho.

Echo [*Within.*]. Ho, ho, ho, ho.

Fort. There, boy.

Echo. There, boy.

Fort. An thou bee'st a good fellow, tell me how call'st this wood.

Echo. This wood.

Fort. Ay, this wood, and which is my best way out.

Echo. Best way out.

Fort. Ha, ha, ha, that's true, my best way out is my best way out, but how that out will come in, by this maggot I know not. I see by this we are all worms' meat. Well, I am very poor and very patient; Patience is a virtue: would I were not virtuous, that's to say, not poor, but full of vice, that's to say, full of chinks. Ha, ha, so I am, for I am so full of chinks, that a horse with one eye may look through and through me. I have sighed long, and that makes me windy; I have fasted long, and that makes me chaste; marry, I have prayed little, and that makes me I still dance in this conjuring circle; I have wandered long, and that makes me weary. But for my weariness, anon I'll lie down, instead of fasting I'll feed upon nuts, and instead of sighing will laugh and be lean, Sirrah Echo.

Echo. Sirrah Echo.

Fort. Here's a nut.

Echo. Here's a nut.

Fort. Crack it.

Echo. Crack it.

Fort. Hang thyself.

Echo. Hang thyself.

Fort. Th'art a knave, a knave.

Echo. A knave, a knave.

Fort. Ha, ha, ha, ha!

Echo. Ha, ha, ha, ha!

Fort. Why so, two fools laugh at one another, I at my tittle tattle gammer Echo, and she at me. Shortly there will creep out in print some filthy book of the old hoary wandering knight, meaning me: would I were that book, for then I should be sure to creep out from hence. I should be a good soldier, for I traverse my ground rarely; marry I see neither enemy nor friends, but popinjays, and squirrels, and apes, and owls, and daws, and wagtails, and the spite is that none of these grass-eaters can speak my language, but this fool that mocks me, and swears to have the last word, in spite of my teeth, ay, and she shall have it because she is a woman, which kind of cattle are indeed all echo, nothing but tongue, and are like the great bell of St. Michael's[1] in Cyprus, that keeps most rumbling when men would most sleep. Echo, a pox on thee for mocking me.

Echo. A pox on thee for mocking me.

Fort. Why so, Snip snap, this war is at an end, but

---

[1] Probably a church in Famagosta, which tradition makes Fortunatus's native place, and which was at one time the chief port and fortress in Cyprus.

this wilderness is world without end. To see how travel can transform : my teeth are turned into nutcrackers, a thousand to one I break out shortly, for I am full of nothing but waxen kernels, my tongue speaks no language but an almond for a parrot, and crack me this nut. If I hop three days more up and down this cage of cuckoos' nests, I shall turn wild man sure, and be hired to throw squibs among the commonalty upon some terrible day.   In the meantime, to tell truth, here will I lie. Farewell, fool !

Echo. Farewell, fool.

Fort. Are not these comfortable words to a wise man ? All hail, signor tree, by your leave I'll sleep under your leaves.   I pray bow to me, and I'll bend to you, for your back and my brows must, I doubt, have a game or two at noddy ere I wake again : down, great heart, down. Hey, ho, well, well.   [*He lies down and sleeps.*

Enter a Shepherd, *a* Carter,[1] *a* Tailor,[2] *and a* Monk, *all crowned ; a* Nymph *with a globe, another with* FORTUNE'S *wheel ; then* FORTUNE. *After her, four* Kings *with broken crowns and sceptres, chained in silver gyves and led by her. The fore-most enter singing.* FORTUNE *takes her chair, the* Kings *lying at her feet so that she treads on them as she ascends to her seat.*

SONG.

Fortune smiles, cry holiday,
Dimples on her cheeks do dwell,
Fortune frowns, cry welladay,
Her love is Heaven, her hate is Hell :
Since Heaven and Hell obey her power.
Tremble when her eyes do lower,

---

[1] " A gardener " in the original, which does not tally with the description given by Fortune on p. 300. *q.v.*

[2] " A smith " in the original, which is again a confusion with the description in the text.

Since Heaven and Hell her power obey,
When she smiles, cry holiday.
  Holiday with joy we cry
  And bend, and bend, and merrily
  Sing hymns to Fortune's deity,
  Sing hymns to Fortune's deity.

Chorus. Let us sing, merrily, merrily, merrily,
  With our song let Heaven resound,
  Fortune's hands our heads have crowned;
  Let us sing merrily, merrily, merrily.

    1*st King.* Accursed Queen of chance, what had we done,
Who having sometimes like young Phaeton,
Rid in the burnished chariot of the sun,
And sometimes been thy minions, when thy fingers
Weaved wanton love-nets in our curlèd hair,
And with sweet juggling kisses warmed our cheeks:
Oh how have we offended thy proud eyes,
That thus we should be spurned and trod upon,
Whilst those infected limbs of the sick world,
Are fixed by thee for stars in that bright sphere,
Wherein our sun-like radiance did appear.
  The Kings. Accursèd Queen of chance, damned sorceress.
  The Others. Most powerful Queen of chance, dread sovereigness.
  Fortune. No more: curse on! your cries to me are music,
And fill the sacred rondure of mine ears
With tunes more sweet than moving of the spheres:
Curse on: on our celestial brows do sit
Unnumbered smiles, which then leap from their throne,
When they see peasants dance and monarchs groan.
Behold you not this globe, this golden bowl,
This toy called world, at our imperial feet?
This world is Fortune's ball, wherewith she sports.
Sometimes I strike it up into the air,

And then create I emperors and kings :
Sometimes I spurn it, at which spurn crawls out
That wild beast Multitude.   Curse on, you fools,—
'Tis I that tumble princes from their thrones,
And gild false brows with glittering diadems.
'Tis I that tread on necks of conquerors,
And when, like demi-gods, they have been drawn
In ivory chariots to the capitol,
Circled about with wonder of all eyes,
The shouts of every tongue, love of all hearts,
Being swoll'n with their own greatness, I have pricked
The bladder of their pride, and made them die,
As water-bubbles, without memory.
I thrust base cowards into Honour's chair,
Whilst the true-spirited soldier stands by
Bare-headed, and all bare, whilst at his scars
They scoff, that ne'er durst view the face of wars.
I set an idiot's cap on Virtue's head,[1]
Turn Learning out of doors, clothe Wit in rags,
And paint ten thousand images of loam
In gaudy silken colours.   On the backs
Of mules and asses I make asses ride,
Only for sport, to see the apish world
Worship such beasts with sound idolatry.
This Fortune does, and when this is done,
She sits and smiles to hear some curse her name,
And some with adoration crown her fame.

     Monk. True centre of this wide circumference,
Sacred commandress of the destinies,
Our tongues shall only sound thy excellence.

     The Others. Thy excellence our tongues shall only
sound.

     2nd King. Thou painted strumpet, that with honeyed
          smiles,

---

[1] An allusion to the coxcomb, the invariable ornament to the
fool's cap, which Virtue wears on her head.   See description,
Scene III.

In triumph at his heels, and there in grief
Dash out thy brains.

    4th King. Oh miserable me !

    Fortune. No tears can melt the heart of destiny :
These have I ruined and exalted those.
These hands have conquered Spain, these brows fill up
The golden circle of rich Portugal,—
Viriat a monarch now, but born a shepherd ;[1]
This Primislaus, a Bohemian king,
Last day a carter ;[2] this monk, Gregory,[3]
Now lifted to the Papal dignity ;—
Wretches,[4] why gnaw you not your fingers off,
And tear your tongues out, seeing yourselves trod down,
And this Dutch botcher[5] wearing Munster's crown,
John Leyden,[6] born in Holland poor and base,
Now rich in empery and Fortune's grace ?
As these I have advanced, so will I thee.
Six gifts I spend upon mortality,
Wisdom, strength, health, beauty, long life, and riches,
Out of my bounty : one of these is thine,—
Choose then which likes thee best.

    Fort. Oh most divine !
Give me but leave to borrow wonder's eye,
To look amazed at thy bright majesty,

---

    [1] Viriathus, a shepherd who became a famous Lusitanian chief in the 2nd century B.C., and long warred successfully against the Romans in Spain.

    [2] Primislaus, a country labourer, who became first Duke of Bohemia, having married the daughter of Croc who founded the city of Prague.

    [3] Gregory VII. (1013—1085).

    [4] Fortune here turns and addresses the four deposed kings again.

    [5] Tailor. See *The Devil's Answer to Pierce Pennylesse* (Dekker's non-dramatic works, The Huth Library, edited by the Rev. A. B. Grosart, vol. ii. p. 147), " That botcher I preferred to be Lucifer's tailor, because he works with a hot needle and burnt thread."

    [6] John of Leyden (John Beccold), b. 1510, d. 1536, a tailor, who became a leader of the Anabaptists and at their head took extra-ordinary possession of the city of Munster, and ruled for a brief space as king there, before constitutional authority was restored and he was seized and put to death.

Wisdom, strength, health, beauty, long life, and riches.
  Fortune. Before thy soul at this deep lottery
Draw forth her prize, ordained by destiny,
Know that here's no recanting a first choice.
Choose then discreetly for the laws of Fate,
Being graven in steel, must stand inviolate.
  Fort. Daughters of Jove and the unblemished Night,
Most righteous Parcae,[1] guide my genius right,
Wisdom, strength, health, beauty, long life, and riches.
  Fortune. Stay, Fortunatus, once more hear me speak ;
If thou kiss Wisdom's cheek and make her thine,
She'll breathe into thy lips divinity,
And thou like Phœbus shalt speak oracle,
Thy Heaven-inspired soul, on Wisdom's wings,
Shall fly up to the Parliament of Jove,
And read the statutes of eternity,
And see what's past and learn what is to come.
If thou lay claim to strength, armies shall quake
To see thee frown : as kings at mine do lie,
So shall thy feet trample on empery.
Make health thine object, thou shalt be strong proof
'Gainst the deep searching darts of surfeiting,
Be ever merry, ever revelling.
Wish but for beauty, and within thine eyes
Two naked Cupids amorously shall swim,[2]
And on thy cheeks I'll mix such white and red,
That Jove shall turn away young Ganymede,
And with immortal arms shall circle thee.
Are thy desires long life ?—thy vital thread

---

[1] The Three Destinies, to whom Fortune herself was sometimes added as a fourth.   Fortunatus here seems to be addressing Fortune and her two attendant nymphs, for no stage direction is specially given for the entrance of the Three Destinies, as in Act II. sc. ii., *q.v.*

[2] See an anonymous poem in *Tottel's Miscellany*, 1557, called "A praise of his Lady," from which Dekker may have borrowed the fancy :—

> "In each of her two crystal eyes
> Smileth a naked boy."

The Kings. We dwell with cares, yet cannot quickly die.   [*Exèunt all singing, except* FORTUNATUS.

Fort. But now go dwell with cares and quickly die? How quickly? if I die to-morrow, I'll be merry to-day: if next day, I'll be merry to-morrow. Go dwell with cares? Where dwells Care? Hum ha, in what house dwells Care, that I may choose an honester neighbour? In princes' courts? No. Among fair ladies? Neither: there's no care dwells with them, but care how to be most gallant. Among gallants then? Fie, fie, no! Care is afraid sure of a gilt rapier, the scent of musk is her prison, tobacco chokes her, rich attire presseth her to death. Princes, fair ladies and gallants, have amongst you then, for this wet-eyed wench Care dwells with wretches: they are wretches that feel want, I shall feel none if I be never poor; therefore, Care, I cashier you my company. I wonder what blind gossip this minx is that is so prodigal; she should be a good one by her open dealing: her name's Fortune: it's no matter what she is, so she does as she says. "Thou shalt spend ever, and be never poor." Mass, yet I feel nothing here to make me rich:— here's no sweet music with her silver sound. Try deeper: ho God be here: ha, ha, one, two, three, four, five, six, seven, eight, nine and ten, good, just ten. It's gold sure, it's so heavy, try again, one, two, &c. Good again, just ten, and just ten. Ha, ha, ha, this is rare: a leather mint, admirable: an Indian mine in a lamb's skin, miraculous! I'll fill three or four bags full for my sons, but keep this for myself. If that lean tawny face tobacconist Death, that turns all into smoke, must turn me so quickly into ashes, yet I will not mourn in ashes, but in music, hey, old lad, be merry. Here's riches, wisdom, strength, health, beauty, and long life (if I die not quickly). Sweet purse, I kiss thee; Fortune, I adore thee; Care, I despise thee; Death, I defy thee.[1]   [*Exit.*

---

[1] Compare Shakespeare's "Crabbed Age and Youth."

SCENE II.—*Outside the House of* FORTUNATUS.

Enter AMPEDO, SHADOW *after him, both sad: then*
ANDELOCIA.

Andel. 'Sheart,[1] why how now: two knights of the
post?[2]

Shad. Ay, master, and we are both forsworn, as all
such wooden knights be, for we both took an oath—
marry it was not corporal, you may see by our cheeks,
that we would not fast twenty-four hours to amend, and
we have tasted no meat since the clock told two
dozen.

Andel. That lacks not much of twenty-four, but I
wonder when that half-faced moon of thine will be at the
full.

Shad. The next quarter, not this, when the sign is in
Taurus.

Andel. Ho, that's to say, when thou eat'st bull beef.
But, Shadow, what day is to-day?

Shad. Fasting day.

Andel. What day was yesterday?

Shad. Fasting day too.

Andel. Will to-morrow be so too?

Shad. Ay, and next day too.

Andel. That will be rare, you slave:
For a lean diet makes a fat wit.

Shad. I had rather be a fool and wear a fat pair of
cheeks.

Andel. Now I am prouder of this poverty, which I
know is mine own, than a waiting gentlewoman is of a
frizzled groatsworth of hair, that never grew on her head.
Sir Shadow, now we can all three swear like Puritans at
one bare word: this want makes us like good bowlers,
we are able to rub out and shift in every place.

Shad. That's not so, we have shifted ourselves in no

---

[1] A corruption of "God's heart."   [2] Hired witnesses.

Dekker.   X place this three months : marry, we rub out in every corner, but here follows no amendment either of life or of livery.

Andel. Why, brother Ampedo, art thou not yet tired with riding post ? Come, come, 'light from this logger-headed jade, and walk afoot, and talk with your poor friends.

Shad. Nay, by my troth, he is like me : if his belly be empty, his heart is full.

Andel. The famine of gold gnaws his covetous stomach, more than the want of good victuals : thou hast looked very devilishly ever since the good angel [1] left thee : come, come, leave this broad-brim fashions ; because the world frowns upon thee, wilt not thou smile upon us ?

Amp. Did but the bitterness of mine own fortunes
Infect my taste, I could paint o'er my cheeks
With ruddy-coloured smiles : 'tis not the want
Of costly diet or desire of gold
Enforces rupture in my wounded breast.
Oh no, our father—if he live—doth lie
Under the iron foot of misery,
And, as a dove gripped in a falcon's claw,
There pant'th for life being most assured of death.
Brother, for him my soul thus languisheth.

Shad. 'Tis not for my old master that I languish.

Amp. I am not enamoured of this painted idol,
This strumpet World ; for her most beauteous looks
Are poisoned baits, hung upon golden hooks :
When fools do swim in wealth, her Cynthian beams
Will wantonly dance on the silver streams ;
But when this squint-eyed age sees Virtue poor,
And by a little spark sits shivering,
Begging at all, relieved at no man's door,
She smiles on her, as the sun shines on fire,
To kill that little heat, and, with her little frown,

---

[1] One of the usual puns on the coin of that name.

Is proud that she can tread poor Virtue down :
Therefore her wrinkled brow makes not mine sour,
Her gifts are toys, and I desire her power.

Shad. 'Tis not the crab-tree faced World neither that makes mine sour.

Andel. Her gifts toys ! Well, brother Virtue, we have let slip the ripe plucking of those toys so long, that we flourish like apple-trees in September, which, having the falling sickness, bear neither fruit nor leaves.

Shad. Nay, by my troth, master, none flourish in these withering times, but ancient bearers [1] and trumpeters.

Andel. Shadow, when thou provest a substance, then the tree of virtue and honesty, and such fruit of Heaven, shall flourish upon earth.

Shad. True ; or when the sun shines at midnight, or women fly, and yet they are light enough.

Andel. 'Twas never merry world with us, since purses and bags were invented, for now men set lime-twigs to catch wealth : and gold, which riseth like the sun out of the East Indies, to shine upon every one, is like a cony taken napping in a pursenet,[2] and suffers his glistering yellow-face deity to be lapped up in lambskins, as if the innocency of those leather prisons should dispense with the cheveril [3] consciences of the iron-hearted gaolers.

Shad. Snudges [4] may well be called gaolers : for if a poor wretch steal but into a debt of ten pound, they lead him straight to execution.

Andel. Doth it not vex thee, Shadow, to stalk up and down Cyprus, and to meet the outside of a man, lapped all in damask, his head and beard as white as milk, only with conjuring in the snowy circles of the field argent, and his nose as red as scarlet, only with kissing

---

[1] Ensign-bearers.

[2] A net the ends of which are drawn together with a string like a purse.

[3] Kid leather (Fr. *chevreau*).   Hence a very flexible conscience was often called a cheveril conscience. — *Halliwell.*

[4] Mean or miserly persons. — *Halliwell.*

the ruddy lips of angels,[1] and such an image to wear on
his thumb, three men's livings in the shape of a seal ring,
whilst my brother Virtue here,—

Shad. And you his brother Vice !

Andel. Most true, my little lean Iniquity—whilst we
three, if we should starve, cannot borrow five shillings
of him neither in word nor deed : does not this vex thee,
Shadow ?

Shad. Not me ; it vexes me no more to see such a
picture, than to see an ass laden with riches, because I
know when he can bear no longer, he must leave his
burthen to some other beast.

Andel. Art not thou mad, to see money on goldsmiths'
stalls, and none in our purses ?

Shad. It mads not me, I thank the destinies.

Andel. By my poverty, and that's but a thread-bare
oath, I am more than mad to see silks and velvets lie
crowding together in mercers' shops, as in prisons, only
for fear of the smell of wax—they cannot abide to see a
man made out of wax, for these satin commodities have
such smooth consciences that they'll have no man give
his word for them or stand bound for their coming forth,
but vow to lie till they rot in those shop counters, except
Monsieur Money bail them.   Shadow, I am out of my
little wits to see this.

Shad. So is not Shadow : I am out of my wits, to see
fat gluttons feed all day long, whilst I that am lean fast
every day : I am out of my wits, to see our Famagosta
fools turn half a shop of wares into a suit of gay apparel,
only to make other idiots laugh, and wise men to cry,
who's the fool now ?   I am mad, to see soldiers beg, and
cowards brave : I am mad, to see scholars in the broker's
shop, and dunces in the mercer's : I am mad, to see men
that have no more fashion in them than poor Shadow,
yet must leap thrice a day into three orders of fashions :

---

[1] See note *ante*, p. 306.

I am mad, to see many things, but horn-mad, that my mouth feels nothing.

Andel. Why now, Shadow, I see thou hast a substance : I am glad to see thee thus mad.

Amp. The sons of Fortunatus had not wont
Thus to repine at others' happiness :
But fools have always this loose garment wore,
Being poor themselves, they wish all others poor.
Fie, brother Andelocia, hate this madness,
Turn your eyes inward, and behold your soul,
That wants more than your body ; burnish that
With glittering virtue, and make idiots grieve
To see your beauteous mind in wisdom shine,
As you at their rich poverty repine.

Enter FORTUNATUS, *gallant.*[1]

Andel. Peace, good Virtue; Shadow, here comes another shadow.

Shad. It should be a chameleon : for he is all in colours.

Amp. Oh, 'tis my father.   With these tears of joy,
My love and duty greet your fair return !
A double gladness hath refreshed my soul ;
One, that you live, and one, to see your fate
Looks freshly howsoever poor in state.

Andel. My father Fortunatus, and thus brave ?

Shad. 'Tis no wonder to see a man brave, but a wonder how he comes brave.

Fort. Dear Andelocia and son Ampedo,
And my poor servant Shadow, plume your spirits
With light-winged mirth ; for Fortunatus' hand
Can now pour golden showers into their laps
That sometimes scorned him for his want of gold.
Boys, I am rich, and you shall ne'er be poor ;
Wear gold, spend gold, we all in gold will feed,
Now is your father Fortunate indeed.

[1] *i.e.* Gallantly attired.

Andel. Father, be not angry, if I set open the windows
of my mind : I doubt for all your bragging, you'll prove
like most of our gallants in Famagosta, that have a rich
outside and a beggarly inside, and like mules wear gay
trappings, and good velvet foot-cloths [1] on their backs,
yet champ on the iron bit of penury—I mean, want coin.
You gild our ears with a talk of gold, but I pray dazzle
our eyes with the majesty of it.

Fort. First will I wake your senses with the sound
Of gold's sweet music : tell me what you hear ?

Amp. Believe me, sir, I hear not any thing.

Andel. Ha, ha, ha. 'Sheart, I thought as much ; if I
hear any jingling, but of the purse strings that go flip
flap, flip flap, flip flap, would I were turned into a flip-
flap,[2] and sold to the butchers !

Fort. Shadow, I'll try thine ears ; hark, dost rattle ?

Shad. Yes, like three blue beans in a blue bladder,
rattle bladder, rattle : your purse is like my belly,
th' one's without money, th' other without meat.

Fort. Bid your eyes blame the error of your ears :
You misbelieving pagans, see, here's gold—
Ten golden pieces : take them, Ampedo.
Hold, Andelocia, here are ten for thee.

Amp. Shadow, there's one for thee, provide thee food.

Fort. Stay, boy : hold, Shadow, here are ten for thee.

Shad. Ten, master ? then defiance to fortune, and a
fig for famine.

Fort. Now tell me, wags, hath my purse gold or no ?

Andel. We the wags have gold, father ; but I think
there's not one angel more wagging in this sacred temple.
Why, this is rare : Shadow, five will serve thy turn, give
me th' other five.

Shad. Nay, soft, master, liberality died long ago. I
see some rich beggars are never well, but when they be

---

[1] Housings hung on horses and mules, and considered a mark of
dignity.—*Halliwell.*

[2] A stick with leather flap for killing flies.

craving : my ten ducats are like my ten fingers, they will not jeopard a joint for you. I am yours, and these are mine; if I part from them, I shall never have part of them.

Amp. Father, if Heaven have blest you once again,
Let not an open hand disperse that store,
Which gone, life's gone ; for all tread down the poor.

Fort. Peace, Ampedo, talk not of poverty.
Disdain, my boys, to kiss the tawny cheeks
Of lean necessity : make not inquiry
How I came rich ; I am rich, let that suffice.
There are four leathern bags trussed full of gold :
Those spent, I'll fill you more. Go, lads, be gallant :
Shine in the streets of Cyprus like two stars,
And make them bow their knees that once did spurn
   you ;
For, to effect such wonders, gold can turn you.
Brave it in Famagosta, or elsewhere ;
I'll travel to the Turkish Emperor,
And then I'll revel it with Prester John,[1]
Or banquet with great Cham [2] of Tartary,
And try what frolic court the Soldan keeps.
I'll leave you presently. Tear off these rags ;
Glitter, my boys, like angels,[3] that the world
May, whilst our life in pleasure's circle roams,
Wonder at Fortunatus and his sons.

Andel. Come, Shadow, now we'll feast it royally.

Shad. Do, master, but take heed of beggary.

         [Exeunt.

[1] One of the followers of Ogier the Dane into India, according to Mandeville, who was given sovereignty there, and is said by tradition to have had seventy tributary kings.

[2] *i.e.* Khan.   [3] Another reference to the gold coins so called.

SCENE III.—*A Wood in Cyprus.*

Music sounds.   Enter VICE *with a gilded face, and horns
       on her head ; her garments long, painted before with
       silver half-moons, increasing by little and little till
       they come to the full ; while in the midst of them is
       written in capital letters, "* Crescit Eundo." * Behind
       her garments are painted with fools' faces and heads ;
       and in the midst is written, "* Ha, Ha, He." * She, and
       others wearing gilded vizards and attired like devils,
       bring out a fair tree of gold with apples on it.*

After her comes VIRTUE, *with a coxcomb on her
       head, and her attire all in white before ; about the
       middle is written "* Sibi sapit." * Her attire behind is
       painted with crowns and laurel garlands, stuck full of
       stars held by hands thrust out of bright clouds, and
       among them is written, "* Dominabitur astris." * She
       and other nymphs, all in white with coxcombs on
       their heads, bring a tree with green and withered
       leaves mingled together, and with little fruit on it.*

After her comes FORTUNE, *with two Nymphs, one
       bearing her wheel, another her globe.*

And last, the Priest.

Fortune. You ministers of Virtue, Vice, and Fortune,
Tear off this upper garment of the earth,
And in her naked bosom stick these trees.

Virtue. How many kingdoms have I measured,
Only to find a climate, apt to cherish
These withering branches ? But no ground can prove
So happy ; ay me, none do Virtue love.
I'll try this soil ; if here I likewise fade,
To Heaven I'll fly, from whence I took my birth,
And tell the Gods, I am banished from the earth.

Vice. Virtue, I am sworn thy foe : if there thou plant,
Here, opposite to thine, my tree shall flourish,
And as the running wood-bine spreads her arms,
To choke thy withering boughs in their embrace,

I'll drive thee from this world : were Virtue fled,
Vice as an angel should be honourèd.

    Fortune. Servants of this bright devil and that poor
        saint,
Apply your task whilst you are labouring :
To make your pains seem short our priest shall sing.

        [*Whilst the* Priest *sings, the rest set the trees into
        the earth.*

SONG.

    Virtue's branches wither, Virtue pines,
      O pity, pity, and alack the time,
    Vice doth flourish, Vice in glory shines,
      Her gilded boughs above the cedar climb.
    Vice hath golden cheeks, O pity, pity,
      She in every land doth monarchize.
    Virtue is exiled from every city,
      Virtue is a fool, Vice only wise.
    O pity, pity, Virtue weeping dies.
      Vice laughs to see her faint,—alack the time.
    This sinks ; with painted wings the other flies :
      Alack that best should fall, and bad should climb.
      O pity, pity, pity, mourn, not sing,
      Vice is a saint, Virtue an underling.
      Vice doth flourish, Vice in glory shines,
      Virtue's branches wither, Virtue pines.

    Fortune. Flourish or wither, Fortune cares not which,
In either's fall or height our eminence
Shines equal to the sun : the Queen of chance
Both virtuous souls and vicious doth advance.
These shadows of yourselves shall, like yourselves,
Strive to make men enamoured of their beauties;
This grove shall be our temple, and henceforth
Be consecrated to our deities.

    Virtue. How few will come and kneel at Virtue's
        shrine ?

    Vice. This contents Virtue, that she is called divine.

Fortune. Poor Virtue, Fortune grieves to see thy looks
Want cunning to entice : why hang these leaves,
As loose as autumn's hair which every wind
In mockery blows from his rotten brows ?
Why like a drunkard art thou pointed at ?
Why is this motley-scorn [1] set on thy head ?
Why stands thy court wide open, but none in it ?
Why are the crystal pavements of thy temple,
Not worn, not trod upon?   All is for this,
Because thy pride is to wear base attire,
Because thine eyes flame not with amorous fire.

    Virtue. Virtue is fairest in a poor array.

    Fortune. Poor fool, 'tis not this badge of purity,
Nor *Sibi sapit*, painted on thy breast,
Allures mortality to seek thy love.
No : now the great wheel of thy globe hath run,
And met this first point of creation.
On crutches went this world but yesterday,
Now it lies bed-rid, and is grown so old,
That it's grown young ; for 'tis a child again,
A childish soul it hath, 'tis a mere fool :
And fools and children are well pleased with toys.
So must this world, with shows it must be pleased,
Then, Virtue, buy a golden face like Vice,
And hang thy bosom full of silver moons,
To tell the credulous world, As those increase,
As the bright moon swells in her pearlèd sphere,
So wealth and pleasures them to Heaven shall rear.

    Virtue. Virtue abhors to wear a borrowed face.

    Vice. Why hast thou borrowed, then, that idiot's hood ?

    Virtue. Fools placed it on my head that knew me not,
And I am proud to wear the scorn of fools.

    Fortune. Mourn in that pride and die, all the world
        hates thee.

    Virtue. Not all, I'll wander once more through the
        world :

---

[1] *i.e.* The fool's cap.

Wisdom I know hath with her blessèd wings
Fled to some bosom : if I meet that breast,
There I'll erect my temple, and there rest.
Fortune nor Vice shall then e'er have the power
By their loose eyes to entice my paramour.
Then will I cast off this deformity,
And shine in glory, and triumph to see
You conquered at my feet, that tread on me.

  Fortune. Virtue begins to quarrel : Vice, farewell.

  Vice. Stay, Fortune, whilst within this grove we dwell,
If my angelical and saint-like form
Can win some amorous fool to wanton here,
And taste the fruit of this alluring tree,
Thus shall his saucy brows adornèd be,
To make us laugh.   *[Makes horns.*

  Fortune. It will be rare : adieu.

  Virtue. Foul, hell-bred fiend, Virtue shall strive with
      you,
If any be enamoured of thine eyes,
Their love must needs beget deformities.
Men are transformed to beasts, feasting with sin ;
But if in spite of thee their souls I win,
To taste this fruit, though thou disguise their head,
Their shapes shall be re-metamorphosèd.

  Vice. I dare thee do thy worst.

  Virtue. My best I'll try.

  Fort. Fortune shall judge who wins the sovereignty.
                    [Exeunt.

ACT THE SECOND.

Enter Chorus.

HORUS. The world to the circumfer-
            ence of Heaven
            Is as a small point in geometry,
            Whose greatness is so little, that a less
            Cannot be made : into that narrow
            room,
Your quick imaginations we must charm,
To turn that world : and turned, again to part it
Into large kingdoms, and within one moment
To carry Fortunatus on the wings
Of active thought, many a thousand miles.
Suppose then, since you last beheld him here,
That you have sailed with him upon the seas,
And leapt with him upon the Asian shores,
Been feasted with him in the Tartar's palace,
And all the courts of each barbarian king :
From whence being called by some unlucky star,—
For happiness never continues long,
Help me to bring him back to Arragon,
Where for his pride—riches make all men proud—
On slight quarrel, by a covetous Earl,
Fortune's dear minion is imprisonèd.
There think you see him sit with folded arms,
Tears dropping down his cheeks, his white hairs torn,
His legs in rusty fetters, and his tongue
Bitterly cursing that his squint-eyed soul

Did not make choice of wisdom's sacred love.
Fortune, to triumph in inconstancy,
From prison bails him: liberty is wild,
For being set free, he like a lusty eagle
Cut with his vent'rous feathers through the sky,
And 'lights not till he find the Turkish court.
Thither transport your eyes, and there behold him,
Revelling with the Emperor of the East,
From whence through fear, for safeguard of his life,
Flying into the arms of ugly Night,
Suppose you see him brought to Babylon ;
And that the sun clothed all in fire hath rid
One quarter of his hot celestial way
With the bright morning, and that in this instant,
He and the Soldan meet, but what they say,
Listen you—the talk of kings none dare bewray. [*Exit.*

SCENE I.—*The Court at Babylon.*[1]

Enter the SOLDAN, Noblemen, *and* FORTUNATUS.

OLD. Art thou that Fortunatus, whose
　　　great name,
　　Being carried in the chariot of the
　　　winds,
　　Hast filled the courts of all our Asian
　　　kings
With love and envy, whose dear presence ties
The eyes of admiration to thine eyes ?
Art thou that Jove that in a shower of gold
Appeared'st before the Turkish Emperor ?
　Fort. I am that Fortunatus, mighty Soldan.

---

[1] In the original story Fortunatus goes to Cairo, and Dekker is
evidently here confusing Egypt with Assyria. Hence the Soldan's
court at Babylon.

Sold. Where is that purse which threw abroad such
    treasure ?

Fort. I gave it to the Turkish Soliman,
A second I bestowed on Prester John,
A third the great Tartarian Cham received :
For with these monarchs have I banqueted,
And rid with them in triumph through their courts,
In crystal chariots drawn by unicorns.
England, France, Spain, and wealthy Belgia,
And all the rest of Europe's blessed daughters,
Have made my covetous eye rich in th' embrace
Of their celestial beauties ; now I come
To see the glory of fair Babylon.
Is Fortunatus welcome to the Soldan ?
For I am like the sun, if Jove once chide,
My gilded brows from amorous Heaven I hide.

Sold. Most welcome, and most happy are mine arms
In circling such an earthly deity ;
But will not Fortunatus make me blessed
By sight of such a purse ?

Fort. Ere I depart,
The Soldan shall receive one at my hands :
For I must spend some time in framing it,
And then some time to breathe that virtuous spirit
Into the heart thereof, all which is done
By a most sacred inspiration.

Sold. Welcome, most welcome to the Soldan's court ;
Stay here and be the King of Babylon :
Stay here, I will more amaze thine eyes
With wondrous sights, than can all Asia.
Behold yon town, there stands mine armoury,
In which are corselets forged of beaten gold,
To arm ten hundred thousand fighting men,
Whose glittering squadrons when the sun beholds,
They seem like to ten hundred thousand Joves,
When Jove on the proud back of thunder rides,
Trapped all in lightning flames : there can I show thee

The ball of gold that set all Troy on fire ; [1]
There shalt thou see the scarf of Cupid's mother,
Snatched from the soft moist ivory of her arm,
To wrap about Adonis' wounded thigh ;
There shalt thou see a wheel of Titan's care,
Which dropped from Heaven when Phaeton fired the
    world : [2]
I'll give thee, if thou wilt, two silver doves
Composed by magic to divide the air,
Who, as they fly, shall clap their silver wings,
And give strange music to the elements ;
I'll give thee else the fan of Proserpine,
Which in reward for a sweet Thracian song,
The black-browed Empress threw to Orpheus,
Being come to fetch Eurydice from hell.

   Fort. Hath ever mortal eye beheld these wonders?

   Sold. Thine shall behold them, and make choice of
    any,
So thou wilt give the Soldan such a purse.

   Fort. By Fortune's blessèd hand, who christened
    me,
The mighty Soldan shall have such a purse,
Provided I may see these priceless wonders.

   Sold. Leave us alone : [*Exeunt* Nobles.] never was
    mortal ear
Acquainted with the virtue of a jewel,
Which now I'll show, out-valuing all the rest.

   Fort. It is impossible.

   Sold. Behold this casket,   [*Draws a curtain.*
Fettered in golden chains, the lock pure gold,
The key of solid gold, which myself keep,
And here's the treasure that's contained in it.

                        [*Takes out the hat.*

   Fort. A coarse felt hat ? is this the precious jewel ?

---

[1] The golden apple which Paris adjudged to Venus.
[2] Alluding to Phaeton's flight, and the fiery disruption of his
chariot.

Sold. I'll not exchange this for ten diadems.
On pain of death, none listen to our talk.

Fort. What needs this solemn conjuration !

Sold. O, yes, for none shall understand the worth
Of this inestimable ornament,
But you : and yet not you, but that you swear
By her white hand, that lent you such a name,
To leave a wondrous purse in Babylon.

Fort. What I have sworn, I will not violate,
But now uncover the virtues of this hat.

Sold. I think none listen ; if they do, they die.

Fort. None listen : tell, what needs this jealousy ?

Sold. You see 'tis poor in show ; did I want jewels,
Gold could beget them, but the wide world's wealth
Buys not this hat : this clapped upon my head,
I, only with a wish, am through the air
Transported in a moment over seas
And over lands to any secret place ;
By this I steal to every prince's court,
And hear their private counsels and prevent
All dangers which to Babylon are meant ;
By help of this I oft see armies join,
Though when the dreadful Alvarado[1] sounds,
I am distant from the place a thousand leagues.
Oh, had I such a purse and such a hat,
The Soldan were, of all, most fortunate.

Fort. Oh, had I such a hat, then were I brave.
Where's he that made it ?

Sold.   Dead, and the whole world
Yields not a workman that can frame the like.

Fort. No, does't ?[2]   By what trick shall I make this
          mine ?   [*Aside.*
Methinks, methinks, when you are borne o'er seas,

---

[1] A martial term, probably of Spanish derivation, for the summons
to battle.

[2] "No does ? " simply in the original, which is not intelligible.
In full it would seem to imply " No, does it not ? "

And over lands, the heaviness thereof
Should weigh you down, drown you, or break your neck.

Sold. No, 'tis more light than any hat beside :
Your hand shall peise [1] it.

Fort. Oh, 'tis wondrous heavy.

Sold. Fie, y'are deceived : try it upon your head.

Fort. Would I were now in Cyprus with my sons.

[*Exit.*

Sold. Stay ! Fortunatus, stay ! I am undone.
Treason, lords, treason, get me wings, I'll fly
After this damnèd traitor through the air.

Re-enter Nobles.

Nobles. Who wrongs the mighty King of Babylon ?

Sold. This Fortunatus, this fiend, wrongs your king.

Nobles. Lock the court gates, where is the devil hid ?

Sold. No gates, no grates of iron imprison him,
Like a magician breaks he through the clouds,
Bearing my soul with him, for that jewel gone,
I am dead, and all is dross in Babylon.
Fly after him !—'tis vain : on the wind's wings,
He'll ride through all the courts of earthly kings.

Nobles. What is the jewel that your grace hath lost ?

Sold. He dies that troubles me : call me not king ;
For I'll consume my life in sorrowing.   [*Exeunt.*

SCENE II.—*Outside the House of* FORTUNATUS.

Enter ANDELOCIA, *very gallant,*[2] *and* SHADOW.

Andel. Shadow ? what have I lost to-day at dice ?

Shad. More than you will win again in a month.

Andel. Why, sir, how much comes it to ?

---

[1] Poise, weigh. "Peise" is still in use in some parts of the
north of England.

[2] *i.e.* Gallantly attired.

Shad. It comes to nothing, sir, for you have lost your wits; and when a man's wits are lost, the man is like twenty pounds' worth of tobacco, which mounts into th' air, and proves nothing but one thing.

Andel. And what thing is that, you ass?

Shad. Marry, sir, that he is an ass that melts so much money in smoke.

Andel. 'Twere a charitable deed to hang thee a smoking.

Shad. I should never make good bacon, because I am not fat.

Andel. I'll be sworn thy wit is lean.

Shad. It's happy I have a lean wit: but, master, you have none; for when your money tripped away, that went after it, and ever since you have been mad. Here comes your brother.

Enter AMPEDO.

Borrow a dram of him, if his be not mouldy: for men's wits in these days are like the cuckoo, bald once a year, and that makes motley so dear, and fools so good cheap.

Andel. Brother, all hail.

Shad. There's a rattling salutation.

Andel. You must lend me some more money. Nay, never look so strange, an you will come off, so; if you will bar me from square play, do. Come, come, when the old traveller my father comes home, like a young ape, full of fantastic tricks, or a painted parrot stuck full of outlandish feathers, he'll lead the world in a string, and then like a hot shot I'll charge and discharge all.

Shad. I would be loth, master, to see that day: for he leads the world in a string that goes to hanging.

Andel. Take heed I turn not that head into the world, and lead you so.

Brother wilt be? Ha' ye any ends of gold or silver?

Amp. Thus wanton revelling breeds beggary.

Brother, 'twere better that you still lived poor.
Want would make wisdom rich : but when your coffers
Swell to the brim, then riot sets up sails,
And like a desperate unskilled mariner
Drives your unsteady fortunes on the point
Of wreck inevitable.   Of all the wealth
Left by our father, when he left us last,
This little is unspent, and this being wasted,
Your riot ends ; therefore consume it all.
I'll live ; or dying, find some burial.

Andel. Thanks for my crowns.[1] Shadow, I . am
villainous hungry, to hear one of the seven wise masters
talk thus emptily.

Shad. I am a villain, master, if I am not hungry.

Andel. Because I'll save this gold. sirrah Shadow, we'll
feed ourselves with paradoxes.

Shad. Oh rare : what meat's that ?

Andel. Meat, you gull : 'tis no meat : a dish of
paradoxes is a feast of strange opinion, 'tis an ordinary
that our greatest gallants haunt nowadays, because they
would be held for statesmen.

Shad. I shall never fill my belly with opinions.

Andel. In despite of sway-bellies, gluttons, and sweet
mouthed epicures, I'll have thee maintain a paradox in
commendations of hunger.

Shad. I shall never have the stomach to do't.

Andel. See'st thou this crusado ?[2] do it, and turn this
into a feast.

Shad. Covetousness and lechery are two devils, they'll
tempt a man to wade through deep matters : I'll do't
though good cheer conspire my death, for speaking treason
against her.

Andel. Fall to it then with a full mouth.

---

[1] In the original these words are assigned to Ampedo, an evident
error.
[2] A Portuguese coin having a cross on one side and worth about
2*s*. 3*d*., but varying in value at different times.

Shad. Oh famine, inspire me with thy miserable
reasons.
I begin, master.

Amp. O miserable invocation.

Andel. Silence!

Shad. There's no man but loves one of these three
beasts, a horse, a hound, or a whore ; the horse by his
goodwill has his head ever in the manger ; the whore
with your ill will has her hand ever in your purse ; and a
hungry dog eats dirty puddings.

Andel. This is profound, forward : the conclusion of
this now.

Shad. The conclusion is plain : for since all men love
one of these three monsters, being such terrible eaters,
therefore all men love hunger.

Amp. A very lean argument.

Shad. I can make it no fatter.

Andel. Proceed, good Shadow ; this fats me.

Shad. Hunger is made of gunpowder.

Andel. Give fire to that opinion.

Shad. Stand by, lest it blow you up.   Hunger is made
of gunpowder, or gunpowder of hunger, for they both eat
through stone walls ; hunger is a grindstone, it sharpens
wit ; hunger is fuller of love than Cupid, for it makes a
man eat himself ; hunger was the first that ever opened a
cook-shop, cooks the first that ever made sauce, sauce
being liquorish, licks up good meat ; good meat preserves
life : hunger therefore preserves life.

Amp. By my consent thou shouldst still live by hunger.

Shad. Not so, hunger makes no man mortal : hunger
is an excellent physician, for he dares kill any body.
Hunger is one of the seven liberal sciences.

Andel. Oh learned !   Which of the seven ?

Shad. Music, for she'll make a man leap at a crust ;
but as few care for her six sisters, so none love to dance
after her pipe.   Hunger, master, is hungry and covetous ;
therefore the crusado.

Andel. But hast thou no sharper reasons than this?

Shad. Yes, one : the dagger of Cyprus had never stabbed out such six penny pipes, but for hunger.

Andel. Why, you dolt, these pipes [1] are but in their minority.

Shad. My belly and my purse have been twenty times at dagger's drawing, with parting the little urchins.

Enter FORTUNATUS.

Amp. Peace, idiot, peace, my father is returned.

Fort. Touch me not, boys, I am nothing but air ; let none speak to me, till you have marked me well.

Shad. (*Chalking* FORTUNATUS' *back.*) Now speak your mind.

Amp. Villain, why hast thou chalked my father's back?

Shad. Only to mark him, and to try what colour air is of.

Fort. Regard him not, Ampedo : Andelocia, Shadow, view me, am I as you are, or am I transformed?

Andel. I thought travel would turn my father madman or fool.

Amp. How should you be transformed? I see no change.

Shad. If your wits be not planet stricken, if your brains lie in their right place, you are well enough ; for your body is little mended by your fetching vagaries.

Andel. Methinks, father, you look as you did, only your face is more withered.

Fort. That's not my fault ; age is like love, it cannot be hid.

Shad. Or like gunpowder a-fire, or like a fool, or like a young novice new come to his lands : for all these will show of what house they come. Now, sir, you may amplify.

Fort. Shadow, turn thy tongue to a shadow, be silent ! Boys, be proud, your father hath the whole world in this compass, I am all felicity, up to the brims.   In a minute

---

[1] " Pies " in the original, an evident misprint.

am I come from Babylon, I have been this half-hour in Famagosta.

Andel. How? in a minute, father? Ha, ha, I see travellers must lie.

Shad. 'Tis their destiny : the Fates do so conspire.

Fort. I have cut through the air like a falcon ; I would have it seem strange to you.

Shad. So it does, sir.

Fort. But 'tis true : I would not have you believe it neither.

Shad. No more we do not, sir.

Fort. But 'tis miraculous and true. Desire to see you, brought me to Cyprus. I'll leave you more gold, and go visit more countries.

Shad. Leave us gold enough, and we'll make all countries come visit us.

Amp. The frosty hand of age now nips your blood,
And strews her snowy flowers upon your head,
And gives you warning that within few years,
Death needs must marry you : those short-lived minutes,
That dribble out your life, must needs be spent
In peace, not travel : rest in Cyprus then.
Could you survey ten worlds, yet you must die ;
And bitter is the sweet that's reaped thereby.

Andel. Faith, father, what pleasure have you met by walking your stations?

Fort. What pleasure, boy? I have revelled with kings, danced with queens, dallied with ladies, worn strange attires, seen fantasticos, conversed with humorists, been ravished with divine raptures of Doric, Lydian and Phrygian harmonies. I have spent the day in triumphs, and the night in banqueting.

Andel. Oh rare : this was heavenly.

Shad. Methinks 'twas horrible.

Andel. He that would not be an Arabian phœnix to burn in these sweet fires, let him live like an owl for the world to wonder at.

Amp. Why, brother, are not all these vanities?

Fort. Vanities? Ampedo, thy soul is made of lead, too dull, too ponderous to mount up to the incomprehensible glory that travel lifts men to.

Shad. My old master's soul is cork and feathers, and being so light doth easily mount up.

Andel. Sweeten mine ears, good father, with some more.

Fort. When in the warmth of mine own country's
      arms
We yawned like sluggards, when this small horizon
Imprisoned up my body, then mine eyes
Worshipped these clouds as brightest; but, my boys,
The glist'ring beams which do abroad appear
In other heavens,—fire is not half so clear.

Shad. Why, sir, are there other heavens in other countries?

Andel. Peace; interrupt him not upon thy life.

Fort. For still in all the regions I have seen,
I scorned to crowd among the muddy throng
Of the rank multitude, whose thickened breath,
Like to condensèd fogs, do choke that beauty,
Which else would dwell in every kingdom's cheek.
No, I still boldly stept into their courts,
For there to live 'tis rare, O 'tis divine;
There shall you see faces angelical,
There shall you see troops of chaste goddesses,
Whose star-like eyes have power, might they still
      shine,
To make night day, and day more crystalline.
Near these you shall behold great heroes,
White-headed counsellors and jovial spirits,
Standing like fiery cherubims to guard
The monarch, who in god-like glory sits
In midst of these, as if this deity
Had with a look created a new world,
The standers by being the fair workmanship.

Andel. Oh how my soul is rapt to a third heaven.
I'll travel sure, and live with none but kings.

Shad. Then Shadow must die among knaves ; and yet
why so ? In a bunch of cards, knaves wait upon the
kings.

Andel. When I turn king, then shalt thou wait on me.

Shad. Well, there's nothing impossible : a dog has his
day, and so have you.

Amp. But tell me, father, have you in all courts
Beheld such glory, so majestical
In all perfection, no way blemishèd ?

Fort. In some courts shall you see ambition
Sit piercing Dedalus' old waxen wings,
But being clapped on, and they about to fly,
Even when their hopes are busied in the clouds,
They melt against the sun of majesty,
And down they tumble to destruction :
For since the Heaven's strong arms teach kings to stand,
Angels are placed about their glorious throne,
To guard it from the strokes of trait'rous hands.
By travel, boys, I have seen all these things.
Fantastic compliment stalks up and down,
Tricked in outlandish feathers, all his words,
His looks, his oaths, are all ridiculous,
All apish, childish, and Italianate.[1]

Enter FORTUNE *in the background : after her* The Three
Destinies,[2] *working.*

Shad. I know a medicine for that malady.

Fort. By travel, boys, I have seen all these things.

[1] A common reproach for the affectation of the courtiers in
Elizabeth's reign.

[2] See note *ante*, p. 301. " The Parcae were generally represented
as three old women with chaplets made with wool, and interwoven
with the flowers of the narcissus. They were covered with a white
robe, and fillet of the same colour, bound with chaplets. One of
them held a distaff, another the spindle, and the third was armed
with scissors with which she cut the thread which her sisters had
spun."—*Lempriere.*

Andel. And these are sights for none but gods and kings.

Shad. Yes, and for Christian creatures, if they be not blind.

Fort. In these two hands do I grip all the world.
This leather purse, and this bald woollen hat
Make me a monarch.   Here's my crown and sceptre !
In progress will I now go through the world.
I'll crack your shoulders, boys, with bags of gold
Ere I depart ; on Fortune's wings I ride,
And now sit in the height of human pride.

  Fortune. (*Coming forward.*) Now, fool, thou liest ;
      where thy proud feet do tread,
These shall throw down thy cold and breathless head.

  Fort. O sacred deity, what sin is done,
That Death's iron fist should wrestle with thy son ?
                    [*All kneel.*

Fortune. Thou art no son of Fortune, but her slave :
Thy cedar hath aspired to his full height.
Thy sun-like glory hath advanced herself
Into the top of pride's meridian,
And down amain it comes.   From beggary
I plumed thee like an ostrich, like that ostrich
Thou hast eaten metals, and abused my gifts,
Hast played the ruffian, wasted that in riots
Which as a blessing I bestowed on thee.

  Fort. Forgive me, I will be more provident.

Fortune. No, endless follies follow endless wealth.
Thou hadst thy fancy, I must have thy fate,
Which is, to die when th'art most fortunate.
This inky thread, thy ugly sins have spun,
Black life, black death ; faster ! that it were done.

  Fort. Oh, let me live, but till I can redeem.

Fortune. The Destinies deny thee longer life.

Fort. I am but now lifted to happiness.

Fortune. And now I take most pride to cast thee
    down.

Hadst thou chosen wisdom, this black had been white,
And Death's stern brow could not thy soul affright.

    Fort. Take this again! (*Offering the purse.*) Give
        wisdom to my sons.

    Fortune. No, fool, 'tis now too late: as death strikes thee,
So shall their ends sudden and wretched be.
Jove's daughters—righteous Destinies—make haste!
His life hath wasteful been, and let it waste.

                [*Exeunt* FORTUNE *and* The Three Destinies.

    Andel. Why the pox dost thou sweat so?

    Shad. For anger to see any of God's creatures have
such filthy faces as these sempsters[1] had that went hence.

    Andel. Sempsters? why, you ass, they are Destinies.

    Shad. Indeed, if it be one's destiny to have a filthy
face, I know no remedy but to go masked and cry
"Woe worth the Fates."

    Amp. Why droops my father? these are only shadows,
Raised by the malice of some enemy,
To fright your life, o'er which they have no power.

    Shad. Shadows?   I defy their kindred.

    Fort. O Ampedo, I faint; help me, my sons.

    Andel. Shadow, I pray thee run and call more help.

    Shad. If that desperate Don Dego[2] Death hath ta'en
up the cudgels once, here's never a fencer in Cyprus dare
take my old master's part.

    Andel. Run, villain, call more help.

    Shad. Bid him thank the Destinies for this.   [*Exit.*

    Fort. Let me shrink down, and die between your arms,
Help comes in vain.   No hand can conquer fate,
This instant is the last of my life's date.
This goddess, if at least she be a goddess,
Names herself Fortune: wand'ring in a wood,
Half famished, her I met.   I have, quoth she,
Six gifts to spend upon mortality,

---

    [1] Sempstresses, alluding to their spinning.
    [2] See *The Devil's Answer to Pierce Pennylesse*, p. 100, "that
great Dego of Devils."—*Dekker's Non-Dramatic Works.*

Wisdom, strength, health, beauty, long life and riches.
Out of my bounty one of these is thine.

   Amp. What benefit did from your choice arise?

   Fort. Listen, my sons! in this small compass lies
Infinite treasure: this she gave to me,
And gave to this, this virtue, Take, quoth she,
So often as from hence thou draw'st thy hand,
Ten golden pieces of that kingdom's coin,
Where'er thou liv'st; which plenteous sure shall last,
After thy death, till thy sons' lives do waste.

   Andel. Father, your choice was rare, the gift divine.

   Fort. It had been so, if riches had been mine.

   Amp. But hath this golden virtue never failed?

   Fort. Never.

   Andel. O admirable: here's a fire
Hath power to thaw the very heart of death,
And give stones life; by this most sacred breath,[1]
See brother, here's all India in my hand.

   Fort. Inherit you, my sons, that golden land.
This hat I brought away from Babylon,
I robbed the Soldan of it, 'tis a prize
Worth twenty empires in this jewel lies.

   Andel. How, father? jewel? call you this a jewel? it's
coarse wool, a bald fashion, and greasy to the brim; I
have bought a better felt for a French crown forty times:
of what virtuous block is this hat, I pray?

   Fort. Set it upon thy head, and wish a wish,
Thou in the moment, on the wind's swift wings,
Shalt be transported into any place.

   Andel. A wishing hat, and a golden mine?

   Fort. O Andelocia, Ampedo, now Death
Sounds his third summons, I must hence! These jewels
To both I do bequeath; divide them not,
But use them equally: never bewray
What virtues are in them; for if you do,
Much shame, much grief, much danger follows you.

---

   [1] Death, in original,—an evident misprint.

Peruse this book; farewell ! behold in me
The rotten strength of proud mortality.   [*Dies.*

  Amp. His soul is wandering to the Elysian shades.

  Andel. The flower that's fresh at noon, at sunset fades.

  Brother, close you down his eyes, because you were his eldest; and with them close up your tears, whilst I as all younger brothers do, shift for myself: let us mourn, because he's dead, but mourn the less, because he cannot revive. The honour we can do him, is to bury him royally ; let's about it then, for I'll not melt myself to death with scalding sighs, nor drop my soul out at mine eyes, were my father an emperor.

  Amp. Hence, hence, thou stop'st the tide of my true
        tears.
True grief is dumb, though it hath open ears.

  Andel. Yet God send my grief a tongue, that I may have good utterance for it : sob on, brother mine, whilst you sigh there, I'll sit and read what story my father has written here.

    [*They both fall asleep :* FORTUNE *and a company*
        of Satyrs *enter with music, and playing*
        about FORTUNATUS' *body, take it away.*
        Afterwards SHADOW *enters running.*

  Shad. I can get none, I can find none : where are you, master? Have I ta'en you napping? and you too? I see sorrow's eye-lids are made of a dormouse skin, they seldom open, or of a miser's purse, that's always shut. So ho, master.

  Andel. Shadow, why how now ? what's the matter ?

  Shad. I can get none, sir, 'tis impossible.

  Amp. What is impossible ? what canst not get ?

  Shad. No help for my old master.

  Andel. Hast thou been all this while calling for help ?

  Shad. Yes, sir : he scorned all Famagosta when he was in his huffing,[1] and now he lies puffing for wind, they say they scorn him.

        [1] Swaggering mood,

Amp. The poison of their scorn infects not him ;
He wants no help.   See where he breathless lies :
Brother, to what place have you borne his body ?

Andel. I bear it ?   I touched it not.

Amp. Nor I : a leaden slumber pressed mine eyes.

Shad. Whether it were lead or latten[1] that hasped
down those winking casements, I know not, but I found
you both snorting.

Amp. And in that sleep, methought, I heard the tunes
Of sullen passions apt for funerals,
And saw my father's lifeless body borne
By Satyrs :   O I fear that deity
Hath stolen him hence !—that snudge, his destiny.

Andel. I fear he's risen again ; didst not thou meet
him ?

Shad. I, sir ? do you think this white and red durst
have kissed my sweet cheeks, if they had seen a ghost ?
But, master, if the Destinies, or Fortune, or the Fates, or
the Fairies have stolen him, never indict them for the
felony : for by this means the charges of a tomb is saved,
and you being his heirs, may do as many rich executors
do, put that money in your purses, and give out that he
died a beggar.

Andel. Away, you rogue, my father die a beggar !
I'll build a tomb for him of massy gold.

Shad. Methinks, master, it were better to let the
memory of him shine in his own virtues, if he had any,
than in alabaster.

Andel. I shall mangle that alabaster face, you whoreson virtuous vice.

Shad. He has a marble heart, that can mangle a face
of alabaster.

Andel. Brother, come, come, mourn not ; our father is
but stepped to agree with Charon for his boat hire to
Elysium.   See, here's a story of all his travels ; this book
shall come out with a new addition : I'll tread after my

---

[1] Ital. *Latta*, tin-plate.

father's steps ; I'll go measure the world, therefore let's
share these jewels, take this, or this !

Amp. Will you then violate our father's will?

Andel. A Puritan!—keep a dead man's will ? Indeed
in the old time, when men were buried in soft church-
yards, that their ghosts might rise, it was good : but,
brother, now they are imprisoned in strong brick and
marble, they are fast. Fear not : away, away, these are
fooleries, gulleries, trumperies ; here's this or this, or I
am gone with both !

Amp. Do you as you please, the sin shall not be mine.
Fools call those things profane that are divine.

Andel. Are you content to wear the jewels by turns ?
I'll have the purse for a year, you the hat, and as much
gold as you'll ask ; and when my pursership ends, I'll
resign, and cap you.

Amp. I am content to bear all discontents.   [*Exit.*

Andel. I should serve this bearing ass rarely now, if I
should load him, but I will not. Though conscience be
like physic, seldom used, for so it does least hurt, yet I'll
take a dram of it. This for him, and some gold : this for
me ; for having this mint about me, I shall want no
wishing cap. Gold is an eagle, that can fly to any place,
and, like death, that dares enter all places. Shadow, wilt
thou travel with me ?

Shad. I shall never fadge [1] with the humour because I
cannot lie.

Andel. Thou dolt, we'll visit all the kings' courts in
the world.

Shad. So we may, and return dolts home, but what
shall we learn by travel ?

Andel. Fashions. [2]

---

[1] Succeed.

[2] Farcy, a disease to which horses are subject, still sometimes
miscalled " Fashions " by country farriers. Dekker puns on it again
in *The Gull's Horn-Book :*—" Fashions then was counted a disease,
and horses died of it : But now (thanks to folly) it is held the only
rare physic, and the purest golden Asses live upon it."

Shad. That's a beastly disease : methinks it's better staying in your own country.

Andel. How? In mine own country—like a cage-bird, and see nothing ?

Shad. Nothing? yes, you may see things enough, for what can you see abroad that is not at home? The same sun calls you up in the morning, and the same man in the moon lights you to bed at night ; our fields are as green as theirs in summer, and their frosts will nip us more in winter : our birds sing as sweetly and our women are as fair : in other countries you shall have one drink to you ; whilst you kiss your hand, and duck,[1] he'll poison you : I confess you shall meet more fools, and asses, and knaves abroad than at home. Yet God be thanked we have pretty store of all. But for punks,[2] we put them down.

Andel. Prepare thy spirits, for thou shalt go with me.
To England shall our stars direct our course ;
Thither the Prince of Cyprus, our king's son,
Is gone to see the lovely Agripyne.
Shadow, we'll gaze upon that English dame,
And try what virtue gold has to inflame.
First to my brother, then away let's fly ;
Shadow must be a courtier ere he die.　　　　　*[Exit.*

Shad. If I must, the Fates shall be served : I have seen many clowns courtiers, then why not Shadow ? Fortune, I am for thee.　　　　　*[Exit.*

---

[1] Bow.　　　　　[2] Prostitutes.

ACT THE THIRD.

SCENE I.—*London. The Court of* ATHELSTANE.

Enter ORLEANS *melancholy*, GALLOWAY *with him; a*
Boy *after them with a lute.*

RLE. Begone : leave that with me, and
leave me to myself ; if the king ask for
me, swear to him I am sick, and thou
shalt not lie ; pray thee leave me.

    Boy. I am gone, sir.   [*Exit.*
    Orle. This music makes me but more
        out of tune.

O, Agripyne.

    Gall. Gentle friend, no more.
Thou sayest love is a madness, hate it then,
Even for the name's sake.

    Orle. O, I love that madness,
Even for the name's sake.

    Gall. Let me tame this frenzy,
By telling thee thou art a prisoner here,
By telling thee she's daughter to a king,
By telling thee the King of Cyprus' son
Shines like a sun, between her looks and thine,
Whilst thou seem'st but a star to Agripyne :
He loves her.

    Orle. If he do : why so do I.

    Gall. Love is ambitious, and loves majesty.

Orle. Dear friend, thou art deceived, love's voice doth
    sing
As sweetly in a beggar as a king.

Gall. Dear friend, thou art deceived : O bid thy soul
Lift up her intellectual eyes to Heaven,
And in this ample book of wonders read,
Of what celestial mould, what sacred essence,
Herself is formed, the search whereof will drive
Sounds musical among the jarring spirits,
And in sweet tune set that which none inherits.

Orle. I'll gaze on Heaven if Agripyne be there :
If not : fa, la, la, sol, la, &c.

Gall. O, call this madness in ; see, from the windows
Of every eye derision thrusts out cheeks,
Wrinkled with idiot laughter ; every finger
Is like a dart shot from the hand of scorn,
By which thy name is hurt, thine honour torn.

Orle. Laugh they at me, sweet Galloway ?

Gall. Even at thee.

Orle. Ha, ha, I laugh at them, are not they mad
That let my true true sorrow make them glad ?
I dance and sing only to anger grief,
That in that anger, he might smite life down
With his iron fist.   Good heart, it seemeth then,
They laugh to see grief kill me : O, fond men,
You laugh at others' tears ; when others smile,
You tear yourselves in pieces : vile, vile, vile !
Ha, ha, when I behold a swarm of fools,
Crowding together to be counted wise,
I laugh because sweet Agripyne's not there,
But weep because she is not anywhere,
And weep because whether she be or not,
My love was ever, and is still, forgot : forgot, forgot, for-
    got.

Gall. Draw back this stream, why should my Orleans
    mourn ?

Orle. Look yonder, Galloway, dost thou see that sun ?

Nay, good friend, stare upon it, mark it well,
Ere he be two hours older, all that glory
Is banished Heaven, and then for grief this sky,
That's now so jocund, will mourn all in black,
And shall not Orleans mourn ? Alack, alack !
O what a savage tyranny it were
T'enforce care laugh, and woe not shed a tear !
Dead is my love, I am buried in her scorn,
That is my sunset, and shall I not mourn ?
Yes, by my troth I will.

  Gall. Dear friend, forbear,
Beauty, like sorrow, dwelleth everywhere.
Rase out this strong idea of her face,
As fair as hers shineth in any place.

  Orle. Thou art a traitor to that white and red,
Which, sitting on her cheeks, being Cupid's throne,
Is my heart's sovereign : O, when she is dead,
This wonder, beauty, shall be found in none.
Now Agripyne's not mine, I vow to be
In love with nothing but deformity.
O fair Deformity, I muse all eyes
Are not enamoured of thee : thou didst never
Murder men's hearts, or let them pine like wax,
Melting against the sun of destiny ;
Thou art a faithful nurse to chastity ;
Thy beauty is not like to Agripyne's,
For cares, and age, and sickness hers deface,
But thine's eternal. O Deformity,
Thy fairness is not like to Agripyne's,
For dead, her beauty will no beauty have,
But thy face looks most lovely in the grave.

Enter the PRINCE OF CYPRUS *and* AGRIPYNE.

  Gall. See where they come together, hand in hand.
  Orle. O watch, sweet Galloway, when their hands do
    part,
Between them shalt thou find my murdered heart.

Cypr. By this then it seems a thing impossible, to know when an English lady loves truly.

Agrip. Not so, for when her soul steals into her heart, and her heart leaps up to her eyes, and her eyes drop into her hands, then if she say, Here's my hand ! she's your own,—else never.

Cyp. Here's a pair of your prisoners, let's try their opinion.

Agrip. My kind prisoners, well encountered ; the Prince of Cyprus here and myself have been wrangling about a question of love : my lord of Orleans, you look lean, and likest a lover—Whether is it more torment to love a lady and never enjoy her, or always to enjoy a lady whom you cannot choose but hate ?

Orle. To hold her ever in mine arms whom I loath in my heart, were some plague, yet the punishment were no more than to be enjoined to keep poison in my hand, yet never to taste it.

Agrip. But say you should be compelled to swallow the poison ?

Orle. Then a speedy death would end a speeding misery. But to love a lady and never enjoy her, oh it is not death, but worse than damnation; 'tis hell, 'tis——

Agrip. No more, no more, good Orleans ; nay then, I see my prisoner is in love too.

Cypr. Methinks, soldiers cannot fall into the fashion of love.

Agrip. Methinks a soldier is the most faithful lover of all men else ; for his affection stands not upon compliment. His wooing is plain home-spun stuff; there's no outlandish thread in it, no rhetoric. A soldier casts no figures to get his mistress' heart ; his love is like his valour in the field, when he pays downright blows.

Gall. True, madam, but would you receive such payment ?

Agrip. No, but I mean, I love a soldier best for his plain dealing.

Cypr. That's as good as the first.

Agrip. Be it so, that goodness I like : for what lady can abide to love a spruce silken-face courtier, that stands every morning two or three hours learning how to look by his glass, how to speak by his glass, how to sigh by his glass, how to court his mistress by his glass ? I would wish him no other plague, but to have a mistress as brittle as glass.

Gall. And that were as bad as the horn plague.

Cypr. Are any lovers possessed with this madness ?

Agrip. What madmen are not possessed with this love ? Yet by my troth, we poor women do but smile in our sleeves to see all this foppery : yet we all desire to see our lovers attired gallantly, to hear them sing sweetly, to behold them dance comely and such like. But this apish monkey fashion of effeminate niceness, out upon it ! Oh, I hate it worse than to be counted a scold.

Cypr. Indeed, men are most regarded, when they least regard themselves.

Gall. And women most honoured, when they show most mercy to their lovers.

Orle. But is't not a miserable tyranny, to see a lady triumph in the passions of a soul languishing through her cruelty ?

Cypr. Methinks it is.

Gall. Methinks 'tis more than tyranny.

Agrip. So think not I ; for as there is no reason to hate any that love us, so it were madness to love all that do not hate us ; women are created beautiful, only because men should woo them ; for 'twere miserable tyranny to enjoin poor women to woo men : I would not hear of a woman in love, for my father's kingdom.

Cypr. I never heard of any woman that hated love.

Agrip. Nor I : but we had all rather die than confess we love ; our glory is to hear men sigh whilst we smile, to kill them with a frown, to strike them dead with a sharp eye, to make you this day wear a feather, and to-morrow a sick nightcap. Oh, why this is rare, there's a certain deity in this, when a lady by the magic of her looks, can turn a man into twenty shapes.

Orle. Sweet friend, she speaks this but to torture me.

Gall. I'll teach thee how to plague her : love her not.

Agrip. Poor Orleans, how lamentably he looks : if he stay, he'll make me surely love him for pure pity. I must send him hence, for of all sorts of love, I hate the French; I pray thee, sweet prisoner, entreat Lord Longaville to come to me presently.

Orle. I will, and esteem myself more than happy, that you will employ me.   [*Exit.*

Agrip. Watch him, watch him for God's sake, if he sigh not or look not back.

Cypr. He does both : but what mystery lies in this ?

Agrip. Nay, no mystery, 'tis as plain as Cupid's forehead : why this is as it should be.—" And esteem myself more than happy, that you will employ me." My French prisoner is in love over head and ears.

Cypr. It's wonder how he 'scapes drowning.

Gall. With whom, think you ?

Agrip. With his keeper, for a good wager : Ah, how glad is he to obey ! And how proud am I to command in this empire of affection ! Over him and such spongy-livered youths, that lie soaking in love, I triumph more with mine eye, than ever he did over a soldier with his sword. Is't not a gallant victory for me to subdue my father's enemy with a look ? Prince of Cyprus, you were best take heed, how you encounter an English lady.

Cypr. God bless me from loving any of you, if all be so cruel.

Agrip. God bless me from suffering you to love me, if you be not so formable.

Cypr. Will you command me any service, as you have done Orleans ?

Agrip. No other service but this, that, as Orleans, you love me, for no other reason, but that I may torment you.

Cypr. I will : conditionally, that in all company I
may call you my tormentor.

Agrip. You shall : conditionally, that you never beg
for mercy.   Come, my Lord of Galloway.

Gall. Come, sweet madam.

[*Exeunt all except the* PRINCE OF CYPRUS.

Cypr. The ruby-coloured portals of her speech
Were closed by mercy : but upon her eye,
Attired in frowns, sat murdering cruelty.

Re-enter AGRIPYNE *and listens.*

She's angry, that I durst so high aspire.
O, she disdains that any stranger's breast
Should be a temple for her deity :
She's full of beauty, full of bitterness.
Till now, I did not dally with love's fire :
And when I thought to try his flames indeed,
I burnt me even to cinders.   O, my stars,
Why from my native shore did your beams guide me,
To make me dote on her that doth deride me ?

[AGRIPYNE *kneels :* CYPRUS *walks musing.*

Agrip. Hold him in this mind, sweet Cupid, I conjure
thee.   O, what music these hey-hos make !   I was about
to cast my little self into a great love trance for him,
fearing his heart had been flint : but since I see 'tis pure
virgin wax, he shall melt his bellyful : for now I know
how to temper him.

[*Exit ; as she departs* CYPRUS *spies her.*

Cypr. Never beg mercy ? yet be my tormentor.
I hope she heard me not : doubtless she did,
And now will she insult upon my passions,
And vex my constant love with mockeries.
Nay, then I'll be mine own physician,
And outface love, and make her think that I
Mourned thus, because I saw her standing by.
What news, my Lord of Cornwall ?

Enter CORNWALL.

Cornw. This fair prince,
One of your countrymen, is come to court,
A lusty gallant brave, in Cyprus' isle,
With fifty bard[1] horses prancing at his heels,
Backed by as many strong-limbed Cypriots,
All whom he keeps in pay : whose offered service,
Our king with arms of gladness hath embraced.
    Cypr. Born in the isle of Cyprus ? what's his name ?
    Cornw. His servants call him Fortunatus' son.
    Cypr. Rich Fortunatus' son ?   Is he arrived ?

Enter LONGAVILLE, GALLOWAY, *and* CHESTER *with
jewels.*

    Longa. This he bestowed on me.
    Chest. And this on me.
    Gall. And this his bounteous hand enforced me take.
    Longa. I prize this jewel at a hundred marks,[2]
Yet would he needs bestow this gift on me.
    Cypr. My lords, whose hand hath been thus prodigal ?
    Gall. Your countryman, my lord, a Cypriot.
    Longa. The gallant sure is all compact of gold,
To every lady hath he given rich jewels,
And sent to every servant in the court
Twenty fair English angels.[3]
    Cypr. This is rare.

Enter LINCOLN.

    Linc. My lords, prepare yourselves for revelling,
'Tis the king's pleasure that this day be spent
In royal pastimes, that this golden lord,
For so all that behold him, christen him,
May taste the pleasures of our English court.
Here comes the gallant, shining like the sun.
                        [Trumpets sound.

---

[1] Barded, or barbed : *i.e.* Adorned with trappings.
[2] The mark was worth 13*s.* 4*d.*
[3] The angel varied from 6*s.* 8*d.* to 10*s.* in value.

Enter ATHELSTANE, ANDELOCIA, AGRIPYNE, ORLEANS,
    Ladies, *and other* Attendants, *also* INSULTADO.
    Music sounds within.

Andel. For these your royal favours done to me,
Being a poor stranger, my best powers shall prove,
By acts of worth, the soundness of my love.
    Athelst. Herein your love shall best set out itself,
By staying with us : if our English isle
Hold any object welcome to your eyes,
Do but make choice, and claim it as your prize.
                    [*The* KING *and* CYPRUS *confer aside.*
    Andel. I thank your grace : would he durst keep his
            word,
I know what I would claim.   Tush, man, be bold,
Were she a saint, she may be won with gold.
    Cypr. 'Tis strange, I must confess, but in this pride,
His father Fortunatus, if he live,
Consumes his life in Cyprus : still he spends,
And still his coffers with abundance swell,
But how he gets these riches none can tell.
                    [*The* KING *and* AGRIPYNE *confer aside.*
    Athelst. Hold him in talk : come hither, Agripyne.
    Cypr. But what enticed young Andelocia's soul
To wander hither ?
    Andel. That which did allure
My sovereign's son, the wonder of the place.
    Agrip. This curious heap of wonders, which an Empress
Gave him, he gave me, and by Venus' hand,
The warlike Amorato needs would swear,
He left his country Cyprus for my love.
    Athelst. If by the sovereign magic of thine eye,
Thou canst enchant his looks to keep the circles
Of thy fair cheeks, be bold to try their charms,
Feed him with hopes, and find the royal vein,
That leads this Cypriot to his golden mine.
Here's music spent in vain, lords, fall to dancing.

Cypr. My fair tormentor, will you lend a hand ?

Agrip. I'll try this stranger's cunning [1] in a dance.

Andel. My cunning is but small, yet who'll not prove
To shame himself for such a lady's love ?

Orle. These Cypriots are the devils that torture me.
He courts her, and she smiles, but I am born
To be her beauty's slave, and her love's scorn.

Andel. I shall never have the face to ask the question
twice.

Agrip. What's the reason ?   Cowardliness or pride ?

Andel. Neither : but 'tis the fashion of us Cypriots,
both men and women, to yield at first assault, and we
expect others should do the like.

Agrip. It's a sign, that either your women are very
black, and are glad to be sped, or your men very fond,
and will take no denial.

Andel. Indeed our ladies are not so fair as you.

Agrip. But your men more venturous at a breach than
you, or else they are all dastardly soldiers.

Andel. He that fights under these sweet colours, and
yet turns coward, let him be shot to death with the
terrible arrows of fair ladies' eyes.

Athelst. Nay, Insultado, you must not deny us.

*Insultad. Mi corazon es muy pesado, mi anima muy a-
tormentada.   No por los Cielos : El pie de Español no
hace musica en tierra ingles.* [2]

Cypr. Sweet Insultado, let us see you dance.
I have heard the Spanish dance is full of state.

*Insultad. Verdad, señor : la danza española es muy
alta,
Majestica, y para monarcas : vuestra Inglesa,
Baja, fantastica, y muy humilde.* [3]

---

[1] Skill.

[2] " My heart is weighed down, my soul much tormented.   No,
by Heaven, the Spanish foot does not beat to music on English
ground. "

[3] " The truth, sir ; the Spanish dance is full of state, majestic, and
fit for monarchs : your English low, fantastic, and very humble. "

Agrip. Doth my Spanish prisoner deny to dance? He
has sworn to me by the cross of his pure Toledo, to be
my servant : by that oath, my Castilian prisoner, I conjure you to show your cunning ; though all your body be
not free, I am sure your heels are at liberty.

*Insultad. Nolo quiero contra deseo ; vuestro ojo hace
conquista á su prisionero : Oyerer la a pavan española ;
sea vuestra musica y gravidad, y majestad : Paje, daime
tabacco, toma my capa, y my espada. Mas alta, mas alta :
Desviaios, desviaios, compañeros, mas alta, mas alta.*[1]

[*He dances.*

Athelst. Thanks, Insultado.

Cypr. 'Tis most excellent.

Agrip. The Spaniard's dance is as his deeds be, full of
pride.

Athelst. The day grows old, and what remains un-
        spent,
Shall be consumed in banquets. Agripyne,
Leave us a while, if Andelocia please,
Go bear our beauteous daughter company.

And. Fortune, I thank thee : now thou smil'st on me.

[*Exeunt* AGRIPYNE, ANDELOCIA, *and* Ladies.

Athelst. This Cypriot bears a gallant princely mind.
My lord, of what birth is your countryman ?
Think not, sweet prince, that I propound this question,
To wrong you in your love to Agripyne :
Our favours grace him to another end.
Nor let the wings of your affection droop,
Because she seems to shun love's gentle lure.
Believe it on our word, her beauty's prize
Only shall yield a conquest to your eyes.
But tell me what's this Fortunatus' son ?

---

[1] " I desire only to please you : your eye has conquered its
prisoner. You shall hear the Spanish Pavan, let your music be
grave and majestic : Page, give me tobacco ; take my cloak and my
sword. Higher, higher : Make way, make way friends, higher,
higher." The Pavan was a stately Spanish dance.

Cypr. Of honourable blood, and more renowned
In foreign kingdoms, whither his proud spirit,
Plumed with ambitious feathers, carries him,
Than in his native country; but last day
The father and the sons were, through their riots,
Poor and disdained of all, but now they glister
More bright than Midas: if some damnèd fiend
Fed not his bags, this golden pride would end.

    Athelst. His pride we'll somewhat tame, and curb the
        head
Of his rebellious prodigality:
He hath invited us, and all our peers,
To feast with him to-morrow; his provision,
I understand, may entertain three kings.
But Lincoln, let our subjects secretly
Be charged on pain of life that not a man
Sell any kind of fuel to his servants.

    Cypr. This policy shall clip his golden wings,
And teach his pride what 'tis to strive with kings.

    Athelst. Withdraw awhile:

                [*Exeunt all except* ATHELSTANE.

None filled his hands with gold, for we set spies,
To watch who fed his prodigality:
He hung the marble bosom of our court,
As thick with glist'ring spangles of pure gold,
As e'er the spring hath stuck the earth with flowers.
Unless he melt himself to liquid gold,
Or be some god, some devil, or can transport
A mint about him, by enchanted power,
He cannot rain such showers.   With his own hands
He threw more wealth about in every street,
Than could be thrust into a chariot.
He's a magician sure, and to some fiend,
His soul by infernal covenants has he sold,
Always to swim up to the chin in gold.
Be what he can be, if those doting fires,
Wherein he burns for Agripyne's love,

Want power to melt from him this endless mine,
Then like a slave we'll chain him in our tower,
Where tortures shall compel his sweating hands
To cast rich heaps into our treasury.   [*Exit.*

SCENE II.—*The same.*

Music sounding still; a curtain being drawn, ANDELOCIA
is discovered sleeping in AGRIPYNE'S *lap; she has
his purse, and she and another lady tie another like
it in its place, and then rise from him. Enter* ATHEL-
STANE.

Agrip. I have found the sacred spring that never ebbs.
Leave us : [*Exit* Lady.]   But I'll not show't your majesty
Till you have sworn by England's royal crown,
To let me keep it.

Athelst. By my crown I swear,
None but fair Agripyne the gem shall wear.

Agrip. Then is this mine : see, father, here's the fire
Whose gilded beams still burn, this is the sun
That ever shines, the tree that never dies,
Here grows the Garden of Hesperides ;
The outside mocks you, makes you think 'tis poor,
But entering it, you find eternal store.

Athelst. Art sure of this?   How didst thou drive it
    out ?

Agrip. Fear not his waking yet, I made him drink
That soporiferous juice which was composed
To make the queen,[1] my mother, relish sleep,
When her last sickness summoned her to Heaven.
He sleeps profoundly : when his amorous eyes
Had singed their wings in Cupid's wanton flames,
I set him all on fire, and promised love,

[1] History does not record that Athelstane had either wife or
daughter.

In pride whereof, he drew me forth this purse,
And swore, by this he multiplied his gold.
I tried and found it true : and secretly
Commanded music with her silver tongue,
To chime soft lullabies into his soul,
And whilst my fingers wantoned with his hair,
T'entice the sleepy juice to charm his eyes,
In all points was there made a purse, like his,
Which counterfeit is hung in place of this.

    Athelst. More than a second kingdom hast thou won.
Leave him, that when he wakes he may suspect,
Some else has robbed him ; come, dear Agripyne,
If this strange purse his sacred virtues hold,
We'll circle England with a wall of gold.   [*Exeunt.*

Music still : *Enter* SHADOW *very gallant, reading a bill,
    with empty bags in his hand, singing.*

    Shad. These English occupiers are mad Trojans : let
a man pay them never so much, they'll give him nothing
but the bag. Since my master created me steward over
his fifty men, and his one-and-fifty horse, I have rid over
much business, yet never was galled, I thank the destinies.
Music ? O delicate warble : O these courtiers are most
sweet triumphant creatures ! Seignior, sir, monsieur,
sweet seignior : this is the language of the accomplish-
ment. O delicious strings ; these heavenly wire-drawers
have stretched my master even out at length : yet at
length he must wake. Master ?

    Andel. Wake me not yet, my gentle Agripyne.

    Shad. One word, sir, for the billets, and I vanish.

    Andel. There's Heaven in these times : throw the
    musicians
A bounteous largesse of three hundred angels.

                       [ANDELOCIA *starts up.*

    Shad. Why, sir, I have but ten pounds left.

    Andel. Ha, Shadow ? where's the Princess Agripyne ?

    Shad. I am not Apollo, I cannot reveal.

Andel. Was not the princess here, when thou cam'st in ?

Shad. Here was no princess but my princely self.

Andel. In faith ?

Shad. No, in faith, sir.

Andel. Where are you hid ? where stand you wantoning ? Not here ? gone, i'faith ? have you given me the slip ? Well, 'tis but an amorous trick, and so I embrace it : my horse, Shadow, how fares my horse ?

Shad. Upon the best oats my under-steward can buy.

Andel. I mean, are they lusty, sprightly, gallant, wanton, fiery ?

Shad. They are as all horses are, caterpillars to the commonwealth, they are ever munching : but, sir, for these billets, and these fagots and bavins ?

Andel. 'Sheart, what billets, what fagots ? dost make me a woodmonger ?

Shad. No, sweet seignior, but you have bid the king and his peers to dinner, and he has commanded that no woodmonger sell you a stick of wood, and that no collier shall cozn you of your measure, but must tie up the mouth of their sacks, lest their coals kindle your choler.

Andel. Is't possible ? is't true, or hast thou learnt of the English gallants to gull ?

Shad. He's a gull that would be taught by such gulls.

Andel. Not a stick of wood ? Some child of envy has buzzed this stratagem into the king's ear, of purpose to disgrace me. I have invited his majesty, and though it cost me a million, I'll feast him. Shadow, thou shalt hire a hundred or two of carts, with them post to all the grocers in London, buy up all the cinnamon, cloves, nutmegs, liquorice and all other spices, that have any strong heart, and with them make fires to prepare our cookery. Ere Fortunatus' son look red with shame,
He'll dress a king's feast in a spicèd flame.

Shad. This device, sir, will be somewhat akin to Lady Pride, 'twill ask cost.

Andel. Fetch twenty porters, I'll lade all with gold.

Shad. First, master, fill these bags.

Andel. Come then, hold up.   How now? tricks, new crotchets, Madame Fortune? Dry as an eel-skin? Shadow, take thou my gold out.

Shad. Why, sir, here's none in.

Andel, Ha, let me see : O here's a bastard cheek, I see now 'tis not mine; 'tis counterfeit, 'Tis so !   Slave, thou hast robbed thy master.

Shad. Not of a penny, I have been as true a steward—

Andel. Vengeance on thee and on thy stewardship ! Yet wherefore curse I thee? thy leaden soul Had never power to mount up to the knowledge Of the rich mystery closed in my purse. Oh no, I'll curse myself, mine eyes I'll curse, They have betrayed me ; I will curse my tongue, That hath betrayed me ; I'll curse Agripyne, She hath betrayed me.   Sirens, cease to sing, Your charms have ta'en effect, for now I see, All your enchantments were, to cozen me. [*Music ceases.*

Shad. What shall I do with this ten pound, sir ?

Andel. Go buy with it a chain and hang thyself. Now think I on my father's prophecy. Tell none, quoth he, the virtue, if you do, Much shame, much grief, much danger follows you. With tears I credit his divinity. O fingers, were you upright justices, You would tear out mine eyes ! had not they gazed On the frail colour of a painted cheek, None had betrayed me : henceforth I'll defy All beauty, and will call a lovely eye, A sun whose scorching beams burn up our joys, Or turn them black like Ethiopians. O women, wherefore are you born men's woe, Why are your faces framed angelical ? Your hearts of sponges, soft and smooth in show, But touched, with poison they do overflow.

Had sacred wisdom been my father's fate,
He had died happy, I lived fortunate.
Shadow, bear this to beauteous Agripyne,
With it this message, tell her, I'll reprove
Her covetous sin the less, because for gold,
I see that most men's souls too cheap are sold.

 Shad. Shall I buy these spices to-day or to-morrow?

+ *Andel.* To-morrow? ay, to-morrow thou shalt buy
  them.

To-morrow tell the princess I will love her,
To-morrow tell the king I'll banquet him,
To-morrow, Shadow, will I give thee gold;
To-morrow pride goes bare and lust acold.
To-morrow will the rich man feed the poor,
And vice to-morrow virtue will adore.
To-morrow beggars shall be crownèd kings,
This no-time, morrow's-time, no sweetness sings:
I pray thee hence; bear that to Agripyne.

 Shad. I'll go hence, because you send me; but I'll go
weeping hence, for grief that I must turn villain as many do,
and leave you when you are up to the ears in adversity.
              [*Exit.*

 Andel. She hath robbed me, and now I'll play the thief,
Ay, steal from hence to Cyprus, for black shame
Here, through my riots, brands my lofty name.
I'll sell this pride for help to bear me thither,
So pride and beggary shall walk together.
This world is but a school of villany,
Therefore I'll rob my brother, not of gold,
Nor of his virtues, virtue none will steal—
But, if I can, I'll steal his wishing hat,
And with that, wandering round about the world,
I'll search all corners to find Misery,
And where she dwells, I'll dwell, languish and die. [*Exit.*

ACT THE FOURTH.

HORUS. Gentles, if e'er you have be-
      held the passions,
    The combats of his soul, who being a
      king,
    By some usurping hand hath been
      deposed
From all his royalties : even such a soul,
Such eyes, such heart swol'n big with sighs and tears,
The star-crossed son of Fortunatus wears.
His thoughts crowned him a monarch in the morn,
Yet now he's bandied by the seas in scorn
From wave to wave : his golden treasure's spoil
Makes him in desperate language to entreat
The winds to spend their fury on his life :
But they, being mild in tyranny, or scorning
To triumph in a wretch's funeral,
Toss him to Cyprus.   Oh, what treachery
Cannot this serpent gold entice us to ?
He robs his brother of the Soldan's prize,
And having got his wish, the wishing hat,
He does not, as he vowed, seek misery,
But hopes by that to win his purse again,
And in that hope from Cyprus is he fled.
If your swift thoughts clap on their wonted wings,
In Genoa may you take this fugitive,
Where having cozened many jewellers,

Dekker.   A A

To England back he comes ; step but to court,
And there disguised you find him bargaining
For jewels with the beauteous Agripyne,
Who wearing at her side the virtuous purse,
He clasps her in his arms, and as a raven,
Griping the tender-hearted nightingale,
So flies he with her, wishing in the air
To be transported to some wilderness :
Imagine this the place ; see, here they come !
Since they themselves have tongues, mine shall be dumb.
                                        [*Exit.*

SCENE I.—*A Wilderness.*

Enter ANDELOCIA *with the wishing hat on, and dragging*
        AGRIPYNE *by the hand.*

GRIP. What devil art thou that affright'st
        me thus,
    Haling a princess from her father's court,
    To spoil her in this savage wilderness?
        Andel. Indeed the devil and the pick-
        purse should always fly together, for
they are sworn brothers : but Madam Covetousness, I
am neither a devil as you call me, nor a jeweller as I
call myself; no, nor a juggler,—yet ere you and I part, we'll
have some legerdemain together.   Do you know me?

Agrip. I am betrayed : this is the Cypriot.
Forgive me, 'twas not I that changed thy purse,
But Athelstane my father ; send me home,
And here's thy purse again : here are thy jewels,
And I in satisfaction of all wrongs—

Andel. Talk not you of satisfaction, this is some recompense, that I have you. 'Tis not the purse I regard : put
it off, and I'll mince it as small as pie meat. The purse?
hang the purse : were that gone, I can make another,

and another, and another, ay, and another : 'tis not the
purse I care for, but the purser, you, ay you.   Is't not
a shame that a king's daughter, a fair lady, a lady not for
lords, but for monarchs, should for gold sell her love,
and when she has her own asking, and that there stands
nothing between, then to cheat your sweetheart?   O fie,
fie, a she cony-catcher?   You must be dealt fondly with.

Agrip. Enjoin what pains thou wilt, and I'll endure
　　them,
So thou wilt send me to my father's court.

Andel. Nay God's lid, y'are not gone so : set your
heart at rest, for I have set up my rest, that except you
can run swifter than a hart, home you go not.   What
pains shall I lay upon you?   Let me see : I could serve
you now but a slippery touch : I could get a young king
or two, or three, of you, and then send you home, and bid
their grandsire king nurse them : I could pepper you, but
I will not.

Agrip. O, do not violate my chastity.

Andel. No, why I tell you I am not given to the flesh,
though I savour in your nose a little of the devil, I could
run away else, and starve you here.

Agrip. If I must die, doom me some easier death.

Andel. Or transform you, because you love picking,
into a squirrel, and make you pick out a poor living here
among the nut trees : but I will not neither.

Agrip. What will my gentle Andelocia do?

Andel. Oh, now you come to your old bias of cogging.[1]

Agrip. I pray thee, Andelocia, let me go :
Send me to England, and by Heaven I swear,
Thou from all kings on earth my love shalt bear.

Andel. Shall I in faith?

Agrip. In faith, in faith thou shalt.

Andel. Hear, God a mercy : now thou shalt not go.

Agrip. Oh God.

Andel. Nay, do you hear, lady? Cry not, y'are best ; no

---

[1] Your old mind (or, more literally, inclination) of cajoling.

nor curse me not. If you think but a crabbed thought of
me, the spirit that carried you in mine arms through the
air, will tell me all ; therefore set your Sunday face upon't.
Since you'll love me, I'll love you, I'll marry you, and lie
with you, and beget little jugglers : marry, home you get
not. England, you'll say, is yours : but, Agripyne, love
me, and I will make the whole world thine.

Agrip. I care not for the world, thou murd'rest me ;
Between my sorrow, and the scalding sun
I faint, and quickly will my life be done,
My mouth is like a furnace, and dry heat
Drinks up my blood. O God, my heart will burst,
I die, unless some moisture quench my thirst.

Andel. 'Sheart, now I am worse than ere I was before :
For half the world I would not have her die.
Here's neither spring nor ditch, nor rain, nor dew,
Nor bread nor drink : my lovely Agripyne,
Be comforted, see here are apple trees.

Agrip. Climb up for God's sake, reach me some of
        them.

Andel. Look up, which of these apples likes thee best ?

Agrip. This hath a withered face, 'tis some sweet fruit.
Not that, my sorrows are too sour already.

Andel. Come hither, here are apples like gold.

Agrip. O, ay, for God's sake, gather some of these.
Ay me, would God I were at home again !

Andel. Stand farther, lest I chance to fall on thee.
                                    [*Climbs up.*
Oh here be rare apples, rare red-cheeked apples, that cry
come kiss me : apples, hold your peace, I'll teach you to
cry.   [*Eats one.*

Agrip. O England, shall I ne'er behold thee more?

Andel. Agripyne, 'tis a most sugared delicious taste in
one's mouth, but when 'tis down, 'tis as bitter as gall.

Agrip. Yet gather some of them. Oh, that a princess
Should pine for food : were I at home again,
I should disdain to stand thus and complain.

Andel. Here's one apple that grows highest, Agripyne;
an' I could reach that, I'll come down.
                    [*Fishes with his girdle for it.*
Agrip. Make haste, for the hot sun doth scald my cheeks.
Andel. The sun kiss thee? hold, catch, put on my hat,
I will have yonder highest apple, though I die for't.
Agrip. I had not wont be sun-burnt, wretched me.
O England, would I were again in thee!   [*Exit.*

ANDELOCIA *leaps down.*

Andel. 'Swounds, Agripyne, stay, Oh I am undone!
Sweet Agripyne, if thou hear'st my voice,
Take pity of me, and return again.
She flies like lightning: Oh she hears me not!
I wish myself into a wilderness,
And now I shall turn wild: here I shall famish,
Here die, here cursing die, here raving die,
And thus will wound my breast, and rend mine hair.
What hills of flint are grown upon my brows?
O me, two forkèd horns, I am turned beast,
I have abused two blessings, wealth and knowledge,
Wealth in my purse, and knowledge in my hat,
By which being borne into the courts of kings,
I might have seen the wondrous works of Jove,
Acquired experience, learning, wisdom, truth,
But I in wildness tottered out my youth,
And therefore must turn wild, must be a beast,
An ugly beast: my body horns must bear,
Because my soul deformity doth wear.
Lives none within this wood?   If none but I
Live here,—thanks Heaven! for here none else shall die.
                    [*Lies down and sleeps under the tree.*

Enter FORTUNE, VICE, VIRTUE, *the* Priest: *and* Satyrs
          with music, playing before FORTUNE.

  Fortune. See where my new-turned devil has built his
      hell.

Vice. Virtue, who conquers now? the fool is ta'en.
Virtue. O sleepy sin.
Vice. Sweet tunes, wake him again.

    [*Music sounds awhile, and then ceases.*

Fortune. Vice sits too heavy on his drowsy soul,
Music's sweet concord cannot pierce his ear.
Sing, and amongst your songs mix bitter scorn.

    Virtue. Those that tear Virtue, must by Vice be torn.

SONG.

Virtue, stand aside : the fool is caught.
Laugh to see him, laugh aloud to wake him ;
Folly's nets are wide, and neatly wrought,
Mock his horns, and laugh to see Vice take him.
Chorus. Ha, ha, ha, ha, ha, laugh, laugh in scorn,
        Who's the fool? the fool, he wears a horn.

        [ANDELOCIA *wakens and stands up.*

Virtue, stand aside, mock him, mock him, mock
    him,
Laugh aloud to see him, call him fool.
Error gave him suck, now sorrows rock him,
Send the riotous beast to madness' school.
Chorus. Ha, ha, ha, ha, ha, laugh, laugh in scorn.
        Who's the fool? the fool, he wears a horn.

Virtue, stand aside : your school he hates.
Laugh aloud to see him, mock, mock, mock him.
Vanity and hell keep open gates,
He's in, and a new nurse, Despair, must rock him.
Chorus. Ha, ha, ha, ha, ha, laugh, laugh in scorn,
        Fool, fool, fool, fool, fool, wear still the horn.

    [VICE *and* VIRTUE *hold apples out to* ANDELOCIA,
        VICE *laughing,* VIRTUE *grieving.*

Andel. O me, what hell is this? fiends, tempt me not.
Thou glorious devil, hence.   O now I see,
This fruit is thine, thou hast deformèd me :
Idiot, avoid, thy gifts I loathe to taste.

Away : since I am entered madness' school,
As good to be a beast, as be a fool.
Away, why tempt you me ? some powerful grace
Come and redeem me from this hideous place.

Fortune. To her hath Andelocia all his life
Sworn fealty ; would'st thou forsake her now?

Andel. Whose blessed tongue names Andelocia ?

Fortune. Hers, who, attended on by destinies,
Shortened thy father's life, and lengthens thine.

Andel. O sacred Queen of chance, now shorten mine,
Else let thy deity take off this shame.

Fortune. Woo her, 'twas she that set it on thy head.

Andel. She laughs to see me metamorphosèd.   [*Rises.*

Virtue. Woo me, and I'll take off this ugly scorn.

Vice. Woo me, and I'll clap on another horn.

Andel. I am beset with anguish, shame and death.
O bid the Fates work fast, and stop my breath.

Fortune. No, Andelocia, thou must live to see
Worse torments, for thy follies, light on thee.
This golden tree, which did thine eyes entice,
Was planted here by Vice : lo, here stands Vice :
How often hast thou sued to win her grace ?

Andel. Till now, I never did behold her face.

Fortune. Thou didst behold her at thy father's death,
When thou in scorn didst violate his will ;
Thou didst behold her, when thy stretched-out arm
Catched at the highest bough, the loftiest vice,
The fairest apple, but the foulest price ;
Thou didst behold her, when thy liquorish eye
Fed on the beauty of fair Agripyne ;
Because th' hadst gold, thou thought'st all women thine.
When look'st thou off from her ? for they whose souls
Still revel in the nights of vanity,
On the fair cheeks of Vice still fix their eye.
Because her face doth shine, and all her bosom
Bears silver moons, thou wast enamoured of her.
But hadst thou upward looked, and seen these shames,

Or viewed her round about, and in this glass
Seen idiots' faces, heads of devils and hell,
And read this " Ha, ha, he," this merry story,
Thou wouldst have loathed her : where, by loving her,
Thou bear'st this face, and wear'st this ugly head,
And if she once can bring thee to this place,
Loud sounds these " Ha, ha, he !"   She'll laugh apace.

   Andel. O, re-transform me to a glorious shape,
And I will learn how I may love to hate her.

   Fortune. I cannot re-transform thee, woo this woman.

   Andel. This woman ? wretched is my state, when I,
To find out wisdom, to a fool must fly.

   Fortune. Fool, clear thine eyes, this is bright Aretë,[1]
This is poor virtue, care not how the world
Doth crown her head, the world laughs her to scorn,
Yet " SIBI SAPIT," Virtue knows her worth.
Run after her, she'll give thee these and these,
Crowns and bay-garlands, honour's victories :
Serve her, and she will fetch thee pay from Heaven,
Or give thee some bright office in the stars.

   Andel. Immortal Aretë, Virtue divine :   [*Kneels.*
O smile on me, and I will still be thine.

   Virtue. Smile thou on me, and I will still be thine :
Though I am jealous of thy apostasy,
I'll entertain thee : here, come taste this tree,
Here's physic for thy sick deformity.

   Andel. 'Tis bitter : this fruit I shall ne'er digest.

   Virtue. Try once again, the bitterness soon dies.

   Vice. Mine's sweet, taste mine.

   Virtue. But being down 'tis sour,
And mine being down has a delicious taste.
The path that leads to Virtue's court is narrow,
Thorny and up a hill, a bitter journey,
But being gone through, you find all heavenly sweets,
The entrance is all flinty, but at th' end,
To towers of pearl and crystal you ascend.

----

[1] Virtue. *Greek.*

Andel. O delicate, O sweet Ambrosian relish,
And see, my ugliness drops from my brows,
Thanks, beauteous Aretë : O had I now
My hat and purse again, how I would shine,
And gild my soul with none but thoughts divine.
　　Fortune. That shall be tried, take fruit from both these
　　　　　trees,
By help of them, win both thy purse and hat,
I will instruct thee how, for on my wings
To England shalt thou ride ; thy virtuous brother
Is, with that Shadow who attends on thee,
In London, there I'll set thee presently.
But if thou lose our favours once again,
To taste her sweets, those sweets must prove thy bane.
　　Virtue. Vice, who shall now be crowned with victory ?
　　Vice. She that triumphs at last, and that must I.
　　　　　　　　　　　　　　　　　　　　[*Exeunt.*

SCENE II.--*London.   The Court of* ATHELSTANE.

Enter ATHELSTANE, LINCOLN *with* AGRIPYNE, CYPRUS,
　　GALLOWAY, CORNWALL, CHESTER, LONGAVILLE *and*
　　MONTROSE.

　　Athelst. Lincoln, how set'st thou her at liberty?
　　Linc. No other prison held her but your court,
There in her chamber hath she hid herself
These two days, only to shake off that fear,
Which her late violent rapture cast upon her.
　　Cypr. Where hath the beauteous Agripyne been?
　　Agrip. In Heaven or hell, in or without the world,
I know not which, for as I oft have seen,
When angry Thamesis hath curled her locks,
A whirlwind come, and from her frizzled brows,
Snatch up a handful of those sweaty pearls,
That stood upon her forehead, which awhile,

Being by the boist'rous wind hung in the air,
At length hath flung them down and raised a storm,—
Even with such fury was I wherried up,
And by such force held prisoner in the clouds,
And thrown by such a tempest down again.

 Cornw. Some soul is damned in hell for this black
  deed.

 Agrip. I have the purse safe, and anon your grace
Shall hear the wondrous history at full.

 Cypr. Tell me, tormentor, shall fair Agripyne,
Without more difference be now christened mine!

 Agrip. My choice must be my father's fair consent.

 Athelst. Then shall thy choice end in this Cyprus prince.
Before the sun shall six times more arise,
His royal marriage will we solemnise.
Proclaim this honoured match! Come, Agripyne,
I am glad th' art here, more glad the purse is mine.

> [*As they are going in, enter* ANDELOCIA *and*
> SHADOW, *disguised as Irish coster-mongers.*
> AGRIPYNE, LONGAVILLE, *and* MONTROSE
> *stay listening to them, the rest exeunt.*

 Both. Buy any apples, feene apples of Tamasco,[1] feene
Tamasco peepins : peeps feene, buy Tamasco peepins.

 Agrip. Damasco apples? good my Lord Montrose,
Call yonder fellows.

 Montr. Sirrah coster-monger.

 Shad. Who calls : peeps of Tamasco, feene peeps :
Ay, fat 'tis de sweetest apple in de world, 'tis better den
de Pome water,[2] or apple John.[3]

---

 [1] In the English translation from the original story of Fortunatus, as published in the Dutch, Andelocia invents the name of
Damascus, or Damasco, for his apples, on the spur of the moment,
so as to give them an air of rarety, the name apparently not being
one previously used for any special kind of apple. In an earlier
English edition of the story, published about 1650, however, they
are otherwise described. It says there :—"They were brought
from Jerusalem, and were from the Holy Garden."
 [2] A large sweet apple, full of juice [see *Bailey's Dictionary*].
 [3] John apple, a good keeping apple, which long retains its fresh-
ness.

Andel. By my trat, madam, 'tis reet Tamasco peepins, look here els.

Shad. I dare not say, as de Irishman my countryman say, taste de goodness of de fruit : no, sayt, 'tis farie teere, mistriss, by Saint Patrick's hand 'tis teere Tamasco apple.

Agrip. The fairest fruit that ever I beheld.
Damasco apples, wherefore are they good ?

Longa. What is your price of half a score of these ?

Both. Half a score, half a score ? dat is doos many, mester.[1]

Longa. Ay, ay, ten, half a score, that's five and five.

Andel. Feeve and feeve ? By my trat and as Creeze save me la, I cannot tell wat be de price of feeve and feeve, but 'tis tree crown for one peepin, dat is de preez if you take 'em.

Shad. Ay fat, 'tis no less for Tamasco.

Agrip. Three crowns for one ? what wondrous virtues have they ?

Shad. O, 'tis feene Tamasco apple, and shall make you a great teal wise, and make you no fool, and make feene memory.

Andel. And make dis fash be more fair and amiable, and make dis eyes look always lovely, and make all de court and country burn in desire to kiss di none sweet countenance.

Montr. Apples to make a lady beautiful ?
Madam, that's excellent.

Agrip. These Irishmen,
Some say, are great dissemblers, and I fear
These two the badge of their own country wear.

Andel. By my trat, and by Saint Patrick's hand, and as Creez save me la, 'tis no dissembler : de Irishman now and den cut di countryman's throat, but yet in fayt

---

[1] "That is too many, master." Dekker's Irish even surpasses his Dutch in unintelligibility, and it would need more space than mere footnotes can afford, to attempt any full elucidation.

he love di countryman, 'tis no dissembler : dis feene
Tamasco apple can make di sweet countenance, but I
can take no less but three crowns for one, I wear out my
naked legs and my foots, and my tods,[1] and run hidder
and didder to Tamasco for dem.

Shad. As Creez save me la, he speaks true : Peeps
feene.

Agrip. I'll try what power lies in Damasco fruit.
Here are ten crowns for three.   So fare you well.

Montr. Lord Longaville, buy some.

Longa. I buy ? not I :
Hang them, they are toys ; come, madam, let us go.

    [*Exeunt* AGRIPYÑE, LONGAVILLE *and* MONTROSE.

Both. Saint Patrick and Saint Peter, and all de holy
angels look upon dat fash and make it fair.

Re-enter MONTROSE *softly.*

Shad. Ha, ha, ha ! she's sped, I warrant.

Andel. Peace, Shadow, buy any peepins, buy.

Both. Peeps feene, feene Tamasco apples.

Montr. Came not Lord Longaville to buy some fruit ?

Andel. No fat, master, here came no lords nor ladies,
but di none sweet self.

Montr. 'Tis well, say nothing, here's six crowns for
        two :
You say the virtues are to make one strong.

Both. Yes fat, and make sweet countenance and strong
        too.

Montr. 'Tis excellent : here ! farewell ! if these prove,
I'll conquer men by strength, women by love.   [*Exit.*

Re-enter LONGAVILLE.

Andel. Ha, ha, ha ! why this is rare.

Shad. Peace, master, here comes another fool.

Both. Peepes feene, buy any peepes of Tamasco ?

---

[1] Stockings probably, from the use of the term for bales of wool.

Longa. Did not the Lord Montrose return to you?

Both. No fat, sweet master, no lord did turn to us :
peepes feene !

Longa. I am glad of it ; here are nine crowns for
three.

What are the virtues besides making fair?

Andel. O, 'twill make thee wondrous wise.

Shad. And dow shall be no more a fool, but sweet face
and wise.

Longa. 'Tis rare, farewell, I never yet durst woo.
None loves me : now I'll try what these can do.   [*Exit.*

Andel. Ha, ha, ha.   So, this is admirable, Shadow,
here end my torments in Saint Patrick's Purgatory, but
thine shall continue longer.

Shad. Did I not clap on a good false Irish face?

Andel. It became thee rarely.

Shad. Yet that's lamentable, that a false face should
become any man.

Andel. Thou art a gull,[1] tis all the fashion now, which
fashion because we'll keep, step thou abroad, let not the
world want fools ; whilst thou art commencing thy
knavery there, I'll precede Dr. Dodipoll[2] here : that
done, thou, Shadow, and I will fat ourselves[3] to behold
the transformation of these fools : go fly.

Shad. I fear nothing, but that whilst we strive to make
others fools, we shall wear the cock's combs ourselves.
Pips fine.   [*Exit* SHADOW.

Enter AMPEDO.

Andel. S'heart, here's my brother whom I have abused :
His presence makes me blush, it strikes me dead,
To think how I am metamorphosèd.
Feene peepins of Tamasco !

---

[1] Dekker uses "Gallant," as an equivalent in *The Gull's Horn-
Book*, but he means something more opprobrious ;—"Masher," as
we would say to-day, a fool of fashion.

[2] An allusion to the comedy *The Wisdom of Dr. Dodipoll.*

[3] *i.e.* Grow jolly, at the spectacle.

Amp. For shame cast off this mask.

Andel. Wilt thou buy any pips?

Amp. Mock me no longer
With idle apparitions : many a land
Have I with weary feet and a sick soul
Measured to find thee ; and when thou art found,
My greatest grief is that thou art not lost.
Yet lost thou art, thy fame, thy wealth are lost,
Thy wits are lost, and thou hast in their stead,
With shame and cares, and misery crowned thy head.
That Shadow that pursues thee, filled mine ears
With sad relation of thy wretchedness,
Where is the purse, and where my wishing hat ?

Andel. Where, and where ? are you created constable ?
You stand so much upon interrogatories.   The purse is
gone, let that fret you, and the hat is gone, let that mad
you : I run thus through all trades to overtake them, if
you be quiet, follow me, and help, if not, fly from me,
and hang yourself.   Wilt thou buy any pippins?   [*Exit.*

Amp. Oh, how I grieve, to see him thus transformed ?
Yet from the circles of my jealous eyes
He shall not start, till he have repossessed
Those virtuous jewels, which found once again,
More cause they ne'er shall give me to complain,
Their worth shall be consumed in murdering flames,
And end my grief, his riot, and our shames.   [*Exit.*

ACT THE FIFTH.

SCENE I.—*London.   The Court of Athelstane.*

Enter ATHELSTANE, *followed by* AGRIPYNE, MONTROSE,
and LONGAVILLE *with horns ; then* LINCOLN *and*
CORNWALL.

THELST. In spite of sorcery try once
again,
    Try once more in contempt of all damned
spells.
    Agrip. Your majesty fights with no
mortal power.
Shame, and not conquest, hangs upon this strife.
O, touch me not, you add but pain to pain,
The more you cut, the more they grow again.
    Linc. Is there no art to conjure down this scorn ?
I ne'er knew physic yet against the horn.

Enter CYPRUS.

    Athelst. See, Prince of Cyprus, thy fair Agripyne
Hath turned her beauty to deformity.
    Cypr. Then I defy thee, Love ; vain hopes, adieu,
You have mocked me long; in scorn I'll now mock
you.
I came to see how the Lord Longaville
Was turned into a monster, and I find
An object, which both strikes me dumb and blind.
To-morrow should have been our marriage morn,

But now my bride is shame, thy bridegroom scorn.
O tell me yet, is there no art, no charms,
No desperate physic for this desperate wound?

    Athelst. All means are tried, but no means can be
        found.

    Cypr. Then, England, farewell : hapless maid, thy
        stars,
Through spiteful influence set our hearts at wars.
I am enforced to leave thee, and resign
My love to grief.

Enter ORLEANS *and* GALLOWAY.

    Agrip. All grief to Agripyne.

    Cypr. Adieu, I would say more, had I a tongue
Able to help his master: mighty king,
I humbly take my leave; to Cyprus I;
My father's son must all such shame defy.   [*Exit.*

    Orle. So doth not Orleans ; I defy all those
That love not Agripyne, and him defy,
That dares but love her half so well as I.
O pardon me ! I have in sorrow's jail
Been long tormented, long this mangled bosom
Hath bled, and never durst expose her wounds,
Till now, till now, when at thy beauteous feet
I offer love and life.   Oh, cast an eye
Of mercy on me, this deformèd face
Cannot affright my soul from loving thee.

    Agrip. Talk not of love, good Orleans, but of hate.

    Orle. What sentence will my love pronounce on me?

    Gall. Will Orleans then be mad? O gentle friend.

    Orle. O gentle, gentle friend, I am not mad :
He's mad, whose eyes on painted cheeks do doat,
O Galloway, such read beauty's book by rote.
He's mad, that pines for want of a gay flower,
Which fades when grief doth blast, or sickness lower,
Which heat doth wither, and white age's frost
Nips dead : such fairness, when 'tis found, 'tis lost.

I am not mad, for loving Agripyne,
My love looks on her eyes with eyes divine;
I doat on the rich brightness of her mind,
That sacred beauty strikes all other blind.
O make me happy then, since my desires
Are set a burning by love's purest fires.

Athelst. So thou wilt bear her far from England's sight,
Enjoy thy wishes.

Agrip. Lock me in some cave,
Where staring wonder's eye shall not be guilty
To my abhorrèd looks, and I will die
To thee, as full of love as misery.

Athelst. I am amazed and mad, some speckled soul
Lies pawned for this in hell, without redemption,
Some fiend deludes us all.

Cornw. O unjust Fates,
Why do you hide from us this mystery?

Linc. My Lord Montrose, how long have your brows
  worn
This fashion? these two feather-springs of horn?

Montr. An Irish kerne sold me Damasco apples
Some two hours since, and like a credulous fool—
He swearing to me that they had this power
To make me strong in body, rich in mind—
I did believe his words, tasted his fruit,
And since have been attired in this disguise.

Longa. I fear that villain hath beguiled me too.

Cornw. Nay before God he has not cozened you,
You have it soundly.

Longa. Me he made believe,
One apple of Damasco would inspire
My thoughts with wisdom, and upon my cheeks
Would cast such beauty that each lady's eye,
Which looked on me, should love me presently.

Agrip. Desire to look more fair, makes me more fool,[1]

---

[1] A play upon "fool" and "foul."

Dekker.   B B

Those apples did entice my wandering eye,
To be enamoured of deformity.

Athelst. This proves that true, which oft I have heard
    in schools,
Those that would seem most wise, do turn most fools.

Linc. Here's your best hope, none needs to hide his
    face,
For hornèd foreheads swarm in every place.

Enter CHESTER, *with* ANDELOCIA *disguised as a* French
Soldier.

Athelst. Now, Chester, what physicians hast thou
    found, ?

Chest. Many, my liege, but none that have true skill
To tame such wild diseases : yet here's one,
A doctor and a Frenchman, whom report
Of Agripyne's grief hath drawn to court.

Athelst. Cure her, and England's treasury shall stand,
As free for thee to use, as rain from Heaven.

Montr. Cure me, and to thy coffers I will send
More gold from Scotland than thy life can spend.

Longa. Cure Longaville, and all his wealth is thine.

Andel. He Monsieur Long-villain,[1] gra tanck you :
Gra tanck your mashesty a great teal artely by my trat :
where be dis Madam Princeza dat be so mush tormenta ?
O Jeshu : one, two : an tree, four an five, seez horn :
Ha, ha, ha, pardona moy prea wid al mine art, for by
my trat, me can no point shose but laugh, Ha, ha, ha, to
mark how like tree bul-beggera, dey stand.   Oh, by my
trat and fat, di divela be whoreson, scurvy, paltry, ill
favore knave to mock de madam, and gentill-home so :
Ha, ha, ha, ha.

Linc. This doctor comes to mock your majesty.

Andel. No, by my trat la, but me lova musha musha
merymant : come, madam, pre-artely stand still, and letta

---

[1] Elucidation of his jargon must be left to the discretion of the
reader.

me feel you.   Dis horn, O 'tis pretty horn, dis be facile,
easy for pull de vey; but, madam, dis O be grand, grand
horn, difficil, and very deep; 'tis perilous, a grand laroone.
But, madam, prea be patient, we shall take it off vell.

Athelst. Thrice have we pared them off, but with fresh
       pain,
In compass of a thought they rise again.

Andel. It's true, 'tis no easy mattra, to pull horn off,
'tis easy to pull on, but hard for pull off; some horn be
so good fellow, he will still inhabit in de man's pate, but
'tis all one for tat, I shall snap away all dis.   Madam,
trust dis down into your little belly.

Agrip. Father, I am in fear to taste his physic.
First let him work experiments on those.

Andel. I'll sauce you for your infidelity.
In no place can I spy my wishing hat.   [*Aside.*

Longa. Thou learned Frenchman, try thy skill on me,
More ugly than I am, I cannot be.

Montr. Cure me, and Montrose wealth shall all be
       thine.

Andel. 'Tis all one for dat ! Shall do presently, madam,
prea mark me.   Monsieur, shamp dis in your two shaps,
so, now Monsieur Long-villain; dis so; now dis; fear
noting, 'tis eshelent medicine ! so, now cram dis into your
guts, and belly; so, now snap away dis whoreson four
divela ; Ha, ha, is no point good ?
              [*Pulls* LONGAVILLE'S *horns off.*

Athelst. This is most strange.
Was't painful, Longaville ?

Longa. Ease took them off, and there remains no pain.

Agrip. O try thy sacred physic upon me.

Andel. No by my trat, 'tis no possibla, 'tis no possibla,
al de mattra, all de ting, all de substance, all de medicine,
be among his and his belly : 'tis no possibla, till me prepare more.

Athelst. Prepare it then, and thou shalt have more gold
From England's coffers, than thy life can waste.

Andel. I must buy many costly tings, dat grow in
Arabia, in Asia, and America, by my trat 'tis no possibla
till anoder time, no point.

Agrip. There's nothing in the world, but may for gold
Be bought in England ; hold your lap, I'll rain
A shower of angels.

Andel. Fie, fie, fie, fie, you no credit le dockature ?
Ha, but vel, 'tis all one for tat : 'tis no mattera for gold !
vel, vel, vel, vel, vel, me have some more, prea say noting,
shall be presently prepara for your horns.

(Aside.) She has my purse, and yonder lies my hat,
Work, brains, and once more make me fortunate.—
Vel, vel, vel, vel, be patient, madam, presently, presently !
Be patient, me have two, tree, four and five medicines for
de horn : presently, madam, stand you der, prea wid all
my art, stand you all der, and say noting,—so ! nor look
noting dis vey. So, presently, presently, madam, snip dis
horn off wid de rushes and anoder ting by and by, by and
by, by and by. Prea look none dis vey, and say noting.

                                        [*Takes his hat.*

Athelst. Let no man speak, or look, upon his life.
Doctor, none here shall rob thee of thy skill.

Andel. So, taka dis hand : winck now prea artely with
your two nyes : why so.
Would I were with my brother Ampedo !

                              [*Exit with* AGRIPYNE.

Agrip. Help, father, help, I am hurried hence perforce.

Athelst. Draw weapons, where's the princess ? follow
          him,
Stay the French doctor, stay the doctor there.

     [CORNWALL *and others run out, and presen'ly re-enter.*

Cornw. Stay him ! 's heart, who dare stay him ? 'tis the
          devil
In likeness of a Frenchman, of a doctor.
Look how a rascal kite having swept up
A chicken in his claws, so flies this hell-hound
In th' air with Agripyne in his arms.

Orle. Mount every man upon his swiftest horse.
Fly several ways, he cannot bear her far.

 Gall. These paths we'll beat.

      [*Exeunt* GALLOWAY *and* ORLEANS.

 Linc. And this way shall be mine.   [*Exit.*

 Cornw. This way, my liege, I'll ride. [*Exit.*

 Athelst. And this way I :

No matter which way, to seek misery. [*Exit.*

 Longa. I can ride no way, to out-run my shame.

 Montr. Yes, Longaville, let's gallop after too ;
Doubtless this doctor was that Irish devil,
That cozened us, the medicine which he gave us
Tasted like his Damasco villany.
To horse, to horse, if we can catch this fiend,
Our forkèd shame shall in his heart blood end.

 Longa. O how this mads me, that all tongues in
  scorn,
Which way soe'er I ride, cry, 'ware the horn !

          [*Exeunt.*

SCENE II.—*An open Space near London : a Prison and
a Pair of Stocks in the background.*

Enter ANDELOCIA *with* AGRIPYNE, AMPEDO *and*
SHADOW *following.*

 Agrip. O gentle Andelocia, pity me,
Take off this infamy, or take my life.

 Andel. Your life ? you think then that I am a true
doctor indeed, that tie up my living in the knots of winding sheets : your life ? no, keep your life, but deliver your
purse : you know the thief's salutation,—"Stand and
deliver." So, this is mine, and these yours : I'll teach you
to live by the sweat of other men's brows.

 Shad. And to strive to be fairer than God made her,

Andel. Right, Shadow : therefore vanish, you have made me turn juggler, and cry " hey-pass," but your horns shall not repass.[1]

Agrip. O gentle Andelocia.

Andel. Andelocia is a nettle : if you touch him gently, he'll sting you.

Shad. Or a rose : if you pull his sweet stalk he'll prick you.

Andel. Therefore not a word ; go, trudge to your father. Sigh not for your purse, money may be got by you, as well as by the little Welshwoman in Cyprus, that had but one horn in her head ;[2] you have two, and perhaps you shall cast both. As you use me, mark those words well, " as you use me," nay, y'are best fly, I'll not endure one word more. Yet stay too, because you entreat me so gently, and that I'll make some amends to your father,—although I care not for any king in Christendom, yet hold you, take this apple, eat it as you go to court, and your horns shall play the cowards and fall from you.

Agrip. O gentle Andelocia.

Andel. Nay, away, not a word.

Shad. Ha, ha, ha ! 'Ware horns !

[*Exit* AGRIPYNE, *weeping.*

Andel. Why dost thou laugh, Shadow ?

Shad. To see what a horn plague follows covetousness and pride.

Amp. Brother, what mysteries lie in all this ?

Andel. Tricks, Ampedo, tricks, devices, and mad hieroglyphics, mirth, mirth, and melody. O, there's more music in this, than all the gamut airs, and sol fa res, in the world ; here's the purse, and here's the hat : because you shall be sure I'll not start, wear you this, you know its virtue. If danger beset you, fly and away : a sort of

---

[1] See *ante*, " They mean to fall to their hey-pass and re-pass."

[2] A reference probably to a woman exhibited at some show in London, and transferred by Dekker, with his usual artistic liberty, to Cyprus.

broken-shinned limping-legged jades run hobbling to seek us. Shadow, we'll for all this have one fit of mirth more, to make us laugh and be fat.

Shad. And when we are fat, master, we'll do as all gluttons do, laugh and lie down.

Andel. Hie thee to my chamber, make ready my richest attire, I'll to court presently.

Shad. I'll go to court in this attire, for apparel is but the shadow of a man, but shadow is the substance of his apparel.   [*Exit* SHADOW.

Andel. Away, away, and meet me presently.

Amp. I had more need to cry away to thee.
Away, away with this wild lunacy,
Away with riots.

Andel. Away with your purity, brother, y'are an ass. Why doth this purse spit out gold but to be spent? why lives a man in this world, to dwell in the suburbs of it, as you do? Away, foreign simplicity, away: are not eyes made to see fair ladies? hearts to love them? tongues to court them, and hands to feel them? Out, you stock, you stone, you log's end: Are not legs made to dance, and shall mine limp up and down the world after your cloth-stocking-heels? You have the hat, keep it. Anon I'll visit your virtuous countenance again; adieu! Pleasure is my sweet mistress, I wear her love in my hat, and her soul in my heart: I have sworn to be merry, and in spite of Fortune and the black-browed Destinies, I'll never be sad.   [*Exit.*

Amp. Go, fool; in spite of mirth, thou shalt be sad.
I'll bury half thy pleasures in a grave
Of hungry flames; this fire I did ordain
To burn both purse and hat: as this doth perish,
So shall the other; count what good and bad
They both have wrought, the good is to the ill
As a small pebble to a mighty hill.
Thy glory and thy mischiefs here shall burn;
Good gifts abused to man's confusion turn.

Enter Longaville *and* Montrose *with* Soldiers.

Longa. This is his brother : soldiers, bind his arms.

Montr. Bind arms and legs, and hale the fiend away.

Amp. Uncivil : wherefore must I taste your spite ?

Longa. Art thou not one of Fortunatus' sons ?

Amp. I am, but he did never do you wrong.

Longa. The devil thy brother has ; villain, look here.

Montr. Where is the beauteous purse and wishing hat ?

Amp. My brother Andelocia has the purse,
This way he'll come anon to pass to court.
Alas, that sin should make men's hearts so bold,
To kill their souls for the base thirst of gold.
The wishing hat is burnt.

Montr. Burnt ? Soldiers, bind him.
Tortures shall wring both hat and purse from you.
Villain, I'll be revenged for that base scorn
Thy hell-hound brother clapped upon my head.

Longa. And so will Longaville.
Away with him !

Montr. Drag him to yonder tower, there shackle him,
And in a pair of stocks lock up his heels,
And bid your wishing cap deliver you.
Give us the purse and hat, we'll set thee free,
Else rot to death and starve.

Amp. Oh tyranny, you need not scorn the badge which
you did bear :
Beasts would you be, though horns you did not wear.

Montr. Drag hence the cur : come, noble Longaville,
One's sure, and were the other fiend as fast,
Their pride should cost their lives : their purse and hat
Shall both be ours, we'll share them equally.

Longa. That will be some amends for arming me.

Enter Andelocia, *and* Shadow *after him.*

Montr. Peace, Longaville, yonder the gallant comes.

Longa. Y'are well encountered.

Andel. Thanks, Lord Longaville.

Longa. The king expects your presence at the court.

Andel. And thither am I going.

Shad. Pips fine, fine apples of Tamasco, ha, ha, ha!

Montr. Wert thou that Irishman that cozened us?

Shad. Pips fine, ha, ha, ha! no not I : not Shadow.

Andel. Were not your apples delicate and rare?

Longa. The worst that e'er you sold; sirs, bind him fast.

Andel. What, will you murder me? help, help, some help!

Shad. Help, help, help!   [*Exit* SHADOW.

Montr. Follow that dog, and stop his bawling throat.

Andel. Villains, what means this barbarous treachery?

Longa. We mean to be revenged for our disgrace.

Montr. And stop the golden current of thy waste.

Andel. Murder! they murder me, O call for help.

Longa. Thy voice is spent in vain; come, come, this
        purse,
This well-spring of your prodigality.

Andel. Are you appointed by the king to this?

Montr. No, no; rise, spurn him up! know you who's this?

Andel. My brother Ampedo? Alas, what fate
Hath made thy virtues so unfortunate?

Amp. Thy riot and the wrong of these two lords,
Who causeless thus do starve [1] me in this prison.

Longa. Strive not y'are best, villains, lift in his legs.

Andel. Traitors to honour, what do you intend?

Longa. That riot shall in wretchedness have end.
Question thy brother with what cost he's fed,
And so assure thou shalt be banqueted.

                [*Exeunt* LONGAVILLE *and* MONTROSE.

Amp. In want, in misery, in woe and care,
Poor Ampedo his fill hath surfeited :

---

[1] This is an imaginative prevision on the part of Ampedo, as
again in his next speech, "My want is famine."

My want is famine, bolts my misery,
My care and woe should be thy portion.
    Andel. Give me that portion, for I have a heart
Shall spend it freely, and make bankrupt
The proudest woe that ever wet man's eyes.
Care, with a mischief! wherefore should I care?
Have I rid side by side by mighty kings,
Yet be thus bridled now? I'll tear these fetters,
Murder! cry, murder! Ampedo, aloud.
To bear this scorn our fortunes are too proud.
    Amp. O folly, thou hast power to make flesh glad,
When the rich soul in wretchedness is clad.
    Andel. Peace, fool, am I not Fortune's minion?
These bands are but one wrinkle of her frown,
This is her evening mask, her next morn's eye
Shall overshine the sun in majesty.
    Amp. But this sad night will make an end of me.
Brother, farewell; grief, famine, sorrow, want,
Have made an end of wretched Ampedo.
    Andel. Where is the wishing hat?
    Amp. Consumed in fire.
    Andel. Accursèd be those hands that did destroy it;
That would redeem us, did we now enjoy it.
    Amp. Wanton, farewell! I faint, Death's frozen hand
Congeals life's little river in my breast.
No man before his end is truly blest.   [*Dies.*
    Andel. O miserable, miserable soul!
Thus a foul life makes death to look more foul.

    Re-enter LONGAVILLE *and* MONTROSE *with a halter.*

    Longa. Thus shall this golden purse divided be,
One day for you, another day for me.
    Montr. Of days anon, say, what determine you,
Shall they have liberty, or shall they die?
    Longa. Die sure: and see, I think the elder's dead.
    Andel. Ay, murderers, he is dead. O sacred Wisdom,
Had Fortunatus been enamourèd

Of thy celestial beauty, his two sons
Had shined like two bright suns.
   Longa. Pull hard, Montrose.
   Andel. Come you to strangle me? are you the hang-
      man?
Hell-hounds, y'are damned for this impiety.
Fortune, forgive me!   I deserve thy hate ;
Myself have made myself a reprobate.
Virtue, forgive me ! for I have transgressed
Against thy laws ; my vows are quite forgot,
And therefore shame is fallen to my sin's lot.
Riches and knowledge are two gifts divine.
They that abuse them both as I have done,
To shame, to beggary, to hell must run.
O conscience, hold thy sting, cease to afflict me.
Be quick, tormentors, I desire to die ;
No death is equal to my misery.
Cyprus, vain world and vanity, farewell.
Who builds his Heaven on earth, is sure of hell.
                                    [Dies.
   Longa. He's dead : in some deep vault let's throw
      their bodies.
   Montr. First let us see the purse, Lord Longaville.
   Longa. Here 'tis, by this we'll fill this tower with gold.
   Montr. Frenchman, this purse is counterfeit.
   Longa. Thou liest.
Scot, thou hast cozened me, give me the right,
Else shall thy bosom be my weapon's grave.
   Montr. Villain, thou shalt not rob me of my due.
                                   [They fight.

Enter ATHELSTANE, AGRIPYNE, ORLEANS, GALLOWAY,
   CORNWALL, CHESTER, LINCOLN, *and* SHADOW *with*
   weapons at one door : FORTUNE, VICE, *and their*
   Attendants *at the other.*

   All. Lay hands upon the murderers, strike them
      down.

Fortune. Surrender up this purse, for this is mine.

All. Are these two devils, or some powers divine ?

Shad. O see, see, O my two masters, poor Shadow's substances ; what shall I do ?   Whose body shall Shadow now follow ?

Fortune. Peace, idiot, thou shalt find rich heaps of
          fools,
That will be proud to entertain a shadow.
I charm thy babbling lips from troubling me.
You need not hold them, see, I smite them down
Lower than hell : base souls, sink to your heaven.

Vice. I do arrest you both my prisoners.

Fortune. Stand not amazed, you gods of earth, at this,
She that arresteth these two fools is Vice,
They have broke Virtue's laws, Vice is her sergeant,
Her jailer and her executioner.
Look on those Cypriots, Fortunatus' sons,
They and their father were my minions,
My name is Fortune.

All. O dread deity !

Fortune. Kneel not to me : if Fortune list to frown,
You need not fall down, for she'll spurn you down ;
Arise ! but, fools, on you I'll triumph thus :
What have you gained by being covetous ?
This prodigal purse did Fortune's bounteous hand
Bestow on them, their riots made them poor,
And set these marks of miserable death
On all their pride, the famine of base gold
Hath made your souls to murder's hands be sold,
Only to be called rich.   But, idiots, see
The virtues to be fled, Fortune hath caused it so ;
Those that will all devour, must all forego.

Athelst. Most sacred Goddess !

Fortune. Peace, you flatterer.
Thy tongue but heaps more vengeance on thy head.
Fortune is angry with thee, in thee burns
A greedy covetous fire, in Agripyne

Pride like a monarch revels, and those sins
Have led you blind-fold to your former shames,
But Virtue pardoned you, and so doth Fortune.

 Athelst. and Agrip. All thanks to both your sacred
  deities.

 Fortune. As for these metal-eaters, these base thieves,
Who rather than they would be counted poor,
Will dig through hell for gold,—you were forgiven
By Virtue's general pardon ; her broad seal
Gave you your lives, when she took off your horns.
Yet having scarce one foot out of the jail,
You tempt damnation by more desperate means,
You both are mortal, and your pains shall ring
Through both your ears, to terrify your souls,
As please the judgment of this mortal king.

 Athelst. Fair Empress of the world, since you resign
Your power to me, this sentence shall be mine :
Thou shalt be tortured on a wheel to death,
Thou with wild horses shalt be quarterèd.

      [*Points to* MONTROSE *and* LONGAVILLE.

 Vice. Ha, ha, weak judge, weak judgment ; I reverse
That sentence, for they are my prisoners.
Embalm the bodies of those Cypriots,
And honour them with princely burial.
For those do as you please ; but for these two,
I kiss you both, I love you, y'are my minions.
Untie their bands, Vice doth reprieve you both.
I set you free.

 Both. Thanks, gracious deity.

 Vice. Begone, but you in liberty shall find
More bondage than in chains ; fools, get you hence,
Both wander with tormented conscience.

 Longa. O horrid judgment, that's the hell indeed.

 Montr. Come, come, our death ne'er ends if conscience
  bleed.

 Both. O miserable, miserable men !

      [*Exeunt* LONGAVILLE *and* MONTROSE.

Fortune. Fortune triumphs at this, yet to appear
All like myself, that which from those I took,
King Athelstane, I will bestow on thee,
And in it the old virtue I infuse :
But, king, take heed how thou my gifts dost use.
England shall ne'er be poor, if England strive
Rather by virtue than by wealth to thrive.

Enter VIRTUE, *crowned :* Nymphs *and* Kings *attending*
on her, crowned with olive branches and laurels ;
music sounding.

Vice. Virtue ? alas good soul, she hides her head.

Virtue. What envious tongue said, " Virtue hides her
head ? "

Vice. She that will drive thee into banishment.

Fortune. She that hath conquered thee : how dar'st
thou come,
Thus tricked in gaudy feathers, and thus guarded
With crownèd kings and Muses, when thy foe
Hath trod thus on thee, and now triumphs so ?
Where's virtuous Ampedo ?   See, he's her slave ;
For following thee, this recompense they have.

Virtue. Is Ampedo her slave ?   Why, that's my glory.
The idiot's cap I once wore on my head,
Did figure him ; those that like him do muffle
Virtue in clouds, and care not how she shine,
I'll make their glory like to his decline.
He made no use of me, but like a miser,
Locked up his wealth in rusty bars of sloth ;
His face was beautiful, but wore a mask,
And in the world's eyes seemed a blackamoor :
So perish they that so keep Virtue poor.

Vice. Thou art a fool to strive, I am more strong,
And greater than thyself ; then, Virtue, fly,
And hide thy face, yield me the victory.

Virtue. Is Vice higher than Virtue ? that's my
glory,

The higher that thou art, thou art more horrid:
The world will love me for my comeliness.

 Fortune. Thine own self loves thyself: why on the
   heads
Of Agripyne, Montrose, and Longaville,—
English, Scot, French—did Vice clap ugly horns,
But to approve that English, French and Scot,
And all the world else, kneel and honour Vice;
But in no country, Virtue is of price!

 Virtue. Yes, in all countries Virtue is of price,
In every kingdom some diviner breast
Is more enamoured of me than the rest.
Have English, Scot and French bowed knees to thee?
Why that's my glory too, for by their shame,
Men will abhor thee and adore my name.
Fortune, thou art too weak, Vice, th'art a fool
To fight with me; I suffered you awhile
T'eclipse my brightness, but I now will shine,
And make you swear your beauty's base to mine.

 Fortune. Thou art too insolent; see, here's a court
Of mortal judges; let's by them be tried,
Which of us three shall most be deified.

 Vice. I am content.

 Fortune. And I.

 Virtue. So am not I.
My judge shall be your sacred deity.[1]

 Vice. O miserable me, I am undone.

       [*Exit* VICE *and her train.*

 All. O stop the horrid monster.

 Virtue. Let her run.
Fortune, who conquers now?

 Fortune. Virtue, I see,
Thou wilt triumph both over her and me.

 All. Empress of Heaven and earth.

---

[1] Virtue here evidently addressed Queen Elizabeth, as she sat in the audience; this direct recognition is kept up to the end of the play.

Fortune. Why do you mock me ?
Kneel not to me, to her transfer your eyes,
There sits the Queen of Chance, I bend my knees
Lower than yours.   Dread goddess, 'tis most meet
That Fortune fall down at thy conquering feet.
Thou sacred Empress that command'st the Fates,
Forgive what I have to thy handmaid done,
And at thy chariot wheels Fortune shall run,
And be thy captive, and to thee resign
All powers which Heaven's large patent have made
   mine.

Virtue. Fortune, th'art vanquished.   Sacred deity,
O now pronounce who wins the victory,
And yet that sentence needs not, since alone,
Your virtuous presence Vice hath overthrown,
Yet to confirm the conquest on your side,
Look but on Fortunatus and his sons ;
Of all the wealth those gallants did possess,
Only poor Shadow is left, comfortless :
Their glory's faded and their golden pride.

Shad. Only poor Shadow tells how poor they died.

Virtue. All that they had, or mortal men can have,
Sends only but a Shadow from the grave.
Virtue alone lives still, and lives in you ;
I am a counterfeit, you are the true ;
I am a shadow, at your feet I fall,
Begging for these, and these, myself and all.
All these that thus do kneel before your eyes,
Are shadows like myself : dread nymph, it lies
In you to make us substances.   O do it !
Virtue I am sure you love, she wooes you to it.
I read a verdict in your sun-like eyes,
And this it is : Virtue the victory.

All. All loudly cry, Virtue the victory !

Fortune. Virtue the victory ! for joy of this,
Those self-same hymns which you to Fortune sung
Let them be now in Virtue's honour rung.

Song.

Virtue smiles : cry holiday,
Dimples on her cheeks do dwell,
Virtue frowns, cry welladay,
Her love is Heaven, her hate is hell.
Since Heaven and hell obey her power,
Tremble when her eyes do lower.
Since Heaven and hell her power obey,
Where she smiles, cry holiday.
    Holiday with joy we cry,
    And bend, and bend, and merrily,
    Sing hymns to Virtue's deity :
    Sing hymns to Virtue's deity.

As they are about to depart, enter Two Old Men.

THE EPILOGUE AT COURT.[1]

1st O. Man. Nay stay, poor pilgrims, when I entered
    first
The circle of this bright celestial sphere,
I wept for joy, now I could weep for fear.
2nd O. Man. I fear we all like mortal men shall prove
Weak, not in love, but in expressing love.
1st. O. Man. Let every one beg once more on his knee,
One pardon for himself, and one for me ;
For I enticed you hither. O dear Goddess,
Breathe life in our numbed spirits with one smile,
And from this cold earth, we with lively souls,
Shall rise like men new-born, and make Heaven sound

---

[1] See note [1] to Prologue.

With hymns sung to thy name, and prayers that we
May once a year so oft enjoy this sight,
Till these young boys change their curled locks to white,
And when gray-wingèd age sits on their heads,
That so their children may supply their steads,
And that Heaven's great arithmetician,
Who in the scales of number weighs the world,
May still to forty-two add one year more,
And still add one to one, that went before,
And multiply four tens by many a ten:
To this I cry, Amen.

    All. Amen, amen!

    1*st O. Man.* Good-night, dear mistress, those that wish
       thee harm,
Thus let them stoop under destruction's arm.

    All. Amen, amen, amen!   [*Exeunt.*

THE WITCH OF EDMONTON.

HE WITCH OF EDMONTON, which was probably first performed in 1623, was not published until thirty-five years later, in 1658. It was then issued in the usual quarto form, with the title : *The Witch of Edmonton :* "A known True Story. Composed into a Tragi-Comedy by divers well-esteemed Poets, William Rowley, Thomas Dekker, John Ford, &c. Acted by the Prince's Servants, often at the Cock-Pit in Drury-Lane, once at Court, with singular Applause." The best modern reprint of the play is that in the Gifford-Dyce edition of Ford, upon which the present version is based.

It is impossible to assign the exact share of the various authors in the play. The business of the Witch, the rustic chorus, and certain other parts mark themselves out as mainly Dekker's. The conception of Sir Arthur Clarington, and the subsidiary domestic plot is no doubt mainly Ford's. Rowley's share is more difficult to ascertain. The intimate collaboration of all three can alone be held accountable for some of the scenes, and indeed in even the passages most characteristic of any one of the authors, the touch of another often shows itself in a chance word or phrase.

The justification for the description of the play as "A known true story" is a pamphlet written by Henry Good-cole, and published at London in 1621, giving an account of one Elizabeth Sawyer, late of Islington, who was "executed in 1621 for witchcraft." See Caulfield's "Portraits, Memoirs, and Characters of Remarkable Persons," 1794. No existing copy of the pamphlet is known, but the British Museum possesses copies of two of Goodcole's other pamphlets on similar subjects.

PROLOGUE.

THE town of Edmonton hath lent the stage
A Devil [1] and a Witch, both in an age.
To make comparisons it were uncivil
Between so even a pair, a Witch and Devil ;
But as the year doth with his plenty bring
As well a latter as a former spring,
So hath this Witch enjoyed the first, and reason
Presumes she may partake the other season :
In acts deserving name, the proverb says,
" Once good, and ever ; " why not so in plays?
Why not in this? since, gentlemen, we flatter
No expectation ; here is mirth and matter.

MASTER BIRD.

The whole argument of the play is this distich.

Forced marriage, murder ; murder blood requires :
Reproach, revenge ; revenge hell's help desires.

[1] An allusion to the popular old play of *The Merry Devil of Edmonton*, written about twenty years previously.

Sir ARTHUR CLARINGTON.

OLD THORNEY, a Gentleman.

CARTER, a rich Yeoman.

WARBECK,
SOMERTON, } Suitors to Carter's daughters.

FRANK, Thorney's Son.

OLD BANKS, a Countryman.

CUDDY BANKS, his Son.

RATCLIFFE,
HAMLUC, } Countrymen.

Morris-dancers.

SAWGUT, an old Fiddler.

A Dog, a Familiar.

A Spirit.

Countrymen, Justice, Constable, Officers, Serving-
men and Maids.

Mother SAWYER, the Witch.

ANN, Ratcliffe's Wife.

SUSAN,
KATHERINE, } Carter's Daughters.

WINNIFRED, Sir Arthur's Maid.

SCENE—The town and neighbourhood of EDMONTON; in the
end of the last act, LONDON.

THE WITCH OF EDMONTON.

ACT THE FIRST.

SCENE I.—*The neighbourhood of Edmonton. A Room in the House of* Sir ARTHUR CLARINGTON.

Enter FRANK THORNEY *and* WINNIFRED, *who is with child.*

FRANK. Come, wench ; why, here's a
    business soon dispatched :
Thy heart I know is now at ease ; thou
    need'st not   [cups
Fear what the tattling gossips in their
Can speak against thy fame ; thy child
    shall know
Whom to call dad now.

   Win.   You have here discharged
The true part of an honest man ; I cannot
Request a fuller satisfaction
Than you have freely granted : yet methinks
'Tis an hard case, being lawful man and wife,
We should not live together.

   Frank.   Had I failed
In promise of my truth to thee, we must
Have then been ever sundered ; now the longest
Of our forbearing either's company

Is only but to gain a little time
For our continuing thrift ; that so hereafter
The heir that shall be born may not have cause
To curse his hour of birth, which made him feel
The misery of beggary and want,—
Two devils that are occasions to enforce
A shameful end.   My plots aim but to keep
My father's love.

  Win.   And that will be as difficult
To be preserved, when he shall understand
How you are married, as it will be now,
Should you confess it to him.

  Frank.   Fathers are
Won by degrees, not bluntly, as our masters
Or wrongèd friends are ; and besides I'll use
Such dutiful and ready means, that ere
He can have notice of what's past, th' inheritance
To which I am born heir shall be assured ;
That done, why, let him know it : if he like it not,
Yet he shall have no power in him left
To cross the thriving of it.

  Win.   You who had
The conquest of my maiden-love may easily
Conquer the fears of my distrust.   And whither
Must I be hurried ?

  Frank.   Prithee do not use
A word so much unsuitable to the constant
Affections of thy husband : thou shalt live
Near Waltham Abbey with thy uncle Selman ;
I have acquainted him with all at large :
He'll use thee kindly ; thou shalt want no pleasures,
Nor any other fit supplies whatever
Thou canst in heart desire.

  Win.   All these are nothing
Without your company.

  Frank.   Which thou shalt have
Once every month at least.

Win.   Once every month !
Is this to have an husband ?
    Frank.   Perhaps oftener ;
That's as occasion serves.
    Win.   Ay, ay ; in case
No other beauty tempt your eye, whom you
Like better, I may chance to be remembered,
And see you now and then. Faith, I did hope
You'd not have used me so : 'tis but my fortune.
And yet, if not for my sake, have some pity
Upon the child I go with ; that's your own :
And 'less you'll be a cruel-hearted father,
You cannot but remember that.
Heaven knows how—
    Frank.   To quit which fear at once,
As by the ceremony late performed
I plighted thee a faith as free from challenge
As any double thought ; once more, in hearing
Of Heaven and thee, I vow that never henceforth
Disgrace, reproof, lawless affections, threats,
Or what can be suggested 'gainst our marriage,
Shall cause me falsify that bridal oath
That binds me thine. And, Winnifred, whenever
The wanton heat of youth, by subtle baits
Of beauty, or what woman's art can practise,
Draw me from only loving thee, let Heaven
Inflict upon my life some fearful ruin !
I hope thou dost believe me.
    Win.   Swear no more ;
I am confirmed, and will resolve to do
What you think most behoveful for us.
    Frank.   Thus, then ;
Make thyself ready ; at the furthest house
Upon the green without the town, your uncle
Expects you. For a little time, farewell !
    Win.   Sweet,
We shall meet again as soon as thou canst possibly ?

Sir Arth. Most provident speed.
Frank, I will be thy friend, and such a friend !—
Thou'lt bring her thither?
 Frank. Sir, I cannot; newly
My father sent me word I should come to him.
 Sir Arth. Marry, and do; I know thou hast a wit
To handle him.
 Frank. I have a suit t'ye.
 Sir Arth. What is't?
Anything, Frank; command it.
 Frank. That you'll please
By letters to assure my father that
I am not married.
 Sir Arth. How !
 Frank. Some one or other
Hath certainly informed him that I purposed
To marry Winnifred ; on which he threatened
To disinherit me :—to prevent it,
Lowly I crave your letters, which he seeing
Will credit; and I hope, ere I return,
On such conditions as I'll frame, his lands
Shall be assured.
 Sir Arth. But what is there to quit[1]
My knowledge of the marriage?
 Frank. Why, you were not
A witness to it.
 Sir Arth. I conceive; and then—
His land confirmed, thou wilt acquaint him throughly
With all that's past.
 Frank. I mean no less.
 Sir Arth. Provided
I never was made privy to't.
 Frank. Alas, sir,
Am I a talker?
 Sir Arth. Draw thyself the letter,
I'll put my hand to't. I commend thy policy;

---

[1] *i.e.* Acquit.

Thou'rt witty, witty, Frank ; nay, nay, 'tis fit :
Dispatch it.

    Frank.   I shall write effectually.   [*Exit.*

    Sir Arth. Go thy way, cuckoo ;—have I caught the
        young man ?
One trouble, then, is freed.   He that will feast
At other's cost must be a bold-faced guest.

        Re-enter WINNIFRED *in a riding-suit.*

Win, I have heard the news ; all now is safe ;
The worst is past : thy lip, wench [*Kisses her*] : I must bid
Farewell, for fashion's sake ; but I will visit thee
Suddenly, girl.   This was cleanly carried ;
Ha ! was't not, Win ?

    Win.   Then were my happiness,
That I in heart repent I did not bring him
The dower of a virginity.   Sir, forgive me ;
I have been much to blame : had not my lewdness [1]
Given way to your immoderate waste of virtue,
You had not with such eagerness pursued
The error of your goodness.

    Sir Arth.   Dear, dear Win,
I hug this art of thine ; it shows how cleanly
Thou canst beguile, in case occasion serve
To practise ; it becomes thee : now we share
Free scope enough, without control or fear,
To interchange our pleasures ; we will surfeit
In our embraces, wench.   Come, tell me, when
Wilt thou appoint a meeting ?

    Win.   What to do ?

    Sir Arth. Good, good, to con the lesson of our loves,
Our secret game.

    Win.   O, blush to speak it further !
As you're a noble gentleman, forget
A sin so monstrous : 'tis not gently done

---

[1] This speech is very corrupt. Dyce suggested " lewdness " in
place of the " laundress " of the old edition.

Car. Double, treble, more or less, I tell you, Master Thorney, I'll give no security. Bonds and bills are but terriers to catch fools, and keep lazy knaves busy; my security shall be present payment. And we here about Edmonton hold present payment as sure as an alderman's bond in London, Master Thorney.

O. Thor. I cry you mercy, sir; I understood you not.

Car. I like young Frank well, so does my Susan too; the girl has a fancy to him, which makes me ready in my purse. There be other suitors within, that make much noise to little purpose. If Frank love Sue, Sue shall have none but Frank. 'Tis a mannerly girl, Master Thorney, though but a homely man's daughter; there have worse faces looked out of black bags, man.

O. Thor. You speak your mind freely and honestly. I marvel my son comes not; I am sure he will be here some time to-day.

Car. To-day or to-morrow, when he comes he shall be welcome to bread, beer, and beef, yeoman's fare; we have no kickshaws : full dishes, whole bellyfuls. Should I diet three days at one of the slender city-suppers, you might send me to Barber-Surgeons' hall the fourth day, to hang up for an anatomy.[1]—Here come they that—

Enter WARBECK *with* SUSAN, SOMERTON *with* KATHERINE.

How now, girls ! every day play-day with you ? Valentine's day too, all by couples ? Thus will young folks do when we are laid in our graves, Master Thorney ; here's all the care they take. And how do you find the wenches, gentlemen ? have they any mind to a loose gown and a strait shoe ? Win 'em and wear 'em ; they shall choose for themselves by my consent.

War. You speak like a kind father.—Sue, thou hear'st
The liberty that's granted thee ; what say'st thou ?
Wilt thou be mine ?

[1] Skeleton.

Sus.   Your what, sir?   I dare swear
Never your wife.

War.   Canst thou be so unkind,
Considering how dearly I affect thee,
Nay, dote on thy perfections?

Sus.   You are studied,
Too scholar-like, in words I understand not.
I am too coarse for such a gallant's love
As you are.

War. By the honour of gentility,—

Sus. Good sir, no swearing ; yea and nay with us
Prevail above all oaths you can invent.

War. By this white hand of thine,—

Sus.   Take a false oath !
Fie, fie ! flatter the wise ; fools not regard it,
And one of these am I.

War.   Dost thou despise me?

Car. Let 'em talk on, Master Thorney ; I know Sue's
mind. The fly may buzz about the candle, he shall but
singe his wings when all's done ; Frank, Frank is he has
her heart.

Som. But shall I live in hope, Kate?

Kath.   Better so
Than be a desperate man.

Som. Perhaps thou think'st it is thy portion
I level at : wert thou as poor in fortunes
As thou art rich in goodness, I would rather
Be suitor for the dower of thy virtues
Than twice thy father's whole estate ; and, prithee,
Be thou resolved [1] so.

Kath.   Master Somerton,
It is an easy labour to deceive
A maid that will believe men's subtle promises ;
Yet I conceive of you as worthily
As I presume you to deserve.

Som.   Which is,

---

[1] Persuaded.

As worthily in loving thee sincerely
As thou art worthy to be so beloved.

Kath. I shall find time to try you.

Som.   Do, Kate, do ;
And when I fail, may all my joys forsake me !

Car. Warbeck and Sue are at it still.   I laugh to myself, Master Thorney, to see how earnestly he beats the
bush, while the bird is flown into another's bosom.   A very
unthrift, Master Thorney; one of the country roaring-
lads : we have such as well as the city, and as arrant
rake-hells as they are, though not so nimble at their
prizes of wit.   Sue knows the rascal to an hair's-breadth,
and will fit him accordingly.

O. Thor. What is the other gentleman ?

Car. One Somerton ; the honester man of the two by
five pound in every stone-weight.   A civil fellow ; he has
a fine convenient estate of land in West Ham, by Essex :
Master Ranges, that dwells by Enfield, sent him hither.
He likes Kate well ; I may tell you I think she likes
him as well : if they agree, I'll not hinder the match
for my part.   But that Warbeck is such another—I
use him kindly for Master Somerton's sake ; for he
came hither first as a companion of his : honest men,
Master Thorney, may fall into knaves' company now and
then.

War. Three hundred a-year jointure, Sue.

Sus.   Where lies it ?
By sea or by land ? I think by sea.

War. Do I look like a captain ?

Sus.   Not a whit, sir.
Should all that use the seas be reckoned captains,
There's not a ship should have a scullion in her
To keep her clean.

War.   Do you scorn me, Mistress Susan ?
Am I a subject to be jeered at ?

Sus.   Neither
Am I a property for you to use

As stale [1] to your fond wanton loose discourse :
Pray, sir, be civil.

War.   Wilt be angry, wasp?

Car. God-a-mercy, Sue! she'll firk him, on my life, if
he fumble with her.

Enter FRANK.

Master Francis Thorney, you are welcome indeed;
your father expected your coming. How does the right
worshipful knight, Sir Arthur Clarington, your master?

Frank. In health this morning.—Sir, my duty.

O. Thor.   Now
You come as I could wish.

War. [*Aside*]   Frank Thorney, ha!

Sus. You must excuse me.

Frank.   Virtuous Mistress Susan,
Kind Mistress Katherine. [*Kisses them.*]—Gentlemen, to
both
Good time o' th' day.

Som.   The like to you.

War.   'Tis he.
A word, friend. [*Aside to Som.*] On my life, this is the man
Stands fair in crossing Susan's love to me.

Som. [*Aside to War.*] I think no less; be wise, and
take no notice on't;
He that can win her best deserves her.

War. [*Aside to Som.*]   Marry
A serving-man? mew!

Som. [*Aside to War.*] Prithee, friend, no more.

Car. Gentlemen all, there's within a slight dinner
ready, if you please to taste of it; Master Thorney, Master
Francis, Master Somerton.—Why, girls! what huswives!
will you spend all your forenoon in tittle-tattles? away!
it's well, i'faith.—Will you go in, gentlemen?

O. Thor. We'll follow presently; my son and I
Have a few words of business.

<hr />

[1] A stalking-horse, cover.

Car.   At your pleasure.

               [Exeunt all but O. THOR. *and* FRANK.

O. Thor. I think you guess the reason, Frank, for which
I sent for you.

    Frank.   Yes, sir.

    O. Thor. I need not tell you
With what a labyrinth of dangers daily
The best part of my whole estate's encumbered ;
Nor have I any clue to wind it out
But what occasion proffers me ; wherein
If you should falter, I shall have the shame,
And you the loss.   On these two points rely
Our happiness or ruin.   If you marry
With wealthy Carter's daughter, there's a portion
Will free my land ; all which I will instate,[1]
Upon the marriage, to you : otherwise
I must be of necessity enforced
To make a present sale of all ; and yet,
For aught I know, live in as poor distress,
Or worse, than now I do.   You hear the sum ?
I told you thus before ; have you considered on't ?

    Frank. I have, sir ; and however I could wish
To enjoy the benefit of single freedom,—
For that I find no disposition in me
To undergo the burthen of that care
That marriage brings with it,—yet, to secure
And settle the continuance of your credit,
I humbly yield to be directed by you
In all commands.

    O. Thor.   You have already used
Such thriving protestations to the maid
That she is wholly yours ; and—speak the truth—
You love her, do you not ?

    Frank.   'Twere pity, sir,
I should deceive her.

                        [1] Make over.

O. Thor.   Better you'd been unborn.
But is your love so steady that you mean,
Nay, more, desire, to make her your wife ?
   Frank.   Else, sir,
It were a wrong not to be righted.
   O. Thor.   True,
It were : and you will marry her ?
   Frank.   Heaven prosper it,
I do intend it.
   O. Thor.   O, thou art a villain !
A devil like a man ! Wherein have I
Offended all the powers so much, to be
Father to such a graceless, godless son ?
   Frank. To me, sir, this ! O, my cleft heart !
   O. Thor.   To thee,
Son of my curse. Speak truth and blush, thou monster !
Hast thou not married Winnifred, a maid
Was fellow-servant with thee ?
   Frank [*Aside*].   Some swift spirit
Has blown this news abroad ; I must outface it.
   O. Thor. D' you study for excuse ? why, all the country
Is full on't.
   Frank. With your licence, 'tis not charitable,
I'm sure it is not fatherly, so much
To be o'erswayed with credulous conceit
Of mere impossibilities ; but fathers
Are privileged to think and talk at pleasure.
   O. Thor. Why, canst thou yet deny thou hast no wife ?
   Frank. What do you take me for ? an atheist ?
One that nor hopes the blessedness of life
Hereafter, neither fears the vengeance due
To such as make the marriage-bed an inn,
Which travellers, day and night,
After a toilsome lodging, leave at pleasure ?
Am I become so insensible of losing
The glory of creation's work, my soul ?
O, I have lived too long !

O. Thor.   Thou hast, dissembler.
Dar'st thou perséver yet, and pull down wrath
As hot as flames of hell to strike thee quick
Into the grave of horror?   I believe thee not;
Get from my sight!

   Frank.   Sir, though mine innocence
Needs not a stronger witness than the clearness
Of an unperished conscience, yet for that
I was informed how mainly you had been
Possessed of this untruth,—to quit all scruple,
Please you peruse this letter; 'tis to you.

   O. Thor. From whom?

   Frank.   Sir Arthur Clarington, my master.

   O. Thor. Well, sir.   [*Reads.*

   Frank [*Aside*].   On every side I am distracted;
Am waded deeper into mischief
Than virtue can avoid; but on I must:
Fate leads me; I will follow.—There you read
What may confirm you.

   O. Thor.   Yes, and wonder at it.
Forgive me, Frank; credulity abused me.
My tears express my joy; and I am sorry
I injured innocence.

   Frank.   Alas! I knew
Your rage and grief proceeded from your love
To me; so I conceived it.

   O. Thor.   My good son,
I'll bear with many faults in thee hereafter;
Bear thou with mine.

   Frank.   The peace is soon concluded.

         Re-enter CARTER *and* SUSAN.

   Car. Why, Master Thorney, d'ye mean to talk out
your dinner? the company attends your coming.   What
must it be, Master Frank? or son Frank? I am plain
Dunstable.[1]

        [1] *i.e.* Blunt and honest.   An old proverb.

O. Thor. Son, brother, if your daughter like to have
it so.

Frank. I dare be confident she is not altered
From what I left her at our parting last:—
Are you, fair maid?

Sus. You took too sure possession
Of an engagèd heart.

Frank. Which now I challenge.

Car. Marry, and much good may it do thee, son.
Take her to thee; get me a brace of boys at a burthen,
Frank; the nursing shall not stand thee in a penny-
worth of milk; reach her home and spare not: when's
the day?

O. Thor. To-morrow, if you please. To use cere-
mony
Of charge and custom were to little purpose;
Their loves are married fast enough already.

Car. A good motion. We'll e'en have an household dinner, and let the fiddlers go scrape: let the bride
and bridegroom dance at night together; no matter for
the guests:—to-morrow, Sue, to-morrow.—Shall's to
dinner now?

O. Thor. We are on all sides pleased, I hope.

Sus. Pray Heaven I may deserve the blessing sent
me:
Now my heart is settled.

Frank. So is mine.

Car. Your marriage-money shall be received before
your wedding-shoes can be pulled on. Blessing on you
both!

Frank [*Aside*]. No man can hide his shame from
Heaven that views him;
In vain he flees whose destiny pursues him. [*Exeunt.*

ACT THE SECOND.

SCENE I.—*The Fields near Edmonton.*

Enter MOTHER SAWYER *gathering sticks.*

OTHER SAWYER. And why on me?
why should the envious world
Throw all their scandalous malice upon
me?
'Cause I am poor, deformed, and ig-
norant,
And like a bow buckled and bent
together
By some more strong in mischiefs than myself,
Must I for that be made a common sink
For all the filth and rubbish of men's tongues
To fall and run into? Some call me witch,
And being ignorant of myself, they go
About to teach me how to be one; urging
That my bad tongue—by their bad usage made so—
Forspeaks [1] their cattle, doth bewitch their corn,
Themselves, their servants, and their babes at nurse.
This they enforce upon me, and in part
Make me to credit it; and here comes one
Of my chief adversaries.

Enter OLD BANKS.

O. Banks. Out, out upon thee, witch!

[1] Another term for "bewitch" commonly in use; the word probably implied the muttering or "forspeaking" of a spell.

M. Saw.   Dost call me witch?

O. Banks. I do, witch, I do; and worse I would,
knew I a name more hateful. What makest thou upon
my ground?

M. Saw. Gather a few rotten sticks to warm me.

O. Banks. Down with them when I bid thee quickly;
I'll make thy bones rattle in thy skin else.

M. Saw. You won't, churl, cut-throat, miser!—there
they be [*Throws them down*]: would they stuck cross thy
throat, thy bowels, thy maw, thy midriff!

O. Banks. Sayest thou me so, hag? Out of my
ground!   [*Beats her.*

M. Saw. Dost strike me, slave, curmudgeon! Now,
thy bones ache, thy joints cramp, and convulsions
stretch and crack thy sinews!

O. Banks. Cursing, thou hag! take that and that.

                                    [*Beats her and exit.*

M. Saw. Strike, do!—and withered may that hand
          and arm
Whose blows have lamed me drop from the rotten trunk.
Abuse me! beat me! call me hag and witch!
What is the name, where and by what art learned,
What spells, what charms, or invocations,
May the thing called Familiar be purchased?

Enter CUDDY BANKS *and several other* Clowns.

Cud. A new head for the tabor, and silver tipping for
the pipe; remember that: and forget not five leash of
new bells.

1st. Cl. Double bells;—Crooked Lane[1]—ye shall
have 'em straight in Crooked Lane:—double bells all, if
it be possible.

Cud. Double bells? double coxcombs! trebles, buy
me trebles, all trebles; for our purpose is to be in the
altitudes.

---

[1] A winding thoroughfare which led from Eastcheap to Fish-street-
hill.

And hated like a sickness ; made a scorn
To all degrees and sexes.   I have heard old beldams
Talk of familiars in the shape of mice,
Rats, ferrets, weasels, and I wot not what,
That have appeared, and sucked, some say, their blood ;
But by what means they came acquainted with them
I am now ignorant.   Would some power, good or bad,
Instruct me which way I might be revenged
Upon this churl, I'd go out of myself,
And give this fury leave to dwell within
This ruined cottage ready to fall with age,
Abjure all goodness, be at hate with prayer,
And study curses, imprecations,
Blasphemous speeches, oaths, detested oaths,
Or anything that's ill : so I might work
Revenge upon this miser, this black cur,
That barks and bites, and sucks the very blood
Of me and of my credit.   'Tis all one
To be a witch as to be counted one :
Vengeance, shame, ruin light upon that canker !

Enter a Black Dog.

Dog. Ho ! have I found thee cursing ? now thou art
Mine own.

   M. Saw.   Thine ! what art thou ?

   Dog.   He thou hast so often
Importuned to appear to thee, the devil.

   M. Saw. Bless me ! the devil ?

   Dog. Come, do not fear ; I love thee much too well
To hurt or fright thee ; if I seem terrible,
It is to such as hate me.   I have found
Thy love unfeigned ; have seen and pitied
Thy open wrongs ; and come, out of my love,
To give thee just revenge against thy foes.

   M. Saw. May I believe thee ?

   Dog.   To confirm't, command me
Do any mischief unto man or beast,

And I'll effect it, on condition
That, uncompelled, thou make a deed of gift
Of soul and body to me.

 M. Saw.   Out, alas!
My soul and body?

 Dog.   And that instantly,
And seal it with thy blood : if thou deniest,
I'll tear thy body in a thousand pieces.

 M. Saw. I know not where to seek relief : but shall I,
After such covenants sealed, see full revenge
On all that wrong me?

 Dog.   Ha, ha! silly woman!
The devil is no liar to such as he loves :
Didst ever know or hear the devil a liar
To such as he affects?

 M. Saw. Then I am thine ; at least so much of me
As I can call mine own—

 Dog.   Equivocations?
Art mine or no? speak, or I'll tear—

 M. Saw.   All thine.

 Dog. Seal't with thy blood.

    [*She pricks her arm, which he sucks.   Thunder
     and lightning.*

       See! now I dare call thee mine!
For proof, command me ; instantly I'll run
To any mischief ; goodness can I none.

 M. Saw. And I desire as little.   There's an old churl,
One Banks—

 Dog. That wronged thee, lamed thee, called thee
    witch.

 M. Saw. The same ; first upon him I'd be revenged.

 Dog. Thou shalt ; do but name how.

 M. Saw.   Go, touch his life.

 Dog. I cannot.

 M. Saw. Hast thou not vowed?   Go, kill the slave!

 Dog.   I wonnot.

 M. Saw. I'll cancel, then, my gift.

M. Saw. I understand thee not ; be plain, my son.

Cud. As a pike-staff, mother. You know Kate Carter ?

M. Saw. The wealthy yeoman's daughter ? what of her ?

Cud. That same party has bewitched me.

M. Saw. Bewitched thee ?

Cud. Bewitched me, *hisce auribus.* I saw a little devil fly out of her eye like a burbolt,[1] which sticks at this hour up to the feathers in my heart. Now, my request is, to send one of thy what-d'ye-call-'ems either to pluck that out, or stick another as fast in hers : do, and here's my hand, I am thine for three lives.

M. Saw. [*Aside*] We shall have sport.—Thou art in love with her ?

Cud. Up to the very hilts, mother.

M. Saw. And thou wouldst have me make her love thee too ?

Cud. [*Aside*] I think she'll prove a witch in earnest. —Yes, I could find in my heart to strike her three quarters deep in love with me too.

M. Saw. But dost thou think that I can do't, and I alone ?

Cud. Truly, Mother Witch, I do verily believe so ; and, when I see it done, I shall be half persuaded so too.

M. Saw. It is enough : what art can do be sure of. Turn to the west, and whatsoe'er thou hear'st Or seest, stand silent, and be not afraid.

[*She stamps on the ground ; the* Dog *appears, and fawns, and leaps upon her.*

Cud. Afraid, Mother Witch !—"turn my face to the west !" I said I should always have a back-friend of her ; and now it's out. An her little devil should be hungry, come sneaking behind me, like a cowardly catchpole, and clap his talons on my haunches—'Tis woundy cold, sure

---

[1] Bird-bolt, arrow ; perhaps more correctly " But-bolt," as emendated by Gifford.

—I dudder and shake like an aspen-leaf every joint of me.

M. Saw. To scandal and disgrace pursue 'em,
            Et sanctibicetur nomen tuum.   [*Exit* Dog.
How now, my son, how is't?

Cud. Scarce in a clean life, Mother Witch.—But did your goblin and you spout Latin together?

M. Saw. A kind of charm I work by; didst thou hear me?

Cud. I heard I know not the devil what mumble in a scurvy base tone, like a drum that had taken cold in the head the last muster. Very comfortable words; what were they? and who taught them you?

M. Saw. A great learned man.

Cud. Learned man! learned devil it was as soon! But what? what comfortable news about the party?

M. Saw. Who? Kate Carter? I'll tell thee. Thou knowest the stile at the west end of thy father's peas-field: be there to-morrow night after sunset; and the first live thing thou seest be sure to follow, and that shall bring thee to thy love.

Cud. In the peas-field? has she a mind to codlings [1] already? The first living thing I meet, you say, shall bring me to her?

M. Saw. To a sight of her, I mean. She will seem wantonly coy, and flee thee; but follow her close and boldly: do but embrace her in thy arms once, and she is thine own.

Cud. "At the stile at the west end of my father's peas-land, the first live thing I see, follow and embrace her, and she shall be thine." Nay, an I come to embracing once, she shall be mine; I'll go near to make at eaglet else.   [*Exit.*

M. Saw. A ball well bandied! now the set's half won; The father's wrong I'll wreak upon the son.   [*Exit.*

---

[1] Peas codlings; green peas.

SCENE II.—CARTER'S *House.*

Enter CARTER, WARBECK, *and* SOMERTON.

Car. How now, gentlemen ! cloudy ?   I know, Master Warbeck, you are in a fog about my daughter's marriage.

War. And can you blame me, sir ?

Car. Nor you me justly.   Wedding and hanging are tied up both in a proverb ; and destiny is the juggler that unties the knot.   My hope is, you are reserved to a richer fortune than my poor daughter.

War. However, your promise—

Car. Is a kind of debt, I confess it.

War. Which honest men should pay.

Car. Yet some gentlemen break in that point now and then, by your leave, sir.

Som. I confess thou hast had a little wrong in the wench ; but patience is the only salve to cure it.   Since Thorney has won the wench, he has most reason to wear her.

War. Love in this kind admits no reason to wear her.

Car. Then Love's a fool, and what wise man will take exception ?

Som. Come, frolic, Ned : were every man master of his own fortune, Fate might pick straws, and Destiny go a-wool-gathering.

War. You hold yours in a string, though : 'tis well ; but if there be any equity, look thou to meet the like usage ere long.

Som. In my love to her sister Katherine ?   Indeed, they are a pair of arrows drawn out of one quiver, and should fly at an even length ; if she do run after her sister,—

War. Look for the same mercy at my hands as I have received at thine.

Som. She'll keep a surer compass ; I have too strong a confidence to mistrust her.

War. And that confidence is a wind that has blown many a married man ashore at Cuckold's Haven, I can tell you ; I wish yours more prosperous though.

Car. Whate'er your wish, I'll master my promise to him.

War. Yes, as you did to me.

Car. No more of that, if you love me : but for the more assurance, the next offered occasion shall consummate the marriage ; and that once sealed—

Som. Leave the manage of the rest to my care. But see, the bridegroom and bride come ; the new pair of Sheffield knives, fitted both to one sheath.

War. The sheath might have been better fitted, if somebody had their due ; but—

Car. No harsh language, if thou lovest me. Frank Thorney has done—

War. No more than I, or thou, or any man, things so standing, would have attempted.

Enter FRANK THORNEY *and* SUSAN.

Som. Good-morrow, Master Bridegroom.

War. Come, give thee joy : mayst thou live long and
        happy
In thy fair choice !

Frank. I thank ye, gentlemen ; kind Master Warbeck,
I find you loving.

War. Thorney, that creature,—much good do thee
        with her !—
Virtue and beauty hold fair mixture in her ;
She's rich, no doubt, in both : yet were she fairer,
Thou art right worthy of her. Love her, Thorney ;
'Tis nobleness in thee, in her but duty.
The match is fair and equal ; the success
I leave to censure. Farewell, Mistress Bride !
Till now elected, thy old scorn deride.   [*Exit.*

Som. Good Master Thorney—

Car. Nay, you shall not part till you see the barrels
run a-tilt, gentlemen.   [*Exit with* SOMERTON.

Sus. Why change you your face, sweetheart?

Frank.   Who, I? for nothing.

Sus. Dear, say not so; a spirit of your constancy
Cannot endure this change for nothing.
I have observed strange variations in you.

Frank. In me?

Sus. In you, sir.
Awake, you seem to dream, and in your sleep
You utter sudden and distracted accents,
Like one at enmity with peace.   Dear loving husband,
If I
May dare to challenge any interest in you,
Give me the reason fully; you may trust
My breast as safely as your own.

Frank.   With what?
You half amaze me; prithee—

Sus.   Come, you shall not,
Indeed you shall not, shut me from partaking
The least dislike that grieves you; I'm all yours.

Frank. And I all thine.

Sus.   You are not, if you keep
The least grief from me: but I find the cause;
It grew from me.

Frank.   From you?

Sus.   From some distaste
In me or my behaviour: you're not kind
In the concealment. 'Las, sir, I am young,
Silly and plain; more, strange to those contents
A wife should offer: say but in what I fail,
I'll study satisfaction.

Frank.   Come; in nothing.

Sus. I know I do; knew I as well in what,
You should not long be sullen.   Prithee, love,
If I have been immodest or too bold,
Speak't in a frown; if peevishly too nice,

Show't in a smile : thy liking is the glass
By which I'll habit my behaviour.

Frank. Wherefore dost weep now ?

Sus.   You, sweet, have the power
To make me passionate as an April-day ;
Now smile, then weep ; now pale, then crimson red :
You are the powerful moon of my blood's sea,
To make it ebb or flow into my face,
As your looks change.

Frank.   Change thy conceit, I prithee ;
Thou art all perfection : Diana herself
Swells in thy thoughts and moderates thy beauty.
Within thy left eye amorous Cupid sits,
Feathering love-shafts, whose golden heads he dipped
In [1] thy chaste breast ; in the other lies
Blushing Adonis scarfed in modesties ;
And still as wanton Cupid blows love-fires,
Adonis quenches out unchaste desires ;
And from these two I briefly do imply
A perfect emblem of thy modesty.
Then, prithee, dear, maintain no more dispute,
For when thou speak'st, it's fit all tongues be mute.

Sus. Come, come, these golden strings of flattery
Shall not tie up my speech, sir ; I must know
The ground of your disturbance.

Frank.   Then look here ;
For here, here is the fen in which this hydra
Of discontent grows rank.

Sus.   Heaven shield it ! where?

Frank. In mine own bosom, here the cause has root ;
The poisoned leeches twist about my heart,
And will, I hope, confound me.

Sus.   You speak riddles.

Frank. Take't plainly, then : 'twas told me by a woman

---

[1] There is a break here in the quarto. It is suggested that the
printer was unable to decipher the first word of the line in the
manuscript.

Known and approved in palmistry,
I should have two wives.

    Sus.   Two wives? sir, I take it
Exceeding likely ; but let not conceit hurt you :
You're afraid to bury me ?

    Frank.   No, no, my Winnifred.

    Sus. How say you? Winnifred ! you forget me.

    Frank. No, I forget myself !—Susan.

    Sus.   In what?

    Frank. Talking of wives, I pretend Winnifred,
A maid that at my mother's waited on me
Before thyself.

    Sus.   I hope, sir, she may live
To take my place : but why should all this move you ?

    Frank. The poor girl !—[*Aside.*] she has't before
        thee,
And that's the fiend torments me.

    Sus.   Yet why should this
Raise mutiny within you ? such presages
Prove often false : or say it should be true?

    Frank. That I should have another wife?

    Sus.   Yes, many ;
If they be good, the better.

    Frank.   Never any
Equal to thee in goodness.

    Sus. Sir, I could wish I were much better for you ;
Yet if I knew your fate
Ordained you for another, I could wish—
So well I love you and your hopeful pleasure—
Me in my grave, and my poor virtues added
To my successor.

    Frank.   Prithee, prithee, talk not
Of deaths or graves ; thou art so rare a goodness
As Death would rather put itself to death
Than murder thee : but we, as all things else,
Are mutable and changing.

    Sus.   Yet you still move

In your first sphere of discontent. Sweet, chase
Those clouds of sorrow, and shine clearly on me.

    Frank. At my return I will.

    Sus.   Return ! ah me !
Will you, then, leave me ?

    Frank.   For a time I must :
But how ? As birds their young, or loving bees
Their hives, to fetch home richer dainties.

    Sus.   Leave me !
Now has my fear met its effect. You shall not ;
Cost it my life, you shall not.

    Frank.   Why ? your reason ?

    Sus. Like to the lapwing have you all this while
With your false love deluded me, pretending
Counterfeit senses for your discontent ;
And now at last it is by chance stole from you.

    Frank. What ? what by chance ?

    Sus.   Your pre-appointed meeting
Of single combat with young Warbeck.

    Frank.   Ha !

    Sus. Even so : dissemble not ; 'tis too apparent :
Then in his look I read it :—deny it not,
I see't apparent ; cost it my undoing,
And unto that my life, I will not leave you.

    Frank. Not until when ?

    Sus.   Till he and you be friends.
Was this your cunning ?—and then flam me off
With an old witch, two wives, and Winnifred !
You're not so kind, indeed, as I imagined.

    Frank. [*Aside.*] And you are more fond by far than I
         expected.—
It is a virtue that attends thy kind—
But of our business within :—and by this kiss,
I'll anger thee no more ; 'troth, chuck, I will not.

    Sus. You shall have no just cause.

    Frank.   Dear Sue, I shall not.
                             [*Exeunt.*

ACT THE THIRD.

SCENE I.—*The Village Green.*

Enter CUDDY BANKS *with the* Morris-dancers.

IRST CLOWN. Nay, Cuddy, prithee do not leave us now; if we part all this night, we shall not meet before day.

2nd. Cl. I prithee, Banks, let's keep together now.

Cud. If you were wise, a word would serve; but as you are, I must be forced to tell you again, I have a little private business, an hour's work; it may prove but an half hour's, as luck may serve; and then I take horse, and along with you. Have we e'er a witch in the morris?

1st Cl. No, no; no woman's part but Maid Marian and the Hobby-horse.

Cud. I'll have a witch; I love a witch.

1st Cl. 'Faith, witches themselves are so common now-a-days, that the counterfeit will not be regarded. They say we have three or four in Edmonton besides Mother Sawyer.

2nd Cl. I would she would dance her part with us.

3rd Cl. So would not I; for if she comes, the devil and all comes along with her.

Cud. Well, I'll have a witch; I have loved a witch

ever since I played at cherry-pit.[1]   Leave me, and get my horse dressed ; give him oats : but water him not till I come.   Whither do we foot it first ?

2nd Cl. To Sir Arthur Clarington's first ; then whither thou wilt.

Cud. Well, I am content; but we must up to Carter's, the rich yeoman ; I must be seen on hobby-horse there.

1st Cl. O, I smell him now !— I'll lay my ears Banks is in love, and that's the reason he would walk melancholy by himself.

Cud. Ha ! who was that said I was in love ?

1st Cl. Not I.

2nd Cl. Nor I.

Cud. Go to, no more of that : when I understand what you speak, I know what you say ; believe that.

1st Cl. Well, 'twas I, I'll not deny it; I meant no hurt in't.   I have seen you walk up to Carter's of Chessum : Banks, were not you there last Shrovetide ?

Cud. Yes, I was ten days together there the last Shrovetide.

2nd Cl. How could that be, when there are but seven days in the week ?

Cud. Prithee peace ! I reckon *stila nova* as a traveller; thou understandest as a fresh-water farmer, that never sawest a week beyond sea.   Ask any soldier that ever received his pay but in the Low Countries, and he'll tell thee there are eight days in the week [2] there hard by. How dost thou think they rise in High Germany, Italy, and those remoter places?

3rd Cl. Ay, but simply there are but seven days in the week yet.

Cud. No, simply as thou understandest.   Prithee look

[1] A children's game, in which cherry-stones are pitched into a small hole.   The suggestion was sometimes a less innocent one, however.   Compare Herrick's quatrain on "Cherry-pit."

[2] Thus Butler :

> "The soldier does it every day,
> *Eight to the week*, for sixpence pay."—*Gifford.*

but in the lover's almanac : when he has been but three
days absent, " O," says he, " I have not seen my love
these seven years : " there's a long cut !   When he comes
to her again and embraces her, " O," says he, " now methinks I am in Heaven ; " and that's a pretty step !   He
that can get up to Heaven in ten days need not repent
his journey ; you may ride a hundred days in a caroche,[1]
and be further off than when you set forth.   But, I pray
you, good morris-mates, now leave me.   I will be with
you by midnight.

1st Cl. Well, since he will be alone, we'll back again
and trouble him no more.

All the Clowns. But remember, Banks.

Cud. The hobby-horse shall be remembered.   But
hark you ; get Poldavis, the barber's boy, for the witch,
because he can show his art better than another.

[*Exeunt all but* CUDDY.

Well, now to my walk.   I am near the place where I
should meet—I know not what : say I meet a thief ? I
must follow him, if to the gallows ; say I meet a horse,
or hare, or hound ? still I must follow : some slow-paced
beast, I hope ; yet love is full of lightness in the heaviest
lovers.   Ha ! my guide is come.

Enter the Dog.

A water-dog !   I am thy first man, sculler ; I go with
thee ; ply no other but myself.   Away with the boat !
land me but at Katherine's Dock, my sweet Katherine's
Dock, and I'll be a fare to thee.   That way ? nay, which
way thou wilt ; thou knowest the way better than I :—
fine gentle cur it is, and well brought up, I warrant him.
We go a-ducking, spaniel ; thou shalt fetch me the ducks,
pretty kind rascal.

Enter a Spirit *vizarded.   He throws off his mask, &c.,
and appears in the shape of* KATHERINE.

Spir. Thus throw I off mine own essential horror,

---

[1] Coach, Fr. *Carrosse.*

And take the shape of a sweet lovely maid
Whom this fool dotes on : we can meet his folly,
But from his virtues must be runaways.
We'll sport with him ; but when we reckoning call,
We know where to receive ; the witch pays for all.

> [*The* Dog *barks.*

Cud. Ay? is that the watchword? She's come. [*Sees the* Spirit.] Well, if ever we be married, it shall be at Barking Church,[1] in memory of thee : now come behind, kind cur.

> And have I met thee, sweet Kate?
> I will teach thee to walk so late.

O, see, we meet in metre. [*The* Spirit *retires as he advances.*] What! dost thou trip from me? O, that I were upon my hobby-horse, I would mount after thee so nimble! "Stay, nymph, stay, nymph," singed Apollo.

> Tarry and kiss me, sweet nymph, stay ;
> Tarry and kiss me, sweet :
> We will to Chessum Street,
> And then to the house stands in the highway.

Nay, by your leave, I must embrace you.

> [*Exit, following the* Spirit.

[*Within.*] O, help, help! I am drowned, I am drowned!

Re-enter CUDDY *wet.*

Dog. Ha, ha, ha, ha!

Cud. This was an ill night to go a-wooing in ; I find it now in Pond's almanac : thinking to land at Katherine's Dock, I was almost at Gravesend. I'll never go to a wench in the dog-days again ; yet 'tis cool enough.—Had you never a paw in this dog-trick? a mange take that black hide of yours! I'll throw you in at Limehouse in some tanner's pit or other.

Dog. Ha, ha, ha, ha!

---

[1] Barking Church stood at the bottom of Seething Lane. It was destroyed in the great fire.—*Gifford.*

Cud. How now! who's that laughs at me? Hist to him! [*The* Dog *barks.*]—Peace, peace! thou didst but thy kind neither; 'twas my own fault.

Dog. Take heed how thou trustest the devil another time.

Cud. How now! who's that speaks? I hope you have not your reading tongue about you?

Dog. Yes, I can speak.

Cud. The devil you can! you have read Æsop's fables, then; I have played one of your parts then,—the dog that catched at the shadow in the water. Pray you, let me catechise you a little; what might one call your name, dog?

Dog. My dame calls me Tom.

Cud. 'Tis well, and she may call me Ass; so there's an whole one betwixt us, Tom-Ass: she said I should follow you, indeed. Well, Tom, give me thy fist, we are friends; you shall be mine ingle :[1] I love you; but I pray you let's have no more of these ducking devices.

Dog. Not, if you love me. Dogs love where they are beloved; cherish me, and I'll do anything for thee.

Cud. Well, you shall have jowls and livers; I have butchers to my friends that shall bestow 'em : and I will keep crusts and bones for you, if you'll be a kind dog, Tom.

Dog. Any thing; I'll help thee to thy love.

Cud. Wilt thou? that promise shall cost me a brown loaf, though I steal it out of my father's cupboard : you'll eat stolen goods, Tom, will you not?

Dog. O, best of all; the sweetest bits those.

Cud. You shall not starve, Ningle[2] Tom, believe that : if you love fish, I'll help you to maids and soles; I'm acquainted with a fishmonger.

Dog. Maids and soles? O, sweet bits! banqueting stuff those.

----

[1] Crony, friend.
[2] Abbreviation for " Mine ingle," as above.

Cud. One thing I would request you, ningle, as you have played the knavish cur with me a little, that you would mingle amongst our morris-dancers in the morning. You can dance?

Dog. Yes, yes, any thing; I'll be there, but unseen to any but thyself. Get thee gone before; fear not my presence. I have work to-night; I serve more masters, more dames than one.

Cud. He can serve Mammon and the devil too.

Dog. It shall concern thee and thy love's purchase.
There is a gallant rival loves the maid,
And likely is to have her. Mark what a mischief,
Before the morris ends, shall light on him!

Cud. O, sweet ningle, thy neuf[1] once again; friends must part for a time. Farewell, with this remembrance; shalt have bread too when we meet again. If ever there were an honest devil, 'twill be the Devil of Edmonton,[2] I see. Farewell, Tom; I prithee dog me as soon as thou canst.   [*Exit.*

Dog. I'll not miss thee, and be merry with thee.
Those that are joys denied must take delight
In sins and mischiefs; 'tis the devil's right.   [*Exit.*

SCENE II.—*The neighbourhood of Edmonton.*

Enter FRANK THORNEY *and* WINNIFRED *in boy's clothes.*

Frank. Prithee no more! those tears give nourishment
To weeds and briers in me, which shortly will
O'ergrow and top my head; my shame will sit
And cover all that can be seen of me.

Win. I have not shown this cheek in company;

---

[1] Or "neif," *i.e.* fist.

[2] The allusion is to Master Peter Fabel, who, as the prologue to the old comedy says, "was called, for his sleights and his magic, "The merry Devil of Edmonton."—*Gifford.*

Pardon me now : thus singled with yourself,
It calls a thousand sorrows round about,
Some going before, and some on either side,
But infinite behind ; all chained together :
Your second adulterous marriage leads ;
That is the sad eclipse, th' effects must follow,
As plagues of shame, spite, scorn, and obloquy.

   Frank. Why, hast thou not left one hour's patience
To add to all the rest ? one hour bears us
Beyond the reach of all these enemies :
Are we not now set forward in the flight,
Provided with the dowry of my sin[1]
To keep us in some other nation ?
While we together are, we are at home
In any place.

   Win.   'Tis foul ill-gotten coin,
Far worse than usury or extortion.

   Frank.   Let
My father, then, make the restitution,
Who forced me to take the bribe : it is his gift
And patrimony to me ; so I receive it.
He would not bless, nor look a father on me,
Until I satisfied his angry will :
When I was sold, I sold myself again—
Some knaves have done't in lands, and I in body—
For money, and I have the hire.   But, sweet, no more,
'Tis hazard of discovery, our discourse ;
And then prevention takes off all our hopes :
For only but to take her leave of me
My wife is coming.

   Win.   Who coming ? your wife !

   Frank. No, no ; thou art here : the woman—I knew
Not how to call her now ; but after this day
She shall be quite forgot and have no name
In my remembrance.   See, see ! she's come.

---

   [1] Frank alludes to the marriage portion which he had just received
with Susan.—*Gifford.*

Enter SUSAN.

Go lead
The horses to th' hill's top ; there I'll meet thee.

Sus. Nay, with your favour let him stay a little ;
I would part with him too, because he is
Your sole companion ; and I'll begin with him,
Reserving you the last.

Frank.   Ay, with all my heart.

Sus. You may hear, if't please you, sir.

Frank.   No, 'tis not fit :
Some rudiments, I conceive, they must be,
To overlook my slippery footings : and so—

Sus. No, indeed, sir.

Frank.   Tush, I know it must be so,
And it is necessary : on ! but be brief.   [*Walks forward.*

Win. What charge soe'er you lay upon me, mistress,
I shall support it faithfully—being honest—
To my best strength.

Sus.   Believe't shall be no other.
I know you were commended to my husband
By a noble knight.

Win.   O, gods ! O, mine eyes !

Sus. How now ! what ail'st thou, lad ?

Win. Something hit mine eye,—it makes it water
     still,—

Even as you said " commended to my husband."—
Some dor [2] I think it was.—I was, forsooth,
Commended to him by Sir Arthur Clarington.

Sus. Whose servant once my Thorney was himself.
That title, methinks, should make you almost fellows ;
Or at the least much more than a servant ;
And I am sure he will respect you so.
Your love to him, then, needs no spur from me,
And what for my sake you will ever do,
'Tis fit it should be bought with something more
Than fair entreats ; look ! here's a jewel for thee,

[1] Cockchafer, beetle.

A pretty wanton label for thine ear ;
And I would have it hang there, still to whisper
These words to thee, "Thou hast my jewel with
   thee."
It is but earnest of a larger bounty,
When thou return'st with praises of thy service,
Which I am confident thou wilt deserve.
Why, thou art many now besides thyself :
Thou mayst be servant, friend, and wife to him ;
A good wife is them all. A friend can play
The wife and servant's part, and shift enough ;
No less the servant can the friend and wife :
'Tis all but sweet society, good counsel,
Interchanged loves, yes, and counsel-keeping.

 Frank. Not done yet?

 Sus. Even now, sir.

 Win. Mistress, believe my vow ; your severe eye,
Were't present to command, your bounteous hand,
Were it then by to buy or bribe my service,
Shall not make me more dear or near unto him
Than I shall voluntary. I'll be all your charge,
Servant, friend, wife to him.

 Sus.   Wilt thou?
Now blessings go with thee for't ! courtesies
Shall meet thee coming home.

 Win.   Pray you say plainly,
Mistress, are you jealous of him ? if you be,
I'll look to him that way too.

 Sus.   Say'st thou so ?
I would thou hadst a woman's bosom now ;
We have weak thoughts within us. Alas,
There's nothing so strong in us as suspicion ;
But I dare not, nay, I will not think
So hardly of my Thorney.

 Win.   Believe it, mistress,
I'll be no pander to him ; and if I find
Any loose lubric scapes in him, I'll watch him,

And at my return protest I'll show you all :
He shall hardly offend without my knowledge.

Sus. Thine own diligence is that I press,
And not the curious eye over his faults.
Farewell : if I should never see thee more,
Take it for ever.

    Frank. Prithee take that along with thee, [*Handing
        his sword to* WINNIFRED.] and haste thee
To the hill's top ; I'll be there instantly.

    Sus. No haste, I prithee ; slowly as thou canst—
                    [*Exit* WINNIFRED.
Pray let him obey me now ; 'tis happily
His last service to me : my power is e'en
A-going out of sight.

    Frank.   Why would you delay ?
We have no other business now but to part.

    Sus. And will not that, sweetheart, ask a long time ?
Methinks it is the hardest piece of work
That e'er I took in hand.

    Frank.   Fie, fie ! why, look,
I'll make it plain and easy to you—farewell !
                    [*Kisses her.*

    Sus. Ah, 'las, I'm not half perfect in it yet ;
I must have it read o'er an hundred times :
Pray you take some pains ; I confess my dulness.

    Frank. [*Aside.*] What a thorn this rose grows on !
           Parting were sweet ;
But what a trouble 'twill be to obtain it !—
Come, again and again, farewell !—[*Kisses her.*] Yet
    wilt return ?
All questions of my journey, my stay, employment,
And revisitation, fully I have answered all ;
There's nothing now behind but—nothing.

    Sus.   And
That *nothing* is more hard than anything,
Than all the everythings. This request—

    Frank.   What is't ?

Dekker.   F F

Sus. That I may bring you through one pasture more
Up to yon knot of trees ; amongst those shadows
I'll vanish from you, they shall teach me how.

Frank. Why, 'tis granted ; come, walk, then.

Sus.   Nay, not too fast :
They say slow things have best perfection ;
The gentle shower wets to fertility,
The churlish storm may mischief with his bounty ;
The baser beasts take strength even from the womb,
But the lord lion's whelp is feeble long.   [*Exeunt.*

SCENE III.—*A Field with a clump of trees.*

Enter the Dog.

Dog. Now for an early mischief and a sudden !
The mind's about it now ; one touch from me
Soon sets the body forward.

Enter FRANK *and* SUSAN.

Frank.   Your request
Is out ; yet will you leave me ?

Sus.   What ? so churlishly ?
You'll make me stay for ever,
Rather than part with such a sound from you.

Frank. Why, you almost anger me.   Pray you be
    gone.
You have no company, and 'tis very early ;
Some hurt may betide you homewards.

Sus.   Tush ! I fear none ;
To leave you is the greatest hurt I can suffer :
Besides, I expect your father and mine own
To meet me back, or overtake me with you ;
They began to stir when I came after you
I know they'll not be long.

Frank. So! I shall have more trouble,—[*The* Dog
rubs against him]—thank you for that : [1]

[*Aside.*] Then I'll ease all at once.   It is done now ;
What I ne'er thought on.—You shall not go back.

Sus. Why, shall I go along with thee ? sweet music !

Frank. No, to a better place.

Sus.   Any place I ;
I'm there at home where thou pleasest to have me.

Frank. At home? I'll leave you in your last lodging ;
I must kill you.

Sus.   O, fine ! you'd fright me from you.

Frank. You see I had no purpose ; I'm unarmed ;
'Tis this minute's decree, and it must be :
Look, this will serve your turn.   [*Draws a knife.*

Sus.   I'll not turn from it,
If you be earnest, sir ; yet you may tell me
Wherefore you'll kill me.

Frank.   Because you are a whore.

Sus. There's one deep wound already ; a whore !
'Twas ever further from me than the thought
Of this black hour ; a whore ?

Frank.   Yes, I'll prove it,
And you shall confess it.   You are my whore.
No wife of mine ; the word admits no second.
I was before wedded to another ; have her still.
I do not lay the sin unto your charge,
'Tis all mine own : your marriage was my theft,
For I espoused your dowry, and I have it.
I did not purpose to have added murder ;
The devil did not prompt me till this minute :
You might have safe returned ; now you cannot.
You have dogged your own death.   [*Stabs her.*

Sus.   And I deserve it ;
I'm glad my fate was so intelligent :

---

[1] The dog is of course supposed invisible.   Frank thanks Susan
for telling him of the threatened arrival of Carter and Old Thorney
which would lead to discovery.

'Twas some good spirit's motion. Die ?   O, 'twas time !
How many years might I have slept in sin,
The sin of my most hatred, too, adultery !

   Frank. Nay, sure, 'twas likely that the most was
      past ;
For I meant never to return to you
After this parting.

   Sus.   Why, then, I thank you more ;
You have done lovingly, leaving yourself,
That you would thus bestow me on another.
Thou art my husband, Death, and I embrace thee
With all the love I have.   Forget the stain
Of my unwitting sin ; and then I come
A crystal virgin to thee : my soul's purity
Shall with bold wings ascend the doors of Mercy ;
For Innocence is ever her companion.

   Frank. Not yet mortal ?   I would not linger you,
Or leave you a tongue to blab.   [*Stabs her again.*

   Sus. Now Heaven reward you ne'er the worse for me !
I did not think that Death had been so sweet,
Nor I so apt to love him.   I could ne'er die better,
Had I stayed forty years for preparation ;
For I'm in charity with all the world.
Let me for once be thine example, Heaven ;
Do to this man as I him free forgive,
And may he better die and better live.   [*Dies.*

   Frank. 'Tis done ; and I am in ! Once past our
     height,
We scorn the deep'st abyss. This follows now,
To heal her wounds by dressing of the weapon.[1]
Arms, thighs, hands, any place ; we must not fail
                 [*Wounds himself.*
Light scratches, giving such deep ones : the best I can
To bind myself to this tree.   Now's the storm,

---

[1] An allusion to an old superstition in which the idea was that
wounds were healed by the turning of the assailant's weapon against
himself so as to cover it with his blood.

Which if blown o'er, many fair days may follow.
> [*Binds himself to a tree ; the* Dog *ties him
> behind and exit.*

So, so, I'm fast ; I did not think I could
Have done so well behind me.   How prosperous
And effectual mischief sometimes is !—[*Aloud*] Help !
Murder, murder, murder !   [help !

Enter CARTER *and* OLD THORNEY.

Car. Ha ! whom tolls the bell for ?
Frank.   O, O !
O. Thor.   Ah me !
The cause appears too soon ; my child, my son !
Car. Susan, girl, child ! not speak to thy father ? ha !
Frank. O, lend me some assistance to o'ertake
This hapless woman.
O. Thor.   Let's o'ertake the murderers.
Speak whilst thou canst, anon may be too late ;
I fear thou hast death's mark upon thee too.
Frank. I know them both ; yet such an oath is passed
As pulls damnation up if it be broke.
I dare not name 'em : think what forced men do.
O. Thor. Keep oath with murderers ! that were a
 conscience
To hold the devil in.
Frank.   Nay, sir, I can describe 'em,
Shall show them as familiar as their names :
The taller of the two at this time wears
His satin doublet white, but crimson-lined,
Hose of black satin, cloak of scarlet—
O. Thor.   Warbeck,
Warbeck, Warbeck !—do you list to this, sir ?
Car. Yes, yes, I listen you ; here's nothing to be heard.
Frank. Th' other's cloak branched[1] velvet, black,
 velvet-lined his suit.

---

[1] *i.e.* Adorned with tufts, or tassels, dependent from the shoulders.
— *Gifford.*

O. Thor. I have 'em already; Somerton, Somerton!
Binal revenge all this. Come, sir, the first work
Is to pursue the murderers, when we have
Removed these mangled bodies hence.

Car. Sir, take that carcass there, and give me this.
I will not own her now ; she's none of mine.
Bob me off with a dumb-show ! no, I'll have life.
This is my son too, and while there's life in him,
'Tis half mine ; take you half that silence for't.—
When I speak I look to be spoken to :
Forgetful slut !

O. Thor. Alas, what grief may do now !
Look, sir, I'll take this load of sorrow with me.

Car. Ay, do, and I'll have this. [*Exit* OLD THORNEY
with SUSAN *in his arms.*] How do you, sir ?

Frank. O, very ill, sir.

Car. Yes,
I think so; but 'tis well you can speak yet :
There's no music but in sound ; sound it must be.
I have not wept these twenty years before,
And that I guess was ere that girl was born ;
Yet now methinks, if I but knew the way,
My heart's so full, I could weep night and day.

[*Exit with* FRANK.

SCENE IV.—*Before* SIR ARTHUR CLARINGTON'S *House*

Enter SIR ARTHUR CLARINGTON, WARBECK, *and*
SOMERTON.

Sir Arth. Come, gentlemen, we must all help to grace
The nimble-footed youth of Edmonton,
That are so kind to call us up to-day
With an high morris.

War. I could wish it for the best, it were the worst

now.   Absurdity's in my opinion ever the best dancer in
a morris.

Som. I could rather sleep than see 'em.

Sir Arth. Not well, sir?

Som. 'Faith, not ever thus leaden: yet I know no
cause for't.

War. Now am I beyond mine own condition highly
disposed to mirth.

Sir Arth. Well, you may have yet a morris to help
      both ;
To strike you in a dump, and make him merry.

Enter SAWGUT *with the* Morris-dancers, *&c.*

Saw. Come, will you set yourselves in morris-ray?[1] the
forebell, second-bell, tenor, and great-bell; Maid Marian[2]
for the same bell.   But where's the weathercock now?
the Hobby-horse?

1st Cl. Is not Banks come yet?   What a spite 'tis!

Sir Arth. When set you forward, gentlemen?

1st Cl. We stay but for the Hobby-horse, sir; all our
footmen are ready.

Som. 'Tis marvel your horse should be behind your
foot.

2nd Cl. Yes, sir, he goes further about; we can come
in at the wicket, but the broad gate must be opened for
him.

Enter CUDDY BANKS *with the Hobby-horse, followed
by the* Dog.

Sir Arth. O, we stayed for you, sir.

Cud. Only my horse wanted a shoe, sir; but we shall
make you amends ere we part.

Sir Arth. Ay? well said; make 'em drink ere they
      begin.

[1] Array.
[2] Maid Marian was always a prominent figure in the morris-dance.
Robin Hood, Friar Tuck, and other characters were also added
according to the humour of the dancers.

Enter Servants *with beer.*

Cud. A bowl, I prithee, and a little for my horse;
he'll mount the better. Nay, give me: I must drink to
him, he'll not pledge else. [*Drinks.*] Here, Hobby
[*Holds the bowl to the Hobby-horse.*]—I pray you: no?
not drink! You see, gentlemen, we can but bring our
horse to the water; he may choose whether he'll drink or
no.   [*Drinks again.*

Som. A good moral made plain by history.

1st Cl. Strike up, Father Sawgut, strike up.

Saw. E'en when you will, children. [CUDDY *mounts
the Hobby.*]—Now in the name of—the best foot forward!
[*Endeavours to play, but the fiddle gives no sound.*]
—How now! not a word in thy guts? I think, children,
my instrument has caught cold on the sudden.

Cud. [*Aside.*] My ningle's knavery; black Tom's doing.

All the Clowns. Why, what mean you, Father Sawgut?

Cud. Why, what would you have him do? you hear
his fiddle is speechless.

Saw. I'll lay mine ear to my instrument that my poor
fiddle is bewitched. I played "The Flowers in May"
e'en now, as sweet as a violet; now 'twill not go against
the hair: you see I can make no more music than a
beetle of a cow-turd.

Cud. Let me see, Father Sawgut [*Takes the fiddle*];
say once you had a brave hobby-horse that you were be-
holding to. I'll play and dance too.—Ningle, away
with it.   [*Gives it to the* Dog, *who plays the morris.*

All the Clowns. Ay, marry, sir!   [*They dance.*

Enter a Constable *and* Officers.

Con. Away with jollity! 'tis too sad an hour.—
Sir Arthur Clarington, your own assistance,
In the king's name, I charge, for apprehension
Of these two murderers, Warbeck and Somerton.

Sir Arth. Ha! flat murderers?

Som. Ha, ha, ha ! this has awakened my melancholy.

War. And struck my mirth down flat.—Murderers ?

Con. The accusation's flat against you, gentlemen.—
Sir, you may be satisfied with this. [*Shows his warrant.*]—
I hope you'll quietly obey my power ;
'Twill make your cause the fairer.

Som. and War. O, with all our hearts, sir.

Cud. There's my rival taken up for hangman's meat ;
Tom told me he was about a piece of villany.—Mates
and morris-men, you see here's no longer piping, no
longer dancing ; this news of murder has slain the morris.
You that go the footway, fare ye well ; I am for a gallop.
—Come, ningle.

[*Canters off with the Hobby-horse and the* Dog.

Saw. [*Strikes his fiddle, which sounds as before.*] Ay?
nay, an my fiddle be come to himself again, I care not.
I think the devil has been abroad amongst us to-day ;
I'll keep thee out of thy fit now, if I can.

[*Exit with the* Morris-dancers.

Sir Arth. These things are full of horror, full of pity.
But if this time be constant to the proof,
The guilt of both these gentlemen I dare take
On mine own danger ; yet, howsoever, sir,
Your power must be obeyed.

War.   O, most willingly, sir.
'Tis a most sweet affliction ; I could not meet
A joy in the best shape with better will :
Come, fear not, sir ; nor judge nor evidence
Can bind him o'er who's freed by conscience.

Som. Mine stands so upright to the middle zone
It takes no shadow to't, it goes alone.   [*Exeunt.*

ACT THE FOURTH.

SCENE I.—*Edmonton. The Street.*

Enter OLD BANKS *and several* Countrymen.

LD BANKS. My horse this morning runs most piteously of the glanders, whose nose yesternight was as clean as any man's here now coming from the barber's; and this, I'll take my death upon't, is long of this jadish witch Mother Sawyer.

1st Coun. I took my wife and a serving-man in our town of Edmonton thrashing in my barn together such corn as country wenches carry to market; and examining my polecat why she did so, she swore in her conscience she was bewitched: and what witch have we about us but Mother Sawyer?

2nd Coun. Rid the town of her, else all our wives will do nothing else but dance about other country maypoles.

3rd Coun. Our cattle fall, our wives fall, our daughters fall, and maid-servants fall; and we ourselves shall not be able to stand, if this beast be suffered to graze amongst us.

Enter HAMLUC *with thatch and a lighted link.*

Ham. Burn the witch, the witch, the witch, the witch!

Countrymen. What hast got there?

Ham. A handful of thatch plucked off a hovel of

hers; and they say, when 'tis burning, if she be a witch, she'll come running in.

O. Banks. Fire it, fire it ! I'll stand between thee and home for any danger. [HAM. *sets fire to the thatch.*

Enter MOTHER SAWYER *running.*

M. Saw. Diseases, plagues, the curse of an old woman
Follow and fall upon you !

Countrymen. Are you come, you old trot ?

O. Banks. You hot whore, must we fetch you with fire in your tail ?

1st Coun. This thatch is as good as a jury to prove she is a witch.

Countrymen. Out, witch ! beat her, kick her, set fire on her !

M. Saw. Shall I be murdered by a bed of serpents ? Help, help !

Enter SIR ARTHUR CLARINGTON *and a* Justice.

Countrymen. Hang her, beat her, kill her !

Just. How now ! forbear this violence.

M. Saw. A crew of villains, a knot of bloody hangmen,
Set to torment me, I know not why.

Just. Alas, neighbour Banks, are you a ringleader in mischief? fie ! to abuse an aged woman.

O. Banks. Woman ? a she hell-cat, a witch ! To prove her one, we no sooner set fire on the thatch of her house, but in she came running as if the devil had sent her in a barrel of gunpowder ; which trick as surely proves her a witch as the pox in a snuffling nose is a sign a man is a whore-master.

Just. Come, come : firing her thatch ? ridiculous !
Take heed, sirs, what you do ; unless your proofs
Come better armed, instead of turning her
Into a witch, you'll prove yourselves stark fools.

Countrymen. Fools ?

Just. Arrant fools.

O. Banks. Pray, Master Justice What-do-you-call-'em, hear me but in one thing : this grumbling devil owes me I know no good-will ever since I fell out with her.

M. Saw. And break'dst my back with beating me.

O. Banks. I'll break it worse.

M. Saw. Wilt thou?

Just. You must not threaten her ; 'tis against law : Go on.

O. Banks. So, sir, ever since, having a dun cow tied up in my back-side,[1] let me go thither, or but cast mine eye at her, and if I should be hanged I cannot choose, though it be ten times in an hour, but run to the cow, and taking up her tail, kiss—saving your worship's reverence —my cow behind, that the whole town of Edmonton has been ready to bepiss themselves with laughing me to scorn.

Just. And this is long of her?

O. Banks. Who the devil else ? for is any man such an ass to be such a baby, if he were not bewitched ?

Sir Arth. Nay, if she be a witch, and the harms she does end in such sports, she may scape burning.

Just. Go, go : pray, vex her not ; she is a subject, And you must not be judges of the law To strike her as you please.

Countrymen. No, no, we'll find cudgel enough to strike her.

O. Banks. Ay ; no lips to kiss but my cow's—!

M. Saw. Rots and foul maladies eat up thee and thine !

[*Exeunt* OLD BANKS *and* Countrymen.

Just. Here's none now, Mother Sawyer, but this gentleman,
Myself, and you : let us to some mild questions ;
Have you mild answers ; tell us honestly
And with a free confession—we'll do our best
To wean you from it—are you a witch, or no ?

M. Saw. I am none.

---

[1] An outbuilding or yard in the rear of a house.

Just.   Be not so furious.

M. Saw.   I am none.
None but base curs so bark at me ; I'm none :
Or would I were ! if every poor old woman
Be trod on thus by slaves, reviled, kicked, beaten,
As I am daily, she to be revenged
Had need turn witch.

Sir Arth.   And you to be revenged
Have sold your soul to th' devil.

M. Saw.   Keep thine own from him.

Just. You are too saucy and too bitter.

M. Saw.   Saucy ?
By what commission can he send my soul
On the devil's errand more than I can his ?
Is he a landlord of my soul, to thrust it,
When he list, out of door ?

Just.   Know whom you speak to.

M. Saw. A man ; perhaps no man. Men in gay clothes,
Whose backs are laden with titles and with honours,
Are within far more crookèd than I am,
And, if I be a witch, more witch-like.

Sir Arth. You're a base hell-hound.—
And now, sir, let me tell you, far and near
She's bruited for a woman that maintains
A spirit that sucks her.

M. Saw.   I defy thee.

Sir Arth.   Go, go :
I can, if need be, bring an hundred voices,
E'en here in Edmonton, that shall loud proclaim
Thee for a secret and pernicious witch.

M. Saw. Ha, ha !

Just.   Do you laugh ? why laugh you ?

M. Saw.   At my name,
The brave name this knight gives me—witch.

Just. Is the name of witch so pleasing to thine ear ?

Sir Arth. Pray, sir, give way, and let her tongue
    gallop on.

M. Saw. A witch ! who is not?
Hold not that universal name in scorn, then.
What are your painted things in princes' courts,
Upon whose eyelids lust sits, blowing fires
To burn men's souls in sensual hot desires,
Upon whose naked paps a lecher's thought
Acts sin in fouler shapes than can be wrought?

    Just. But those work not as you do.

    M. Saw.   No, but far worse
These by enchantments can whole lordships change
To trunks of rich attire, turn ploughs and teams
To Flanders mares and coaches, and huge trains
Of servitors to a French butterfly.
Have you not city-witches who can turn
Their husbands' wares, whole standing shops of wares,
To sumptuous tables, gardens of stolen sin ;
In one year wasting what scarce twenty win?
Are not these witches?

    Just.   Yes, yes ; but the law
Casts not an eye on these.

    M. Saw.   Why, then, on me,
Or any lean old beldam?   Reverence once
Had wont to wait on age ; now an old woman,
Ill-favoured grown with years, if she be poor,
Must be called bawd or witch.   Such so abused
Are the coarse witches ; t'other are the fine,
Spun for the devil's own wearing.

    Sir Arth.   And so is thine.

    M. Saw. She on whose tongue a whirlwind sits to
       blow
A man out of himself, from his soft pillow
To lean his head on rocks and fighting waves,
Is not that scold a witch? The man of law
Whose honeyed hopes the credulous client draw—
As bees by tinkling basins—to swarm to him
From his own hive to work the wax in his ;
He is no witch, not he !

Sir Arth.   But these men-witches
Are not in trading with hell's merchandise,
Like such as you are, that for a word, a look,
Denial of a coal of fire, kill men,
Children, and cattle.

   M. Saw.   Tell them, sir, that do so :
Am I accused for such an one ?

   Sir Arth.   Yes ; 'twill be sworn.

   M. Saw. Dare any swear I ever tempted maiden
With golden hooks flung at her chastity
To come and lose her honour ; and being lost,
To pay not a denier [1] for't ?   Some slaves have done it.
Men-witches can, without the fangs of law
Drawing once one drop of blood, put counterfeit pieces
Away for true gold.

   Sir Arth.   By one thing she speaks
I know now she's a witch, and dare no longer
Hold conference with the fury.

   Just.   Let's, then, away.—
Old woman, mend thy life ; get home and pray.

                   [Exeunt SIR ARTHUR *and]* Justice.

   M. Saw. For his confusion.

               Enter the Dog.

                 My dear Tom-boy, welcome !
I'm torn in pieces by a pack of curs
Clapt all upon me, and for want of thee :
Comfort me ; thou shalt have the teat anon.

   Dog. Bow, wow ! I'll have it now.

   M. Saw.   I am dried up
With cursing and with madness, and have yet
No blood to moisten these sweet lips of thine.
Stand on thy hind-legs up—kiss me, my Tommy,
And rub away some wrinkles on my brow
By making my old ribs to shrug for joy

          [1] Penny.   Lat. *Denarius.*

Of thy fine tricks.   What hast thou done? let's tickle.
Hast thou struck the horse lame as I bid thee?

Dog.   Yes;
And nipped the sucking child.

M. Saw.   Ho, ho, my dainty,
My little pearl! no lady loves her hound,
Monkey, or paroquet, as I do thee.

Dog. The maid has been churning butter nine hours;
but it shall not come.

M. Saw. Let 'em eat cheese and choke.

Dog.   I had rare sport
Among the clowns i' th' morris.

M. Saw.   I could dance
Out of my skin to hear thee.   But, my curl-pate,
That jade, that foul-tongued whore, Nan Ratcliffe,
Who, for a little soap licked by my sow,
Struck and almost had lamed it;—did not I charge thee
To pinch that queen to th' heart?

Dog.   .   Bow, wow, wow! look here else.

Enter ANN RATCLIFFE *mad.*

Ann. See, see, see! the man i' th' moon has built a
new windmill; and what running there's from all quarters
of the city to learn the art of grinding!

M. Saw. Ho, ho, ho! I thank thee, my sweet mongrel.

Ann. Hoyda! a pox of the devil's false hopper! all
the golden meal runs into the rich knaves' purses, and
the poor have nothing but bran.   Hey derry down! are
not you Mother Sawyer?

M. Saw. No, I am a lawyer.

Ann. Art thou? I prithee let me scratch thy face;
for thy pen has flayed-off a great many men's skins.
You'll have brave doings in the vacation; for knaves and
fools are at variance in every village.   I'll sue Mother
Sawyer, and her own sow shall give in evidence against
her.

M. Saw. Touch her. [*To the* Dog, *who rubs against her.*

Ann. O, my ribs are made of a paned hose, and they break ![1] There's a Lancashire hornpipe in my throat; hark, how it tickles it, with doodle, doodle, doodle, doodle ! Welcome, sergeants ! welcome, devil !—hands, hands ! hold hands, and dance around, around, around.

[*Dancing.*

Re-enter OLD BANKS, *with* CUDDY, RATCLIFFE, *and* Countrymen.

Rat. She's here ; alas, my poor wife is here !

O. Banks. Catch her fast, and have her into some close chamber, do ; for she's, as many wives are, stark mad.

Cud. The witch ! Mother Sawyer, the witch, the devil !

Rat. O, my dear wife ! help, sirs !

[ANN *is carried off by* RATCLIFFE *and* Countrymen.

O. Banks. You see your work, Mother Bumby.[2]

M. Saw. My work? should she and all you here run mad, Is the work mine ?

Cud. No, on my conscience, she would not hurt a devil of two years old.

Re-enter RATCLIFFE *and* Countrymen.

How now ! what's become of her ?

Rat. Nothing; she's become nothing but the miserable trunk of a wretched woman. We were in her hands as reeds in a mighty tempest : spite of our strengths away she brake ; and nothing in her mouth being heard but " the devil, the witch, the witch, the devil ! " she beat out her own brains, and so died.

Cud. It's any man's case, be he never so wise, to die when his brains go a wool-gathering.

---

[1] Paned hose were made of stripes (panels) of different-coloured stuff stitched together, and therefore liable to break or be seam-rent. Thus counterpane.

[2] Farmer Banks is very familiar with the names of old plays (or rather of the supposed witches who gave names to the plays). *Mother Bombie* is the title of one of Lyly's comedies, of which she is the heroine ; as is *Gammer Gurton* of the farcical drama, *Gammer Gurton's Needle*, to which Old Banks presently refers.

O. Banks. Masters, be ruled by me; let's all to a justice.—Hag, thou hast done this, and thou shalt answer it.

M. Saw. Banks, I defy thee.

O. Banks. Get a warrant first to examine her, then ship her to Newgate; here's enough, if all her other villanies were pardoned, to burn her for a witch.—You have a spirit, they say, comes to you in the likeness of a dog; we shall see your cur at one time or other: if we do, unless it be the devil himself, he shall go howling to the gaol in one chain, and thou in another.

M. Saw. Be hanged thou in a third, and do thy worst!

Cud. How, father! you send the poor dumb thing howling to the gaol? he that makes him howl makes me roar.

O. Banks. Why, foolish boy, dost thou know him?

Cud. No matter if I do or not: he's bailable, I am sure, by law;—but if the dog's word will not be taken, mine shall.

O. Banks. Thou bail for a dog!

Cud. Yes, or a bitch either, being my friend. I'll lie by the heels myself before puppison shall; his dog-days are not come yet, I hope.

O. Banks. What manner of dog is it? didst ever see him?

Cud. See him? yes, and given him a bone to gnaw twenty times. The dog is no court-foisting hound that fills his belly full by base wagging his tail; neither is it a citizen's water-spaniel,[1] enticing his master to go a-ducking twice or thrice a week, whilst his wife makes ducks and drakes at home: this is no Paris-garden bandog[2] neither, that keeps a bow-wow-wowing to have butchers bring their curs thither; and when all comes to all, they

---

[1] A breed of dogs, in great request for hunting ducks in the ponds at Islington and other outlying regions of London at this period.

[2] A fierce kind of mastiff kept to bait bears. Paris-garden, where these brutal sports were regularly exhibited, was situated on the Bankside in Southwark, close to the Globe Theatre.—*Gifford.*

run away like sheep : neither is this the Black Dog of Newgate.[1]

O. Banks. No, Goodman Son-fool, but the dog of hell-gate.

Cud. I say, Goodman Father-fool, it's a lie.

All. He's bewitched.

Cud. A gross lie, as big as myself. The devil in St. Dunstan's will as soon drink with this poor cur as with any Temple-bar laundress that washes and wrings lawyers.

Dog. Bow, wow, wow, wow !

All. O, the dog's here, the dog's here.

O. Banks. It was the voice of a dog.

Cud. The voice of a dog? if that voice were a dog's, what voice had my mother ? so am I a dog : bow, wow, wow ! It was I that barked so, father, to make coxcombs of these clowns.

O. Banks. However, we'll be coxcombed no longer : away, therefore, to the justice for a warrant ; and then, Gammer Gurton, have at your needle of witchcraft !

M. Saw. And prick thine own eyes out. Go, peevish fools !

[*Exeunt* OLD BANKS, RATCLIFFE, *and* Countrymen.

Cud. Ningle, you had liked to have spoiled all with your bow-ings. I was glad to have put 'em off with one of my dog-tricks on a sudden ; I am bewitched, little Cost-me-nought, to love thee—a pox,—that morris makes me spit in thy mouth.—I dare not stay ; farewell, ningle ; you whoreson dog's nose !—Farewell, witch !   [*Exit.*

Dog. Bow, wow, wow, wow.

M. Saw. Mind him not, he is not worth thy worrying ; Run at a fairer game : that foul-mouthed knight,

---

[1] There is a tract, in prose and verse, attributed to Luke Hatton, entitled *The Black Dog of Newgate ;* and we learn from Henslowe's *Diary* that there was a play by Hathway, Day, Smith, and another poet, with the same title.—*Dyce.*

Scurvy Sir Arthur, fly at him, my Tommy,
And pluck out's throat.

    Dog. No, there's a dog already biting,—'s conscience.

    M. Saw. That's a sure bloodhound. Come, let's home
      and play;

Our black work ended, we'll make holiday.   [*Exeunt.*

SCENE II.—*A Bedroom in* CARTER'S *House. A bed thrust
    forth, with* FRANK *in a slumber.*

Enter KATHERINE.

    Kath. Brother, brother! so sound asleep? that's well.

    Frank. [*Waking.*] No, not I, sister; he that's wounded
      here
As I am—all my other hurts are bitings
Of a poor flea;—but he that here once bleeds
Is maimed incurably.

    Kath.   My good sweet brother,—
For now my sister must grow up in you,—
Though her loss strikes you through, and that I feel
The blow as deep, I pray thee be not cruel
To kill me too, by seeing you cast away
In your own helpless sorrow. Good love, sit up;
And if you can give physic to yourself,
I shall be well.

    Frank.   I'll do my best.

    Kath.   I thank you;
What do you look about for?

    Frank.   Nothing, nothing;
But I was thinking, sister,—

    Kath.   Dear heart, what?

    Frank. Who but a fool would thus be bound to a bed,
Having this room to walk in?

    Kath.   Why do you talk so?
Would you were fast asleep!

Frank.   No, no; I'm not idle.[1]
But here's my meaning; being robbed as I am,
Why should my soul, which married was to hers,
Live in divorce, and not fly after her?
Why should I not walk hand in hand with Death,
To find my love out?
   Kath.   That were well indeed,
Your time being come; when Death is sent to call
     you,
No doubt you shall meet her.
   Frank.   Why should not I
Go without calling?
   Kath.   Yes, brother, so you might,
Were there no place to go when you're gone
But only this.
   Frank.   'Troth, sister, thou say'st true;
For when a man has been an hundred years
Hard travelling o'er the tottering bridge of age,
He's not the thousand part upon his way:
All life is but a wandering to find home;
When we're gone, we're there.   Happy were man,
Could here his voyage end; he should not, then,
Answer how well or ill he steered his soul
By Heaven's or by Hell's compass; how he put in—
Losing blessed goodness' shore—at such a sin;
Nor how life's dear provision he has spent,
Nor how far he in's navigation went
Beyond commission: this were a fine reign,
To do ill and not hear of it again;
Yet then were man more wretched than a beast;
For, sister, our dead pay is sure the best.
   Kath. 'Tis so, the best or worst; and I wish Heaven
To pay—and so I know it will—that traitor,
That devil Somerton—who stood in mine eye
Once as an angel—home to his deservings:
What villain but himself, once loving me,

---

[1] *i.e.* Wandering.

With Warbeck's soul would pawn his own to hell
To be revenged on my poor sister !

 Frank.   Slaves !
A pair of merciless slaves ! speak no more of them.

 Kath. I think this talking hurts you.

 Frank. Does me no good, I'm sure ;
I pay for't everywhere.

 Kath.   I have done, then.
Eat, if you cannot sleep ; you have these two days
Not tasted any food.—Jane, is it ready ?

 Frank. What's ready ? what's ready ?

 Kath. I have made ready a roasted chicken for you :

Enter Maid *with chicken.*

Sweet, wilt thou eat ?

 Frank. A pretty stomach on a sudden ; yes.—
There's one in the house can play upon a lute ;
Good girl, let's hear him too.

 Kath.   You shall, dear brother. [*Exit* Maid.
Would I were a musician, you should hear
How I would feast your ear ! [*Lute plays within*]—stay
   mend your pillow,
And raise you higher.

 Frank.   I am up too high,
Am I not, sister now ?

 Kath.   No, no ; 'tis well.
Fall-to, fall-to.—A knife ! here's never a knife.
Brother, I'll look out yours.   [*Takes up his vest.*

Enter the Dog, *shrugging as it were for joy, and dances.*

 Frank.   Sister, O, sister,
I'm ill upon a sudden, and can eat nothing.

 Kath. In very deed you shall : the want of food
Makes you so faint. Ha ! [*Sees the bloody knife*]—here's
   none in your pocket ;
I'll go fetch a knife.   [*Exit hastily.*

 Frank.   Will you ?—'tis well, all's well.

FRANK *searches first one pocket, then the other, finds the*
   knife, and then lies down.—The Dog *runs off.—The*
   spirit of SUSAN *comes to the bed's side ;* FRANK *stares*
   at it, and then turns to the other side, but the spirit is
   there too.   Meanwhile enter WINNIFRED *as a page,*
   *and stands sadly at the bed's foot.—*FRANK *affrighted*
   sits up.   The spirit vanishes.

   Frank. What art thou ?
   Win.   A lost creature.
   Frank.   So am I too.—Win ?
Ah, my she-page !
   Win.   For your sake I put on
A shape that's false ; yet do I wear a heart
True to you as your own.
   Frank.   Would mine and thine
Were fellows in one house !—Kneel by me here.
On this side now ! how dar'st thou come to mock me
On both sides of my bed ?
   Win.   When ?
   Frank.   But just now :
Outface me, stare upon me with strange postures,
Turn my soul wild by a face in which were drawn
A thousand ghosts leapt newly from their graves
To pluck me into a winding-sheet !
   Win.   Believe it,
I came no nearer to you than yon place
At your bed's feet ; and of the house had leave,
Calling myself your horse-boy, in to come,
And visit my sick master.
   Frank.   Then 'twas my fancy ;
Some windmill in my brains for want of sleep.
   Win. Would I might never sleep, so you   could
         rest !
But you have plucked a thunder on your head,
Whose noise cannot cease suddenly : why should you
Dance at the wedding of a second wife,
When scarce the music which you heard at mine

Had ta'en a farewell of you?   O, this was ill!
And they who thus can give both hands away
In th' end shall want their best limbs.

Frank.   Winnifred,—
The chamber-door's fast?

Win.   Yes.

Frank.   Sit thee, then, down;
And when thou'st heard me speak, melt into tears:
Yet I, to save those eyes of thine from weeping,
Being to write a story of us two.
Instead of ink dipped my sad pen in blood.
When of thee I took leave, I went abroad
Only for pillage, as a freebooter,
What gold soe'er I got to make it thine.
To please a father I have Heaven displeased;
Striving to cast two wedding-rings in one,
Through my bad workmanship I now have none;
I have lost her and thee.

Win.   I know she's dead;
But you have me still.

Frank.   Nay, her this hand
Murdered; and so I lose thee too.

Win.   O me!

Frank. Be quiet; for thou my evidence art,
Jury, and judge: sit quiet, and I'll tell all.

While they are conversing in a low tone, enter at one door
    CARTER *and* KATHERINE, *at the other the* Dog,
    pawing softly at FRANK.

Kath. I have run madding up and down to find
        you,
Being laden with the heaviest news that ever
Poor daughter carried.

Car.   Why? is the boy dead?

Kath.   Dead, sir!
O, father, we are cozened: you are told
The murderer sings in prison, and he laughs here.

This villain killed my sister see else, see,

> [*Takes up his vest, and shows the knife to her father, who secures it.*

A bloody knife in's pocket !

   Car.   Bless me, patience !

   Frank. [*Seeing them.*] The knife, the knife, the knife !

   Kath. What knife ?   [*Exit the* Dog.

   Frank.   To cut my chicken up, my chicken ;
Be you my carver, father.

   Car.   That I will.

   Kath. How the devil steels our brows after doing ill !

   Frank. My stomach and my sight are taken from me ;
All is not well within me,

   Car. I believe thee, boy ; I that have seen so many
moons clap their horns on other men's foreheads to strike
them sick, yet mine to scape and be well; I that
never cast away a fee upon urinals, but am as sound as
an honest man's conscience when he's dying ; I should
cry out as thou dost, "All is not well within me," felt I
but the bag of thy imposthumes. Ah, poor villain ! ah,
my wounded rascal ! all my grief is, I have now small
hope of thee,

   Frank. Do the surgeons say my wounds are dangerous,
      then ?

   Car. Yes, yes, and there's no way with thee but one.

   Frank. Would he were here to open them !

   Car. I'll go to fetch him ; I'll make an holiday to see
thee as I wish.

   Frank. A wondrous kind old man !

   Win. [*Aside to* FRANK.]   Your sin's the blacker
So to abuse his goodness.—[*Aloud*] Master, how do
      you?

   Frank. Pretty well now, boy ; I have such odd qualms
Come cross my stomach.—I'll fall-to ; boy, cut me—

   Win. [*Aside.*] You have cut me, I'm sure ;—A leg or
      wing, sir ?

   Frank. No, no, no ; a wing—

ACT THE FIFTH.

SCENE I.—*The Witch's Cottage.*

Enter MOTHER SAWYER.

OTHER SAWYER. Still wronged by
    every slave, and not a dog
    Bark in his dame's defence? I am
      called witch,
    Yet am myself bewitched from doing
      harm.
    Have I given up myself to thy black
Thus to be scorned? Not see me in three days! [lust
I'm lost without my Tomalin; prithee come,
Revenge to me is sweeter far than life;
Thou art my raven, on whose coal-black wings
Revenge comes flying to me. O, my best love!
I am on fire, even in the midst of ice,
Raking my blood up, till my shrunk knees feel
Thy curled head leaning on them: come, then, my
      darling;
If in the air thou hover'st, fall upon me
In some dark cloud; and as I oft have seen
Dragons and serpents in the elements,
Appear thou now so to me. Art thou i' th' sea?
Muster-up all the monsters from the deep,
And be the ugliest of them: so that my bulch [1]

---

[1] Literally, a bull-calf, sometimes used, as here, as an expression
of kindness; but generally indicative of familiarity and contempt.—
Gifford.

Show but his swarth cheek to me, let earth cleave
And break from hell, I care not ! Could I run
Like a swift powder-mine beneath the world,
Up would I blow it all, to find out thee,
Though I lay ruined in it. Not yet come !
I must, then, fall to my old prayer :
Sanctibicetur nomen tuum.
Not yet come ! the worrying of wolves, biting of mad
dogs, the manges, and the—

Enter the Dog *which is now white.*

Dog. How now ! whom art thou cursing ?
M. Saw. Thee !
Ha ! no, it is my black cur I am cursing
For not attending on me.
Dog.   I am that cur,
M. Saw. Thou liest: hence ! come not nigh me.
Dog.   Baw, waw !
M. Saw. Why dost thou thus appear to me in white,
As if thou wert the ghost of my dear love ?
Dog. I am dogged, and list not to tell thee ; yet,—to
torment thee,—my whiteness puts thee in mind of thy
winding-sheet.
M. Saw. Am I near death ?
Dog. Yes, if the dog of hell be near thee ; when the
devil comes to thee as a lamb, have at thy throat !
M. Saw. Off, cur !
Dog. He has the back of a sheep, but the belly of an
otter ; devours by sea and land. " Why am I in white ?"
didst thou not pray to me ?
M. Saw. Yes, thou dissembling hell-hound !
Why now in white more than at other times ?
Dog. Be blasted with the news ! whiteness is day's
footboy, a forerunner to light, which shows thy old
rivelled face : villanies are stripped naked ; the witch
must be beaten out of her cockpit.

Dog. Right ; I served her to that purpose ; 'twas part
of my wages.

Cud. This was no honest servant's part, by your leave,
Tom.   This remember, I pray you, between you and I ;
I entertained you ever as a dog, not as a devil.

Dog. True ;
And so I used thee doggedly, not devilishly ;
I have deluded thee for sport to laugh at :
The wench thou seek'st after thou never spak'st with,
But a spirit in her form, habit, and likeness.
Ha, ha !

Cud. I do not, then, wonder at the change of your
garments, if you can enter into shapes of women too.

Dog. Any shape, to blind such silly eyes as thine ; but
chiefly those coarse creatures, dog, or cat, hare, ferret,
frog, toad.

Cud. Louse or flea ?

Dog. Any poor vermin.

Cud. It seems you devils have poor thin souls, that
you can bestow yourselves in such small bodies.   But,
pray you, Tom, one question at parting ;—I think I shall
never see you more ;—where do you borrow those bodies
that are none of your own ?—the garment-shape you may
hire at broker's.

Dog. Why would'st thou know that, fool? it avails
thee not.

Cud. Only for my mind's sake, Tom, and to tell some
of my friends.

Dog. I'll thus much tell thee : thou never art so
         distant
From an evil spirit, but that thy oaths,
Curses, and blasphemies pull him to thine elbow ;
Thou never tell'st a lie, but that a devil
Is within hearing it ; thy evil purposes
Are ever haunted ; but when they come to act,—
As thy tongue slandering, bearing false witness,
Thy hand stabbing, stealing, cozening, cheating,—

He's then within thee : thou play'st, he bets upon thy part ;
Although thou lose, yet he will gain by thee.

Cud. Ay ? then he comes in the shape of a rook ?

Dog. The old cadaver of some self-strangled wretch
We sometimes borrow, and appear human ;
The carcass of some disease-slain strumpet
We varnish fresh, and wear as her first beauty.
Did'st never hear ? if not, it has been done ;
An hot luxurious lecher in his twines,
When he has thought to clip his dalliance,
There has provided been for his embrace
A fine hot flaming devil in her place.

Cud. Yes, I am partly a witness to this ; but I never
could embrace her ; I thank thee for that, Tom.   Well,
again I thank thee, Tom, for all this counsel ; without a
fee too ! there's few lawyers of thy mind now.   Certainly,
Tom, I begin to pity thee.

Dog. Pity me ! for what ?

Cud. Were it not possible for thee to become an
honest dog yet ?—'Tis a base life that you lead, Tom, to
serve witches, to kill innocent children, to kill harmless
cattle, to stroy[1] corn and fruit, etc. : 'twere better yet to
be a butcher and kill for yourself.

Dog. Why, these are all my delights, my pleasures, fool.

Cud. Or, Tom, if you could give your mind to ducking,
—I know you can swim, fetch, and carry,—some shopkeeper in London would take great delight in you, and
be a tender master over you : or if you have a mind to
the game either at bull or bear, I think I could prefer you
to Moll Cutpurse.[2]

---

[1] *i.e.* Destroy.

[2] A notorious character of those days, whose real name was Mary
Frith.   She appears to have excelled in various professions, of which
far the most honest and praiseworthy was that of picking pockets.
By singular good fortune she escaped the gallows, and died, "in a
ripe and rotten old age," some time before the Restoration.   Moll
is the heroine of *The Roaring Girl*, a lively comedy by Middleton
and Dekker, who have treated her with kindness.—*Gifford.*

Dog. Ha, ha ! I should kill all the game,—bulls, bears, dogs and all ; not a cub to be left.

Cud. You could do, Tom ; but you must play fair ; you should be staved-off else. Or if your stomach did better like to serve in some nobleman's, knight's, or gentleman's kitchen, if you could brook the wheel and turn the spit—your labour could not be much—when they have roast meat, that's but once or twice in the week at most : here you might lick your own toes very well. Or if you could translate yourself into a lady's arming puppy, there you might lick sweet lips, and do many pretty offices ; but to creep under an old witch's coats, and suck like a great puppy ! fie upon't !—I have heard beastly things of you, Tom.

Dog. Ha, ha !
The worse thou heard'st of me the better 'tis
Shall I serve thee, fool, at the selfsame rate ?

Cud. No, I'll see thee hanged, thou shalt be damned first ! I know thy qualities too well, I'll give no suck to such whelps ; therefore henceforth I defy thee. Out, and avaunt !

Dog. Nor will I serve for such a silly soul :
I am for greatness now, corrupted greatness ;
There I'll shug in,[1] and get a noble countenance ;[2]
Serve some Briarean footcloth-strider,[3]
That has an hundred hands to catch at bribes,
But not a finger's nail of charity.
Such, like the dragon's tail, shall pull down hundreds
To drop and sink with him :[4] I'll stretch myself,
And draw this bulk small as a silver wire,

---

[1] Creep in.

[2] Patronage, protection, responsibility.—*Gifford.*

[3] Footcloths were the ornamental housings or trappings flung over the pads of state-horses. On these the great lawyers then rode to Westminster Hall, and, as our authors intimate, the great courtiers to St. James's. They became common enough in aftertimes.— *Gifford.* Briareus, the hundred-handed giant. The allusion is obvious.

[4] Compare " Revelation," ch. xii.

Enter at the least pore tobacco-fume
Can make a breach for :—hence, silly fool !
I scorn to prey on such an atom soul.

Cud. Come out, come out, you cur ! I will beat thee
out of the bounds of Edmonton, and to-morrow we go in
procession, and after thou shalt never come in again : if
thou goest to London, I'll make thee go about by Tyburn,
stealing in by Thieving Lane.   If thou canst rub thy
shoulder against a lawyer's gown, as thou passest by
Westminster-hall, do ; if not, to the stairs amongst the
bandogs, take water, and the Devil go with thee !

[*Exit, followed by the* Dog *barking.*

SCENE II.—*London.   The neighbourhood of Tyburn.*

Enter Justice, SIR ARTHUR, SOMERTON, WARBECK,
CARTER, *and* KATHERINE.

Just. Sir Arthur, though the bench hath mildly censured
your errors, yet you have indeed been the instrument
that wrought all their misfortunes ; I would wish you
paid down your fine speedily and willingly.

Sir Arth. I'll need no urging to it.

Car. If you should, 'twere a shame to you; for if I
should speak my conscience, you are worthier to be
hanged of the two, all things considered ; and now make
what you can of it : but I am glad these gentlemen are
freed.

War. We knew our innocence.

Som.   And therefore feared it not.

Kath. But I am glad that I have you safe.

[*A noise within.*

Just. How now ! what noise is that?

Car. Young Frank is going the wrong way.   Alas, poor
youth ! now I begin to pity him.

Enter OLD THORNEY *and* WINNIFRED *weeping*.

    O. Thor. Here let our sorrows wait him ; to press
       nearer
The place of his sad death, some apprehensions
May tempt our grief too much, at height already.—
Daughter be comforted.
    Win.   Comfort and I
Are far too separated to be joined.
But in eternity : I share too much
Of him that's going thither.
    Car. Poor woman, 'twas not thy fault ; I grieve to see
thee weep for him that hath my pity too.
    Win. My fault was lust, my punishment was shame.
Yet I am happy that my soul is free
Both from consent, foreknowledge, and intent
Of any murder but of mine own honour,
Restored again by a fair satisfaction,
And since not to be wounded.
    O. Thor.   Daughter, grieve not
For what necessity forceth ;
Rather resolve to conquer it with patience.—
Alas, she faints !
    Win.   My griefs are strong upon me ;
My weakness scarce can bear them.
    [*Within.*] Away with her ! hang her, witch !

Enter to execution MOTHER SAWYER ; *Officers* with
halberds, followed by a crowd of Country-people.

    Car. The witch, that instrument of mischief ! Did
not she witch the devil into my son-in-law, when he
killed my poor daughter ?—Do you hear, Mother Sawyer ?
    M. Saw. What would you have ?
Cannot a poor old woman have your leave
To die without vexation ?
    Car. Did not you bewitch Frank to kill his wife ? he
could never have done't without the devil.

M. Saw. Who doubts it? but is every devil mine?
Would I had one now whom I might command
To tear you all in pieces? Tom would have done't
Before he left me.

Car. Thou didst bewitch Ann Ratcliffe to kill herself.

M. Saw. Churl, thou liest; I never did her hurt:
Would you were all as near your ends as I am,
That gave evidence against me for it!

1st Coun. I'll be sworn, Master Carter, she bewitched
Gammer Washbowl's sow to cast her pigs a day before
she would have farrowed: yet they were sent up to
London and sold for as good Westminster dog-pigs at
Bartholomew fair as ever great-bellied ale-wife longed
for.

M. Saw. These dogs will mad me: I was well resolved
To die in my repentance. Though 'tis true
I would live longer if I might, yet since
I cannot, pray torment me not; my conscience
Is settled as it shall be: all take heed
How they believe the devil; at last he'll cheat you.

Car. Thou'dst best confess all truly.

M. Saw.   Yet again?
Have I scarce breath enough to say my prayers,
And would you force me to spend that in bawling?
Bear witness, I repent all former evil;
There is no damnèd conjuror like the devil.

All. Away with her, away!   [*She is led off.*

Enter FRANK *to execution,* Officers, &c.

O. Thor. Here's the sad object which I yet must meet
With hope of comfort, if a repentant end
Make him more happy than misfortune would
Suffer him here to be.

Frank.   Good sirs, turn from me:
You will revive affliction almost killed
With my continual sorrow.

O. Thor.   O, Frank, Frank!

Kath.   I will pray for you
For her sake, who I'm sure did love you dearly.

Sir Arth. Let us part friendly too ; I am ashamed
Of my part in thy wrongs.

Frank.   You are all merciful,
And send me to my grave in peace. Sir Arthur,
Heaven send you a new heart !—Lastly, to you, sir ;
And though I have deserved not to be called
Your son, yet give me leave upon my knees
To beg a blessing.   [*Kneels.*

O. Thor.   Take it ; let me wet
Thy cheeks with the last tears my griefs have left me.
O, Frank, Frank, Frank !

Frank.   Let me beseech you, gentlemen,
To comfort my old father, keep him with ye ;
Love this distressèd widow ; and as often
As you remember what a graceless man
I was, remember likewise that these are
Both free, both worthy of a better fate
Than such a son or husband as I have been.
All help me with your prayers.—On, on ; 'tis just
That law should purge the guilt of blood and lust.

                    [*Exit, led off by the* Officers.

Car. Go thy ways ; I did not think to have shed one
tear for thee, but thou hast made me water my plants
spite of my heart.—Master Thorney, cheer up, man ;
whilst I can stand by you, you shall not want help to
keep you from falling : we have lost our children, both
on's, the wrong way, but we cannot help it ; better or
worse, 'tis now as 'tis.

O. Thor. I thank you, sir ; you are more kind than I
Have cause to hope or look for.

Car. Master Somerton, is Kate yours or no ?

Som. We are agreed.

Kath. And but my faith is passed, I should fear to be
married, husbands are so cruelly unkind. Excuse me
that I am thus troubled.

Som. Thou shalt have no cause.

Just. Take comfort, Mistress Winnifred : Sir Arthur,
For his abuse to you and to your husband,
Is by the bench enjoined to pay you down
A thousand marks.[1]

Sir Arth.   Which I will soon discharge.

Win. Sir, 'tis too great a sum to be employed
Upon my funeral.

Car. Come, come ; if luck had served, Sir Arthur, and
every man had his due, somebody might have tottered
ere this, without paying fines, like it as you list.—Come
to me, Winnifred ; shalt be welcome.—Make much of
her, Kate, I charge you : I do not think but she's a good
wench, and hath had wrong as well as we. So let's every
man home to Edmonton with heavy hearts, yet as merry
as we can, though not as we would.

Just. Join, friends, in sorrow ; make of all the best :
Harms past may be lamented, not redrest.   [*Exeunt.*

EPILOGUE.

Spoken by WINNIFRED.

I am a widow still, and must not sort
A second choice without a good report ;
Which though some widows find, and few deserve,
Yet I dare not presume, but will not swerve
From modest hopes.   All noble tongues are free ;
The gentle may speak one kind word for me.

                                        PHEN.

---

[1] The mark was worth 13*s.* 4*d.*

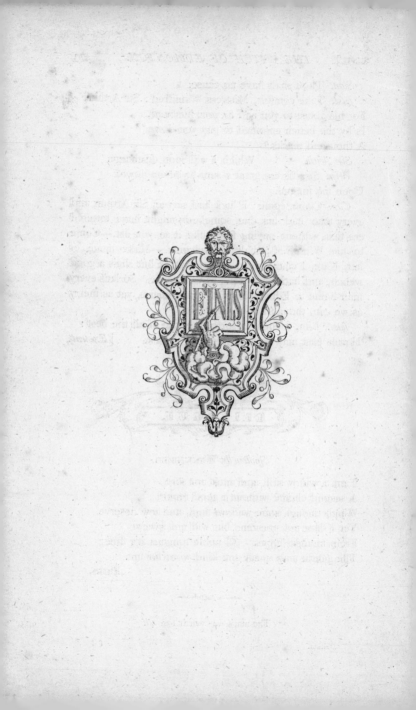